The ENDS Of TIME

The ENDS Of TIME

Life and Work in a Nursing Home

Joel S. Savishinsky

BERGIN & GARVEY

New York
Westport, Connecticut
London

Library of Congress Cataloging-in-Publication Data

Savishinsky, Joel S.
    The ends of time : life and work in a nursing home / Joel S.
Savishinsky.
        p.   cm.
    Includes bibliographical references and index.
    ISBN 0-89789-226-7 (alk. paper).—ISBN 0-89789-229-1 (pbk: alk.
paper)
    1. Nursing homes—Social aspects.   2. Nursing home patients—
Social life and customs.   3. Nursing homes—Employees—Social life
and customs.   I. Title.
RA997.S25   1991
362.1'6—dc20   91-10660

British Library Cataloguing in Publication Data is available.

Library of Congress Catalog Card Number: 91-10660
ISBN: 0-89789-226-7 (hb.)
        0-89789-229-1 (pb.)

First published in 1991

Bergin & Garvey, One Madison Avenue, New York, NY 10010
An imprint of Greenwood Publishing Group, Inc.

Printed in the United States of America

The paper used in this book complies with the
Permanent Paper Standard issued by the National
Information Standards Organization (Z39.48-1984).

P

Copyright Acknowledgments

Excerpts from "The Waste Land" and "Gerontion" from COLLECTED POEMS, 1909–
1962 by T. S. Eliot, copyright 1936 by Harcourt Brace Jovanovich, Inc., copyright © 1964,
1963 by T. S. Eliot, reprinted by permission of the publisher.

Excerpts from "Sailing to Byzantium," "Quarrel in Old Age," and "The Wild Old Wicked
Man" reprinted with permission of Macmillan Publishing Company from THE POEMS
OF W. B. YEATS: A NEW EDITION, edited by Richard J. Finneran. Copyright 1919,
1933 by Macmillan Publishing Company, renewed 1947. © 1961 by Bertha Georgie Yeats.
Copyright 1928 by Macmillan Publishing Company, renewed © 1956 by Georgie Yeats.

To my grandmothers—
Mindel Alsofrom
and
Lillian Savishinsky

And my mentors—
Burt Aginsky
and
Morris Opler

And Jacob called unto his sons,
and said: "Gather yourselves together,
that I may tell you that
which shall befall you in
the end of days. . . . "

Genesis 49:1

CONTENTS

Figures   xi

Preface   xiii

Acknowledgments   xix

1   Introduction   1

2   The Visits   27

3   Meanings and Losses   54

4   The Residents   69

5   Memories and Symbols   107

6   Silence and Stigma   124

7   The Staff   143

8   Roles and Realities   176

9   The Volunteers   200

10 Altruism and Aging   223

11 Conclusions and Recommendations   238

Notes   259

References   265

Index   273

FIGURES

2.1 The Front Lobby   38

4.1 The Screen   70

6.1 Bulletin Board   130

7.1 Elmwood Grove Nursing Home: Selected Residents
     and Staff   145

8.1 Patient Review Instrument   182

PREFACE

This book is about two kinds of relationships: the ties between generations, and the bonds between species. It examines life in an American nursing home by detailing the experiences of the residents, staff, and visitors whose lives converge within one institution. The research upon which it is based, however, began as a study of an innovative program for helping institutionalized people, namely, the use of pet therapy to reduce some of the physical and social losses which older people face in nursing facilities. In the early part of the study, my students and I worked as volunteers in a companion animal program. In this capacity, we regularly visited a number of geriatric facilities in our community, and got to know something of the nature of life and work within these institutions. In particular, we identified a number of the significant ways in which pets, and the volunteers who brought them, affected the people whom they visited each week.

The nursing home which this book describes—a place I will call Elmwood Grove—was one of the facilities we originally studied. It was the institution I became most deeply involved in, and the information presented here draws on seven years of experience with the people who came within its walls. I chose Elmwood for two reasons. First, its small size—84 beds—made it more feasible to know in an intimate way than would have been true with a larger home. And second, as a nonprofit facility, Elmwood shared the reputation that such voluntary institutions have gained for being well run. I wanted to see how a "good" home operated.

While the animals provided the initial impetus for this work, they proved to be just the starting point for a widening circle of concerns and questions. The research soon moved beyond the initial focus on pet therapy to explore why elderly individuals had come to live at Elmwood Grove and how they felt about being there. Work with residents also brought us into contact with their families, which provided insight

into how these people viewed the institution and the lives of their relatives. In what felt like a logical or natural progression, we moved on to
examine the personal and working world of the staff members who
served the residents. We gave special attention to how employees' experiences shaped their attitudes towards aging and institutionalization, and
how these women and men coped with the demands of their jobs. Finally, the study turned to a consideration of why community volunteers
offered their time to help elderly individuals living in the nursing home.
Among the major concerns here were the questions of what these visitors expected and what they got out of their work, why some stayed
with it, and why others dropped out.

The nature of the study thus continued to expand over time, spiraling
outward from the animals to include the residents, the relatives, the staff,
and the volunteers. This kind of movement is very much in the spirit of
anthropology, which tries to look at social life in a holistic way by taking
into account all the relevant features of human experience. In this book,
then, I have attempted to treat Elmwood Grove Nursing Home as a whole,
as a small-scale culture, by considering the significance of its three primary
populations—those who lived, those who worked, and those who visited
there.

This book's format mirrors the progress of the study. Chapter 1, "Introduction," briefly examines the image and nature of late life in modern
times, and considers some of the theories and research that illuminate aging
in general and nursing homes in particular. It describes the process and the
methods by which the study presented here was carried out. The next nine
chapters, the heart of the volume, follow a rhythm of counterpoint. In
alternating sections, they move from descriptive and biographical data on
people associated with the home—first residents, then staff, and finally
volunteers—to an analysis of how these individuals have been affected by
their relationship to the institution.

Chapter 2, "The Visits," describes the weekly pet sessions at Elmwood Grove conducted by people and animals from the local community. It includes material on the structure of pet visits, the nature of
interactions between people and animals, and the personalities of some
of the regular participants. In the course of these descriptions, the history and organization of Elmwood Grove itself are also sketched in.
The third chapter, "Meanings and Losses," examines the moral and
personal issues that the animal visits evoked for residents. It gives special consideration to people's feelings about their families, their losses,
and the very idea of domesticity. I argue there that the deceptive simplicity of pet sessions overlaid a much more complex set of experiences:
animals tapped into the memories and the moral meanings that residents
held to—sentiments which might have been left unarticulated were it

not for the opportunities offered by the pets.

The fourth chapter, "The Residents," describes the histories and current lives of four people living at the home. The experiences of two women and two men are related largely in their own words, supplemented with comments from staff and family members. These accounts draw on material from daily events, life-history interviews, and many informal visits with these residents over a period of two to seven years. The fifth chapter, "Memories and Symbols," develops a number of issues raised by the residents in their stories. In particular, it examines how these people talk about their lives and how they relate to one another. The specific issues analyzed include the nature and use of their memories, the routes by which they entered Elmwood Grove, their relations with roommates, and their responses to the loss of home, privacy, and autonomy. The sixth chapter, "Silence and Stigma," shifts attention to those residents who could not readily talk about their lives, such as those who suffered from Alzheimer's disease, dementia, or other communicative disorders. It considers the kind of stigma under which they lived, the forms of contact and communication that were available to them, and the reactions that people in American and other societies have had to individuals whose silence or unpredictability violate the norms of everyday life.

The viewpoints and experiences of employees are the subject of the seventh chapter, "The Staff." Four individuals—three women and one man—are considered: a physical therapist, a nurse, a social worker, and an administrator. The makeup of the home's work force changed a good deal during the period of the study, a pattern of high turnover which is typical of many nursing facilities. The four people featured here were selected for emphasis, in part because they had had a significant amount of experience at Elmwood Grove and, in some cases, at other geriatric facilities as well. In the eighth chapter, "Roles and Realities," the focus is on how these staff members saw their jobs, and how their expectations about working with the elderly had fared in the face of reality. Their sources of satisfaction and disappointment, the tension between caring and curing, and people's methods for coping with the stresses of work, are given particular attention.

The last major population presented is "The Volunteers." The ninth chapter gives three women and one man from this group a chance to describe their unpaid work at Elmwood Grove. They speak about their motives for volunteering and the nature of their relationships with the elderly. The following chapter, "Altruism and Aging," centers on a major dilemma faced by these people and their colleagues, that is, the inherent contradiction of what one volunteer, Janice Ashler, called their "selfish altruism." The analysis examines the rewards and costs for volunteers of visiting the home, and identifies the factors that led some of them to continue their work and others to burn out. The age of the volunteers themselves, and not just that of the people they visited, turned out to be a significant factor in this equation.

Finally, in Chapter 11, "Conclusions and Recommendations," four tasks are undertaken. First, the major findings of the book are summarized. The points developed here deal with the impact and effectiveness of pet therapy for the elderly; the way older people adjust to institutionalization and interpret it within the context of their histories; the qualities that shape the nature of work for staff members and volunteers; and the effect that living and working in a nursing home had on people's attitudes towards aging and institutionalization.

The second task of this chapter is to identify the practical applications that this study had for the lives of people at Elmwood Grove. During the course of the research, results were periodically shared with individuals and groups at the facility. This led to several changes, including better support systems for volunteers, more appropriate formats for visitors and residents to meet in, and an enhanced recognition of the impact of reminiscence and role expectations on people's behavior.

The third section of the chapter compares the findings and applications that were developed at Elmwood Grove with studies that have been done on other nursing facilities.

The last task of this last chapter is to offer a caveat and several recommendations. No single nursing home can be typical of all such institutions, and the twelve people from Elmwood Grove featured here—four residents, four staff, and four volunteers—are themselves drawn from a total of over 200 individuals who variously lived in, worked at, or visited this facility. They were chosen not because of their typicality, but because, in their variety, they reflected the range of individuals and experiences to be found at the home. While this institution had its unique character and its characters, however, it also shared many features with other geriatric facilities that have been studied. These commonalities suggest several ways for improving the quality of life and work in nursing homes, and for supporting staff, volunteers, and family members in their difficult roles as caregivers. The final chapter therefore offers proposals for dealing with some basic institutional issues, including conflict, death, social support, and recreational therapy.

The various findings, applications, and recommendations presented here are based on a particular anthropological method, a way of approaching institutional life through direct observation and participation. It also rests upon a long-term, seven-year involvement in the life of this small world— the type of time commitment that has long characterized the way anthropologists study human society. Beyond its methods, the book also draws on a distinct perspective. Its emphasis is on meaning as much as on truth. Whereas people's accounts of their pasts often could not be verified, it *was*

possible to examine the significance that individuals found in their recollections. Their speech, their actions, and their silence all yielded clues to
how, in every sense of the word, they made sense of their world.[1] This
book, then, also demonstrates the uses of anthropology for helping us to
understand the culture of nursing homes and their place in the human
community. The conclusion argues that anthropologists can play a signif
icant role in illuminating not only the lives of the elderly, but also the
institutions in which they live and the people who care for and serve them.

ACKNOWLEDGMENTS

I aged seven years in the course of this study, incurred many debts, and saw a number of people enter and leave my life. I want to acknowledge here some of what I lost and found during that time.

Ithaca College and its gerontology program gave valuable support to the project through faculty development and research grants. The genesis of the study itself owed much to the help of numerous colleagues and friends, especially Jules Burgevin, Janet Fitchen, Bea Goldman, Garry Thomas, and the late Chet Galaska. I am indebted to seven of my students who participated directly in the research: Nordica and Susan Holochuck, Mari Kobayakawa, Rich Lathan, Andrea Nevins, Lisa Sahasrabudhe, and Tu Vu offered their data and their insights. Maria Vesperi made many suggestions that improved an early draft of the manuscript. In the agencies and institutions that serve the elderly in Tompkins County, I was fortunate to have the assistance of Peg Hopper and Laura Weinberger. All of these people lent not just expertise, but encouragement and candor. I discovered that they, and many others whom I met, had stories of their own to tell about their aging relatives and friends. The result was that when people heard about the subject of my work, they often volunteered their tales without urging. In several ways, then, this book was shaped by the climate of concern and caring that I found in my own community.

Many of the elderly residents who appear in these pages have died in the years since I began this study. Their loss has been one of the personal costs of doing this kind of anthropology, just as their friendship has provided me one of its special rewards. I have changed the names and certain details of the nursing home, its residents, staff, and visitors in order to protect everyone's privacy. Though I cannot thank the people of "Elmwood Grove" directly, then, I nevertheless owe them all a great deal of gratitude for their patience and openness. Without their willingness, their honesty, and their humor, this project would never have been completed.

Finally, I owe a comparable debt to my family—Susan, Jacob, Max and our cats Eppis and Izzy—for helping me to appreciate the meaning of "home." Life with them has enabled me to appreciate what the residents of Elmwood Grove have lost and how they have tried to reclaim it.

The ENDS Of TIME

1 INTRODUCTION

BEYOND MYTH AND METAPHOR

Anthropologists are supposed to study myths, not live by them. But an anthropologist without myths would be a person without a culture, and as an American I have been raised on the myths that shape my society. To many of my compatriots, old age is joyless and terrible, and nursing homes only make a bad situation worse. Such institutions are seen as the last resort of those who can no longer help themselves. In the apparent uselessness of one's later years, they symbolize rejection, and they sometimes rub the salt of neglect into the moral wounds of marginality. This sad, spoiled image of late life contrasts with the equally extreme myth of the golden age of old age, a once hallowed but now suspect truth that people no longer believe in. The imagination of our culture has transformed the old dream into a new nightmare.

Both literature and the social sciences have provided some of the substance on which this new image feeds. Novels, poems, and drama portray the desperation of the aged, the indifference of some who could help them, the impotence of others who try. With less vividness but more detail, researchers have tried to record the realities of older people living in their own communities, as well as those who lack the grace of independence and must make their home in an institution.

The imaginative and scholarly results often have a tragic ring. This may be because Western writers warm to the theme of decline and fall, be it of empires, generations, or individuals. Literary figures have been partial to seasonal metaphors, picturing the autumn years as a prelude to the winter of our discontent (Simone de Beauvoir 1972). And historians have frequently used the human life cycle and its inevitable outcome as a metaphor for the birth and death of civilizations. In the hands of Oswald Spengler (1926), Arnold Toynbee (1934–1954), and others, the collapse of great cultures becomes the analog of age and senescence. The old become models of loss, their twilight a lesson in how failing nations also fall into eclipse.

The social scientists who look at the aged try to see them as flesh and blood and spirit rather than as mere metaphor. Anthropologists, for example, have documented the great variety of ways in which the elderly have fared in both traditional and modern societies. They have described gerontocracies among people as disparate as the hunting-gathering Tiwi of Australia and the rural Irish of the prewar period. Their studies document the great respect and longevity enjoyed by older people in the Abkhasian communities of Soviet Georgia and in the peasant region of Vilcabamba in highland Ecuador. Important spiritual, family, and advisory roles have been reserved for aged individuals among the Samoans, the Druze of Lebanon, the Japanese, the Chinese, and many Native American peoples. There were also societies, such as the Inuit (Eskimo), where the old sometimes had to be sacrificed—and yet such death had meaning and the grace of altruism, with its sting drawn off by the Inuit belief in reincarnation.[1]

Cataloging cultures that accorded their elderly considerable power or respect is not to claim that the aged were well treated in every non-Western or premodern society. There were also peoples—such as the Siriono of Bolivia, the Tasmanians of the South Pacific, and the Xosa of South Africa— who neglected, abused, or disparaged the few old people they had. The Siriono saw the aged as "excess baggage." They were "relegated to a position of obscurity," and weeded out when frailty set in (Alan Holmberg 1969: 225). Elderly Tasmanians were deposited in hollow trees or under rock ledges "to pine and die" (H. L. Roth 1890: 73). And while the Xosa respected their patriarchs, the lot of their old women is described as "sad indeed. . . . They were frequently left to starve or die of exposure." When their use was considered over, females became "cast-off things" (Dudley Kidd 1904: 22).[2] The cultures with more positive attitudes, then, are not necessarily typical. Rather, their value is that they show us what is humanly possible, and serve to set off what is characteristic of our own society and time in history. The modern marginality of the old is a hallmark of the very first century to see the elderly become a sizable, problematic portion of the population, with ill-defined roles and responsibilities. The present-day picture of the aged is a complex, broken landscape of many parts. There are older people living in their own homes or apartments, in retirement communities, in senior citizens' housing complexes, and in nursing homes. There are those steeped in an ethnic identity and others devoid of such a heritage. The category of "the elderly" includes rich and poor, sick and well, sane and demented; it embraces both the relatively healthy "young old" between 60 and 75, and the more vulnerable "old old" who have gone beyond their eighth decade. There are those connected to kin and community, and others cut off from their families. There are the active and the disengaged, the ardent and the hopeless.

Many of the recent studies that have been done of older people develop this theme of extremes. In some, the emphasis falls on how time and society mortify the body or try the spirit. Some of the pictures painted of retirement communities cast a critical, often lifeless light. In a Sun Belt development given the ironic pseudonym Fun City (Jerry Jacobs 1974), retired people were shown to be leading a joyless, isolated existence. The well-to-do, all white couples that went there brought with them similar class and social backgrounds, but were unable to build any sense of community on that basis. Living in separate homes behind wide, empty streets and green gravel "lawns," they found themselves in a cemetery for the living which Jacobs condemned as a "false paradise."

There is nothing inherently depressing or deathlike about a community of older people, however. In *Number Our Days*, Barbara Myerhoff wrote evocatively about an enclave of elderly East European Jews in the Los Angeles area (1978). Poor in health and finances, but rich in spirit and identity, this neighborhood's people were full of passionate intensity. Using the local Jewish community center as a second home and focus for their lives, they reveled there in *Yiddishkeit*, argued vehemently about politics, and created their own rituals to celebrate long-held values of learning, generosity, and religiosity.

Although they lived in the same region of the country, the people of Fun City and *Number Our Days* were at the opposite extremes of economy and emotion. Vibrant communities of older people have also been found in other settings. Situations as varied as a Parisian residence for retired laborers, an American mobile home park and an apartment building for seniors, and a subsidized housing complex for elderly Jews in Leeds, England, have all been shown to promote a strong spirit of connectedness for residents.[3] Politics, common cultural roots, and similar class origins were among the factors fostering a sense of identity in these far-flung places. Some of the same forces work to the benefit of older people who continue to live near their kin in their community of origin. Studies of various ethnic groups in the United States, including Italians, blacks, and Native Americans, show persistent qualities of pride, respect, and authentic family roles for older people.[4]

When it comes to nursing homes, however, the overriding theme of much that has been written is rejection. The verdict these institutions teach journalists about Western society is the same one that William Butler Yeats ([1927] 1983: 193) passed on Byzantium: "That is no country for old men." Books with such telling titles as *Tender Loving Greed* (Mary Mendelson 1975), *Why Survive?* (Robert Butler 1975), *Unloving Care* (Bruce Vladeck 1980), *Nobody Ever Died of Old Age* (Sharon Curtin 1972), *The Last Segregation* (Claire Townsend 1971), and *Sans Everything* (Barbara Robb 1968) expose the inhumanity of some of the worst places on the landscape.

Novelists have taken up this same topic, and in the hands of a writer such as May Sarton, the elderly who have been consigned to a nursing home can speak with eloquence. Seventy-six-year-old Caro Spencer, the protagonist of Sarton's *As We Are Now* (1973), is a woman of refinement and awareness, cast off by her last relative into the crude world of a rural institution. She watches the aged people around her slip deeper into senility and inaction each day, while fiercely trying to preserve her own memory, sanity, and sense of self by starting a diary. But the erosion of hope and purpose is relentless: Caro's privileges and contacts with the outside are cut off by her keepers, and her cold descent is tempered only by the occasional presence of a cat that wanders into Caro's room at night. Finally, even that small pleasure, that fleeting source of touch, is banned by the home's owner. Demeaned beyond the reach of meaningful life, feeling that the living around her are morally dead already, Caro settles on a last act of will and destroys herself, the home, and all its inhabitants in a holocaust.

Novels, like Caro herself, take a kind of license in their treatment of reality. But we now have sources other than journalism and fiction to turn to if we want some insight into what goes on inside real nursing homes. A number of anthropologists and gerontologists have studied these facilities with an eye to documenting how people have come to live and work there, and how residents and staff adapt to the regime of institutional life. Nursing homes are a specific instance of what Erving Goffman (1961) has called "total institutions." Like mental hospitals, prisons, army barracks, nunneries, and the old workhouse, nursing homes are "total" in that they completely isolate, control, and reconstitute the daily lives of those who reside in them. Goffman has documented the stripping away and recreating of people's identities that goes on in such settings; the rituals of initiation and degradation that residents may be subjected to; and the participation of patients, inmates, and others in behaviors for gaining privilege and manipulating the system.

While the linking of nursing homes with asylums and prisons may seem extreme, the point is that institutional life—regardless of the particular kind of institution at issue—presents some common features. These include the residents' loss of control and self, their separation from society, and the precedence of institutional routines over individual needs.[5] Furthermore, there are cases where the prisonlike potential of geriatric facilities becomes manifest. The strange and often involuntary route by which some older people end up in institutions has been explored by Nancy Scheper-Hughes (1979). In a study of schizophrenia and hospitalization in rural Ireland, she has documented the "warehousing" of the elderly in mental institutions. Families that were reluctant to care for their aged kin, or those who coveted their land, pushed for psychiatric assessments of older relatives in order to have these people hospitalized. Though most of the elderly were guilty of no more than eccentricity, the shortage of nursing home beds and the convenience of their kin led to questionable diagnoses and equally questionable institutionalization. Comparable situations have been described in England and the United States, suggesting an image of the old as a disposable commodity.[6]

Anthropologists have written about the insides of nursing homes from a number of different vantage points. One of the most unusual, highly personalized, and detailed sets of observations has been given by Carobeth Laird (1979). At the age of 79, in failing health, this American anthropologist was placed in Golden Mesa, a 110-bed Arizona geriatric facility. Several months later, following her discharge, she began to write *Limbo*, a book pointedly subtitled *"A Memoir about Life in a Nursing Home by a Survivor."* Laird incisively described several basic experiences common to institutionalized residents. In her own case these included the loss of control over her daily life, a ubiquitous preoccupation with eating and excretion, financial insecurity, the fragile nature of her sanity and sense of time, and her social isolation. These were partially offset by the support she received from staff—support that was mitigated, however, by the frequent turnover in the home's personnel.

Laird survived long enough for several events to interrupt and reverse her decline. Deprived of her familiar possessions when she first entered the home, she began to claim as her own a hairbrush, a notebook, a typewriter, and other ingredients for a new identity kit. The opportunity to attend church services, which she first responded to with indifference, eventually enabled Laird to rediscover a sense of her own religiosity. Her recovery of hope was bolstered by the attention she got from visitors and new acquaintances. And at a point where she had begun to doubt her accounts of her own past, her identity as a writer was tangibly reaffirmed by the arrival of the galley proofs for her next book. She had indeed become the author of her own being. Finally, some friends learned belatedly of Laird's situation. They offered her a room in their home, thus rescuing her from the limbo into which her life had fallen.

Taking the role of a nurse's aide, anthropologist Maria Vesperi (1983) studied staff as well as patients in Martindale, a 50-bed geriatric facility in New England. She identified various institutional factors that contributed to the physical and mental deterioration of residents there. These included the infantilizing and depersonalization to which people were subjected, and the overuse of sedation and restraints. Vesperi noted the recourse of patients to incontinence and self-starvation as methods for both asserting control over their lives and protesting the conditions of their treatment. She also examined the low levels of pay, education, and cohesiveness among Martindale's direct care staff, arguing that each of these features fed into people's negative work attitudes and the high rate at which they resigned. Furthermore, she observed a basic contradiction between the expectations of patients and the goals of staff. Employees had been trained to pursue a medical model of curing, but gave up on this with patients because of their feeling that the elderly could never fully recover. Thus, they were not highly motivated to help people simply regain a modicum of health. Many residents, however, had entered the home with the desire to convalesce, and with the assumption that rehabilitation would eventually enable them to leave. But because treatment did not work toward these objectives, it was often reduced to the level of custodial care. This lack of emphasis on restoring people's health defeated the best hopes of residents and intensified their tendency to decline.

In the American Midwest, Jaber Gubrium (1975) participated in and observed the routines of a 360-bed church-run institution he called Murray Manor. Much of his research centered on the cognitive organization of life and labor in this geriatric facility. He described the structural divisions between "top staff" and "floor staff"; the conduct of "bed-and-body" work by caregivers; the ritual outings of residents and the status gained by those who received visitors; and the indirect as well as overt ways that people laid claim to chairs, lounge areas, and other forms of personal space. While Murray Manor's administrators espoused an ethic of sensitive, individualized care, they were so removed from the workaday world of floor staff that they rarely saw how patients were treated. And the reality of residents had other nuances. Among the relatively healthy, it included the sobering realization that transfer to the home's upper floors was usually a terminal voyage of no return, the start of what patients called "really dying" (Gubrium: 200).

The subtleties of behavior and morale in geriatric institutions have been the subject of research by Bethel Powers (1988a, b). A registered nurse and anthropologist, Powers used participant-observation, mapping, and interviewing to study the social networks of elderly people in a 212-bed, health-related facility in upstate New York. She found considerable diversity in the kinds of support systems that residents developed. There were "institution-centered" networks focused on people's ties to staff and other patients; "kin-centered" support systems that stressed an individual's relationships with family members outside the facility; and the "balanced networks" of people with a mix of ties to residents, staff, kin, and friends. Her most basic finding—the lack of a uniform pattern of adjustment among the elderly—supports the conclusions of other researchers who have studied the highly individualized adaptations of older people to such diverse settings as apartment buildings, domiciliary facilities, and skid row neighborhoods.[7]

At the nursing facility Powers examined, she also discovered a significant discrepancy in the way certain residents and staff looked at issues of dependency and intimacy. Employees often insisted that people do the maximum they were capable of for themselves in terms of dressing, eating, and other daily activities. Some personnel discouraged residents from turning to staff or other patients for help with these tasks. But while caregivers saw this as a way of enhancing people's independence, some residents felt that getting assistance was also a way to create and express social bonds with others. Certain residents believed that employees, in their insistence on maximizing self-sufficiency, were interfering with the ties that they, as patients, were trying to maintain. Thus, when a staff member declined to help a person for a "good" reason, that same resident may have experienced this refusal as a form of rejection.

Several institutions that have been examined in depth have had a distinct ethnic or religious makeup. One of these was Bethany Manor (Mary O'Brien 1989), a 230-bed East Coast nursing home whose funding, supervisory staff, and clientele were primarily drawn from the local Catholic community. Bethany's religious atmosphere and services were important to many residents, who were found to have a very accepting attitude towards death. If anything, there was a greater "fear of not dying," of "surviving with a lingering cognitive deficit" (O'Brien: 96) and being transferred to the third floor—an event that "was decidedly viewed as a fate worse than death" (O'Brien: 32). Even confused residents found reassurance in comparing themselves with those who were worse off, deriving comfort from what O'Brien called an attitude of "relative deprivation" (O'Brien: 39).

Ethnicity and identity in late life were two of the issues emphasized by Renee Rose Shield (1988) in her study of Franklin Nursing Home, a nonprofit Jewish facility located in a northeastern city. With over 200 residents, Franklin was a well-run institution offering patients a good quality of care. But while residents shared a common religious background, what Franklin could not provide them with was a sense of community, or a meaningful way to ease their transition to old age. Shield traced these deficits to several factors: the controlling nature of institutional regulations; the inability of residents to reciprocate what others gave them; the tendency of patients to preserve their autonomy by remaining aloof from one another; and the lack of staff consensus over whether Franklin itself was a hospital or a home. The result of these rules, inequities, and contradictions was to place residents and staff in an adversarial relationship, one in which nursing home life became a "ritual-less rite of passage" between adulthood and death (Shield: 22).

A number of anthropologists have done *comparative* studies of geriatric facilities. One of the first of these was conducted by Jules Henry (1963), who examined differences in the treatment of elderly patients in three American settings: an urban hospital and two nursing homes. The three presented a continuum in the quality of care, with the hospital standing midway between a relatively comfortable, humane institution and another home characterized by Henry as "hell's vestibule" (Henry: 406). The latter reduced people to the level of animals through a combination of hunger, filth, neglect, and personal degradation. The hospital, though less abusive, was simply more benign in its control over patients. It enforced a kind of quietude upon residents in order to preserve the orderliness of the institutional regime. Even the best of the three facilities, in Henry's judgment, rendered people obsolete, petty, and inactive by denying them human dignity and depriving them of purpose, stimulation, and meaningful contact with other individuals.

A different kind of comparison was undertaken by Wilbur Watson and Robert Maxwell (1977), who were concerned with the influence of ethnic and racial factors on the organization of nursing home behavior. They studied two American geriatric facilities, a Jewish home for the aged with 328 residents, and a 190-bed facility for black elderly. In the Jewish home, with a racially mixed staff, higher status nurses distanced themselves from extremely disabled patients, leaving most direct-care responsibilities in the hands of lower-level personnel. The people who were most impaired, and those most likely to die, were placed in rooms furthest from nursing stations. Employees also used physical objects, architectural features, and patient sedation to increase their separation from the most deteriorated. These findings echo other studies that document the tendency of medical staff to distance themselves from the terminally ill and dying (Barney Glaser and Anselm Strauss 1968: 62–63).

Behavior and staffing patterns were both quite different at the Afro-American home that Watson and Maxwell studied. Its work force was primarily black, and nurses and aides there were physically and emotionally more involved with the most disabled. While the black facility was severely understaffed, many of its personnel had the same racial and cultural background as the residents they cared for. This "status parity" (Watson and Maxwell: 108) promoted a sense of solidarity among the two groups, whereas racial attitudes in the Jewish home made it more difficult for patients and minority staff to relate.

A cross-cultural view of nursing homes is provided in the work of Jeanie Kayser-Jones (1981). She studied two facilities: Pacific Manor, a privately owned 85-bed home in California; and Scottsdale, a 96-bed continuing care institution operated by the National Health Service in Scotland. From comparing the quality of care in these two facilities, she found that Scottsdale consistently provided more satisfactory food, social activities, and medical treatment. Scottish residents got out into the community more, experienced less turnover among staff, and had access to more services and disposable income. They and their caregivers also developed a deeper sense of camaraderie and reciprocity. In contrast to this, the California nursing home depersonalized, infantilized, and victimized its residents. Patients at Pacific Manor rarely got out of the facility, were frequently demeaned, and often had their few possessions stolen.

Analyzing her data in the light of social exchange theory, Kayser-Jones argued that the lack of social and monetary resources among the California elderly heightened their dependency on staff: it intensified the latter's power over patients, thereby lowering the quality of care that residents received. Also contributing to these distinctive experiences of institutionalization were policy differences in how American and British societies support elderly people and their caregivers. Compared to the American stress on private medicine, Kayser-Jones found that public support for geriatric care in Great Britain has meant better salaries for nursing staff and a more coherent approach to the financing and organization of health services. These, in turn, reflect and reinforce a stronger cultural emphasis upon community responsibility for older people in that country.[8]

BODY, MIND AND SPIRIT

That much of the literature on aging has been written by or about women—or by *and* about them—is probably not coincidental. Females outnumber males in our population, and the size of the women's majority steadily increases in the older segments of the population. Widows, spinsters, elderly mothers, and grandmothers are thus more likely than their male compatriots to spend the end of their days in nursing homes, and to live to tell or write their stories. The kin who previously cared for them, and the strangers who staff the facilities they now find themselves in, are also overwhelmingly female in number.

The themes that emerge from studies of institutional life, however, center on problems that confront the elderly of both sexes, and they touch on the lives of more individuals than is usually recognized. Government statistics released in 1990 showed approximately 1,553,000 people residing in America's 25,646 nursing homes. The cost of their care, which came to 38.1 billion dollars, accounted for 8.1 percent of the nation's total expenditure on health. Seventy-nine percent of these individuals lived in privately owned institutions, 17 percent in voluntary, nonprofit ones, and the remaining 4 percent in government-run facilities (United States Bureau of the Census 1990: 93, 104, 112).

Though only 5 percent of those over 65 were in long-term care on any given day, that figure is a deceptive one. For all persons who entered the 65-plus age bracket in 1990, 43 percent will eventually reside for some time in a nursing home, and two-thirds of them will be female. A quarter of those in institutions will pass at least 12 months there, while almost 10 percent will be patients for five or more years (Peter Kemper and Christopher Murtaugh 1991:597). An individual's chances of being in a geriatric facility will increase with age. Approximately 22 percent of the elderly population will spend some time in one after they reach 85 (Jacob Siegel and Cynthia Taeuber 1986: 101). Thus, while most older people live *outside* nursing homes and *in* contact with their families (Ethel Shanas 1979), the potential for institutionalization remains a haunting possibility. And for each person in a facility, perhaps a score of individuals on the outside—

family, friends, neighbors, clergy, social workers, lawyers, and doctors—
will be directly touched by their fate.

That fate is a product of people's aging bodies, minds, and social worlds;
institutionalization, in turn, affects all three of these domains. At the level
of the body, frailty can take many forms: there are strokes, arthritis, broken
limbs, osteoporosis, incontinence, respiratory ailments, circulatory problems, malnutrition, and iatrogenic disorders. Most nursing home residents
have multiple chronic conditions, the kind that medical professionals are
often not well trained or motivated to treat (Colleen Johnson and Leslie
Grant 1985: 33–36). Physical problems can be accompanied by or contribute
to psychological ones, with depression, confusion, Alzheimer's disease, and
other forms of dementia being among the most common. Any of these
assaults on the body or the psyche can lead to a dismaying loss of self-
sufficiency. Dependency, however, does not necessarily lead to institutionalization: for every elderly person in an institution, there are two individuals
of comparable age and disability who remain in the community thanks to
the care and support of spouses, kin, friends, or local agencies that provide
meals, housekeeping, nursing, or other services. But when the frailty becomes pronounced, or when a spouse dies, or when the caregivers have
burned out themselves, their families, or their finances, a nursing home
may be one of the few alternatives left. A considerable number of people
enter institutions, then, not because of illness alone, but due to their social
isolation or lack of outside supports (Johnson and Grant: 37–63).

People moving to such facilities may do so willingly or under duress.
They may have had a say in the choice of home or been left out of the
decision. Some have come from their own place of residence, some from
a hospital, and others from an institution where they were getting a lower
level of care. People may have understood what was happening or have
been confused. They may have seen their new environment as temporary
or permanent, as a haven or a prison. Numerous studies have shown that
residents who feel they had some control over the decision to enter a facility
tend to do better and live longer (Judith Rodin 1986).

Even under the best and most hopeful of circumstances, the emotional
consequences of entering a nursing home can be manifold. For many, dependency may soon be married to embarrassment: needing the help of others
to feed, bathe, dress, and toilet themselves reverses some of maturity's
earliest and hardest-won accomplishments. At the level of social life and
habit, they are separated from all that had once been familiar, including
family, friends, home, neighborhood, and belongings. With the loss of
these may go the sense of belonging itself.

The effects of all these changes on a person's outlook and self-image defy
simple summary. There are those who enter the nursing home with a sense
of relief: after the trauma of a hospital stay or the uncertainties of life at
home, the 24-hour-a-day care, the company, the meals, the laundry service,

and the possibility of improved health are a source of security and comfort. People's quality of life, and their peace of mind, may be better than anything they have recently experienced. But for others there may be a sense of abandonment and betrayal, feelings of anger or depression, the slow erosion of hope, and a growing lack of faith in their own senses and memories and identities. If mortality now looms larger, it can magnify the triumphs and failures by which people measure their lives. The confrontation with frailty can also be clouded with financial worries: residents are often monetarily as well as medically vulnerable, concerned about their ability to pay for the care they know they must have.

The emotions that people feel after entering a home are colored by their personalities and history, by the type of family support they get, and by the nature of the facility they are in. The quality of institutional care varies tremendously from one home to another, though it is usually only the worst places that reach public awareness when a scandal erupts. Such facilities compound the psychological toll of institutionalization with neglect and abuse. Even some of the better homes may be understaffed and their employees overworked and underpaid. The latter conditions are most likely to be true for those personnel giving direct care to residents. Critics also note the irony that while staff may have more responsibilities than they can handle, residents often have too little to do. A state of inactivity can reinforce a sense of uselessness. In the saddest instances—the kind described by Henry (1963), Laird (1979), Vesperi (1983), and others—a dim and threatening present stretches out in the mind to the pointless, painful days to come.

ANIMALS AND THE AGING ANTHROPOLOGIST

I came to the subject of elderly people in middle age and entered the world of the nursing home by a back door. Earlier in my career I had done archaeology in Turkey and ethnographic work in the Bahamas and the Canadian Arctic. None of that research had taken me inside a medical institution, or raised aging as a primary issue. In Turkey, during 1966, I was part of an expedition to Sardis, the capital of King Croesus's Lydian Empire: there I had been responsible for excavating and analyzing the bones of humans and animals, deciphering what they could tell us about people's lives, diets, and rituals (George M. A. Hanfmann 1972). The Arctic was a very different enterprise. Between 1967 and 1971 I made two field trips to the Northwest Territories of Canada, living with a small, isolated community of Hare Indians who subsisted primarily by hunting, fishing, and trapping (Joel S. Savishinsky 1974). The Hare spent over half of each year following a seminomadic existence, traveling by dogsled and snowshoe through the northern forests to reach the best areas for taking caribou and moose, trout and pike, marten and beaver. What impressed me was not only their ability to survive physically, but their psychological resilience and humor in the face of a harsh environment and a highly mobile, frequently solitary life.

Several years later, with a group of my students, I went to study a network of small communities on Cat Island in the east central Bahamas (Savishinsky 1978). The settlements there were off the main tourist routes, and their inhabitants—the descendants of slaves freed a century and a half before—had developed an economy that combined slash-and-burn farming with goat herding and offshore fishing. Despite the benign appearance of the island's tropical environment, most people there were poor, and we found that family ties, values, and religion were as much a part of what sustained them as their crops and animals and technology.

By 1982, the worlds of Turkey, the taiga, and the tropics were well behind me. At the age of 38, I had a family with two children, and a wife with a career. I could not uproot and transplant my life with the ease I had known in the past. Not only had I settled down after years as an academic nomad, I was also being haunted, each semester, by my students' insistent questions about the relevance of anthropology to their own society. Pushed by them, pulled by my surroundings, I was ready to see how field work might be applied to some of the problems of my own culture and community.

But neither the elderly in general, nor nursing homes in particular, were on my mind at the time. I had never given either much thought. My parents, both in their early seventies then, were in relatively good health. For better or worse, none of my grandparents had ever lived in a geriatric facility. One grandfather had passed away before I was born, the other died at his home of a heart attack in my childhood. My two grandmothers, both of whom I had been close to, had lived until I was in my twenties, and then died in hospitals after brief illnesses. The only relative of mine who had lived out the last part of his life in an institution was my great uncle Joseph. Like my grandparents, he had immigrated to this country from Eastern Europe as a young adult. He had gone through his mature years as a quiet tailor and closet scholar. In his seventies, a pious, childless widower, he had been compelled to move from his Bronx apartment into that borough's Jewish Home for the Aged. From a combination of Parkinson's disease and phlebitis he had become too frail to care for himself. But during the final months of his life, when I would go to see him at the home, I was struck by the new role he had taken on. Despite his declining health and quivering hands, he had become a kind of moral anchor for the other residents. They valued his Talmudic wisdom, his relentless advocacy of their needs, the articulate advice he gave in his still-strong voice. It was as if he had found a rabbinical calling in those final years, called to it by those around him who were in greater need than he himself. At his funeral service, people who had once been strangers to him stood up spontaneously: they shuffled to the front of the chapel and told the simplest of anecdotes to eulogize his *chesed*, his loving-kindness, and his *rachmones*, his gift of compassion.

Ten years passed after those visits to my great uncle, and in that decade I did not once step inside a nursing home. When I finally did go back to an institution, it was in a different role and in different company. The occasion was an unusual letter from some people in my community: they had recently formed an organization called the Companion Animal Program (CAP), whose purpose was to provide weekly pet visits to elderly individuals living in local nursing homes. They had contacted me because they were trying to find a social scientist willing to study the impact of their efforts, to tell them what was actually going on for residents during the pet sessions. Their group was primarily a volunteer organization: it had a paid, part-time director, but was otherwise staffed by 60 community members and college students. The letter explained that each of these people donated part of one afternoon or evening a week to visit a particular nursing facility. They brought their own animals, or borrowed one from a neighbor, and then spent an hour or two with the elderly residents.

When I met with the director and several volunteers to discuss their request, I learned that the organization had begun six months before as the brainchild of Patricia Arveli, a veterinary student. She and her dog had at first gone to the nursing homes on their own, but her idea and example had quickly caught the interest of a number of others: students, local animal rights advocates, and a cohort of community activists had all been drawn to it. What impressed me at our first few meetings was how ardently these people believed in what they were doing, but how unsure they were of its effectiveness. They were asking for feedback, but hoping for reassurance.

There were several reasons why studying this program interested me. First, I was quite taken by the members' enthusiasm. Having done volunteer work with another organization, I felt sympathy for the impulses of volunteers, and curiosity about how their experience affected them. Second, I saw such a project as a chance to move from the scholarly to the practical. Much of my previous research had been in exotic places: while personally and scientifically rewarding, it had been remote from the problems of my own society. This, however, was an opportunity to do something that had both tangible value and local meaning.

But there was also a third reason, one related to a cultural issue that had long intrigued me: this was the relationship between humans and domesticated animals. While I believed, with Alexander Pope, that "the proper study of mankind is man," I also knew there were situations where people revealed themselves through their ties to other creatures. In Turkey I had excavated the remains of classic civilizations where beasts were slaughtered not only for food but for ritual and sacrificial purposes. Their forms appeared in relief on monumental architecture, on mosaic tiled floors, and on the refined gold and bronze of jewelry and ornaments. In the Bahamas, I had lived with people who had subsisted, in part, on goat herds, who traveled to and from their farm fields on horseback and who used cats and dogs to protect their homes and storehouses from vermin. The life of the Arctic community I had studied was the most dramatic in this regard, for it was built around the dogsled as an essential means of transportation. Canines were valued there not only as economic resources, however, but as companions, as sources of pride, and as creatures to whom people could express anger, affection, and reverence.

In the months prior to being contacted by CAP, I had delivered several talks on the topic of human-animal relations, and published an essay on the significance of pet keeping in American and non-Western cultures (Savishinsky 1983). One of my earlier presentations had even found its curious way onto the front page of the *Wall Street Journal,* where an article appeared on the stress-reducing value of animals (John Helyar 1981). It was these activities which had brought me to the pet program's attention, and it was my desire for relevance which in turn made CAP's work attractive to me.

Part of this attraction lay in the challenge of understanding the moral meanings that people attribute to animals. Though they are not human, pets tend to be humanized by their owners, who in turn feel humanized by their presence. People have discovered virtues of tranquillity, companionship, love, loyalty, and humor in their animals, and in America they have elevated them to the status of family members.

Furthermore, pet owners are clearly partisan about the worth of creaturely comforts, and many have turned activist in recent years. They have become both proponents of animal rights and promoters of pets as a form of therapy for the handicapped, the isolated, and the disadvantaged. They have championed recreational and therapeutic programs with animals for the developmentally and physically impaired, and for imprisoned, elderly, institutionalized, and emotionally disturbed populations. At the heart of their advocacy lie certain assumptions drawn from personal experience and everyday life: pets alleviate loneliness and promote sociability; they instill confidence and self-worth; and they offer opportunities to love and be loved. If they provide such benefits to people living in normal circumstances and reasonable health, then proponents urge us to consider what pets could do for individuals deprived of social contacts and physical or mental well-being.

The conviction that animals have the power to bestow social and emotional gifts on people has resulted in a striking growth of pet-facilitated therapy in recent decades.[9] There has been both a humanitarian and an ideological—almost a missionary—strain among those who have promoted this development. The call to help the less fortunate, and the use of animals to achieve this goal, have given the movement a potent combination of sentiment and moral attribute. Furthermore, the fact that many of the pet programs have been initiated and largely staffed by nonprofessional volunteers has placed them close to the heart of an American ethic of self-help and community organizing.

These developments were very much in evidence in my hometown of Ithaca, a community with a long, sustained history of activism. When Patricia Arveli began CAP in the summer of 1982, she had been able to draw on the strength of that local tradition. A third-year veterinary student, she had more energy than money at her disposal, but backed by a modicum of publicity, the support of pet owners, and a small grant from her college, she convinced the administrators at several nursing homes to give her idea a try. The veterinary school eliminated one area of concern by offering to give participating animals a free medical screening. The program's reception during its first months was enthusiastic on the part of both the elderly people it reached and the institutional staff who worked with them. Arveli's efforts quickly evolved into a formal organization. Within the space of three months CAP had four geriatric facilities on its weekly calendar of visitations, and was developing plans to reach out to others in the future. The sessions it held were meant to humanize environments that were potentially alien-ating, places which—at the very least—were lacking in certain key expe-riences that had once been part of most people's everyday lives. The organization's first publicity flyer stated its philosophy and purpose in con-cise, evocative terms:

> As animal lovers we can sympathize with those individuals who, despite their wishes, do not know the joy of "a cold nose and a warm heart." We know intuitively that pets add something important to our lives and the lives of others. In fact, recently there have been fascinating reports about the potential human health benefits that companion animals can provide. We are anxious to put these concepts to good use. Our efforts will be directed towards co-ordinating a pet visitation program at each of the local nursing homes—Hillview, Cranford, Riverside, and Elmwood Grove. We hope to arrange weekly visits to each, utilizing several animals and, thus, several volunteers. The animals may the volunteers' own pets, previously screened by CAP, or animals that CAP can provide. Preferably, the same animals and the same volunteers will return each week in order to establish a sense of continuity and expectation in the nursing home residents.

Though the people in the organization knew what they were doing and why they were doing it, their request to me showed their uncertainty over whether they were going about their work in the best way and whether they were accomplishing their purpose. That was the reason they wanted a study that could answer the questions their project had raised. How many persons were in fact being reached by the visits and how did they really feel about the program? What actually went on between residents and pets during the sessions? And how did this whole effort fit into people's experiences of aging and institutional life?

PEOPLE AND PROCESS

The approach that I took to these issues began with two concepts at the very heart of pet therapy—companionship and domesticity. Companionship refers not simply to people's association with one another; it also means, in its original sense, the sharing of bread (from Latin *panis*, "bread" [Eric Partridge 1966: 468]). But since animal companionship was obviously a bond with a different form and substance, it seemed important to examine, firsthand, what actually happened when humans and pets were brought together. The concept of domesticity also required some rethinking. To domesticate literally means to attach or bring into one's *domus*—the Latin word for "house" (Partridge: 162)—a wild animal or plant. But the pet program took creatures out of their home, put them in an alien environment, and tried to render more homelike a place that was foreign to visitors and residents alike. Its object, then, was to employ animals to domesticate a home rather than utilize the home as a way to tame the wild. It was also important, therefore, to explore the relationship between pets and domesticity, and to understand what the presence of animals meant to elderly people whose home was now an institution.

In the broadest terms, I came to realize that the study had to be a cultural and not just a behavioral one. It had to look at meanings and not simply actions. That meant viewing animal companionship as an expression of our society, as an innovative type of intimacy, and as a response to institutions and the dilemmas of old age. It also meant learning something about voluntarism as a social ethic and its role in people's search for fulfillment.

To begin the study, I enlisted myself as a volunteer. My cat Izzy went through the screening process, and within a few weeks he and I had attended sessions at all four of the nursing homes. My son Jacob, seven years old at the time, offered to accompany me some weeks, and he became a fairly regular feature at Elmwood Grove, the facility where I eventually focused most of my energies. Three of my advanced students also became interested in the work, and at my urging they undertook studies of two of the other facilities. In their dual roles as volunteers and researchers, they each brought not only a pet, but a distinct kind of ethnic and inside experience. Mari Kobayakawa, a Japanese-American, had previously worked at one of these institutions as a nurse's aide. Andrea Nevins, raised in an East European family, had taught a poetry class at another of the homes the year before. And Rich Lathan, a native of Bermuda, had once served as recreation aide at a nearby psychiatric hospital. The following year, after these three graduated, another trio stepped in to carry on: Nordica Holochuck, whose ethnic roots were Finnish; Lisa Sahasrabudhe, born in the United States of an

Indian father and a Jewish mother; and Tu Vu, Vietnamese, who had escaped his homeland with his family in the last agonies of the Vietnam war. Said one of the other volunteers to me, "You've brought the United Nations in here to study us."

There were a number of important preparatory rituals to be accomplished in the early part of the research. Before the active phase of the study began, I met with and secured approval from administrators at each of the nursing homes. Then, as my students and I made our initial rounds of the facilities during the next few weeks, we explained to the residents, the other volunteers, and the staff we met both who we were and what we were doing.

Most of the people were at first strikingly indifferent to us in our roles as anthropologists, and I think this was because they were so much more interested in and appreciative of us as volunteers. Though we occupied both of these statuses, it was in the latter guise, armed with pets rather than notebooks, that they recognized us. Six months later, when we gave a progress report on our work at a volunteers' meeting, one woman in the audience commented, "You know, until you stood up this evening and began to speak, I had completely forgotten why you had joined us in the first place."

Our role was not always that simple or unobtrusive. One man, a very dedicated volunteer and hard-nosed scientist named Ray, was mystified by our methods: he could not understand what anthropologists did, or what results we could achieve. Watching, participating, keeping field journals, and making maps of the homes all seemed beside the point to him. When I asked, as gently as I could, what "point" he had in mind, his body language stuttered a bit and he finally offered, "You know, to show how much we help the old people." I suggested that this was a question, not a conclusion. Yet I also had to admit that we were not trying primarily to measure how much the program did, but to identify how it worked and how it was being responded to.

While we were mainly concerned with the qualities of people's experience—not their quantity—I was able to offer Ray one rather unexpected and useful statistic. For several weeks my students and I had been mapping each of the nursing homes and tracking the way volunteers moved about them during their visits. At one institution—the facility that Ray himself went to—we found that there was an entire wing of one floor that was practically never touched. Almost no one had realized this when I mentioned it, and that was because the lack of coverage was an artifact of architecture rather than avoidance. We had found that the pattern of elevators, corridors, and lounges in this building invariably channelled visitors to a "crossroads" area on this particular floor, a place where its two main wings intersected. Most of the nurses and more mobile residents congregated there, and so visitors rarely went beyond its vicinity. But there was a third unit, one that could only be reached either by a back elevator or through an obscure doorway at the end of one corridor. The result was that practically none of the volunteers knew of this wing's existence. In the weeks after we pointed this out, volunteers were able to change their movements and reach a number of residents who had rarely been seen before.

On the same evening that we unveiled the hidden wing, I reported another finding to the volunteers. My students and I had become aware that there were a number of visitors and residents who wanted to have more individualized time with one another. Meeting together in large groups, which was the prevailing format for pet sessions at several homes, was not meeting their needs. We therefore suggested that the pattern be varied to allow volunteers the option of seeing residents in the privacy of their rooms. Once this had been arranged, it gave these individuals the more personalized contacts they had wanted. These practical results were well received and fairly easy to implement, and they took people by surprise mainly because of their simplicity and obviousness. While such outcomes also quieted our critic Ray, however, I was never convinced that they satisfied his doubts about what we were up to.

The nursing homes were such a brave new world to me that at times I had my own doubts about what we were doing. So to monitor the research I developed a policy of periodically sharing the results of our work with the facilities and the pet program. This took several forms. I occasionally gave talks to the volunteers, had meetings with their director and with administrators at the institutions, and wrote brief articles for the newsletters that were published by CAP and the nursing facilities. Twice, at the end of the first and the second years of the study, my students and I produced detailed reports summarizing our work up to those times. These, as well as several articles I published during this period, were also shared with the homes and the pet program.[10] The process of giving and soliciting feedback in these ways usually worked well: People were informed of what we were finding, and they were able to put into practice several of our recommendations. We, in turn, were able to check out our perceptions and hear about new issues that deserved our attention. There was, however, one glaring exception to the fruits of dialogue, and it sobered me about the sensitivity of people who worked in nursing homes.

In one of our annual reports, each of my students wrote a life history of an individual resident, and provided "a day in the life" account of that person to convey what normal routines were like in the facilities. Names and other details were changed to protect identities, but people's more pointed comments were left in place. One man spoke about the food at his home at some length. While this was an issue that many patients brought up at each of the institutions, this man's words were particularly critical. When one of the administrators at his facility saw the quotation in our report, he was outraged. Writing to me in considerable anger and distress, he argued that nursing homes had a hard enough time getting a fair public hearing, and that a report such as this, quoting the bitter comments of a particularly disgruntled resident, hardly did his institution, or its dietary staff, justice.

While the quote was not in error, I had to recognize, in retrospect, that there had been an error of judgment. The nursing home at issue was a decent one, and though there was no such creature as a representative patient, it would have been more balanced in the report to have offered the views of a number of people on the question of food—or at least to have acknowledged that meals were a convenient place for many residents to displace their other displeasures with life. The lesson that I took most to heart was the image-consciousness of staff who work at and run geriatric facilities. Living in an age of bad press and poor politics for their professions, they were understandably sensitive to any slight—real or imagined—that threatened to make a difficult situation even worse. Though I vowed not to censor my findings, I would at least be approaching my work now with a new awareness of what was at stake for people and the risks I ran in writing about them.

There were also emotional costs to doing the research, and my students and I sometimes paid in the coin of discomfort, disillusionment, and uncertainty. From the very start there was the question of whether people could really be happy living in such places. Roles and rewards were also a puzzle. Mari, who had recently worked as a nurse's aide, wondered how the older women who had been her colleagues could support a family on their salaries. Rich raised the issue of where the limits of our responsibility lay. "What should I do," he asked, "when Eddie wants me to call his lawyer about the deed to his house—is that part of my job?" Andrea fumed and shook her head over "why Charlie doesn't get any visitors when he has a son and two sisters?" There were also layers of pain. Tu once walked into my office, ashenfaced. "I just watched Kate change the dressing on Yvonne's foot. It was a—," and he silently cupped his hands, making the shape of a shallow wedge.

"Decubitus?" I offered.[11]

"Yeah, a decubitus sore. I could barely look—it was so purple, just like a war wound. How can Kate do that? How can Yvonne stand it?"

There were strange, sometimes disconcerting moments when my students and the elderly reached out to but moved beyond one another like boats signaling in the night. Nordica was a junior, a novice to fieldwork, an ardent young woman who had spent years in classrooms but little time in institutions. The residents she first met enjoyed her visits, but dismayed her by failing to remember her name from one session to the next. She would sigh about that in our conferences, but then be unable herself to recall the names of staff members whom she had conferred with that same week. It was not always clear whose forgetfulness was more alarming for Nordica—her own or that of the elderly.

I had asked Nordica to keep a field journal, but advised her not to take notes while she was with people. When I suggested that instead she should just open up all her senses, attend to as much as she could, and only record her observations later on, she balked at the idea. "How can I ever remember so much—all those people, all that talk—hours afterwards?" I taught her some of my techniques, such as inventing mnemonics to recall a series of names, and keeping a small notepad in a pocket to write down key words, topics, and snatches of dialogue whenever I had a moment to myself. But I emphasized that no such memory aides were as important as simply paying full attention to each moment's occurrences, consciously registering the words, the looks, and the actions in one's mind for later recall. It meant appreciating the rich details of experience, respecting their place in the fabric of everyday life, and valuing these phenomena for the potential meaning they had. The key was to develop a kind of discipline, an ethnographic mindfulness.

One day, after weeks of watching, talking, writing, and wrestling with her attentiveness, Nordica marched into my office and proudly announced, "It's finally happening! I ask myself what went on and now I can remember. The words come back, or at least enough of them for me to piece conversations together. Now I know what I've had a chance to know—even when I write about people who don't know me." It was a bittersweet realization, a discovery of her own mind's capabilities in the midst of getting to know people faced with the desertion of memory itself.

METHODS AND ISSUES

The study started with the novelty of animals but went on to the reality of people. It grew in an organic way, unfolding outward to take in the personalities of residents, the presence or absence of their families, the responsibilities of staff, and the hopes of visitors. Beyond the pets, then, there were these other bodies and rhythms, their voices and routines. Home life included the pacing of meals and the spacing of medicines, the sounds of the elderly and their histories, the self-selected community of volunteers, and the vocabularies of people's faces and professions. There were also the messages of room decorations, the replay of recollections, the catalogue of ills and indignities to which the aged are heir, and the shifting mood and morale of staff—each of which appeared as background on some days, at center stage on others.

There was more than one method to how we studied all of these facets, but the basic techniques were relatively simple and largely qualitative. We treated the nursing homes as expressions of American society, as microcosms of the culture, the people, and the values that shaped and shared them. Adopting the approach that anthropologists have perfected in examining whole communities and other societies, we functioned primarily as participant–observers in a wide range of activities that residents, staff, pets, and visitors engaged in. Besides making the rounds of the homes each week with our animals, we visited at other times to eat meals with patients, watch their physical therapy, read books and write poetry with them, and attend holiday parties. We also went on outings, drank coffee with staff, hung out in lounges and nursing stations, sat on the lawns with patients in summer, and chatted with family members. We mapped the facilities and how people used space in them, kept records of who attended pet sessions and other programs, and followed the shifting alliances of roommates and relationships.

As we got to know individual residents better, we collected some of their life histories, often using tape recorders. After I began to concentrate my own efforts on Elmwood Grove, I also conducted interviews with staff, volunteers, and visitors from that facility. While most of these were done at the institution itself, I sometimes met with people at their own homes for greater convenience and privacy. For the formal interviews, I developed protocols so that comparable kinds of information could be gathered for each group. Residents were asked to recount the basic facts of their lives, including their memories about families, pets, education, and jobs. I encouraged their recollections about the best and worst periods from their past. They were also asked to discuss the process that had led to their move into Elmwood Grove, their ties to other residents and staff, and the most difficult and most rewarding things about life within the institution. Finally, drawing on my role as a teacher and parent, I asked them what advice they would have me give to young people today, based upon their years of experience and their acquaintanceship with age.

Discussions with family members centered on how the decision to move their relative to Elmwood had been made, and how this had affected the family as a whole. We also examined their feelings about the institution and about how their relative had adapted to life there. Volunteers were, of course, a very different kind of visitor, and interviews with them emphasized their motives and their experiences at the home, and the way the latter had affected their views on aging and institutional care. This last issue was also raised with staff. In addition, employees were asked about their previous job experiences, their methods for coping with stress, and their relationships with residents and co-workers. In the end, I had them talk about whether they would ever want to live in a nursing home themselves.

What emerged from my own work was a small-scale portrait of the culture that framed the lives of the aged and that, in the act of framing them, set these people off with greater clarity. I realized at one point that Elmwood Grove actually had the same size population as the Arctic and Bahamian communities I had once worked in, and that this undoubtedly (and unconsciously) made it easier for me to feel at home there. The decision, however, to emphasize qualitative methods in the study—participating, talking, visiting, interacting, interviewing, observing—was quite conscious, and it admittedly ran against the grain of current trends in social research. The behavioral sciences today have made quantification a very seductive approach, and many people assume that to count is, somehow, to comprehend. My own feeling is that technique can then become a substitute for understanding, just as the design of instruments replaces the role of the imagination. These are the dangers when the rules of measurement become the rule of thumb itself. But because my students and I were mainly interested in the qualities of life, the methods we used were themselves mostly qualitative in nature. And because what we wanted to explore was the story of the old, their institutions, and those who try to humanize such people and places, I have opted here for narrative rather than numbers to tell their tale.

The small world of the nursing home raises some large issues. No single study can address all the questions about aging that geriatric facilities suggest, but the questions themselves put the experience of institutionalization into a broad cultural context. Early in our work, for example, we found ourselves asking whether this was the way it had to be. Why do people end up in such facilities, how do they feel about them, what—if any—were their alternatives? We noted certain ambiguities that other researchers have also identified: the fact that some geriatric staff think of an institution as a home where others see it as a hospital (Shield 1988); the emphasis of some employees on humanitarian care while their colleagues stress curing (Vesperi 1983); and the tensions between those who follow a social as opposed to a medical model of treatment (Robert L. Kane and Rosalie Kane 1978). Recognizing that nursing homes themselves are a relatively recent development in industrial societies, we wondered how other cultures view the process of growing old, and how they respond to those who can no longer lead a fully active life or care for themselves.

The theory of "disengagement" has been proposed as one answer to some of these questions (Elaine Cumming and William Henry 1961). It argues that aging individuals, and those around them, undergo a process of "inevitable mutual withdrawal" as people enter late life (Cumming and Henry:14). In contrast to the "activity" theory of aging, which proposes a "positive relationship between activity and life satisfaction" (Bruce Lemon, Vern Bengtson, and James Peterson 1972: 511), disengagement interprets decreases in the elderly's social involvement as a universal outcome brought on by declining health, diminished vigor, reduced capacity for economic self-sufficiency, and a psychological reorientation to more inward-looking concerns as the life cycle draws to a conclusion. In effect, the old and their society agree to part company.

Responding to the debate over disengagement versus activity theory, anthropologists have qualified the argument by noting that there are certain cultures that enable the elderly to retain wealth and power or assume positions of spiritual and moral leadership.[12] A number of these cases were referred to earlier. In traditional rural Ireland, for example, elderly parents dominated their farms and families well past the point where they ceased active involvement in agriculture and household life (Conrad Arensberg 1937). Retired French laborers have been found to be very engaged in the daily social relations and ideological debates of their community (Jennie Keith 1982). Among the Druze, a militant Islamic people living in Israel and Lebanon, old men hold onto considerable influence in religious and village affairs after they have withdrawn from military and political concerns (David Guttman 1976). And the Tiwi of North Australia, a hunting and gathering group, developed a male gerontocracy in which older men exercised significant control over marriageable women and other tribal resources until the very end of their lives (C. W. M. Hart and Arnold Pilling 1979).

These are just a few instances of cultures in which aging has not meant an inevitable divorce from power or participation. These cases have been explained, in part, by "social exchange theory" (James Dowd 1975), which argues that the status of the old depends on their ability to control valued commodities—be these people, goods, or knowledge—for use in social relations. When confronted, then, with frail elderly Americans residing in institutions where they have little authority and few possessions, one cannot help but question how voluntary and reciprocal their disengagement from life has really been. Their lack of resources has been used to explain the extreme dependency of residents in several institutions, including Pacific Manor (Kayser-Jones 1981) and Franklin (Shield 1988). The powerlessness of such people leads to even broader questions about the place of the old in the larger society. As the aged portion of this country's population increases in the decades ahead, this "graying of America" will force more and more of us to reexamine how involved the elderly can or should be in defining the conditions of their own existence.

In the course of our work my students and I also became aware of the special, protean relationship that the elderly had with their caregivers and the animals. The visiting pets had a strong emotional valence for residents. This was connected not only to the other animals people had once owned, but was somehow subtly bound up with their childhoods, marriages, homes, and earlier domestic lives. We began to wonder how the pets, and the stroking and caressing words they evoked, were related to these other forms of intimacy from the past. What made the pets of strangers morally meaningful? What made their presence not only memorable, but also a stimulus to memories of other times and ties?

The segregation of over one and a half million Americans in geriatric facilities has also generated a large, specialized work force to deal with the needs of residents. Nothing comparable to the array of doctors, dietitians, therapists, nurses, and aides exists in traditional societies, which tend to care for the aged within the community and the extended family. If older

Americans often feel neglected or overlooked, our work led us to suspect that the same is true of those who work with and care for them. If the elderly do not often get heard, what about those who attend to them but go unrecognized in the day-to-day operation of the institutions? Specifically, what is it like to work with the elderly, be it as an employee or a volunteer? How do such people feel about their roles and responsibilities, about the aged whom they serve, about the images and the rewards of what they do?

The issue of image was not as ephemeral or insubstantial as it appeared to be. Simone de Beauvoir has argued that the elderly are invisible, that we see death "with a clearer eye" than old age itself (1972: 4). But when one looks at how people look at the elderly, the relationship between appearance and reality shifts from being a philosophical puzzle to a matter of practical importance. That is, the way the aged are perceived by those who are younger and healthier—including such people as my students, my own children, and a middle-aged anthropologist such as myself—affects the way we behave towards them. One way I tried to develop some insights into this issue of image was to involve people of various ages in the research itself. During the study I was in my late thirties and early forties. My students were half my age, most of the elderly we worked with were twice my age. My son Jacob, who accompanied me to many pet sessions at Elmwood, passed his eighth, ninth, tenth, and eleventh birthdays during this period. At the other extreme of age was Nora Randall, a veteran Elmwood resident, who celebrated her 100th year on earth in the course of the study. One virtue of bringing these extremes together was the candor it sometimes evoked. When Jacob heard about Nora's birthday party, his eyebrows rose and his jaw dropped in awe; he whispered to me, like a conspirator let in on a dark secret, "I didn't think people were allowed to live that long!"

SEGREGATION AND INSTITUTIONALIZATION

While aging is a universal experience, it is the special qualities of old age in modern America that give this study its focus. Recent increases in life expectancy mean that greater numbers of people will survive to an advanced age. Many of those who do will spend some part of their later years in a geriatric facility, heirs to those disabilities that still lie beyond the curative powers of medicine or the scope of what home care could cope with. While most older individuals would prefer to remain in their own residences, nonmedical as well as health factors often contribute to their placement in an institution. For example, community-based services to assist the elderly and their families with home care are frequently inadequate or unaffordable. In other instances, there may simply be no one at home to help provide for an older person. This is because the changed structure of domestic life in America now frequently separates the elderly from those who were once their caregivers. The mobility and dispersion of people's grown children, and the fact that adult daughters and daughters-in-law are more likely to have jobs and careers, means that there are fewer kin at home to offer company, meals, and bodily assistance. In yet other cases elderly individuals have chosen to enter an institution rather than become a burden on their grown children and relatives.

For all these older people—be they voluntary or involuntary residents of a nursing home—the very option of moving to an institution comes from a redirection of society's economic resources. The geriatric facilities of today have been financially underwritten by new forms of capital investment, charity, private insurance, and public support, including Medicare and Medicaid. The fact that government and private forms of health coverage rarely defray the costs of prolonged hospitalization or home care increases the likelihood that a family will choose institutionalization. As the nature of economic policies, local services, and family life patterns suggest, long-term care is a social, not just a medical, phenomenon.[13]

By whatever route people have come to a nursing facility, the residents there do not constitute the only group of Americans living in an age-segregated setting. College dormitories, army barracks, trendy neighborhoods, and retirement communities all share the same characteristic. More of the American population, and more of the country's daily life, is segregated by the criterion of age than many of the segregants realize.

But this kind of generational pattern can have many meanings. Dormitories and retirement complexes, for example, are entered into willingly by people who choose to live with their peers. Elsewhere in the world, there are other societies that also stratify and separate their members by age, but do so primarily for ideological reasons. East African peoples, such as the Nyakyusa, form distinct "age villages" for males of the same generation. This enables group members to be collectively initiated, educated, and then welded into a community whose residents will work and live together throughout their adult lives (Monica Wilson 1963). Similarly, the Israeli kibbutzim organize children born around the same time into social units called *kevutza*. From infancy until late adolescence, members of these peer groups live and attend school together, experiencing the collective bonds that lie at the heart of kibbutz values (Melford Spiro 1965). In both these cultures, segregation becomes a means to solidarity.

What is distinctive about the American nursing home experience, then, is not segregation, but the added element of institutionalization, that is, life in a setting over which the residents have minimal control. Not that institutions are unique to the elderly in Western culture. Other populations that are socially or physically stigmatized, or that cannot be cared for or treated in the community, have also traditionally undergone institutionalization. These include criminals, orphans, the handicapped, the insane, and the developmentally impaired. Putting people with stigmatized or "spoiled"

identities away has become a fairly pervasive response to the socially marginal in the West (Goffman 1963; Michel Foucault 1973, 1979). So while
the ailing aged do not share many of the deviant qualities of the other groups
mentioned, there are parallels in the total way their respective institutions
define their daily routines, provide for their basic needs, and set limits to
their freedom.

The rise of the nursing home, then, has been the outgrowth of several
medical and social transformations. These include the increased longevity
of current generations, the progressive graying of the population, the decline
of the extended family as a care-giving unit, and the growing use of financial
resources to pay for institutions as an alternative way to house the old.
While describing these trends in broad terms puts nursing facilities into a
social context, it does not tell us what the human impact of these developments has been. What follows is an attempt to tell part of that story by
describing one institution. If my students and I had known what was in
store for us when we set out on this study, we probably would have thought
twice about it, questioning in particular our ability to confront what our
own lives might have in store for us. But what we found was the kind of
learning that historian Daniel Boorstin has called the heart of a true education, which is the process of learning about things you didn't even know
you didn't know.

2 THE VISITS

A START

The first time I went to Elmwood Grove Nursing Home was on a late Friday afternoon in January 1983. By 4:00 P.M. at that season of the year, the sky in upstate New York is being drained of light, and the air tastes like evening. I had driven to the small village of Shelby, just ten miles outside of Ithaca, where Elmwood was located. Walking from the home's lamplit parking lot, I stepped over the remnant patches of snow, and moved past the main entrance. On the glass door fronting the lobby was a small, permanently fixed sign which said "No Pets Allowed."

The irony of the message was hard to miss: as a calling card for that first visit, I had brought my cat, who lay curled up inside his carrying case. But breaking regulations was the least of my anxieties. It was the residents on the inside, rather than the house rules, which preoccupied me the most.

The pet program I had come to study was only several months old, while the elderly people it served ranged in age from their sixties to their nineties. At Elmwood, they were all receiving "skilled nursing" care, that is, their physical disabilities required that they have medical services available to them 24 hours a day. In some cases, I had been told, mental losses compounded the physical ones. There were people suffering from confusion, Alzheimer's disease, depression, and stroke. A number of the residents could move about unaided, but most used walkers or wheelchairs. Among them were individuals coping with incontinence, the loss of speech, and the failed capacity to bathe, feed, or care for their other daily needs.

As compelling as these disabilities were, CAP was more concerned with other kinds of losses. In particular, it tried to address the emotional, social, and sensory deficits of institutional life. The project's volunteers felt that they could help alleviate these by using pets to engage and stimulate. Their most basic idea was that animals offered the elderly an opportunity to touch, talk, and experience some small reminders of domesticity from the outside world and their own pasts.

Elmwood Grove was one of four nursing homes in the county visited by them. Being a "skilled nursing facility" (or SNF) meant that its residents were in much greater need of medical and practical help than either the mildly impaired people living in "health-related facilities" (HRFs), or the relatively self-sufficient individuals at "domiciliary" institutions. Elmwood had an 84-bed capacity, and some of its patients had come to it from facilities where they had been receiving a lower level of care. The home was almost always full. Its residents lived, and its staff worked, in a two-story gray stone structure set in a neighborhood of family homes. Elmwood's building was situated only five streets from the edge of the village's business district, and yet it could claim a distinctly countrified air. The facility sat in the midst of its own block, bounded on one side by a small parking lot and on the other three by a spacious lawn studded with mature, stately trees. The elms that had bestowed their name on the home had long ago succumbed to disease, but large shady maples had since grown up in their stead.

In the weeks preceding my visit, I had thought a lot about what the home would be like. CAP's director had explained to me that pet sessions there were held in the recreation room on late Friday afternoons, and lasted an hour and a half. Approximately six volunteers, an equal number of cats and dogs, and some four to ten residents attended them. While these statistics gave an idea of the scale of visits, I knew the latter were only a small part of the facility's total life. Besides, it was hard to paint a picture of the home by the numbers: what information I had been given about Elmwood kept getting crowded out of view by my overworked imagination. The media, my reading, and my own fears about institutions had done a good job of shaping my worst expectations. The night before that first session I had dreamed a vision of bedlam on the home's inside—bodily smells, moans, people in grotesque postures, hands reaching out. The portrait's outline stayed long after the dream's end, its theatrical image printed on my mind's eye.

When I approached Elmwood the next afternoon, I did not enter the home's main doorway. Instead, as I had been instructed to beforehand, I walked around the building's outside to the back entrance of the rear wing. There, through a window at the top of a small ramp, I had a view of the recreation room: its contents pushed last night's vision aside like a screen. Six elderly people sat in a circle in the middle of the area. Most were in wheelchairs, and these faced inward, directing the residents' attention to a group of animals and people in the space before them. Opening the outside door and stepping into the room, I got a clearer look at what they were watching.

At the center of gravity inside the ring of wheelchairs, two small acts were being performed: in one a pair of dogs was wrestling on the ground, and in the other a collie was begging biscuits from a resident. The woman with the food, who looked to be in her eighties, was wearing a flower-print housedress. She said to a young man standing beside her, "I once had a cat that begged like this dog. It was very cute but very confused: It didn't know what kind of animal it was. But its species didn't much matter because I think it was mostly stomach." Her remark got a chorus of laughter and a bark, and she paid off the collie with a biscuit.

The only person in the room I knew was Cathy Montoya, a volunteer who had helped arrange my visit to the home. She walked over and began introducing me to people. In front of us was Eddie: silent, beatific smile, a stroke patient. Next to him sat Tilly, whose small-framed body bent to one side like a wind-shaped tree. She had salt-and-pepper hair and appeared younger than the others. Her lively eyes looked out over a warm voice whose slurred words I could barely understand. Not knowing what to do when she spoke and looked to me for a response, I nodded as if I agreed with her, and worried whether my answer was correct, or the pretense too obvious. To Tilly's right, in the print dress, was Bonnie, the critic of canine behavior. She said some things to me about the animals, and then the weather, and then my clothes. She talked readily, if disconnectedly, seeming genuinely pleased by the company and the conversation.

Having covered half the residents there, Cathy paused in her introductions and suggested that I take my cat out of his carrier. When I put the box down and opened the lid, Izzy, my six-month-old kitten, was crouched in a corner. He was fawn-colored, thick-furred, and usually calm to the point of being comatose. But the car trip, the strange environment, and the sound of dogs had all combined to make him alert, defensive, and fearful. Coaxing and then coercing him, I got Izzy into my arms, eased him a bit with some strokes, and approached the next resident. Cathy introduced him as Dave Dorenberg, a native of New York and a newcomer to the home. "I didn't know they boarded animals here too," he observed. "If I knew that, I would have brought my brother-in-law and rented a cage for him." He knew he had an audience and seemed to enjoy using the kitten as straight man. "He isn't really so bad, my brother-in-law. And actually he likes cats. It's people he isn't too good with."

Mainly because he did almost all the talking, Dave put me at my ease. Even when he spoke directly to me, he took everyone into his confidence, accomplishing this with his loud voice and the well-timed nods of his head, which he swung to make eye contact with others. I had begun by putting the kitten in Dave's lap. And though the cat had prompted his first brother-in-law remarks, Izzy quickly receded in importance. Dave's talk moved on to his marriage, his daughter's success as a professor, his own political opinions. Yet he kept stroking the animal absentmindedly; during lulls in the conversation he rediscovered him and asked rhetorically, "You're pretty happy here, aren't you? Not bad to have a lap, and be petted and cared for, eh?"

By now the dogs had gotten bored with begging and wrestling, and one of them took his restlessness across the circle to investigate Izzy. It was the collie. He stretched his muzzle up towards Dave's lap, but when his nose touched Izzy's paw, the cat's eyes flashed open and his whole body bristled. Izzy pulled himself up into battle position, his arched back curved like a bowstring, rising up to block Dave's view. The man asked what was happening, but before anyone could answer there was a loud hiss, a quick swipe with a paw, and a nick in the collie's nose from the cat's claw. The dog howled, throwing the room into silence.

The first person to speak was Denise Valensky, Elmwood's activities director. She had been hovering behind the circle of chairs, and now moved in to reassure the residents that the collie was alright. But it turned out that people were more amused than upset, and Denise's remarks faded underneath their comments. Bonnie, musing on the dog's injury, offered the pun that "this is what happens when you get too nosy." Dave was more sociological:

> You bring together people—or animals—who are so different, and sooner or later the differences come out. Just like cats, I think most people want to be with their own. You crowd them with strangers and they strike out at them. Now where I grew up in New York, Hell's Kitchen, we had all kinds: Italians, Poles, Jews, the Irish. We actually got along pretty well, but that was by sticking mostly with our own. Anyway, that's the way it seemed to me. . . . So there's nothing more for me to say.

It was an opening Denise could not resist. "Dave," she interjected, "having nothing to say never stopped you from talking."

He laughed and turned a smile to me, as if his vice was really a hidden virtue. "These women, especially this one," he said, indicating Denise, "they never stop. I've always had something going with them. They don't leave me alone."

"I think it's more that you don't leave *us* alone," responded Denise. "What do you think, Tilly? Do women bother men the way cats bother dogs?"

"People are basically good," Tilly began, adding something to the effect that they only troubled others if they themselves were troubled. She spoke some more, but I couldn't understand her. I turned to Steve, another of the volunteers, and gave him a puzzled look. He translated for me: "She says all God's creatures are good in their hearts. People can be that way too 'if they believe in the Lord.' Then, she says, they can all be 'as innocent as animals.' "

Moving me back a bit from the wheelchairs, Steve explained about Tilly's religiosity: there was her faith in prayer, in Jesus, in people's goodness, and her tendency not to proselytize but to urge others to see the merit of her own beliefs. He felt that Tilly found few candidates for redemption, and yet she was neither discouraged nor disliked. Perhaps, he guessed, her methods were "sincere and soft enough not to offend people."

A large German shepherd trailed Steve as he walked over to a window. Luna, a seven-year-old female, was one of two dogs that came with him each week, and they were sometimes accompanied by Beth, Steve's wife. When I asked how long he had been volunteering, Steve said it had been "about six months, almost from the very start of the program."

> It was actually Beth who got us involved, at least indirectly. She has a grandmother, Laura Johanson, who lives here, and we'd been coming to visit her—though Beth found this a hard place to be. There was too much sadness, too much death.
>
> Then I heard about this pet program at my department—I'm doing graduate work, but with plants, not animals. Still, they had this notice up on the bulletin board about visiting the elderly once a week, and there was a meeting for new people. So we had these two dogs who were eating us out of house and home, and needed to get out more anyway because we're gone all day: I'm in class and the lab, and Beth's a secretary. So I went to the meeting, and when I heard they did visits here, it seemed like the perfect solution.

When I asked how it had worked out, he said:

> Pretty good, though not perfect. It's been easier coming with the dogs than without them—easier to meet and chat with people because the dogs are an instant conversation piece. This one, Luna, even does a few simple tricks. Those paled after a while, but by then I'd found I'd gotten to know some residents and we could talk, dog or no dog, tricks or not. But Beth still finds it upsetting to be here, so while she does come, it's really to see her grandmother. The others are now in the background.

The shepherd had dropped down to the floor near us, obediently waiting, sprawled out on its belly with its head laid across its front legs. Steve gave it a look of mock despair, and with a snap of his fingers, he had her standing up and alert again. The three of us moved back towards the circle, where there were still several residents whom I had not yet met. A few feet away Denise was leaning over a wheelchair, talking to a white-haired, neatly dressed man. He had glasses with a hearing aide attached, and a substantial, well-manicured moustache that seemed to raise the end of his nose up to a slightly aristocratic bent. Luna stuck her own nose between Denise's stomach and the man's knees, slowly insinuating the whole front of her body between them. "Denise," sighed the man, "this is the end of our affair."

He spoke with a European accent of uncertain provenience. "This gentleman," said Denise, bowing towards him with a touch of courtliness, "is

Mr. Costa, Stavros Costa. He's from Turkey originally, and Greece, but he has lived here for many years." Denise then introduced me and explained briefly about the research. "Ah, a professor," he responded. "You have come to study us, the specimens of old age. There is not much that life has left us, as you can see, but you have come to the right place." I was embarrassed at his candor, but then discovered he was teasing—or at least willing to continue on a note of humor. "Don't worry, you won't catch what we have, at least not for many years. With us, your youth is safe. But outside of here. . . . " He finished the phrase with a wave of his hand, taking in the wider world of time. The dog's head jerked up to follow the sweep of his arm, and then rolled back to lie on Stavros's thigh.

The cautionary words left me with an instant feeling of age. Not knowing how to respond, I instead looked in distraction at the others around me. There was only one resident remaining in the room whom I had not spoken with, and Denise, sensing my unease, walked me over to her. The woman's name was Greta, and unlike the others, she was on a mobile bed rather than a wheelchair. She had a peaceful face with a pasty complexion. Lying on her left side, she stared into the center of the room. But her look was not vacant, and her eyes showed a quiet interest. Mandy, one of the volunteers, was standing by Greta's side, holding her hand. She told me that a stroke had left Greta largely immobilized, that she had not spoken a word in over a year. Denise urged me to take Izzy from Dave's lap, where he had dozed off beneath the petting, and place him on Greta's bed. I found a place for the cat inside the curve made by the arc of Greta's legs and belly and chest. He hung like warm dough when I carried him over, but then curled into a more animate shape when I placed him on the blanket. Mandy took the hand of Greta's she had been holding and placed it on the cat's back. It rested there, rising and falling with the animal's breathing. Leaning over, Mandy spoke into Greta's ear, telling her to feel how soft and warm the cat was. Except for a slight lift of her brow, however, the woman's face never changed expression. In a few moments her eyes closed in a kind of sleep.

From somewhere just beyond the room there came a rolling, rhythmic hum and beneath that noise the sound of singing. The roll and the song grew louder, echoing in the passageway outside. Then the two swinging doors from the corridor abruptly banged inward, and a wheelchair appeared: first the foot rests, next the knees, and then two energetic arms launched straight ahead from propelling the wheels a last turn. The new arrival was a seventyish man with a luminous crown of white hair. Surveying the room, he observed, "Ah, a traveling zoo." He wore amber-framed glasses, below which two deep vertical creases went down and out from the bridge of his nose, setting off his cheeks like a potter's mark. From where I stood I could see Bonnie, Denise, Tilly, and Steve smiling at the dramatic entrance.

Though no one needed the name except me, Denise announced, "And this is Frank."

"My friends," the man opened, "I don't quite see the point of all this. But maybe there doesn't have to be any." Frank spoke like someone well experienced at sizing up his audience. "We get out of our rooms, the animals escape their cages, we meet and mingle. I feel," he added as he pushed himself to an opening in the circle near Greta's bed, "I feel at least we are in good company. Now don't get me wrong, young lady," he was addressing Cathy now, "I hold no brief for old age. If anything, it holds me. No, but I do consider where we all might be if we weren't here—I mean the older among us. My sister, for example, lives in a retirement community in northern Florida. But I consider that to be just a prison with palm trees."

From Greta's bedside, Mandy asked Frank what he thought about life at Elmwood. "There are nice people and no palms—and thank God for both of those things," he replied. "It is an institution, of course, though not a prison . . . even though a prison is an institution too. . . . " He paused to test the drift of his own words. "I think this [conversation] is beginning to sound like some lost part of *Alice in Wonderland*. Anyway, I am digressing. To answer you: I am well taken care of here. And the staff is very good. . . . But what I miss most in my life no one can give me, which is the use of my legs and my own place to live. So except for complaining, I can't complain."

No one in earshot took exception to Frank's judgment. It sounded a bit rehearsed but nonetheless honest. Perhaps it was also hard to argue with a man in a wheelchair, yet what I really sensed on people's faces was simply an appreciation for his candor. From Denise's and Steve's nods I read agreement: what is lost is lost; false optimism would only offend. If Frank had the courage not to deny his lot, denial from any of us would be patronizing, cowardly.

There was a ginger cat named Yussy, who had been offstage all hour, sulking in a box on a table by the door. Mandy, who brought him each week, saw that time was running out for the visit and made a last attempt to coax the cat into the room. She finally succeeded in getting him up and bringing him over to Frank. The cat turned around several times in the man's lap, unable to settle down, and then spotted Izzy a few feet away on Greta's bed. The ginger cat's back arched, and he hissed a loud challenge. Izzy leaped to his feet and moved to attack, but I reached over the bed and grabbed him. He squirmed in my arms and scratched through my shirt; the sudden shot of pain made me drop him. He fell to the linoleum floor and tried to run, his paws skittering on the smooth surface; then he found enough traction to flee to a neutral corner.

Standing there empty handed, I felt conspicuous as well as bruised. But no one else seemed especially aware of either emotion: my small wounds lay hidden beneath my sleeve, my self-consciousness simply part of the invisible clothing of a first-time visitor. Bonnie made a joke about letting sleeping cats as well as sleeping dogs lie. Denise explained what had just happened to Eddie, and when he began to say something in response, she bent over to hear him better. Steve was busy with his two dogs while Frank, with Mandy's help, was calming the ginger cat. Unable to shake off my looking-glass self, however, I looked around to see who might be looking at me. I caught Tilly's eyes and crossed over to her. "I know what it's like to be scared like your cat," she confided. "But if you bring him back next week, maybe he'll get used to the other animals." "Tilly," threw in Denise, "you get along better with people here than most other residents. Maybe you could give the cats lessons in coexistence."

There was a bank of high windows running the length of the west wall of the room we were in. Daylight, always at a premium this time of winter, had faded into a lead-pipe gray since the start of the session. Now the large, globe-shaped lights at ceiling height, unnoticed an hour ago, gave us more to see by than the sun. Some people—Eddie and Bonnie—were beginning to nod off, while Stavros, fully alert, wanted to know how long it was until dinner. Cathy looked at the clock and told him half an hour, adding that the bus would be arriving soon to pick up her and Mandy. Residents and visitors alike were visibly getting ready to move on to the next part of their day.

The bus Cathy mentioned was run by a community agency, and offered free transportation to elderly and handicapped people and to those who worked with them. Tilly, for example, told me it took her to her "school" on weekdays, though I did not know at the time what she was referring to by that. Cathy explained that several of the students who volunteered at Elmwood were picked up and later let off at their campus by the bus each Friday afternoon. En route, it also stopped to get the animals that families in the community offered the program for its use each week.

With the session about to end and the bus due in just a few minutes, Denise asked if we could help her take the residents back to their rooms. I agreed to this with the others but told Cathy, who stood near me, that I wasn't sure what to do. So she showed me how to release the brakes on Bonnie's wheelchair, and suggested that the two of us follow her and Tilly because they would be passing right by Bonnie's room.

At the end of the first corridor Bonnie told me she wasn't sure what her room number was but not to worry, that she could direct me to it as we moved through the hallways. She dropped gossipy comments as we passed other residents along the way.

The man in that room is a screamer: he yells at people, and sometimes he just shouts out over and over again even if nobody is there. I don't mean to sound cruel, but it's almost like a dog barking or howling. . . . That woman in the hall there is very nice: she was a teacher like me, though she taught in a different school. . . . No, actually, I'm not sure of her name. . . . That other one, the woman in the yellow dress, is Eva: she's two rooms down from me and wanders all the time—just like the way she's walking now, rubbing along the walls. You have to watch her. She goes into your room and opens drawers to take things. Of course she doesn't know what's she's really doing, yet you still can't help but be upset sometimes. . . . Everyone else here, all these nurses and maids and aides you see going about their business, they're working to get things ready for dinner, I guess.

It seemed, in fact, a very busy time of day. Floor staff were moving people to the dining room, kitchen workers were in the final stage of meal preparation, and late afternoon visitors were taking their leave. My brief walk between the recreation area and Bonnie's first floor room was sufficient to give me a strong first impression of the home's physique. The building's age was apparent in its tight layout and spaces, its well-worn paint and fixtures, its old-style beds and sinks. I knew that parts of the structure dated back to the 1920s. Though institutional and old, however, the building did not feel cold or impersonal. Perhaps it was the lack of spit and polish, the absence of fluorescent glows and a nailed-down appearance. It had, for a home, a homey feel.

There were, nevertheless, an assortment of sights, sounds, and smells that jarred my senses. No amount of reading prepares you for the unmistakable odor of urine, and there was a puddle beneath the chair of one man sitting in the hallway. In one room we passed there was a woman, whom I could not see, rhythmically calling out, "Nurse! Nurse!" Sitting along the sides of the corridor were several residents with silent, unmoving faces: I did not know what to think of or say to them.

When I got back to the recreation room and had packed my cat in his case, I felt quiet and ready to retreat. The scratches on my arm, like small scars of initiation, itched like something unresolved. The other volunteers were talking and joking, but it was hard for me to join them: in my mind, I was already trying to sort out the details of the visit and the sights of that brief, concluding walk. I knew it was premature to try understanding any of these, yet it was just as hard to resist the desire for instant insight. I comforted myself instead with the prospect of going home, opening my field journal, and writing out a description of that first afternoon's events. Before I left, however, Denise invited me to come visit her the next week to tour the home and learn its history.

THE HOME

Elmwood Grove Nursing Home was as old as some of its residents. The facility occupied a two-story, Y-shaped building whose oldest wing dated back to 1927. Denise explained that when it was founded, the institution had a very different purpose and clientele than at present. It had grown out of the private efforts of Lucille Westman, a minister's wife and local resident, who had begun to take a small number of tubercular children into her parish home for care and rehabilitation. With support and funds from the surrounding communities, a building was added on to her personal residence in the village of Shelby in 1927, marking the formal birth of the institution. In subsequent decades, the scope of the facility's program expanded to include both adults and children with respiratory problems, and "The Grove" became a private, not-for-profit home governed by a board of directors. The original Westman house eventually had to be razed when a wing was added in the 1950s to provide more residential space for children and a new dining room.

During the 1960s and 1970s, Elmwood underwent a major change in its programs and patients. With the decline of tuberculosis as a significant health problem, and with the rise of more specialized respiratory centers in the region, the treatment programs for children and adults were phased out. By the early 1970s, in fact, children were no longer being accommodated in the home, and the institution was gradually converted into a geriatric facility. In the next few years the nature of this elderly population also began to change. By the mid-1980s, the residents were generally older and more debilitated than their counterparts had been some 15 years ago. The average age in the 1980s was itself in the mid-eighties, and most residents had chronic, incurable illnesses. Skilled nursing care had become the order of the day . . . and night.

Gordon Morrell, the assistant administrator, argued in fact that the home could now most appropriately be called "a chronic hospital." He noted that few people were discharged or moved to a lower level of care. The medical conditions that brought them there were disabling ones that interfered with what are technically called the ADL, the "activities of daily living." These comprise the basic abilities to eat, walk, dress, toilet, and bathe oneself. The incapacitating illnesses ran the gamut from osteoporosis, diabetes, arthritis, and skin disorders to emphysema, multiple sclerosis, stroke, heart ailments, malnutrition, and Alzheimer's disease. Over 50 percent of the residents had been diagnosed with some form of dementia, 25 percent were being spoon-fed, and about 10 percent were classified as abusive. Marian Portline, the director of nursing, observed that "we have the sickest people [of any institution] in the area. Some of the other homes, for instance, won't take a patient who can't swallow and is on an NG [naso-gastric] tube, because it's too complicated and expensive to care for someone like that."

The home served an elderly population drawn largely from the towns and rural communities of Tompkins County, but it also had residents from other parts of the United States who had moved to the area late in life to be near their families. Though most of the people living at Elmwood were white, rural, and Protestant, the total population represented a range of social and class backgrounds: city and country, black and white, well-to-do and poor, Christian and Jewish. There were native speakers of Hungarian, Yiddish, Italian, and Greek, people who had been housewives, teachers, farmers, and merchants.

Numbers usually dress up a story rather than tell it, but some figures did convey significant information about the scale and character of the home. By the mid–1980s, it cost about $33,000 per year to keep a person in the facility, and the institution's annual budget of $2,500,000 supported 84 residents and 120 staff. The average length of stay at Elmwood was usually two and a half to three years, but Gordon quickly noted that this was not a very meaningful statistic: at the time he gave me this figure, for example, the people living at Elmwood had been there anywhere from one month to 19 years. During the period of research, there were usually about 20 residents who were paying the full costs of care themselves, and the rest— some 75 percent—were on Medicaid. The latter program paid for medication, therapies, bed, and board; but since Medicaid payments did not cover the full price of actually maintaining a person in the institution, operationally the home was really losing money—about $25 each day—on three-quarters of its residents. This was one factor that limited the payscale of employees, for 72 percent of the cost of running the home went into salaries.[1]

The home was largely a female world. Among its seven dozen residents, women usually outnumbered men by a ratio of two or three to one. The situation among staff was even more one-sided: of the 120 people employed there, approximately 18 females could be counted for every male on the payroll. The racial makeup of the institution presented a similar picture. At any one time, there were usually four to six blacks among its residents and a comparable number of minorities on the staff. For a few of the white residents, such as Dave Dorenberg—who believed in "sticking with your own"—this was a point of complaint, though one that was usually stated by them in muted, confiding tones.

The largest department at Elmwood was, predictably, nursing. Its head oversaw 78 employees, including an assistant director, supervisors, charge nurses, registered and licensed practical nurses, and nurse's aides. The next biggest divisions of staff were the dietary department, which had 14 people, and housekeeping and maintenance, with 12 employees. The home's administration had nine members, including a director, an assistant administrator, a head of personnel, and an activities director. Finally, there were a number of professional specialists and consultants who served the residents, including a physical therapist, an audiologist and speech therapist, a social worker, an occupational therapist, and a medical director.

Department sizes varied tremendously, with the 78 employees of nursing at one extreme, and, at the other, the one-person (usually one woman)

Figure 2.1
The Front Lobby

department of social work. Over half of Elmwood's staff, about 70 people, were represented by a union. The latter covered the workers in dietary, housekeeping, maintenance, and nursing up to the level of licensed practical nurses (LPNs). Registered nurses, administrative staff, and professional consultants were nonunion, and they dealt directly with the chief administrator. He, in turn, was responsible to a board of directors whose membership included local business people, civic leaders, human service professionals, and the relatives of residents. The board was organized into a series of committees which monitored such areas as patient care, finance, planning, and personnel. Since the home was a private, nonprofit one, its corporate identity rested in this board, whose members were legally responsible for its solvency and operation.

Elmwood Grove had a strong sense of its own history. This stemmed not only from its unusual child-centered past, but also from its physical and social place on the landscape. Set in a village neighborhood of a civic-minded community, run by board members from the professional, business, and service sectors, and employing and housing mostly local people, it had a considerable visibility in the area. On an early visit Denise took me to a basement room where many of the home's records were stored. In one corner she showed me an old oak bookcase that housed a kind of institutional archive. It held a series of scrapbooks containing news articles, documents, letters, posters, and special announcements that went back to the home's Depression-era youth and extended up to its most recent fund drives. An American vice president had once walked through its doors on a visit, a Nobel Prize winner had been registered among its residents. For six decades, a series of people had cared enough about Elmwood's accomplishments to save, annotate, and mount all this memorabilia.

Over the next few months, conversations that I had with staff at different levels made it clear that they took pride in the home's reputation. Louise Santorini, a charge nurse who had worked there for almost a decade, observed that "professors and business people come to this home, or they send their parents to live here, even though there're more modern and fancy institutions around. I think it's because they know the care is decent, the location's convenient, and we try to make it as homelike as possible." Most of the residents I spoke to, even those unhappy at being in an institution, agreed that their treatment was good (see Figure 2.1—the front lobby easily informed residents, staff, and visitors of events and accomplishments at the home).

But there were other facets to Elmwood's identity. These included a number of long-term employees who had worked there for 15 years or more. Some of these women labored alongside coworkers who were also their relatives—mother with daughter, aunt next to niece, sister with sister. These people and their families had a strong sense of identification with the home. The institution's image was also shaped by its cadre of volunteers. There were a number of community organizations that regularly offered special events at the facility: holiday parties, musical programs, and outings were organized by service clubs, church groups, and local schools. There was also a special body of volunteers—the Westman Club—that had been established in the home's early years and named after the institution's founder. This group was originally created to serve the young tuberculosis patients, but continued to operate after Elmwood's conversion to a nursing home. The Westman volunteers were a largely female club comprising, as one member put it, "a kind of ladies auxiliary." They helped with fundraising and public relations, but also worked with residents during weekly activities.

Though pride in the home was widespread among staff, patients, and volunteers, the institution was not a perfect place in anyone's eyes. Employees, for example, had their issues with work conditions, the style of management, and the conflicting attitudes of administrative and direct-care staff. Certain supervisors faulted workers for inefficiency, while the latter felt victim to insensitivity from above. There were also cliques, gossip, and small plots, all common enough in an organization of this size, but troublesome nonetheless.

For some of the volunteers, the very idea of institutionalization was problematic. It hovered over their work like an uncertain cloud, shadowing their feelings about what they were doing there. Some of the more articulate residents concurred and could point out places where their treatment, basically good in nature, could have been made better. But the criticisms and caveats from each of these quarters were somehow distinct from people's generally positive feelings about the home as a home, their view of the institution as a fixture and a tradition in the community. This seemed to protect it from some of the sting in what was said, as if the home were a person and remarks about it were not to be taken personally. A sense of loyalty or connection to the very idea of Elmwood, or to some of the people living or working within it, helped many to see past, or discount, its shortcomings.

The history of Elmwood Grove Nursing Home encapsulated one of the major medical trends of twentieth-century American society. Just as maples had supplanted the elms on its lawn, the home's meaning had changed with time. It began as a treatment facility to help young children reclaim their lives from the effects of tuberculosis, an infectious disease; and it evolved into a nursing home to serve elderly people afflicted with the noncontagious ravages of age. It had thus gone from young to old, from acute to chronic, from rehabilitation to maintenance.

The pet therapy program I had begun to study was an innovative idea, meant to ameliorate some of the drawbacks of institutional life. Though my first exposure to the animal visits had left me scratched and uncertain about their impact, weekly sessions over the next few months were increasingly rewarding. I got to know a number of residents, formed close ties with a core of volunteers, and slowly became acquainted with members of the staff. I began to visit the home at different times on various days of the week to see more about its general operation, and I accompanied both residents and staff to learn their daily routines. Nina Breckner, Elmwood's social worker, helped me to identify a number of people willing to provide me with life-histories. In addition to hearing both the rich and the mundane contents of people's pasts, another dividend of the time invested was the opportunities it gave me to meet the friends and families of residents when they came to visit: spouses, children, grandchildren, nieces, nephews, and neighbors became part of the home's cast of characters for me.

Week by week I was able to put more names to faces and relate people to their responsibilities. I made a conscious effort to get to know a cross section of the work force, and over the years—and countless cups of coffee—I became familiar with Rachel Ortend, the speech therapist; Nina, in social work; the head of the activities department, Denise; the physical therapist, Claire Lannahan; Louise Santorini in nursing; and a number of other women from among the aides and the housekeeping staff. Trying to move up as well as down in the hierarchy, I also got close to the home's assistant administrator, Gordon Morrell, and the president and several members of the board of directors.

There were times when studying a nursing home came quite close to the kind of traditional anthropology I had previously done in the Arctic and the Bahamas. Each place presented life on a small, very human scale. At Elmwood, besides getting to know people's roles and feelings and relationships, I found I also needed to learn the "native" language. But this time it was the vocabulary of medical and institutional care: it consisted of both technical terms and an alphabet soup of abbreviations and acronyms for treatment procedures, official documents, and government programs. In addition to ADLs, SNFs, HRFs, and NG tubes, Gordon Morrell explained that the level of patient care and reimbursements at Elmwood depended on Medicare, Medicaid, DRGs, RUGs, CMIs, and PNAs. Medicare provided skilled nursing for all people, regardless of income, but only for one hundred days after a hospital discharge. Medicaid covered long-term nursing home stays for the medically indigent or needy, but compelled people with assets to "spend down" and impoverish themselves before qualifying for this program. The term DRGs referred to government-established Diagnosis-Related Groups of illnesses, which set limits to how much—and for how long—hospitals would be paid for providing acute care. This had a direct bearing on Elmwood, Gordon noted, because this cost containment strategy encouraged hospitals to discharge elderly patients in frailer condition more rapidly than would have been true in the past. This, in turn, meant that such people then came to the nursing home in a more debilitated state "than would have characterized 'intakes' a decade ago. We get them sicker, quicker, and for longer."

The level of nursing home care that a person required was determined by "The Screen," an assessment form used by the hospital and institution to determine a patient's medical condition, treatment needs, and ADL capabilities. Once admitted, the amount that Elmwood received for its Medicaid clients depended on which of the RUGs a person fit into. This acronym stood for Resource Utilization Groupings, which were categories established by New York State for clinical disabilities that required comparable levels of care. The home's actual level of state reimbursement, however, was more complex and depended on a formula called the CMI—the Case Mix Index—which reflected the average level of disability among its current load of patients. And whatever Elmwood received under the RUGs, Medicare, Medicaid, and CMI systems, the individual resident was still entitled to a PNA—a Personal Needs Allowance—which came to about $40 per month for clothes, stationery, haircuts, and toiletries.

Upon admission to the home, a new resident was discussed at Thursday Review. This was a regular staff meeting at which "care plans" were developed and periodically reviewed for each person living in the institution. The plan specified, for example, which treatment modalities a resident would be getting, such as PT (physical therapy), OT (occupational therapy), or ST (speech therapy); it indicated what foods and medications were to be administered; and it identified treatment goals which, if achieved, would allow a person to leave the facility for either a lower level of care or her own home. The latter details constituted a "discharge plan." Once these treatments and procedures had been formalized, a PRI—a Patient Review Instrument—was developed for each resident: this document would become a running record of all the therapies, treatments, and activities that each person was involved in every day of the year.

The PRI was itself a compilation of the records kept by each department at Elmwood on what individual residents received from them in the way of exercise, medicine, food, recreation, and therapy. In PT, for example, Claire made a note whenever she treated someone for a decubitus sore or did a debridement—a procedure that involved cutting away the dead tissue from the area around an infection or lesion. She encouraged people to do "range of motion" exercises to enhance the flexibility and reach of their limbs. One of her primary goals was "ambulation," which meant helping people recover the ability to walk. Louise, as a charge nurse, had primary responsibility for keeping up-to-date "med sheets" for all the residents on her unit: these records detailed the medicines and dosages each patient received, and they had to be marked with a PC (physician cancelled) whenever a doctor altered a course of treatment. Furthermore, she had to use her judgment when the med sheets said PRN, which meant to administer drugs as needed. The aides who worked under Louise's supervision each cared for six to eight patients, and had to learn a great variety of procedures, including how to do proper "transfers," the term for moving a resident from one position to another, such as wheelchair to bed, or bed to commode. The aides also became familiar with various materials and technologies, such as enemas, dialysis, catheters, NG tubes, tracheotomies, respirators, and "geri-chairs," which were specially equipped with wheeled legs and a tray across the armrest fronts to provide both a restraint and a surface for magazines, meal trays, and other objects.

The most controversial medical items were the DNRs—the Do Not Resuscitate orders—which instructed caregivers to withhold cardiopulmonary resuscitation from a dying patient. These documents, authorized by only some residents and families, variously pleased or dismayed the nursing staff, among whom there were sharp differences about the morality of placing limits on what they could do. For some, DNRs were the height of caring, and for others a form of suicide, the very antithesis of nursing itself. This same issue divided the aides, and sometimes put a nurse at odds with an aide on her own unit. Elmwood's official policy, however, was to carefully respect such orders, and this is what usually happened. The effect of DNRs on those from outside the home was less ambiguous: while some families would not hear of such a form, Elmwood's policy earned it the unequivocal gratitude of relatives who had agreed to these directives.

On a more mundane level, the daily life of the home also involved diversion and instruction. Denise in the Activities Department had to develop a recreation plan for every resident, as well as keep a record of their attendance at the events she organized. This was true whether the occasion was a church service, a pet visit, a game, or reality orientation, which was a class to help confused residents keep aware of the date, the season, the next holiday, and their own names and room numbers. And all staff regularly participated in "in-service" which, as Denise once joked, was their own form of reality orientation: it consisted of on-going training in everything from fire safety to changes in state "regs" to the use of new equipment.

Though learning the vocabulary was basic to understanding the rules, regimes, and responsibilities of the institution, the life of Elmwood could not be reduced to such a word list or shorthand. During the first year and a half of the study, as I was absorbing the language and getting to know staff, I built up a knowledge of day-to-day experience in the facility by concentrating on the residents, the pets, and the volunteers who brought them. The very concept of pet therapy with the elderly continued to intrigue and puzzle me. I realized, as I got more comfortable with each session, that there was more to this idea than just good intentions and cute moments that were touching in both senses of that undervalued word. Residents, volunteers, and the staff who dropped in on visits all related to one another, not just to the pets. Some of the more withdrawn patients grew animated during sessions. Conversations, often prosaic and pleasant, sometimes dull, periodically grew intense, moralistic, and confessional. Though the visits constituted only a few hours plucked from the week's routine, they called out an affinity between species and generations. Even my cat calmed down.

While there was no such thing as a typical hour at the home, the pet sessions there shared a number of features. Not only did they have a standard format, but they exhibited similarities in the content and rhythm of what took place. The types of talk often repeated themselves, as did the ebb and flow of energy. Since these visits constituted my real introduction to the world of the elderly, they remain vivid in both my notes and my memory. Bonnie's funny, often disconnected anecdotes, Eddie's cowboy songs, Frank cutting people down while Tilly boosted them up—these were all a piece of the pattern. The following group portrait, drawn as a composite from several weeks, shows something of the form and flavor of what developed there.

A PIECE OF THE PATTERN

The central image of the pet sessions was a circle, the ring of wheelchairs that formed a rough corral for the animals. But there were sounds as memorable as the sights. The accent of visits was marked by barks, laughter, whispers, and the occasional strains of a harmonica.

It was Eddie who made the music. He always had his instrument in a shirt pocket, but invariably declined the first few requests to play. Frieda, one of the older volunteers, often took the role of urging him on. One afternoon she pointed out how lazy and shameless the dogs were, lying on the floor either half asleep or spread-eagled on their backs. Poppy, the collie brought by Cathy, was in the latter posture, and Frieda asked Eddie to "get our minds off this display and give us a song instead." Eddie was not coy, but he needed this rite of encouragement. Finally he agreed, and in a slow but faultless manner, played "Red River Valley." There was a round of applause and his blush spread into a smile. Denise came up from behind Eddie's chair and gave him a hug.

At the age of 78, Eddie had seniority over the building, most of its visitors, and all of its staff. Of the outsiders on the inside of the room, the one who came closest to him in age was Frieda. A retired, 67-year-old widow, she had moved to the area two years ago to be near her daughter, and had volunteered after hearing about the pet program from a colleague at her part-time job. She always brought her roommate Colette, a toy poodle, who traveled in a large pocketbook that hung from Frieda's shoulder. Of the other visitors there, those from college were about a quarter of Eddie's age. The youngest, at 19, was Cathy, a prevet student who came each week with her neighbor's dog, Poppy. Twenty-one-year-old Mandy, majoring in physical therapy, had brought Yussy, a ginger-colored cat borrowed from a family in the village. Another volunteer, Steve, helped fill in the middle range of the age spectrum. At 32, he was the most senior of the students: married, a doctoral candidate in agriculture, he contributed his two dogs, Luna and Samba. And later in the afternoon there was usually Janice, a slightly breathless, middle-aged woman whose cat and dog and waves of activism filled her life in the way her children once had.

Almost all the residents at the pet session arrived in the same way—by wheelchair—though their reasons for attending were diverse. Several came out of an interest in animals, some because they had gotten to know the volunteers, yet others simply because the staff had urged them to. For many, events such as this on the activities calendar simply helped to structure their days: the calendar's entries—as varied as movies, cooking, picnics, and day trips—were a mix of the routine, the seasonal, and the unexpected.

The room had fallen quiet after Eddie's solo, but the silence was broken now by scratching sounds on the outside door. Steve opened it to let in his dogs, who had been relieving themselves on the lawn. Samba, a male retriever, rushed over to Eddie's wheelchair and rubbed his muzzle against the man's knees and thigh. Eddie's smile broadened, and he reached down a hand to stroke Samba's head. Cathy walked over, knelt down by the dog, and asked Eddie how his week had been. Her hand rhythmically moved along Samba's back as Eddie talked in brief, slurred phrases about the last few days. His voice was low, and Cathy leaned closer to hear how impressed he had been with Wednesday's snowstorm, to learn about the swelling on his wrist, to see the pin he had made in art class.

Then the inside doors from the corridor swung open, and Denise's assistant Martha wheeled Yvonne into the room, moving her to a position just a few feet to one side of Eddie. The two residents were a contrast not just in gender but in almost every other visual quality: Eddie—slightly bent over, bald and pale skinned, an inward expression of quiet on his face; and Yvonne—an alert black woman, a widowed grandmother with a tight cap of gray curls atop a poised head and straight torso. She had the patience and presence of a matriarch.

The remaining dogs, Luna and Poppy, both made a rush for Yvonne, and Luna, the larger of the two, raised her front legs onto the woman's lap. Yvonne had the effusiveness of an animal lover and, unembarrassed, announced her enthusiasm to anyone willing to listen. Luna, paws on lap, strained for Yvonne's face; and the woman, sensing the dog's excitement, exclaimed, "You sure know who likes you, dearie, don't you, don't you!" Turning to Mandy, who had moved over to take Luna's feet down, she continued, "Oh, that's okay, that's all right. Her, she knows—animals know—when they see people who take to them." Shifting her gaze back to Luna, Yvonne slipped again into the parental language of pet lovers: "We understand one another, don't we? Huh? We sure do."

Once she started, Yvonne needed no prompting. She began to tell Mandy and Martha about having lived most of her life on a farm. She enumerated the cats, cows, dogs, and horses she had dealt with and cared for. Then her voice abruptly moved to a lower register and she described, at some length, how differently she, her brother, and her father had treated the horses they had owned. It was a tale built around gradations of violence. She had been gentle and talkative with the horses, her brother quiet, stern, and demanding, and her father: "Well, he would shout at and beat them like *they* were all that was wrong with the world." Her whole life, she said, she had been puzzled by the paradox of "a man with such a kind soul who could be such a beast to his animals."

While Yvonne was talking, Denise had gone out of the room to get Bonnie. Silver-haired, ruddy-cheeked, Bonnie offered a different kind of enigma. Her talk was sometimes Mississippi smooth and easy, with curves of Southern accent and wit; at other times it would break, slapped shut with a memory lapse, or bumped along by quick leaps from topic to topic. Before Bonnie's wheelchair had been settled in its place in the circle, Poppy and Samba, who had been quietly walking around the room, made a beeline for it. Poppy, bulkier and more assertive, displaced Samba, and the latter's instant air of insult brought a laugh from those who were watching. Bonnie, pleased to be the center of attention and competition, teased Samba for "being pushed around by a woman." Cathy brought over a chair to join Bonnie, and stroking Samba with one hand, she asked her if "women couldn't be as strong as men." Bonnie answered, "Sure, but it depends on the woman, of course. Now my mother, she was a person who knew her own mind. And she had a lot of energy to go with it. Not that she had a career or a profession, you understand, because in her day it wasn't all that easy for women to do that. But she raised four children and ran our house. The amount of work—the physical work—she did, why it would exhaust you just to hear it."

Bonnie continued talking about the house she had grown up in and her parents' marriage. But suddenly her face froze in pain. Only her mouth moved, testing and rejecting syllables. Bonnie's left hand, which had been petting Poppy, stopped in the air above the animal's head, and her whole body seemed suspended with it as her mind searched for a lost word. The story about her mother slipped away. Cathy, who had been speaking with her, now seemed confused herself. She shot a helpless look at Denise, who stepped across the circle. Taking Bonnie's raised hand in one of hers, Denise started to soothe and then prompt her, offering the names of people in Bonnie's family in an attempt to rethread the story line.

For an endless minute, the educated guesses rose and fell. Then success. "Sarah, yes Sarah," said Bonnie, "my mother's name," and the muscles of her face uncoiled as her hand came down. Two deep breaths and she was able to pick up the tale where she had left it. Comparing her own and her mother's generations to Cathy's, Bonnie observed how few of her contemporaries had been able to get a full education. She herself had been an exception, but even she had given up a teaching career to raise a family.

She spoke wistfully about what she might have done with her years had she been born in a different time. Nodding her head towards Poppy, she said, "Now everyone's liberated, even that dog, and it's too late for me." Unable to resist, Cathy protested that "it's never too late." But Bonnie raised her eyebrows, as if to say, "Oh, really?"

Whenever Greta's mobile bed was rolled into the room, I found it hard to take my eyes from hers. Speechless, pale, dreamy, she had a hungry, liquid gaze. Staff members made a special effort to bring her out of the seclusion of her stroke. From time to time she came to sessions, using the muscles and senses that survived. From the height of her bed, however, she could not easily see the dogs on the floor, and so today Mandy went over to Eddie's chair and borrowed Yussy, a lap cat, for her. Propped up by pillows, Greta's body lay curved on its left side, and Mandy placed the cat in the arc formed by her arm and leg. After several months of visits, the marriage of curve and cat had become a fixture. Standing at the head of the bed, Mandy reached over to place Greta's right hand on Yussy's flank. The cat slowly edged up towards the older woman's face, and on her own initiative, Greta shifted her right hand so that she would not lose touch with the fur. Coming around the bed to face her, Mandy asked Greta how it felt to pet the cat. Greta answered with her eyes, bringing them up to meet the voice. "He's very soft," Mandy offered. "It almost looks like he's kissing your chin." The well-timed words did their work. From the surface of the bed, the fist of Greta's left hand uncurled, stretching its fingers towards Mandy. The student placed her own hand in the open palm, and Greta's grip closed around it, holding strong for a long moment.

The volunteers sometimes played like an ensemble, moving in to fill the spaces left by others. Across the room from Mandy, Frieda had seen Eddie sitting alone, and she came over to him with Colette in her arms. She pulled up an empty chair alongside and got the dog to sit on its seat, enabling Eddie to look at the poodle face-to-face. Man and dog quietly studied one another, occasionally nodding their heads in a kind of pantomime: one moved and the other mimicked.

For a minute there was almost no other movement in the room. Except for hands passing over fur, the scene had the poise of a still life: Eddie and Colette gazing at one another; Frieda watching them watch; Yvonne and Steve talking about farm animals with Luna at their feet; Bonnie stroking Samba, speaking of women's lives with Cathy; and Greta lying by Yussy, holding Mandy's hand, gazing off into her own space.

The quietest arrival of the afternoon was Stavros Costa, who was wheeled in a few moments later by Denise. As she shifted the chairs in one part of the circle to make room for him, he gave apologetic looks to Frieda and Steve, who were helping. In a softly accented voice, Stavros remarked, "So much trouble for one old man."

"You know," he confided to Steve, "I'm really not that interested in animals. I like them, but not so much—the way some people here do—to make a big show of it. I come because Denise asks me. I oblige her. And it does not cost me anything. I have," he wryly observed, "no other major commitments in my life just now."

Poppy walked over and dropped herself at the foot of Stavros's chair. "Despite your American saying, I think a dog's life is not so bad," the elderly man continued.

> But I don't know enough to say. When I was a young boy—11 or 12—I spent the summers at the home of my uncle. He lived in the country, in Turkey, where he was a farmer, and he gave me the job to care for his animals: there were sheep, goats, a few chickens. It was supposed to be good for a "city boy" like me to be doing that kind of labor. Who knows? Most days I took the sheep out to where they could graze. It was not hard work and, except for the chickens, I enjoyed it. However, I never did anything like that again. Outside of some cats in my childhood, and then later a few that my wife kept, animals have never been prominent in my life.

"Perhaps you just come to be sociable, then," offered Steve.

"Maybe," Stavros replied after a moment's pause, smiling at the pun to come, "I go where they herd me."

Few residents at Elmwood had the ability to get around themselves. Those with strength in their arms could make slow progress turning the wheels of their chairs. Tilly was an exception. Her means, however, lay in a machine rather than her own muscles. She had a motorized wheelchair, and under the timbre of voices, its low sound could be heard in the corridor. When the doors swung in and Tilly entered, Claire from PT followed her. They had just finished with the whirlpool, which Tilly worked in twice each week for the circulation in her arms and legs. Pausing at the entrance to survey the room, Tilly listed so far to her left that she almost covered the wheelchair's controls. Her right hand, the one that she had some use of, rested on the lever. Framed in the doorway, she and Claire composed a portrait of contrasts. At five feet ten inches, with broad shoulders and strong, expressive hands that carved the air when she spoke, Claire moved and talked with grace. She had to bend over Tilly's condensed and skewed form so that they could hear one another. Yet for all their differences in stature, the two women shared qualities of character: they were animated, articulate, and full of faith.

Tilly was a regular participant—outgoing, inquisitive, undeterred by a voice shaped from birth by cerebral palsy. Whereas other residents had said little to one another upon entering, Tilly greeted each of them by name, and asked Stavros about the pain in his legs. He smiled and shrugged. She reassured him that God cared, and he shrugged again. "Maybe he cares, but does he cure?"

"He does better than that," she answered. "He saves."

Stavros was unmoved. He was no atheist, but neither did he find God an anesthetic for his pain. Tilly's pieties, well meant and gently put, pushed him past the comforts of belief and brought him back to the merits of a dog's life. "Look at what is here before us," he said, pointing to Poppy asleep on the floor. "She needs no care, she *has* no cares. God may have made her for us to play with, but then he made us for his own amusement. Unfortunately, old age is no game and I, for one, am not amused."

Claire began to respond, arguing that "what really matters is how—" but whether her words were meant to defend Tilly, or God, or both, was never made clear, because she was cut off in midsentence by a loud scuffle at the outside door. It was the opening bars of a dogfight. A large Irish setter had come in and Samba, snapping and glaring, had rushed over to challenge him. But a woman's voice quickly cut through the barks and restored a measure of order. The speaker was Janice, a 43-year-old volunteer, who packaged her weekly visits in among a round of chores for her teenage children and her church. She brought Striker, the setter, and Midnight, her tabby. For a person with a commanding voice, Janice stepped in with a distracted air about her: each part of her hair seemed to have a life of its own, and the fake fur of her jacket lay in a dozen different directions, merging at points with the dark coat of the cat she was holding.

The appearance of Striker had brought the other dogs to life. Playful rather than hostile now, they raced through the room, did half turns in the air, tested out their dominance patterns. The short barks and scuffling sounds bounced off the walls. "I didn't know we had paid for a dog show," remarked Bonnie, who looked a bit uneasy at all the tumult.

But most of the others enjoyed it. Yvonne commended the animals for "being so full of life," and Janice went over to joint her, settling Midnight into the older woman's lap. The two began to talk of how hard it was for dogs to be kept indoors for a long time. "When I was a child," Yvonne recalled, "winter in the farmhouse was like that for me. I felt real warm, like bread at first, and then all restless and yeasty by March. 'Ready to jump out of your skin,' my mother'd say."

"Sometimes, now, I can still feel like that . . . right in this chair . . . just like those dogs."

A young woman came into the room—neatly dressed, clipboarded, purposeful—and walked straight across to the far end of the circle. Deep in conversation with Cathy, Tilly did not at first notice the newcomer standing nearby. But when Poppy rose from Cathy's side and moved over to sniff and rub his head against the woman's leg, Tilly looked up to see Rachel Ortend, her speech therapist. She started to introduce her "teacher" to the volunteers. Tilly put as much pride as care into the pronunciation of her words now. While there was no stigma to having a therapist in a place where everyone was being treated for something, Tilly chose to emphasize the quality of learning over that of treatment. For her, speech therapy was education more than correction. Rachel just stood and let Tilly do the talking. The older woman's vowels, drawn out and rounded just a bit beyond the norm, took on a life of their own.

Language was dramatic both for its presence and its absence in the room. Stavros's accent and eloquence, Greta's silence, Tilly's efforts to pronounce, Bonnie's struggle to remember—these were some of the guises and disguises that speech assumed. Rachel sometimes asked the more articulate residents she worked with to tell her the most memorable quote, or saying, or homespun piece of advice that had shaped their approach to life. Much of it was prosaic, but some of the answers opened up their minds to her like "light going through a crystal." She kept a notebook filled with their answers. Yet it was the residents without speech who perhaps awed Rachel the most. She once asked me, rhetorically, "What happens to people when they can no longer put what wisdom they have into words? What is it like to be a prisoner inside your own mind?" Today, however, she herself said very little, letting Tilly hold the floor. Rachel only spoke, in fact, to commend the older woman's progress. But eventually she announced that she had come to work with rather than praise her pupil, and so after a few more minutes, she wheeled Tilly from the room so they could practice in the quiet of her office.

By the time they left, light from the windows had begun to cast shadows across Greta and the others on the west side of the circle. Like the light, Greta was beginning to sink deeper into her pillows. She raised her eyebrows to Denise, who read the fatigue in her look. "I think you had a good visit," Denise suggested, "and we can go back now. But you'll have to let go of Mandy's hand first, dear, alright?" Greta's grip relaxed, but instead of dropping her fingers back on the sheets, she raised them towards Mandy's face. With the same motion she had used a moment before to caress Yussy, she stroked the young woman's cheek. Mandy smiled and lifted the cat, and Denise, nodding at Greta for reaching out to person and pet, rolled her bed from the room.

Like a good editor of scripts, Denise provided much of the continuity at sessions. She responded to people's comments and connected them up to those made by others. She wove what might have been scattered threads of talk into a social fabric. Knowing each resident's character and history better than anyone else in the room, she could introduce good topics, defuse outbursts, and help explain the meaning of words, gestures, or whole patterns of speech when they escaped the ken of a novice volunteer. Despite all of her skills as an organizer, catalyst, translator, and character reference, however, Denise once confided to me that she labored under a kind of professional stigma. Not only at Elmwood, she said, but at other nursing homes too, there was the common idea that "recreation staff are childish." It was based on a facile equation of their personalities with the games they sometimes played. They were dismissed as bingo callers, crayon pushers, song leaders. Lost among the epithets was the art that the best possessed to animate interests and nurture the creativity of residents. But faced with this perception, Denise fought to endure, hoping to outlive her unsought title as "the play lady."

A few minutes after she had left with Greta, Denise returned with two new people. One was Nina, Elmwood's social worker, and the other Karl, a man who had recently moved to the facility. Stavros, one of Karl's roommates, had confided to me a few days before that he found his new neighbor "well meaning and gentle," but complained that the man rarely spoke. Karl had never been to a pet session before, and had barely put in an appearance at any activity in his first two weeks at the home. Nina had offered to accompany him today because she wanted to help familiarize Karl with the building and introduce him to some other people. She announced his name to the residents and volunteers as she approached the circle. "I told him I thought this would be more fun than those soaps he was watching on TV. Besides," she explained, "he was all alone in the lounge."

Karl's face was impassive, hard to read. His chair had been wheeled over to where Bonnie and Cathy were talking. Cathy turned to greet him, nudging Luna over next to this chair. When she asked Karl if he liked dogs, he said, "Not that much." But he reached out a hand and patted Luna on the head a few times. "I like cats better, but he seems like a nice dog."

"It's a 'she'," explained Denise form across the room. "Her name is Luna."

"Louis? What kind of name is that for a girl?" asked Karl.

"No," Cathy offered, "her name is Luna. L–u–n–a. It rhymes with tuna."

"Luna, tuna," said Karl, "it's still strange. But she's okay. Very steady."

Luna stood still for only another minute, however, and then belied Karl's compliment by wandering off to lie down next to Samba. Janice saw this and borrowed Midnight from Yvonne's lap. "I heard you like cats," she said to Karl, "so I thought you'd like to meet this one. Her name is Midnight." Pliant as a blanket, the cat folded herself on top of Karl's thighs.

"How does that feel?" Janice asked.

"Nice. Very nice. Very soft."

"Did you ever have a cat yourself, Karl?"

"Yes, I have quite a few," he answered. "I mean I used to. When I lived in the country. It was easy to keep them there, you know. They could go in and out, catch mice. I had one who was a great mouser. My wife, she loved the cat but hated the mice." He laughed once over the memory and then fell silent.

"Where were you living when you had that cat?" asked Janice.

"Where did I live, you say? Where did I live? We lived . . . let me see

here. It was north of this place, you know. The name . . . it was. . . . " Karl
tapered off, tapping his head with two fingers. "Sometimes I can't . . . can't
. . . the . . . I know I . . . I. . . . "

He was quiet again for a moment. But this time, before words could
break the silence, his cheek muscles began to move and a shudder rose up
from his shoulders, passing through his jaw and brow. In a second, with
a groan, the first wave of crying welled up. His fingers flew back to his
forehead, tapping once more, the hand vibrating with the sobs. The sound
was soft but audible enough for others in the room to hear. Quickly, moving
against the rhythm of pain, Nina and Denise were across the floor and
beside Karl's chair. Nina's right arm curved around the back of his shoulders, trying to comfort, and she told him, "It's okay, it's okay, you don't
need to be upset." But the effect of her soothing was minimal, and she
soon saw this. She had witnessed the strength of Karl's despair before, and
knew there was little she could do at such times. So she decided to return
him to his room and just stay with him for a while. Claire, needing to get
back to PT, said she would walk with them. Each woman put a hand on
one of Karl's shoulders, resigned to the fact that there was nothing else they
could offer. Denise bent over to lift the cat from Karl's lap, and Nina rolled
the wheelchair away.

In the wake of Karl's emotions, stillness reduced the room again to a
tableau. Samba lay in the center of the floor while Cathy stroked him.
Stavros and Mandy sat next to each other, silently watching Cathy pet and
murmur to the dog. Behind them, Poppy and Luna were curled up near a
radiator. Within the ring of chairs, Frieda and Colette had moved alongside
Bonnie, and to their left, Eddie held Yussy on his knees as he talked with
Steve. After Karl's exit, Denise had taken Midnight back to Yvonne, and
now the cat sat posed on her lap. And over by one of the windows, Striker
stood at attention and faced the outside. His head made small, machinelike
jerks, following the staccato moves of birds jockeying for position in a
nearby tree.

The afternoon's quiet was then broken for the last time. Frank Healey
rolled into the room, wheeled by Louise, the charge nurse on his wing.
Even before he appeared at the door, Frank could be heard mimicking the
cadence and nasal tones of his roommate. Louise halfheartedly urged him
to hush, but she could not quite repress her own laughter at his pitch-perfect
imitation. And riding on the air with his words was another quality, that
of anticipation, for Frank's reputation as well as his voice preceded him.

Frank was the residents' resident critic. Few individuals who lived in or
visited the home escaped his judgment. At the very least he subjected most
people's character to some form of characterization. He had once known a
professor from my college who had gained, in Frank's estimation, an un-
deserved renown. "He didn't know what he was talking about half the
time, but man, he sure knew *how* to talk. It was his way with words which

made all the difference. Not too many people noticed what an unoriginal, second-hand thinker he was. It was all there except the footnotes. He would have made a great politician."

Today Frank settled into his editorial style by recounting the telephone call he had gotten that afternoon. "It was my brother, the actor from Syracuse, with this week's excuse for why he can't visit me. He feels he's so convincing! You'd think, for an actor, he'd realize he's on the phone, not on stage. I swear in my mind I can actually see him posturing at the other end. But the truth is he just can't come across over the wire. He has to be *seen* to be believed."

Behind Frank's sardonic tone there was also a note of dismay. He was, in truth, hurt by his brother's repeated failures to materialize, and Denise, who knew Frank well, was more attuned to this than most of the others in the room. She tried to soften the blow by highlighting another victim. "It's a shame he can't come 'cause your roommate, Mr. Carmichael, really enjoys his visits too." Frieda picked up on this and took the calculated risk of asking how Mr. Carmichael was. Frank gave her what she must have expected. "I used to have a terrible roommate, you know. Now I only have a pathetic one. It's all that pissin' and moanin', if you'll excuse my metaphor. And when he isn't complaining he's bragging about all the stupid—I think invented—things he says he's done. Even if most of it's true, after a lifetime he still can't tell the difference between being notable and just being notorious."

When Frank got into this kind of comic, poisonous mood, people knew he could not be distracted. They simply let him go on until he was done. Most of them found most of it entertaining, and by the end of the tirade he had usually talked himself through his bitterness. By the time he finished off his roommate this afternoon, he had also taken his audience through the last part of the visit. The hour was late, and only the last touches of daylight and five residents remained in the room. A few moments later the sound of the bus's horn outside made the end official: Cathy and Mandy had to leave, and the other volunteers took this as their cue to pack up their pets.

Coats on, cats in hand, four dogs in tow, and one in a pocketbook, people said their separate good-byes. "Take care of your wrist," Janice called to Eddie, and he waved his bandaged hand to her in response. Cathy reminded Bonnie that she had not forgotten their unfinished conversation about women, work, and liberation. "To be continued," Cathy promised. "You and I are going to talk about this next Friday."

"If I'm still here, dear," answered Bonnie, "If I'm still here."

3 MEANINGS AND LOSSES

Aging in Western culture is often perceived as a series of losses. The gains of freedom and spontaneity that can come with late life are often overshadowed in people's minds by the vulnerabilities of the old. Strength, health, independence, sensory acuity, and financial security may all decline as time passes. Social losses add another dimension to the experience. Agemates of the elderly may enter institutions, go into retirement communities, or move to age-segregated housing. Eventually, the contemporaries of older people start to die. By this time in a person's life, younger family members may have moved away or, at the very least, established separate lives and residences of their own.

The emphasis on loss, however, can distract us from the fact that aging is not the exclusive province of the aged. It is a long-term process that begins, some would argue, at the very start of the life cycle itself. A more culturally rooted view holds that "we spend about one quarter of our lives growing up and three quarters growing old" (D. Bromley 1966: 13). Aging, seen in either biological or social terms, is thus a continuum. What *old* age does is intensify the losses and declines that have often been in process for decades.

Institutionalization will be the fate of approximately 43 percent of all older Americans (Kemper and Murtaugh 1991: 597). While only 5 percent of those over 65 are in a nursing home on a given day, as noted before better than one of every five elderly individuals who reach 85 will spend some time in a geriatric facility (Siegel and Taeuber 1986: 101). Entering such an institution can come about for one or a combination of reasons. It may be a product of physical or mental impairments, as well as an experience that aggravates the consequences of these losses. An individual's social isolation, or changes in a frail person's support system—such as the death or illness of a spouse, or the move of a grown child who had been a caregiver—

can also contribute to an admission. Both family and medical circumstances are thus potential causes.

The behavioral accompaniments are similarly varied. Mobility, social contacts, touch, and other forms of stimulation may all be diminished as a prelude to or a result of institutional life. The move to a facility may trigger or deepen depression. These physical and emotional factors combine to produce what has variously been called "admissions trauma," "transplantation shock," or "relocation effect"—concepts that suggest that the very process of moving to an institution may be at least as stressful as the actual experience of living in one (Sheldon Tobin and Morton Lieberman 1976: 19–20; Watson and Maxwell 1977: 116). Such experiences contribute to the 33 percent death rate that characterizes nursing home patients in the first twelve months following their admission (Butler 1975: 267).

In recent years, as gerontologists and nursing home staff have become increasingly sensitive to such changes, they have developed new therapeutic programs to try to help residents contend with their situation. But patients react to these efforts in different ways. The losses they have experienced lend shape not only to their speech and their bodies, but also to the attitudes they bring to the special activities now being offered to them in nursing homes. A central issue in studies of the institutionalized aged is the meanings that they find in the losses they have been through, and the effect of these experiences on their current behavior and morale. One way to investigate how residents cope is to examine how they respond to situations that precipitate the recall and discussion of loss. Such recreational activities as reminiscing groups, poetry classes, and life-history courses provide the elderly with occasions where memory and meaning can both be crystallized. Another type of program that has recently been introduced to many geriatric facilities is the kind of pet therapy that was being offered at Elmwood Grove.

While the primary goal of most pet programs is to give residents social and sensory stimulation, a number of investigations have found that companion animal visits also provide opportunities for reminiscing, life review, and evaluations of loss. Such reflections on the past have been recognized as a critical way for older people to create a meaningful account of their lives.[1] Experiences with pets and volunteers at Elmwood also exhibited many other subtleties: the sessions led residents to make moral judgments, to offer character assessments of friends and relatives, to consider their own mortality, and to reflect on the nature of domesticity itself. These themes of loss and memory, morality and mortality, and domesticity and sociability will each be examined here.[2]

MEMORIES

Animals were center stage at pet sessions, but they were far from being the sum of the drama that was acted out each week. Visits presented a variety of ways for residents to address their social, physical, and emotional needs. Patients enjoyed the bodily contact with animals, an experience that restored an element of touch to the lives of people who were more often handled than held. Furthermore, sessions involved them in encounters not only with volunteers, but also with staff and their fellow residents. By providing a shared source of interest, pets were thus a catalyst for increased sociability among all these groups.

Only some residents at Elmwood chose to relate to the animals and volunteers, but the 60 percent who did developed an expectation for ongoing contacts with the same individuals and pets, and looked forward to their weekly visits. In many cases the animals who had served to bring people together receded into the background over the months, and patients then related primarily to the volunteers who brought them. In the course of their conversations, and in their evolving relationships, residents brought up a vast array of topics. The issues they raised ranged from such mundane matters as the weather, recent holidays, and food to more personal and philosophical ones such as family relations, medical problems, religious beliefs, and politics. While elderly participants often chose to talk about the earlier bonds and losses they had experienced with humans and animals, then, these were only two of many concerns brought up by them over the course of time.

The presence of pets nevertheless made animals an obvious and easy topic of conversation. More noteworthy and more unexpected was the process by which residents connected the pets in the room to family memories from their past. Much of their talk, initially centered on the animals before them, eventually shifted to a concern with their former pets and, from this, to their reflections on a range of personal and domestic issues. This shift usually occurred without any urging from volunteers, suggesting a natural tendency to link pets in the present with events of the past. One of the most common and emotional endpoints of this process was the focus of patients on child-hood memories of animals, through which they detailed the membership and lifestyles of the families they had grown up in.

Stavros's usual indifference to animals could be overcome by just such an association. He once told Mandy:

The color of your cat is just like the one my mother kept when I was a boy. She called it Voúturos, which is Greek for "butter". It was her favorite. My mother was very strict around the kitchen, keeping us children away from her work, but she would let that cat climb on everything. He was like the royal taster of food that kings used to have. She would ask him, "And how is that, 'Turos? More basil do you think?" When I helped my mother cook, she would give me the task of cutting up tidbits of chicken for the cat. I can still see her and Voúturos in the kitchen. And smell her cooking. I remember once asking her—I must have been five or six—why she didn't give as much attention or food to the other cat we had. She said, "Everyone has their favorites, even mothers." And she kissed me on the head.

While conversations were full of personal details, certain patterns and sequences tended to recur. Stavros's leap from Mandy's cat to his mother's kitchen showed how animals could bring out family tales told with strong emotional coloring. Furthermore, when reminiscing, many residents tended to talk more about their childhood than their adulthood. Such individuals were inclined to discuss ties to their parents rather than their relations with spouses or their own children. This skipping of a generation was also noted by O'Brien in her observations on reminiscence at Bethany Manor (1989: 186). For the pet program participants at Elmwood Grove, several factors helped to explain this tendency for animals to conjure up youthful associations rather than memories from later periods of development. Some life-long pet owners there indicated that their most intense and personalized ties to animals occurred in childhood, while a small number of individuals indicated that they had only had pets as youngsters, not as adults. Furthermore, there were some individuals, such as Bonnie, whose memories of recent years were far less acute than their recall of the more remote past. Pets and the distant times they stood for were much more vivid in their minds.

The images that residents had of their childhoods, families, and later life were expressed in certain themes that ran through their conversations. Major emphases included the role of pets in people's humor and occupations, in their personal accomplishments and marriages, and in their experiences of loss and moral uncertainty. Many, for example, portrayed animals as the source of domestic comedy. With considerable relish, Yvonne recalled:

> My father didn't want any kittens. So he was always giving the female cats away. But those "males" we kept just went right on having litters. He never could tell the difference between males and females. Every time some new ones were born he would get angry and we would just laugh.

People from rural backgrounds often combined their memories of pets with stories about their work experience with farm animals. Such associations ranged from the prosaic to the sensual. Individuals talked with pride, as well as nostalgia, about the physical demands of agriculture, and their special achievements were sometimes directly linked to laboring with animals. Karl spoke in this way, though it took several weeks of visiting before he became comfortable enough with the volunteers to open up about his past. Once he did, however, he frequently repeated the story of his horse Branch and the large number of acres he had plowed with her when a teenager. He always added, "I was the only one of my brothers who could control that critter." Eddie, whose powers of voice and speech were slowly declining, expressed himself well in a poetry group, often choosing animals for his subject. He once wrote a simple, evocative quatrain:

> I can remember
> When I milked the cows
> It made me feel good
> Especially on a warm day.

Whether through laughter, stories, or poems, then, retelling was a way for residents to appreciate their pasts, their pets, and their work.

It was rare to find married couples living together at Elmwood, and Dave and Mollie Dorenberg were one of only two such pairs there during the years I studied the home. Most days, however, their number was increased for a few hours by people who regularly visited a spouse in residence at Elmwood. On many occasions, married partners spoke at length about the pets they had owned. Several couples, in fact, had a stock set of stories about their animals, and they shared this repertoire with new volunteers and anyone else willing to listen. In certain tales, each person had favorite lines that he or she reserved for the telling, with the result that these spouses related their anecdotes like a well-practiced ensemble. Dave and Mollie, for example, played the following duet. Its theme, always introduced by him, began, "When our kids were young we had a summer cottage on the lake."

"And," Mollie went on, "we always took Toby, our spaniel, with us. He was very sleek and sweet-tempered."

"I never thought he had the talent to catch anything," continued Dave. "He was fast, but his legs were quicker than his brain. And then one day he caught a duck—a duckling, really—and brought it home, proud as a hunter. . . ."

Then Mollie, without missing a beat: "The kids were so upset when they saw him prancing up towards the dock with the bird in his mouth. And then he dropped it near the fishing gear. But when they saw it was still alive, shaking its wings, they screamed. So they came running to the house, yelling to us to 'Save the duck, save the duck!' "

"We brought it inside and nursed it. I remember all the fuss the kids made over who would feed it. Even Toby was concerned, watching everything we did for it."

"You see," Dave would explain, "he was more of a retriever, not a killer or a hunter—it was like he just found that duck somehow and brought it back to us. So I think it was more in shock than in pain when we got it. We couldn't see any wounds."

The first notes of the coda then belonged to Mollie. "Finally, one morning, when the kids took it down to the beach, it just flew off. They screamed and cried and applauded till it was out of sight. They didn't know whether to be happy or heartbroken." And Dave would finish the tale in tone poem fashion: "Toby must have adopted the duck in some way, because all that day he kept looking for it around the porch where we kept it. When he realized it was gone for good, he fell into this sulk, depressed for what seemed like forever, which was something we could never remember him doing before. He lay by its box on the porch, as if keeping a vigil."

The animals that widows and widowers spoke of were also connected by them to their spouses. It would be "the tabby that my wife took in" or "the hound that always sat on the tractor with George." Single, married, and widowed individuals frequently had photographs of former pets on their walls, or in wallets and albums, and these were shown to visitors with marked enthusiasm. Since these pictures usually juxtaposed kin or spouses with animals, the pet stories that accompanied them broadened out into marital and family histories. Using the photographs as a point of departure, a woman might describe the houses and vacation spots her family lived in with a dog, the children born during a cat's life, the favoritism that a spouse had felt for a particular pet or, reversing the emphasis, the animal's partiality for a certain person.

Frank, for example, who usually avoided sentiment as if it were a blemish, had two nostalgic photos he liked to show off and narrate. They faced one another in the plastic pages of his wallet, one showing the Cape Cod-style house that he had his family had lived in, and the other a much-fingered photo of their cat, Harry. He would point to a second floor dormer and explain how Harry had learned to climb the nearby maple—visible along the photo's right edge—and get into the house by crawling from a long branch through a bedroom window. Listening to him, there was little in Frank's words to betray what he felt, but he invariably gave himself away—both the pride and amusement—in the tone of his voice and the playful light in his eyes.

Such reminiscences constituted more than travelogues or a series of tableaux: people wove into them an affirmation of marital and domestic life, drawing, in part, on the animals who had shared the family's more positive and memorable moments. In an institutional world whose residents did not enjoy a common history, an activity such as this provided them with a shared experience through which they could at least come to know something of one another's pasts. Stories such as Frank's, and the more-than-twice-told tales of Dave and Mollie, had the quality of portraiture: they recalled the paintings that landed gentry once commissioned to show off the house, the spouse, the offspring, and the pets who comprised their accomplished, domestic world.[3]

DOMESTICITY

An administrator at Elmwood Grove once characterized the experience of entering a nursing facility by the graphic term "stripping": people lose their homes, most of their familiar belongings, much of their privacy, a good deal of their freedom, many of their friendships, their regular contacts with family, and, in some cases, their pets. While most of the residents felt that Elmwood itself was a decent home, they were more troubled by the very idea of institutionalization than by the quality of the institution itself. As good as a facility may be, in Stavros's words, "It will never be like home."

People tried to cope with this loss of domesticity in several ways. One of their most visible adaptations consisted of efforts to domesticate their immediate environment. They rendered rooms more homelike with family photographs, Bibles, posters, knickknacks, greeting cards, and plants. The ubiquity of interest in animals was reflected in the large number of stuffed pets, plastic beasts, and animal photographs that decorated their walls, bureaus, and beds. Just as petkeeping attempts to tame the wild by bringing it inside, many residents tried to tame institutional space by populating it with animal images and similar props.

Pet sessions also revealed attempts by the elderly to promote a familial intimacy with people who had once been strangers. Their desire for contact with volunteers often exceeded their interest in animal companionship. Some residents, noting that pet visitors came to see them more regularly than their own relatives, began to refer to these community members as their "second family" or, with a touch of hyperbole, their "real" family. Volunteers were sometimes surprised by the strong expectations that patients had for ongoing, personalized contacts, and found that they needed to reconceptualize their role into that of human companions for the elderly rather than as mere transporters of animals. At Elmwood Grove, where most visits occurred in a group format, the presence of a regular corps of volunteers, residents, and pets each week created what Yvonne and others called, a "family atmosphere."

A particularly striking sign of people's desire for human company was their tactile response to visitors. Not only did the residents love to caress and hold the animals, but some of them also "petted" the volunteers by stroking their arms, holding their hands, and feeling their faces. Greta, reaching out of her silence to Mandy, was not alone in this. Visitors and pets were sometimes treated as if they shared a single, undifferentiated body that could be touched and fondled without regard for boundaries.

Over time, many volunteers came to accept and reciprocate this familial definition of their role. They recruited such "significant others" as spouses, children, girlfriends, and roommates to accompany them, transforming sessions into a shared experience. Such visits took on an added dimension for residents too, who found themselves the focus of "family attention." On the all-too-rare occasions when young children were brought to sessions, they evoked very strong responses of interest and delight: even if toddlers paid the old only scant attention, patients still enjoyed watching them interact with the pets and play among themselves. Children and animals also provided one measure of how sessions promoted a degree of reality orientation among residents: certain people saved up candy and treats from their snacks to give to youngsters and pets, which required that they plan, anticipate, and keep track of the days of the week.

The way volunteers handled their "presentation of self" offered further evidence of their desire to be perceived as family by the elderly (Goffman 1959). The companion animal program once considered having its members wear name tags during visits so that residents could more easily identify them. But many volunteers vehemently objected to the proposal, arguing that such tags would make them resemble staff and therefore cloud rather than clarify their identity. At the meeting where the idea was being debated, Janice expressed the majority's feeling about their special status: "We are more like friends or kin to people there, and it's important that they feel free to treat us that way. Some residents get quiet or shy when staff are around, and we would not want that to happen with us."

Volunteers not only wished to be seen as family, they also tended to identify the elderly with their own relatives. Since a fair number of the pet visitors were college students geographically separated from their kin, residents served in loco familias by becoming parental and grandparental figures for them. This convergence in how volunteers and patients perceived their relationship yielded a shared definition of the situation. These two age groups, many of whom were deprived of large extended families—one set because of old age and institutionalization in a home, the other because of youth and the institutionalization of higher learning—thus helped to reproduce a family experience for one another.

Bringing animals into the presence of the elderly, then, did more than just revive memories. It helped to recreate an element of past domesticity that people could actively participate in. For many residents, the pets answered a need that photographs and flowers alone could not satisfy, a desire, as Tilly once expressed it, for "something living that I can name."

MORTALITY

Behind many of the animal tales told by residents, there was an implicit question: How shall we mark and mourn the dead? The death of their pets was a topic frequently and spontaneously raised by the elderly, and the circumstances of these losses were often described by them in considerable detail. The richness and emotiveness with which people communicated these sometimes distant events was particularly striking in the case of individuals who had poor short-term memory.

In recalling animals from the past, residents commonly discussed the circumstances of their pets' deaths at the very beginning of conversations. Details of what the relationship had been like usually came later. At one of their first meetings, Frank said to Janice, "Oh, I once had a dark gray cat like yours. He died of some kind of kidney disease. Nothing seemed to help and finally the vet had to put him down." A few minutes later he added, "You've heard of a one-man dog? Well, that was a one-man cat. He wouldn't let anyone else pick him up but me. You'd get a good clawing for your trouble if you tried. . . . He loved cheese, but would eat almost anything, and he begged at the table like a natural actor."

As in Frank's account, it was a common conversational sequence for death to precede life in people's narratives. Residents often discussed the passing of their animals, and the subsequent burials, with great specificity. Bonnie, how described her Mississippi backyard as a "pet cemetery," once painted a picture in the air with her hands, telling us how and where all her animals had been laid to rest, and listing their names and the years of their deaths. When she reproduced this picture several weeks later, none of the names or dates had been changed. Such details became even more dramatic in light of the fact that Bonnie could often not remember who had visited her last month, or when she had received her most recent haircut.

People often interpolated comments about deceased family members who were connected to the animals being discussed. Bonnie, for example, recalled how much her husband had hated the task of digging the animals' graves. "Yet he was a real pillar of our Baptist church, and even served on their Burial Society, and so he went to more funerals for them than I can count." But the links that residents made between pet death and human loss were often more subtle than simple associations between specific people and animals who had died. Deceased pets were also a subject that engendered thoughtfulness about broader issues of human mortality and morality. Some of the elderly emphasized the longevity of animals they had owned, showing a special pride in the exceptional lifespans these pets achieved. Implicitly or explicitly, people took some of the credit for successfully sustaining their lives for so long. Recalling the cat that caught the mice his wife disliked, Karl once noted that it had lived "for almost 18 years because we fed her so well: fresh bits of fish, kidneys my wife'd cut up. No cans. Homemade. It's what comes, I guess, from good care." For individuals in frail health, surrounded by the death and decline of others, speaking about pets in this way was an indirect opportunity to express some of their own hopes about life expectancy. It was a positive element in their image of both the past and the self.

The animals whose lives and losses were being remembered also had intrinsic meanings of their own. Pets were recalled and mourned not only because they were a connecting thread to memorable experiences and deceased persons. They had their own virtues, such as innocence, courage, trust, and vitality; and they were also creatures with whom people shared their values and hopes, their dreams and their failures, transforming the animals into significant others. The elderly talked *about* them, just as they had once talked *to* them, in a natural, domestic dialogue.

The perception of pets as members of the household also allowed residents to project onto their deaths a range of personal and familial meanings. A small number of people told tales of the demise of cherished animals whom they had never replaced because, as Frank put it in one of his softer moods, he "just couldn't take the thought of losing another one like that." Creatures who were believed to have died from loneliness and grief, and littermates who passed away in relatively rapid succession, were thought to mirror the way in which people responded to the loss of family members. Discussing such experiences among pets enabled certain individuals to share, or anticipate, their own grief. A poignant example was provided by Mrs. Briggs, an Elmwood resident, and Will, her husband, who visited her each day. They were a devoted couple and avid, lifelong cat lovers. They commonly spoke of not being able to imagine living without one another. In discussing their marriage and their former home, they described the antics of their two favorite cats, a brother-sister team, whom they had kept a remarkable 19 years. They invariably ended their stories by noting that "when the brother died, the sister was so sad that she passed away within the week." The pets thus prefigured the kind of terrible grief they anticipated for themselves.

Laura Johanson, the grandmother of Steve's wife Beth, spoke of several losses she had already experienced. During her first two years at Elmwood, within a period of five months, she had suffered the deaths of one sibling and two roommates. She was quite graphic in recalling how depressed and isolated she had felt, picturing herself as "the last old tree in a blown-down forest." But she was later given a new roommate, Jan, with whom she developed a close, mutually sustaining friendship; in retrospect, that development further highlighted how empty her life had been before Jan had come to join her. Later still, when a goldfish they had been keeping in their room died, Laura analyzed its death in the following words: "I think it died because it was all alone. It was cut off like I had been, swimming there by itself in that big globe." The fish had become another way for her to speak about her loneliness as a near fatal experience.

Frank once drew an even more subtle connection between animal death and human loss. Despite his reliance on a wheelchair he was fairly mobile, and he had taken to leaving out food each day for some of the wild animals—the squirrels, birds, and a neighborhood raccoon—that visited the lawn and trees surrounding the nursing home. He had recently begun to worry about whether these creatures were becoming dependent on him, and one day expressed his concern that they would die if he either forgot to feed them or himself passed away. With hardly a pause, he went on to relate that after putting the food out that morning, he had gone to visit a friend of his on Elmwood's first floor, only to be told that this man had died earlier in the week. It was then that Frank remembered he had known this fact for several days, but had somehow forgotten or repressed it. His embarrassment was mixed with the sharp anxiety that he was losing his own mind. Within one narrative event, then, he had drawn together the potential demise of animals, the real death of a friend, his tenuous hold on responsibility, and the possible loss of his own memory.

These confrontations with mortality were not always that easy for people to put into words. One way they accomplished this was to move back and forth between human and animal deaths as they talked, or to alternate the recall of loss with the reassurance, and momentary distraction, of petting the animal that was at their feet or in their laps. The counterpoint of different memories, or of talk and touch, eased the pain of reminiscence. Once, when Frank was recounting to Steve the harsh discipline and academic failures he had gone through in elementary school, he periodically interrupted himself to pet Luna, the dog at his side, and speak for a few moments about her coat, color, and demeanor. The digressions were not the product of a meandering or unfocused mind. Rather, the alternation of subjects made it easier for Frank to address, leave, and return to the difficult memories that were emerging. For still other residents, humor softened the impact of loss. Laura, the woman whose goldfish had died several months ago, once dealt with the very same memory in a very different vein. "I had a thought about what might have killed the one I lost last spring. You know I used to talk to it all the time. Not that she answered, but I liked to speak to her all the same. Well, I think I talked her to death."

People's past experience with pet loss also colored their response to new opportunities to be with animals. Most individuals reached by the program showed no long-term effects from earlier deaths. They welcomed a chance to spend time with animals again, and some indicated that they would enjoy living with a pet once more if the home's policies permitted this. But for others, the loss of old companions was an impediment to accepting new ones. Charlie, a man who repeatedly declined offers to be taken to the pet visits, explained: "That's very kind, but I'd rather you didn't. Animals are too sad for me. I mean they remind me too much of the ones I had." In a similar frame of mind, Carobeth Laird once wrote of refusing to go on an outing to a zoo while a patient at Golden Mesa: "I felt too much like a caged animal myself to enjoy looking at other caged animals" (1979: 112).

In contrast to the tone of Charlie's and Laird's experiences, other residents at Elmwood recalled that even after they had decided not to replace an "irreplaceable" pet, they eventually did so, and were able to create a strong emotional bond with the new animal. In some cases, people compared this to their second marriages or the slow, almost reluctant creation of friendships within the nursing home itself. For Laura, shaken after the deaths of two roommates, Jan's arrival had been "like the pup I got when I was ten: It could not replace the dog I had just lost, but it was a new start; it made me hopeful despite myself."

Most volunteers had also been through the death of a pet, and so they brought to their work their own interpretations of this experience. They readily commiserated with residents on their losses, but tended to stress to them the positive value of creating new ties with other animals. In promoting pet companionship, some visitors actually reversed the emphasis by underlining the benefits of such ties for the animals, and not just the people. By means of this reversal, they tried to show patients that they could offer something of value to other creatures—a self-affirming opportunity that was often lacking in their daily lives. Janice exemplified this when she told a group of residents the story of how severely depressed and withdrawn her dog Striker had become "after the death of his sister" in a hit-and-run accident. A few months later, when she began to bring Striker to the pet program, the sociability of being with people and animals had helped to "draw him out again." The moral that Janice drew from her story had a familial theme: people were not alone in suffering loss, for animals experienced the same kind of devastation when, as she put it, "their loved ones die." In the view that Janice tried to get her elderly companions to share, the reengagement offered by pets could be as therapeutic for the animals as for the people they visited.

MORALITY

Deceased pets were also remembered and spoken of as sources of moral value. Elderly participants praised them for giving and eliciting love, for demonstrating loyalty and trust, for teaching people how to care and be kind, and for offering opportunities to engage in life in a positive way. Human-animal companionship was portrayed both by volunteers and its elderly advocates as a paradigm for caring, dedicated, and life-sustaining relationships among people. Some residents—Bonnie and Yvonne, for example—made a point of contrasting the moral meaning of pets with the values that characterized certain humans. Such individuals, in fact, measured the moral stature of relatives and other people by the way these men or women had treated animals.

The theme of kindness and cruelty underlay many of these tales, highlighting in some instances an ambiguity that defied resolution. Yvonne, raised on a farm, compared her own gentleness with horses to the harsh way her father handled these animals. He "talked love but delivered hate," she observed, whereas, "Animals that cannot speak cannot lie." Yvonne's recurring bits of monologue suggested that her father's character was a lifelong puzzle she was still trying to piece together, that the horses were not the end but the means of doing it.

In another story, one that carried its own *Animal Farm* brand of justice, Bonnie pictured animals as exemplars of a kind of domestic moral order that her own grandfather had lost sight of:

My uncle was a farmer, and my grandfather before him. My grandfather, though, was not very good. He refused to believe that cows had any mind or feelings of their own. He slaughtered a calf once, right in front of its own mother. I tell you, that cow never forgave him. She was a great milker, probably a champion. But every time after my grandfather had killed her calf, whenever he'd milk her, she's stick her foot in the bucket of milk or kick it over.

Residents told stories such as these as more than just pieces of family history, then: They were parables through which the characters of their own kin could be described and judged. And in them, purportedly "dumb" animals were portrayed as having a kind of moral intelligence. In other instances, people alternately discussed humans and pets in a way that allowed their respective fates to mirror one another. Yvonne once launched into a lengthy castigation of people who mistreated animals—the latter "were made to be loved, not abused," she proclaimed—and went on to pepper her monologue with brief comments about how much she had been mistreated as a child by the aunt and uncle with whom she had been sent to live for a year. Bonnie's roommate Barbara Hernstein, perplexed at how certain people willingly acquire animals and then neglect them, once interrupted a diatribe on this with criticisms of her own sister for "abandoning" her at Elmwood. While there were residents who praised family members for taking in the pets they had been forced to give up on entering the institution, there were also individuals such as Barbara who noted, ironically, that they had relatives who paid more attention to their pets than to their ailing kin. In Barbara's words, "They kept the dog and got rid of me."

When the elderly juxtaposed their own experiences with those of pets, they often projected parts of themselves onto these animals. In some of these projections, people also portrayed other members of their family. One of Eddie's roommates, Tom Shaugnessy, occasionally related a tale that combined a cat, his kin, and his own severed body. He was an elderly, diabetic man, an amputee now who had once traveled widely, and he was in the habit of telling lengthy stories about the feral cats and dogs who had lived near his country home. He detailed his adventures with one particular cat whom he managed to partially tame, but who remained "very wild, a real scrapper, a womanizer." Tom would then go on to talk about his second marriage and his "hell-raising father-in-law," a widower who "would not settle down." He described this man in some of the same terms—and in much the same spirit of admiration and envy—he had used for the cat. The two tales of wildness were intertwined both narratively and thematically: they spoke of individuals who shared a great deal of freedom, enjoying life on the fringes of the domestic world. When he finished talking, Tom would look down at his wheelchair and the empty space where his right leg had been. As he once said, he had "seen the last of his travels." The cat and his father-in-law had known capabilities that "were no longer part of life for me."

Pet visits confirmed that elderly people, when given the opportunity, could talk at great length and with great intensity about all phases of their lives. It was not the only type of activity at Elmwood which gave them a chance to do this, but it was a particularly successful kind because it also brought volunteers and staff into the picture, and allowed visitors and residents to create meaningful bonds with one another. The reminiscing that took place was part of a relationship, then, not a reverie, and this made it a richer and more continuous experience. The animals facilitated both the socializing and the remembering by providing a common set of interests and a path to the past. They helped to make the process of recollection a dialogue rather than a soliloquy.

Of comparable importance was the fact that the staff and visitors became witnesses to what the elderly had lived through. As Laura explained: "I have many happy memories, but I now have few friends who are old enough to remember them with me." Stavros noted that while institutional life had few responsibilities, it also bestowed little freedom: its routines were dull, and so reminiscing helped "to anchor the goings-on." Pets did more than simply foster this process, however. They symbolized the animals who were once a part of people's households, and thus provided associations through which residents could recall, evaluate, and project the history of family life.

CONCLUSION

People had a kind of freedom when they spoke about and remembered their pets. They could not only select or invent memories, but they could only be contradicted by themselves. As Yvonne confessed, "One reason I love animals so much is that they don't talk back."

There was no definitive way to assess the accuracy of what residents said about their pasts. A more feasible and more important task was to appreciate what their accounts and their memories meant to them. In Frank's words:

> No one ever really knows what happened anyway. We just have our stories about it, our recollections. The so-called "facts" are just someone else's memories. You pay your money and you take your choice, I guess. Me, I'll take my own memories: I believe them, and they're free.

The animal visits were not originally intended to be a stimulus for reminiscence, or a vehicle for patients and outsiders to form friendships. That they turned out this way indicates the power of people to redefine situations and get from them what they need. As Powers noted in the nursing home she studied, "Planned activities hold different meanings for residents and are not supportive per se"; their significance depends on how individuals react to them (1988a: 50). At Elmwood, patients found opportunities for conversation, humor, touch, and ongoing relationships with others. They also rediscovered pets and pieces of their past and a chance to reflect on their significance for the present.

For some people, animals who were remembered in these ways were also a touchstone for reflections on the virtues and failings of humans. The relations between people and pets were also seen as encapsulating lessons about mortality and moral value. Losses that occurred months, years, or decades ago continued to shape people's views of life, themselves, and others. In this process of recall and interpretation that animals evoked, residents bore out Kierkegaard's observation that "life is lived forward but understood backward" (Clifford Geertz 1971: 60). It was this moral and historical dimension of animals, not just their companionship, that enhanced their stature as "significant others" in the minds of the elderly.

4 THE RESIDENTS

At the individual level, history has a way of not repeating itself. Its great repetitions—its cycles, returns, and reprises—may affect the world at large, but they do not enter much into the way Western people envision their own lives. Individuals are more likely to admit that they are creatures of habit than that they are creations—or recreations—of history. With some justice, and a sense of investment, people choose to see their lives as unique. The articulate residents of Elmwood Grove were no exception. The three main things they had in common were age, infirmity, and institutionalization. While the trajectories of the past had brought them to the same station in life, they felt they had followed very different paths to arrive there. In the process, they had become distinct individuals, and each brought a unique mosaic of feelings about spending the last part of life in a nursing home.

If few people anticipate passing their final years in such an institution, it is also rare for their relatives and friends to expect to be visiting them there. At Elmwood Grove, these unexpected outcomes gave rise to two types of tales. There were those of the insiders, told in the shadow of death, which dwelt on such themes as human dignity, emotional hunger, battles with the powers of mind and body, and finished or unfulfilled dreams. And there were the accounts of the outsiders, told as a form of witness, in which visitors spoke of their frustration, advocacy, guilt, and gratitude.

The lives of residents were absorbing because beneath the deceptively simple style in which they told their stories, there was often the depth of passion, or the moral twists of fable, or the one small detail which transformed the meaning of all the other details. This was evident in some people's reminiscences about their families and their animals. It was there in Stavros's moment in the kitchen with his mother's cat, in Eddie's poem about the feel of cows in summer, in Yvonne's horse sense about the char-

Figure 4.1
The Screen (Selected Items)

```
                                               Page 1
   IDENTIFICATION
     Facility     Patient Name
     Person completing SCREEN
     Date of SCREEN      Date of PRI

   DEMENTIA QUALIFIER

   REVIEW FOR MENTAL ILLNESS
     Mental disorder
     Inpatient experience          HOME ASSESSMENT
     Neuroleptic or antipsychotic drugs    Person understands information
                                           & strongly opposes placement
   REVIEW FOR MENTAL RETARDATION/     Person is aware of cost of
   DEVELOPMENT DISABILITY               community services & desires
     Diagnosis                          to use private resources for
     Current services                   home care or an Adult Care
     Mental/developmental history       Facility
                                      Person has good informal
   MEDICAL CONDITION QUALIFIERS         support system -- willing &
     Qualification for convalescent care  capable (physically &
     Serious illness                    mentally) of caring for the
     Terminal illness                   person's needs

   DANGER TO SELF OR OTHERS          ADL ASSESSMENT

   REFERRALS                         HOME & CAREGIVING ARRANGEMENTS
                                       Hours required
                                       Need & availability of
                                         restorative services
                                       Risk to person or others of
                                         community placement

                                     PATIENT/PERSON DISPOSITION
                                       Home
                                       Adult Care Facility
                                       Health-Related Facility
                                       Skilled Nursing Facility

                                     PATIENT/PERSON OR
                                     REPRESENTATIVE
                                     ACKNOWLEDGEMENT

                                     UPDATE
```

acter of her father. In the biographical sketches which follow, four residents—Stavros, Tilly, Frank, and Bonnie—tell their stories of past and present largely in their own words. In particular, they reflect on what it has been like to move into and make a new life for themselves in a nursing home. But a second perspective on Elmwood is also provided here by recounting the experiences of some of their most frequent visitors—Stavros' daughter Katina, Tilly's neighbor Ruth, Frank's son Patrick, and Bonnie's niece Emma. By joining the accounts of insiders and outsiders, the institution's impact on several groups is revealed. What emerges is not a consensus, but a series of truths about the meaning of the home for those who reside there and for those who care about them. Figure 4.1, The Screen, contains the intake information compiled for all residents; it shows the medical background to their stories.

STAVROS COSTA

"Age Hangs on the Walls"

As a young man, Stavros Costa had migrated across the countries of the Old World, trying to escape the plagues of war and injustice. As an old man, he entered the brave new world of a New York nursing home, the inroads of age having caught up with his body. Where he had once won out against outside forces to find freedom and found a family, he now felt betrayed by his own bones.

It was mainly his legs and spine. By his early sixties there was arthritis in the hip and knee joints and a collapsed vertebra in his lower back: the latter pinched the nerves to the point where the pain sometimes prevented him from standing. After his wife died, he moved in with Katina, his married daughter. Within a year, the blackouts and falls began, and he was in danger of breaking a hip, or an arm, or a leg. Then there were the short journeys from Katina's home to the hospital for tests, and, finally, the ride from the hospital to Elmwood. An adulthood that had begun with the hopeful crossing of oceans was finishing with sad trips across town.

Stavros's ancestry was Greek, but he had been born and raised in the Hellenic area of western Turkey. His parents were shopkeepers, and he grew up during the early years of the century in a middle class, minority world where "the threat of persecution was part of the air we breathed."

When I was very young I don't think I was so aware of it. Who notices the air? But when I was in the gymnasium—which is somewhat like your high school—there was teasing, and nasty comments from my teachers. Finally, they made me to know that almost no Greeks could hope to go to university to study medicine, which was my dream. They had a quota system, and things got worse with time, not better. This was after the First World War. So I took some courses in accounting, and my parents arranged for me to go into the business of an uncle of mine who was in Greece. It was not my chosen career, you understand, but it was a living. He had a son who was a lawyer, quite successful but quite uninterested in the business, and so my uncle made me to understand that it would be made over to me some day, with my cousin keeping a part ownership. All this was much better than I could have hoped for in Turkey, so I stayed in Salonika.

Once I knew I could remain there I began to think about having a family. It was a strange time. The political troubles in Europe were getting as bad as the economic ones, but that did not stop a young man from doing what his heart told him to. Politics and romance did not speak the same language. . . .

Two years later I had a wife and a daughter, and it was time to start taking the world more seriously. The business was doing alright—not great, but alright—and by then people were talking about "the next war." My wife's family urged us to leave, but it was not so easy—politics, again, visas and bureaucrats. My cousin was a well-placed lawyer and finally, with patience and the proper use of money, he got us the papers we needed.

By then the war was well under way, and it proved as hard to get across the Atlantic as it had been to get out of Greece. The family traveled to Portugal, "but then we had to stay there for almost four months to get more papers and a boat. The first one we were scheduled to take was torpedoed by the German U-boats on its way to Lisbon. From that you can see how vulnerable we felt, living with the knowledge that only a small part of our fate was in our hands."

Like others who have come to English as a new language in their maturity, Stavros spoke it with a mixture of precision and expressiveness. He seemed to wrap himself possessively around some words before letting them go. To him, the ocean journey to America was a long, forbidding one, "yet we languished on that ship because we did not know what to do with ourselves except worry. . . . We had to bury an elderly woman at sea, which was such an empty, such a forlorn ceremony to witness, that people suffered even more then from melancholy."

Stavros brought his wife and daughter to Ithaca—a Greek name, he proudly pointed out, the home of Ulysses—because they had relatives there. These people were part of a sizable Greek community in the town, and in lieu of the money Stavros had been compelled to leave in his homeland, these compatriots provided a kind of social capital with which he was able to start a new business. His daughter eventually went to college, getting the kind of education he had once been denied. She married, and gave him and his wife grandchildren. Stavros benignly watched them grow up and then, helplessly, he watched himself grow old: infirmity, widowhood, disability, and then finally the nursing home, a new kind of melancholy.

There were few victories over disease at Elmwood Grove. At best it was more likely for someone to make a successful compromise with frailty. For Stavros part of the accommodation consisted in religiously following a routine. Each afternoon he would usually participate in an activity "just to please Denise." In the hour before dinner he liked to sit in the hallway, watching the others and guiding the confused. He called it his "patrol." Stavros's day was also built around meals and medication, as well as daily visits or telephone conversations with Katina, his daughter. Most mornings, when he was not in physical therapy, he moved his wheelchair near the nursing station so that he could get or make calls on the phone there. He had always liked the telephone as a medium: in business and at home, it had been his favorite way of staying on top of things and keeping in touch at a distance. Among his peers at Elmwood, Stavros's situation was unusual. Only a handful of people there had such regular contact with a close relative.

Having company yielded at least two benefits: one was pleasure, the other was power. The resident with an attentive family member enjoyed a certain amount of leverage, especially if the visitor was willing to engage with staff and, on occasion, be assertive with them. Once, for example, Stavros was having trouble with an aide who tended to ignore his requests to be taken to the toilet. Katina confronted both the aide and her supervisor about this. Stavros was subsequently transferred to a different staff member's care, and the problem never recurred. Another time, when meal service was disrupted because of a breakdown in some kitchen equipment, Katina was able to get her father fed in the employees' dining room as a special favor. Furthermore, because Katina herself was well liked by staff, and socialized with many of them on her daily visits, workers were more aware of Stavros: they stopped to talk to him whether his daughter was there or not. Katina's presence thus gave her father both greater visibility and more attentive care.

Stavros himself, however, deserved much of the credit for the way staff treated him. Although his life had been a solidly middle-class one, his European background and accent gave him a touch of elegance and sophistication in the eyes and ears of his caregivers. There was an Old World manner and graciousness to Stavros's speech that endeared him to many. Proper titles and terms of address mattered to him. People were "Doctor" or "Sir," "Mrs." or "Miss," and such politeness extended to the floor staff as well as administrators. I was always "Professor" to him, whereas American-born residents, some of whom I was less intimate with, easily and invariably called me Joel.

Katina was often surprised by her father's success with personnel. His shyness, and the differences of class and culture that lay between him and his caregivers, struck her as major barriers. To an extent, she was right: Stavros found some of the staff and their language crude, and he was especially disturbed when, as he expressed it, "They treat me like a mental case, or a moron." But when things troubled him he was more likely to complain to his daughter rather than to the employee who was responsible. He missed "the right" ethnic food, for example—"too much Italian, not enough Greek; more lemon and basil, less tomatoes," he'd say—but only Katina, and no one in dietary, actually heard this remark. His daughter simply arranged to bring him some lemons each week to put on his chicken and fish. Such indirection spared Stavros's relationship with the housekeepers and aides, whom he rarely confronted. His charm, his passivity, and Katina's role as advocate, all stood him in good stead.

While Stavros was relatively successful at getting along with staff, he was less effective connecting with other residents. His grace and accommodating style, and his daughter's diplomacy, were modest assets among his peers. He had a quick if quiet wit, and he was very articulate once he got started; but he found many people unwilling or unable to talk. He and his roommate

Karl never hit it off, not because they were incompatible, but because they could not break the silence. Stavros's shyness made it hard for him to make overtures to others, and when he took the risk and got no response, he withdrew. The retreat was moralistic in tone. He attributed the quiet of others not to age or upbringing, but to a defect of human nature. "I have lived in Europe, and the Middle East, and America, and you know I found there are stupid people in all countries."

But it was not just defects of character that were at issue. By the time he moved to Elmwood, Stavros's hearing had weakened, and so trying to speak with others who could also not hear well compounded the difficulty—and the embarrassment—of communication. Katina, observing some of her father's failed attempts to reach out, once noted that raised voices, unanswered questions, and self-consciousness "move in a vicious cycle that finally stop people from trying to talk to one another."

Stavros's history and expectations also shaped his relationships. The very first time I met him was just a few weeks after his admission, and I asked him whether he would be willing to do an interview. "That will be hard," he answered. "I have a full schedule. We are very busy here doing nothing." His wonderful accent could do little to hide the tone of self-mockery. Over a year later, adjusted and resigned, he shared with me his feeling that he would "never be at home" in Elmwood because his sense of domesticity had died when his wife passed away. "Living without her wipes out the very idea of home. There is no home like home. If somebody expects that here he will be disappointed. 'Home'—that is a very distinguished word, and no nursing institution can be that. Here, instead of paintings, age hangs on the walls."

It was not just his ties to his wife that Stavros had lost with her death: she had also been the sociable member of the pair, the one who spoke to and drew in the friends and relatives who made up Stavros's world of family. He had liked people to come and talk with him, but that had happened most often at events planned by his wife. Then he could sit or serve food, and guests would approach him. His wife hovered and chatted, and he mixed the drinks while she mixed the people. But without her, his natural reticence quietly reasserted itself. He would ask me, self-deprecatingly, "Who would want to talk with me?" Yet he remained hungry for people to speak with. His problem was that he wanted them to talk first.

Fortunately, all was not silent, and time, the staff, and his daughter brought Stavros into contact with residents who did not mind making the opening remarks. Yvonne always had a greeting for him, and Frank was especially outgoing. Even Eddie, whose speech was faint and halting, could be called on to ask Stavros about his health. And ironically, Stavros himself was drawn to a few of the residents who were beyond language. The Alzheimer's victims made him feel especially perplexed and compassionate, prompting him to help calm and guide them as they wandered about the halls.

Among the more articulate, he found a form of friendship. On some mornings the northeast corner of the dining room became a male kaffee-klatsch: Stavros, Frank, and Dave Dorenberg would talk over their cake and coffee, discussing their work lives, their children, their ailments. One day when I joined them, Stavros swept his hand in a circle to indicate his two companions and himself, then offered a judgment on what their fate portended for others.

> Nature is cruel, but science is neglectful. People do not worry about the problems of the old, and scientists do not pay much attention to them. In this country, money is what rules. If there are funds to do research on children or some popular disease, that's what the doctors do. You have a "book of the month" and "hit of the week" here, and it is the same with illness: people only care about—they only know about—what is on the cover of the latest magazine. By the time the doctors get old enough to realize what life has in store for them, it's too late for them to do anything about it. Then they will join us here and, perhaps, curse their neglect.

After several months of visiting her father at Elmwood, Katina had joined Stavros as a connoisseur of the nuances of institutional life. There was the unconscious, well-meaning, but infantilizing habit of addressing residents with unearned terms of endearment: "honey," "love," "sweetie," and "dear" were patronizing to the ear and, as Katina heard them, "wounding to the spirit." "Maybe they do fit someone like Sarah Kavalick," she said, "the old woman on South Two, who is sweet and just sits with her teddy bear all day. But those words don't belong to everyone."

Father and daughter also became sensitive to the tendency of some staff to fall into a mind-body confusion when dealing with residents. Certain caregivers regularly attributed the complaints of patients to mental lapses and disorientation. But it was an open question, Katina argued, whether this confusion was itself a ploy by the staff to confuse people's families. Stavros, for example, was supposed to walk for twenty minutes each morning, and one day he told Katina that no one had taken him for his exercise. An aide dismissed the charge, saying Stavros had forgotten that he had been out with her. But later that week Katina confided to me:

> There are certain things that Dad's supposed to do every day. And if they don't do it, they say yes, they did it, and that he doesn't know what he's talking about. I told [the aide], "Don't give me that nonsense." There's nothing wrong with his mind. I'd prefer if they'd tell me honestly that they didn't have the time to do it because I'd be willing to come and walk him.
>
> It's not his mind that's affected; it's his body. Yes, the pain medication he's on does make him drowsy sometimes. And sure, he forgets things occasionally, but so do I. Unfortunately there are a few people here who deal with residents on a kindergarten level, who assume everybody has a mental problem. And some of them always shout because they assume the patients don't

hear well. Daddy claims that when I'm there the attitude changes completely, which is interesting if it's true. Because I say things to him like, "Well, she's so nice." And he answers, "Yes—because you're here. As soon as you're gone, her tone of voice changes."

Of course I can't be sure. I can't be in two places at once—there and not there. But if I believe the good parts of what Dad tells me, I have to be prepared to believe the bad parts too.

The best part for Katina was that the care and the staff as a whole were fine. This was reassuring to Stavros and a relief to her. Elmwood was usually clean and orderly, meals were wholesome and on time, the nursing was conscientious. These virtues allowed father and daughter to live with the occasional excuses, the lapses to patronizing language, the raised voices. Stavros, who once rebuked Tilly's faith in a god who cared but did not cure, was resigned to the fact that the nursing home was a place where he would not truly convalesce, that is, begin to grow strong again. In lieu of that hope, he and his daughter took refuge in Elmwood's other strengths. They both made note, for example, of the flexibility they found in the details of the daily routine. Stavros said he was pleased that "the aides went along with changing the panels on the side of my bed . . . so I can get up and reach for a drink at night without calling a nurse." Katina added, "They bend the rules and are accommodating. At least they are with Dad. . . . Basically the staff is very kind and nice, even with all the 'bumps on the log.' Let's face it: nothing is every one hundred percent smooth. Why should it be different here?"

KATINA GLOVER

If Stavros's first weeks in a nursing home were difficult for him, they were probably even harder for his daughter. He was somewhat dazed and depressed, but she was distraught. Where he had entered an institution, she felt she had crossed into a moral no-man's land. It was not that she had done something bad in placing her father there; she had done something unimaginable. Unable to find or afford adequate care for Stavros in her own house, Katina and her family had placed him in a nursing home as a last resort.

We had hired a series of women to come in and help care for my father at home. Some turned out not to be well trained, or not very sensitive, and the good ones moved on. So it was not just expensive, it was so unreliable. There was the constant aggravation of looking and interviewing, and the hiring, the firing, and the quitting. I didn't know whether I was running an employment agency or a drop-in center.

Moving Dad here was something that was against all our principles. It was a very difficult decision for me, for Alan [her husband], and for my children— even though the children were grown and not living at home by the time. I had never dreamt of either side of the family putting a parent in a nursing home, much less having someone *want* to go into one. But Dad wanted to go. It wasn't even a case of our making the decision. This was my father's choice. Once he got the catheter, and once he realized that there was no way he would be able to walk on his own, it became an ordeal for him as well as for us. So he said, when he was in the hospital, "Look, you can't handle this. Nor can I. It's out of the question. I want to go to a nursing home."

Maybe the fact that he said it made it easier for us. I don't know. But it was still the last possible decision we could have come to. When we went to look at nursing homes, I cried through the whole thing. I didn't want it, but there it was; there was no alternative.

Katina and I spoke about her feelings quite often as the months passed—a few times at her home, more commonly in a corner of Elmwood's dining room over coffee. The sounds of home which had at first startled or distracted her—the rattling carts, the public address system, the television—eventually became background noise. Katina's dismay had also slipped into the past, largely because of her own emerging sense of belonging there. At one point, well into the second year of Stavros's residency, she said:

I don't feel so guilty about it, and it's not so alien to me now. Maybe that's because I'm quite involved with many of the others here, the residents as well as the staff. We've become friends. What it amounts to is that I don't feel like a stranger. When I go down to visit Dad and kid around with people, for me it's the nucleus of having a kind of family with him again.

Honestly, when I first looked at homes for my father, I chose this one partly because it was in a good location for me to visit him. And while I had heard some positive things about it, there was the simple fact that they had an opening at the time we needed it. So, to be frank, it was at least as much an accident as a choice. But now, if someone asked me about it for a relative, I could recommend it.

Katina's humor was a balm laid on the skin of Stavros's self-effacement: it swaddled him and held the world's candor at bay. She teased smiles out of her father and joked with the aides. Stavros would air his discontents to Katina and then ask her, unconvincingly, not to trouble herself or others with changing things. She would reassure him, and then set about making the world as right as she could: a new place for his call bell, an addition to his diet, a word to the nurses about the catheter.

Eventually, Katina found that visiting Elmwood with almost daily regularity made her feel redeemed rather than depressed. It was an edge of permanence against the slow slip of time. What mattered to visitors like her was the difference between caring *for* someone and caring *about* someone. Demonstrating the latter had to compensate for Katina's inability to do the former. Furthermore, she valued her rapport with people at the home; she needed the sense of being helpful. On some days, beyond spending the

afternoon with Stavros, she assisted at activities or visited residents who
had no relatives. And she paid attention to the staff and their cares.

> I really do try to reciprocate, to talk to the people who work here and ask
> them how their lives are. I've gotten close to several of the aides, and so I
> know what their home situation is like: single parents, or uneasy marriages,
> or young families and in-laws all crowded into a small house. Plus, their's is
> such a stressful job, and I give them a lot of credit for doing it. The people
> here are not always easy to take care of. Old age is not all "sweetness and
> light," all "meek and mild," and now I can understand why. I don't know
> that I would be able to live here or do most of the things these women do.
> It's hard work, day in, day out: the tasks never change, and the pay is poor,
> and few show them much gratitude. I feel that a little kindness goes a long
> way for them.

Rapport with residents, and regard for staff, brought Katina halfway to
terms with her father's fate. But these same experiences also heightened a
private death wish she harbored for herself.

> I'll be honest. I also feel like the proverbial hick in New York City: "It's a
> nice place to visit but I wouldn't want to live there." When I think about
> growing old—which is a bit more often now—my thought is the same as my
> mother's was: I want to go quickly. My mother got her wish, a heart attack,
> but its suddenness made it a very traumatic time for the rest of us. It took me
> almost two years to accept the fact that my mother was gone. And it was
> after she died that my father's health began to go. Maybe his decline was just
> coincidence, but probably not. You know, this business of having a very
> close family is marvelous. It's wonderful for the children and the grandchil-
> dren. But when something like my mother's death, or my father's going into
> a home happens, in a way it's that much more difficult than if there had been
> no family to fall apart at the start.

Once I asked Katina what her experiences at Elmwood had taught her
about herself. "I never even thought of that question," she confessed, and
was silent for a moment. Then her face brightened.

> I guess I'm a gutsy old lady. I didn't think I had it in me. Digging deep down,
> I didn't think I could deal with this. . . . I hate to give in to things, and this
> was giving in to something that I had no control over: putting my father in
> a home and having to accept it. I'm a stubborn old mule and I like to fight
> to the bitter end. With this situation I just couldn't win. I fought not only
> with myself but I fought with my father—to try to get *him* to fight a little
> harder so maybe he wouldn't have to go to a nursing home. But I—and he—
> we just weren't able to. I eventually accepted it. But it took a long, long
> time. Months later, I'd suddenly have a flash, not believing it was true.
>   Even now sometimes I dream about it. I'm back there in time, arguing—
> in the dream—with my mother. "Can I do this to Dad?" I cry to her. But

my face is down in her lap and I can't see her expression. I can smell her perfume the way I used to, but she's not saying anything. I'm afraid to look up. I'm afraid of how she'll judge me and I start shaking . . . and then I wake up.

It's against all the principles I've ever grown up with. It's very hard to explain because this is a typical American phenomenon, this nursing home business. In Europe, it's true, I was a child when we left, but I don't believe institutions like this existed there. I don't know whether they do today or not.

In the old country, my grandmother lived with my aunt and after the war, when she came to this country, she moved in with us. The only thing I can compare it to is what the Chinese used to have: one generation lived with the other generation. And for me it was a lovely thing to grow up in a family where Grandma was in the same house together with Mother and Dad. We learned so much from her. It never occurred to me that I would ever have to face a situation like this. Once my mother-in-law—who was American and a lot older than my parents—once she told me, "Well, some day, if I get really sick, I'll go to a nursing home." And I said to her, "How could you even think of such a thing! You have children! Why would you go to a nursing home?" It was an idea that just wouldn't have occurred to someone from my background. But of course *she* died in her sleep, while *my* father is here.

The memories of her dream, her grandmother, and then her mother-in-law had each darkened Katina's face by a shade. But then her optimism, the side she wished the world to see, regained its customary control.

I am amazed that I have had the strength to do what I have done. Now I would feel guilty if I *didn't* go to visit the home. I guess the guilt itself never leaves: it just changes shape with age. . . . It's funny: Elmwood had been in this village all of the years we lived here before my father's illness, but it never would have occurred to me to go down to a place like this, to volunteer, or to just see what was going on. It was like moving again to a foreign country for my father and me, but this time the country was here.

TILLY LARSON

A Dying Wish

While most residents grow old in a nursing home, Tilly Larson grew up in one. Though she entered it as an adult, aged 59, it was only after moving in that she learned to take care of herself, that she learned to write, that she literally learned to speak. Her new life, her re-birth, began with the death of her mother.

To the uninformed eye and ear, Tilly had little to be thankful for. Crippled from birth with cerebral palsy, she was a hemiplegic: neither her left arm or leg had ever been of use to her. Her head and face leaned to that side and lay on her shoulder, and while the surface muscles of the upper body were unimpaired, the speech that came from within was warped by the damaged nerves and tissues inside. Despite the drapery of her limbs on the chair and the bends in her voice, Tilly had her special poise. It came from the set of her eyes and the lines of her face—each of which was strong and deep, holding you to her look, attaching you to her presence. She did not lecture, but managed to say with the tone and language of the body: Take me for a lesson.

Compared to Stavros, who came to English as an immigrant, picked up the new speech second-hand, and mastered it with relative ease, Tilly had been forced to fight for every word of her native tongue. For the first six decades of her life, the only person who could fully understand her painfully wrought words was her mother. There were other contrasts that made Tilly's struggles a much more local affair than those of other residents. Whereas Stavros had spent his life crossing boundaries, Tilly had never left the county in which she had been born. She had never even gone on a vacation. Unlike Frank, Stavros, Bonnie, and most other patients, Tilly did not enter Elmwood from a hospital or another facility. She came directly from her own home—a transition that was usually more difficult for people than the switch from one institution to another. But for Tilly the move was less of an uprooting. While her mother's house had been her sole residence for her entire life, it was a place where Tilly's dependency was a fixture. Moving to the nursing home, then, did not deprive her of autonomy, for she had never had any.

Whereas some people were grateful for being taken care of in Elmwood, and others felt the facility to be a form of imprisonment, Tilly was thankful for the freedom it had given her. The expansion of her life had occurred on such basic levels—learning to talk, to read, to write, and to work—that it was hard for others to imagine what her existence had been like for the preceding sixty years. She had never attended school or held a job, nor had she received any special tutoring or help with her disabilities. In recalling those times, she said, "It was awful hard because my mother was the only person who understood me. I went to church and people could figure out my words a little, but not much. Mostly I just prayed there."

During the first two years I knew her, Tilly maintained that her mother had never let her go to school. "I don't know why. I would have liked to," she claimed. She later confessed, however, that she had gone, just one time, but that the teacher had objected so vehemently that she was never allowed to return. "The teacher sent me home because of the way I act and talk, and the way I look. They didn't let me in that school too because of my wheelchair. 'Too many problems,' said that teacher."

The picture that Tilly gave of her home life was a minimalist one. Working from her seat, she said, she had helped her mother "with everything." But this was a favorite figure of speech for Tilly, and the details of her account suggest that she was only able to manage a token amount of cooking and cleaning, and the folding of some laundry. She recalled spending much of her time as a child "cutting up papers with a scissor." There was no father, few visitors, and no therapists to help with either her speech or her limbs. She lived, labored, and to a degree languished in a safe, protected world of her mother's making.

Tilly rarely went out in those years, but when she did it was to attend church. Sunday outings brought her in touch not only with other people, but with a faith that was to be her most loyal, lifelong companion. Most of the congregation that Tilly had known when she was growing up were now dead. But she still carried the Bible she had held as a young adult, plus a trust in Christ's promise of everlasting life for those who believe. Her knowledge of scripture was wide but founded on pure memory: never having learned to read, she had been read to by others, and had thus built up a rich oral tradition of her own. Tilly's pattern of Sunday service and Bible study, begun in her youth, was still part of her regular routine. But now the Sabbaths had become daylong Sundays. Each week, at nine in the morning, she was picked up by a woman from her fundamentalist church, and then she prayed, studied, socialized, and ate with congregation members until returned by them to the nursing home at seven that night. Worship bracketed time within its weekend borders.

Given the history of her days and years and decades, there was proportion in Tilly's judgement that the two best periods of her life had been "going to church and moving to Elmwood." Both had been acts of obedience: one to God's will, the other to maternal wish. When her mother was nearing the end of her last illness, she asked Tilly, her only child, to make her a promise: " 'Tilly, will you do one thing for me after I die?' And I said 'Yes, I will.' And my mother said: 'See that you go to Elmwood Grove to live.' "

While God had given Tilly solace, the home provided her with security, skills, and a social world. She received physical therapy and exercise on a regular basis. Though she knew she would remain in a wheelchair for the rest of her days, she learned, with Claire's support, to manage a few steps— the only ones of her whole life—on the parallel bars. The most profound change for Tilly after coming to Elmwood, however, had been learning to speak. The slow, arduous work of teaching untrained muscles, of giving articulate shape to a voice heard only in the home-bound, two-character play of mother and daughter—that had been one of the most gratifying and remarkable experiences not only for Tilly, but also for Rachel Ortend, her therapist.

Reflecting on their work together—an enterprise which was then in its third year—Rachel once said:

> By the time Tilly and I started I had done therapy with many older people.
> But for the most part they were individuals with much more modest im-

pairments. Or, if they could barely speak, it was usually because a stroke had deprived them of something they had possessed and taken for granted for almost their whole lives. They were working to recover an ability they had already known. But Tilly, she was trying to develop something new, something she had only heard.

For Tilly, "Rachel has been my best, my most important teacher. The greatest thing about coming here was I learned to talk, and that helped me to do things for myself. That's what I like most—to do everything on my own. Now I can speak and tell people what I want." To Tilly, then, speech was the equivalent of action, it was the *act* of speech: to be able to ask was an act of doing.

Besides her therapist, Tilly had other helpers, companions, and teachers. After her speech became clear enough for people to understand her, she began a job at a sheltered workshop in the community. The same bus system that brought the student volunteers to Elmwood also transported Tilly and other wheelchair users to the workshop each weekday. Tilly was employed at simple, manual tasks there, such as stuffing envelopes and staining wood. She enjoyed the pay, the sense of being productive, and especially the sociability of coffee breaks and meal times. But when funding problems forced this facility to cut back on its programs, Tilly—encouraged by Rachel—decided to try school.

It was not simple to move from piecework to classroom, and will alone was not enough. Tilly was told she needed to be able to read before she could attend the adult courses sponsored by the board of education. So she began the battle for literacy with Lorraine, a tutor who came to see her at Elmwood each week. They sat together in the dining room between meals, turning a corner table into a study hall with books, crayons, and large pieces of paper spread out on the Formica surface. Over the noise of the kitchen and loudspeaker, Tilly learned to put faces on the sounds that Rachel had taught her to pronounce.

Tilly was hungry for the world which literacy promised her. For decades she had harbored a childhood envy of the agemates who had gone to school when she had stayed at home. Now, with her eyes and mind, she devoured letters, primers, readers, a steady diet of print that rarely dulled her appetite. Perhaps with her special sense of the commonplace gift of speech, Tilly felt with Sigmund Freud that "Writing was in its origins the voice of an absent person" (1961: 38).

When she graduated from reading to writing, Tilly needed more than instruction and motivation: she needed muscle. What her mind could grasp had to be translated into the grip of her fingers. So she trained with Barbara Edson, Elmwood's occupational therapist, to gain the dexterity to hold and control a pen. Tilly's medication was reassessed, and a new drug tried that helped to relieve the tremors in her hands. In her spare time she practiced the alphabet. A tray laid across the arms of her wheelchair gave her a writing surface to work on. She usually parked herself in the lounge outside the home's office where Elena, one of the secretaries, would talk to her and help her pronounce words and shape letters. Drawing again on her stock of superlatives, Tilly recalled: "Elena was my best friend, she was the most important person in my life because she helped me to talk and write. Oh, I'll never forget the first time I wrote my name—it was there with her. I laughed and laughed, I was so happy. And I said, 'Amen! Amen!'"

Three years after she entered Elmwood, Tilly became, for the first time, a full-time student. She enrolled in a special education program, and was bused to a local school each weekday. Along with one teacher and five much younger pupils, she studied art, arithmetic, music, reading, and writing. Learning elementary subjects at the age of 62 was, for her, a source of pride, not shame. "You're never too old to study these things," she proclaimed. The identity of being a student was one she had waited and worked too long for to disavow. From then on, when Tilly moved about the home and the community, she carried a handbag on the side of her wheelchair filled with her books and notebooks. The tools and badges of accomplishment traveled with her everywhere.

For many people, the move into late life, and especially the move into a nursing home, has meant the loss or weakening of human ties. But for Tilly, who rarely got out while her mother was alive, the changes wrought by time and place had expanded the world. She now had her days at school, the Sabbath at church, and the evenings for homework and talk. Living at Elmwood brought her roommates, aides, therapists, teachers, fellow students, coworkers, and friends. She enjoyed the sociability of the workshop and classroom, as well as the times when staff wheeled her to Shelby's small downtown so that she could sit in the park, watch parades, or simply window-shop.

The closest of comforts to hand for her was Vivian Grote, one of her three roommates. A widower, Vivian had entered Elmwood a year after Tilly, and had brought with her the wealth of experience that Tilly's birth had denied her. Vivian had known marriage, motherhood, travel, and a career as a bookkeeper. But then, in her early seventies, osteoporosis had put her in a wheelchair, and her husband's subsequent death put her in the home. Despite their worldly and bodily differences, the two women created a kind of kinship. At first Vivian played the Stoic to Tilly's Christian. But as they grew to appreciate one another's strengths and insights, the intersection of their lives steadied them both. Vivian was not so much converted by Tilly as calmed by her. She made Tilly into both a friend and a cause. She assisted her in learning to write, and the two took turns reading to one another. Tilly brought back her stories from the outside, and Vivian helped her make sense of them. Tilly borrowed some of Vivian's clothing and in return gave her a model of resilience. Symmetry kept reappearing in new forms. The reciprocity between them was not so much that of sisters, but of two travelers befriended by the journey itself.

Although Tilly had adjusted well to the nursing home and thrived there, she was often painfully aware of how difficult a place it was for others. She read, in some of their lives, a text of dismay that had emotional symptoms and a spiritual cause.

> When people first come here they don't know how to act, how to do anything. And they don't know what's going to happen. Some don't even know what's going on. A lot of what they see is strange. So I just try to calm them down and talk to them. When I first came here it felt funny because I'd never been away from home in my life. I couldn't do anything. I couldn't even talk. Lots of them can . . . but they don't know what to say. People here helped me, and so the new residents, I try to be a friend to them.

Though the problems of adjustment for residents were considerable, Tilly felt they were overshadowed by the dilemmas of their faith. In her view the hardest thing about being an older person, whether in or out of the institution, was that "many are afraid to die. They're scared to death of dying."

> That ruins their lives because they think about it so much. And I try to talk to them here and tell them, "Don't be afraid to die. Everything will be okay." But they don't have what I have in my heart. I am happy and I know where I am going—that's how I say it to them. . . . I'm at peace because I know I'll be in heaven. Look at me. I have one good hand. I can't stand on my own two feet. But it doesn't matter. I was born this way and I know I'm bound to stay this way all my life. But then I will be with God, and see my mother and grandmother. I'll be with them in my new home in heaven.

Sometimes, however, when Tilly talked to other people about this, to win them over to the peace within, she found that:

> They don't believe what I say. I tried to tell this to Eddie. Also to Stavros and Katina. They listened. They're very nice people. But I couldn't do much. I pray for them every day, for all the ones here who help me, for the aide who puts me to bed at night. . . . That's all I can do. A lot of people don't know where they're going, but they don't want to talk about it. That makes me feel bad. I want them to believe what I do, in everlasting life, but I can't. I don't want to see them go to hell. It's burn, burn, burn all the time. . . .

God offered Tilly a sense of hope. Tilly repaid God with a sense of mission. She found the religious services at Elmwood pallid and uninspired, and felt she could offer others more in her own quiet way. From her wheelchair she reached out to what she saw as a frightened flock, the people she felt were scared by the specter of their own mortality. She knew that the faith that sustained her was usually not one of their possessions, that she had to deal with the fact that few were willing or able to accept it from her as a gift. Having a sense of purpose in her life, she was in no rush to pass on, but neither did she want to slow time down. She claimed that age did not bother her. "When you know what's coming," she said "I feel you might as well not worry. Vivian, she says, 'We all start aging the day we're born.' But me, I say, 'I won't get old till the day I die.' "

Beyond the surety of faith, Tilly's case was also unambiguous in one other important way. Unlike other residents with relatives who might have cared for them at home, she had been very much alone since her mother's death. Coming to Elmwood was not only her mother's dying wish for her, it was probably one of Tilly's only options. And as much as she had loved and appreciated her mother's care, she felt she was living in a present that was far better than any past she had ever had. That, too, took the fear out of the future. If other people could not see their own prospects in the same light that Tilly did, that was partly because they had not brought with them the same body of history, nor had they lived through the same history of the body.

RUTH KARLSON

What Tilly could bring out in others was evident when others came in to see her. She had no immediate family, but enjoyed more visitors and outings than most residents. Never having traveled, lacking the ability to set down a foot to stand on her own home ground, Tilly had still succeeded in developing a sense of place for herself, both in the community and in the lives of her neighbors. Through a combination of longevity, notoriety, and dignity, she had become a person of local renown, someone like William Faulkner's Emily Grierson who, in *A Rose for Emily*, had evolved into "a tradition, a duty, and a care; a sort of hereditary obligation upon the town" (1931: 433).

Ruth Karlson, one of Tilly's more frequent callers, was a member of her church. But their visits were social, not religious: they did not pray or even take out Tilly's Bible. Ruth herself admitted there was more gossip than gospel.

> We just talk a lot about the people we know. Tilly is really interested in them—what they're doing, who said what, how everyone is. It's not all "holier-than-thou" between us, believe me. We laugh a lot. Tilly is no saint and she knows it. That's why I like her. For someone who has led what most would call a sheltered life, she sees a lot about human nature. I don't know where she picked it all up. Maybe it's an art for her, an inborn talent, a reward for all the inborn damage she's had to bear.

"She understands so much about the people in this place," Ruth continued. Her look traveled slowly over the faces of three residents sitting across
the lounge from us. "You could learn a lot from her. I do. I honestly don't
think I'd have Tilly's peace or will—but she's had a whole lifetime to develop
them, whereas if you're born normal—I mean, healthy—then you just go
along, and grow and grow up, and you don't have to fight and find strength
every step of the way. Sometimes I get tired just thinking about what she's
gone through."

One afternoon, Ruth and I sat over coffee in the back of the dining room.
She was in her late thirties, a part-time teacher's aide, the married mother
of two. She had just spent an hour with Tilly, helping her write a letter,
and she looked more tired than the task or the hour of the day would have
suggested. She was very good at being composed, but the ritual of the cups
and the rising steam began to uncoil her.

> Being with her today got to me. First, getting the words down was simple,
> but then halfway through I took a step back—in my mind—and I saw what
> she had to overcome to do this, how happy she was to be able to write, and
> how much we take something that easy for granted. I almost cried, but I
> didn't want to embarrass Tilly.
>
> It is hard for me at times here, though it feels good to do it because I like
> Tilly so much. She's like a pet project in our congregation. I know that's a
> bad pun, but you understand what I mean. People do what they can for her.
> And this is my small piece.
>
> It's easier to come to see someone you already know in a place like this
> than to walk up to people who are practically strangers. I guess I come here
> to be with Tilly, not to visit the nursing home, if you can see the difference.
> I mean, that's the way I think about it. Otherwise I'd find this too depressing
> a prospect.

Perhaps it was her own sense of propriety that made Ruth quickly add:

> I know that's not the way I'm supposed to feel. People here do have hope
> . . . at least some do, I know. But it still tears me up if I look around a lot
> and see all their faces. Tilly is such a bright star. She makes the others harder
> to think about.
>
> Rachel, Tilly's speech therapist, once said to me—it was only half a joke—
> that Tilly was a "success story." And if you listen to Tilly, she feels that her
> life is better here than it was before. Also, when we talk, she asks me about
> my life. Imagine her having enough thoughtfulness to do that. I like telling
> her about the school I work at, and my children. I say hello to a few others
> here, but I don't really visit with them. As it is, I have all I can handle and I
> need to stay focused.

When Ruth got confessional, when she spoke openly about her limits in
this way, she often followed the admission with an evangelical note—as if

trying to cancel out one song by singing another. Pushing past her judgment of Tilly as a good but less than saintly person, Ruth would then praise the saving grace of Tilly's belief and the healing lesson of her life. She sat and spoke in a kind of awe about the quiet power of faith inside her friend's body of weak and wayward muscles. Once, after she had gone on like this quite eloquently for some time, she looked at me and said disarmingly, "You don't really share this kind of faith, do you?" She had seen right through my earnest, practiced politeness. And while I fumbled for something to say, she gently cut off my useless search. "That's alright, you know. You just have to believe that Tilly believes."

FRANK HEALEY

A Painter's Eye

When Frank Healey was young, he wanted to shape his life into a work of art. He grew up in poverty in a small, upstate city, sometimes literally begging for his supper on streetcorners. When he was eight years old he drew and painted pictures—country scenes that he himself had never seen—and sold them to shoppers near the downtown stores. He brought the coins he collected home to his widowed mother in their tenement. There was a kind of dark poetry to the images he would later etch of his childhood: pictures of him and his brothers in a clean, sparse apartment; a precious, patched overcoat; an overworked and worried parent; meager meals. His words had the black-and-white-and-shadowed tones of a Jacob Riis photograph.

Dreams of artistry competed with poverty in Frank's reminiscences. Painting, singing, and acting were the talents he recalled as his endowment. But life was more distracting and demanding than art. He served in the First World War as a young man and later married, raised a family, and held a series of retail jobs. The wish for a career on the stage or in the studio became a bittersweet memory, a naive nostalgic hope he would later smile about and shake his head over. In his old age, in his wheelchair, the desire to create was still alive, but it had become less compelling than the wish to be able to walk.

Elmwood Grove was not the first nursing institution that Frank had lived in. Four years after his wife's death, afflicted with diabetes and an arthritic condition in his knees, he moved to a health-related facility near his daughter's house in Syracuse. Several themes dominated his accounts of that institution: he remembered that many refined people lived there; that the residents included "quite a few attractive women"; that "there wasn't enough therapy to help me use my legs"; and that "almost everyone was very nice"—though he "could have done with fewer Republicans."

When his daughter had to leave the Northeast because of her own health problems, the family decided to move Frank to a home near Ithaca, where his married son was living. By then the arthritis had worsened and Frank had also developed a recurring kidney disorder. His doctor recommended that he enter a skilled nursing facility. "I'll be very honest," Frank confided, "this place is much better than that other one. I wasn't happy there. My son Patrick took it upon himself to get me into this home so that I could see somebody [from the family] every week. My daughter used to visit regularly. Now I'm here because my son decided he'll be the one to see me."

Frank told the story of his move with some pride, choosing to view it as both an improvement in his situation and a testimony to his children's sense of responsibility. For those reasons, he did not shy away from using a passive voice in discussing the transfer: he described the decision as one that *they* had made *for him*. And unlike some other residents, who complained that their families had abandoned them or taken control of their lives and homes, Frank praised Patrick and his daughter-in-law Effie for their conduct. "They come several times a week. She buys me new clothes when I need them. And my son is a very fine person. I am proud of what he has done for me."

But Frank spoke in other voices too. His assessment of his son was sincere, yet it was not the whole story. He periodically complained to Patrick and Effie about this "better" home he was so content to be in. Food, roommates, and rules were high on his list of Elmwood's shortcomings. And when his family could not change things to his satisfaction, he would sometimes criticize them to Nina in social work. She would hear him out, commiserating with his outbursts without encouraging them: she knew the place he had made for her in the geometry of his anger. She acknowledged:

> Frank has a way with words, and he's good at telling tales about us to one another. Patrick and I hear about each other's faults through Frank's good graces. When he deals with people like us—who he thinks have more power than he does—and then finds we can't deliver what he wants, he boils over. The home is bound to fail him some of the time because he wants what no institution can give him: his health, his freedom, his passion. Who wouldn't want those things, or feel cheated at their loss?

Just as Frank chose his moments and his targets with care, he was also conscientious in selecting the words and qualities to describe his own character. He was emphatic, for example, to distinguish himself from certain residents and their disabilities. "Mr. Costa over there is a fine man," he once told me, "but thank God I don't have to carry a urine bag like him and some of the others. The important parts of me still obey. . . . I know that at my age I'm considered an old man. I admit it. But I have all my faculties, if you know what I mean. I'm not like Mr. Howard, next door, the one who shouts and falls so much they keep him tied down, or Sarah, the one who sits and smiles all day at her teddy bear. Or that woman with the red robe from the first floor . . . "

"Eva? Mrs. Rayburn?"

"Yes. Her. She doesn't mean any harm: all smiles too, but not much left in the mind. She wanders and babbles. Pathetic. What can you do with a person like that? What can you do *for* her? Fortunately, I'm not here for my brain. I may get cranky, but I'm not crazy. And I thank God for that."

Besides strength of brain and body, there were other pieces out of which Frank built an identity for himself. Age having divested him of most of his former roles, he created new ones out of fragments of his history. At 90, he was no longer a worker or a husband, and though still a father, his children—the one son and one daughter—were themselves now parents in their own right. So two of the parts of his past that Frank elaborated on when presenting himself were his roles as a painter and performer. In explaining how he had ended up in the first nursing home he had lived in, in fact, he made the decision sound like an audition.

> They wanted someone who could sing and, well, I could sing. And they needed someone who could act, and I could do that too. So I appeared in five plays and I also sang. I even painted the scenery for them. People gave me a lot of applause. One woman who I liked a lot told me how talented I was. Now that was generous, but I don't think she was just being kind. Something else happened to me there that had never been done for anyone else. When they knew I was going away they gave a party. I was the first one they ever did that for, with pictures on the walls and signs saying "We'll miss you." So I couldn't have been such a bad person.

Frank was too bright not to be aware of his impact on people, and not being "such a bad person" had an unmistakably defensive ring. He knew he could grate as well as charm. When weighing the merits and defects of his own character, however, he also laid claim to one special virtue: that of gratitude.

> God is good to me because I've had five operations and I got away with every one of them. I'm still alive. Last year I was operated on for stones in my kidney, in the urinary passage. Well, I stopped breathing during the operation and the surgeons walked away. They thought I was dead. But then, after a minute, I started to belch, so they knew I was alive. I know I have been very fortunate. God has been kind to me. You have to have gratitude after all that I've been through. If you don't feel grateful after five operations, then you're not a good person.

In his milder moods, Frank suggested that there was nothing hard about being in a nursing home. He avoided all but a few organized activities, and other than for meals, baths, and PT, he could usually be found in his room.

Having lived for four years in another facility, he said he had made his peace with institutional life. He argued that "if you follow the rules and act nice to people, they will treat you well." He still loved to paint and draw, and spent several hours a week making sketches and watercolors. A can of brushes and a stack of pads stood on his bureau. Seated in his room, or at a small table in a back lounge, he lost himself in the flow of lines, the spread-out sheets of paper, the choice of brushes, the search for the right shades. His work hung on several of Elmwood's bulletin boards and in his son's house. When people noticed his paintings and complimented them, he feigned indifference but treasured the praise.

The emotional chemistry of Frank's life, however, was not as simple as water and color, or gratitude and accommodation. He was a man of intense feelings, possessed of passion, sadness, and a sense of life's own injustice. When the emotions erupted, there could be laughter, pathos, wonderment, and sharp recoil. There were times when Frank's constant striving for the bon mot, the proper put-down, the turn and twist of phrase, drove people away: it was metaphor as illness. He once overheard Mrs. Briggs complain that her son, a local professor, had not come to visit her in over a week. Frank could not resist remarking that "academics get so lost in their oak-lined studies that they can't see their relatives for the trees." When he added, intemperately, that this was a case where "the bookworm has turned," Mrs. Briggs had had enough, and shouted at him to mind his own business.

Staff and visitors were intrigued as well as troubled by Frank because of his depth and unpredictability. Janice, a volunteer who shared his interest in art, once observed to me that spending time with Frank was a bit like walking into a cubist painting. Different angles and surfaces presented themselves all at once, each demanding attention—not as separate facets, but as parts of a whole that depended on the visitor—as viewer—for their integrity. When Frank spoke, the painting came alive, bringing the inside onto the surface like an X ray etched in words. Once, in a conversation with Janice, Frank used art itself to talk about how he and time had changed one another.

> When I was young, I loved to go to exhibits and museums, and I would walk through the rooms for each painter in chronological order. That's how I studied their lives. But in the last few years I found myself doing it in reverse, taking the last paintings first, and then looking at everything else—back and back through the rooms to the beginning: it was a way to understand what had been done at the end.

With his painter's eye, Frank could be very tender in the way he saw and spoke about his own history. Once, describing his 35-year marriage, a slip of mind-and-tongue revealed how much he identified with his wife. "She was a wonderful person, very gracious and delicate and giving, but it didn't last. What could you do? She died . . . she died . . . It was. . . . " He paused, upset, searching my face for the date. "Not to remember the year!" He hit his forehead with his palm. "When you lose somebody like that it's a big part of your life that's gone. Over thirty years of marriage, two children plus grandchildren. Believe me: it's not easy seeing a coffin that your wife is in lowered through the ground. It ended," he said, sliding unawares into his wife's persona, "it ended because cancer got into my blood and I died. It was terrible to watch, to see a person go like that: wasting, draining away, all the color gone, scraped down right to your poor bones. Thank God, though, my children were both still alive. . . . " He stopped, shifted back into his own shape, continued: "I ordered a gravemarker, but I had it cut with both our names, hers on the right side. I will be there with her on the left some day, in the ground *and* on the stone."

Though Frank's sense of loss was genuine, it had not extinguished the passionate part of his nature. Recounting the last two decades of his life, right down to the present of his 91st year, he painted a self-portrait of a romantic, lusty, but respectful man.

Let me get personal. In this nursing home and in the first one, there are people I've been in love with. That's a big thing. You can understand that, I hope. You know that I lost my wife many years ago. I did not want to marry another woman then but also I did not stop living. It seems to me, and I think you'll agree, that a lot of things in this life are sex. It's crazy, I know. Sex is crazy, but it's important all the same. It's nonsense about old people not feeling anything that way. Frankly, I had relations with widows—only with women whose husbands had passed away. I didn't do anything with a married person—I'm not that kind of man. A woman who is married, she belongs with her husband. It's none of my business. But a widow . . . it's her own life. Anyway, I was familiar with three women at different times. Once a funny thing happened. I came to the house of this woman I'd been seeing, and there was a little boy, her grandson, about 11 years old, who hollered, "That man's here again!" It was like a little boy telling on his big sister!

As far as I'm concerned, there's nothing new about sex. If widows accepted me, alright; if they didn't, I didn't hang around. But there's another thing. When a woman told me she was keeping company again, I stayed away. I wanted to give her and the man she was seeing a full life. I wouldn't interfere. That's because I think it's wonderful when a woman who's a widow finds a person who she might marry. One lady told me it wouldn't make any difference to her, but I said as far as I'm concerned, if you're serious about this other man, then I take myself out of the picture. No one has a right to stand in the way of that just for his own pleasure. I respect that.

Separate from sex, for Frank, was the experience of romance. He was a person who, in the face of age and all its insults, still wanted to be dying for love.

Maybe I'm stupid, but I was always in love with some kind of woman. I like women! It wasn't just ten years ago: it could be five years ago or even now.

When I came to this place, my friends—they know me—they said, "Don't forget to find a beautiful woman you can be in love with." Of course they kidded me. But always I've had a tendency to fall in love very easily. Half the time, to tell you the truth, I think I'm a damn fool because falling in love seems to be such a big thing in my life!

Looking back over his years as a widower, Frank had one regret: he should have remarried.

I think every man should be with a woman. Maybe I'm wrong, but I feel it's in our nature. First of all, if people didn't get together there wouldn't be any more children. And it's a marvelous thing to be in love. I think marrying is a proper answer. . . . After I'd been a widower for two years my daughter told me, "Get yourself another wife." But I didn't. At the time I didn't care to. But I'll be honest with you. I made a mistake. I should have taken another wife. I would have had a home. And it's possible the woman you marry has money, which doesn't hurt. Like my daughter says, I should have waited a couple of years and found another wife. But now I'm going to be 91 and it's too late . . . I think.

He hesitated, and then added the redemptive observation: "Well, at least I've had the blessing of six grandchildren . . . I'm happy about that. You would be too, because if you don't have grandchildren the world would come to an end. You should have children," he directed me. "If you do, see that they stay healthy. Then, with the help of God, you'll never regret your life."

The accounts that Frank gave of his own life alternated between accomplishments and lost chances, between the artistic career and second marriage that never occurred, and the loves and the grandchildren that did. As his tenure in Elmwood reached into its second year, there were more and more moments when the balance of memory and emotion fell to the negative side. There was a great deal in late life that oppressed him: some was of his own making, and some was in his surroundings. At the home, what closed in around him was not darkness but light: the noise of neon, the shine of the floor, the dull, diffused colors of the walls. His painter's sense was offended. But what most often tipped the scales for him was his passionate sense of too much life left unlived, and the painful, present state of his body, with its confinement in home and wheelchair. The first time I met him was eight days after he had moved into the institution, and he vowed he would walk again. He said, "I'm positive I will walk because I started off life without this machine, and I will finish it in the same way. They only put me in this full-time after the kidney operation. Now I am in physical therapy, and someday I'm going to walk like a regular person."

But it never happened. In the next and final three years of his life, Frank suffered the last ironies of art and desire: Elmwood gave him several performances at which to sing, but he had to sit at center stage, and never stood there again. The legs could not carry like the voice. He found the applause both a tribute and a trial.

The bitter fruit of disability for Frank was sometimes anger, an all-too-human lashing out at those around him, including the innocent and the guilty, those who cared and those who gave care. The charge nurse was periodically harangued for being too late or too early with his medicine. He threw a brush at a housekeeper for moving his sketchpads and slippers beyond his reach. And Frank struck one of the aides who he felt handled him roughly during a transfer from the wheelchair to his bed. Unless one made exceptional allowance for the frustrations of a lively spirit caught in an aging body, none of these outbursts were warranted by what the staff had done.

But Frank's sense and expression of rage were not entirely his own creation. Sometimes others helped or provoked him. For a while there was John Carmichael, his blind roommate who, despite or because of his limits, saw through many of Frank's vulnerabilities. John was irritated by Frank's quick judgments and urbane airs, and took whatever opportunities he could to deflate and mock them. Knowing, for example, that Frank disdained television watchers, especially those addicted to "the nonsense of quiz shows," John—who could not watch and rarely listened—would periodically launch into detailed descriptions of questions, answers, and prizes from programs he had overheard. He climaxed his accounts with falsetto imitations of squealing contestants. His monologues worked. Frank would erupt, yelling at him to shut up, upbraiding him for sharing in such stupidity, counting him among the curses which an unkind fate had visited upon him: useless legs, undervalued talent, and the company of fools. Staff on the floor had to drop their tasks, rush in to mediate, and call upon an arsenal of appeasement, threat, and distraction to quiet the conflict. The result was a truce, however, never a permanent peace between these two: the underlying issues—their personalities and values, the anger of age, and the inevitable frictions of coexistence—invariably reasserted themselves.

The struggle was not as one-sided as it sometimes seemed. Though John joked about and teased Frank, he also envied him his sight, his assertiveness, his convictions, and his visitors. When the staff finally settled the two men into new rooms with different roommates, John was relieved but, in the end, muted. His world became quiet as well as dark. He had lost his goad, his spark.

Frank furnished his own flame. He laughed and raged and enjoyed his lustful memories until an embolism ended life in the midst of his third year at Elmwood. He was rarely neutral—about religion, politics, or affairs of the heart—and few of the people around him were indifferent to his presence or his passing. He had his strain of bigotry, and unlike some of his quieter, equally prejudiced peers, he did not hesitate to say how ill at ease he was at being cared for by black aides. Yet among those who found his death the hardest to bear were the staff who had also found him the most difficult to deal with. But this was no late-hour guilt on their part. They found his attachment to life a challenge, his appreciation as ardent as his anger.

Though he often read the Bible and thanked God, Frank was emphatically a creature of this world, a man more attuned to the pleasures and indignities of the flesh than the doubtful promise of the spirit. Like Yeats's "Wild Old Wicked Man," he would have preferred to "forget it all awhile / Upon a woman's breast" than catch "lightning / From the old man in the skies" ([1938] 1983: 311). A few months before he died, we had a conversation which slowly turned into an account of the emotional debts and credits of his life: he cursed his legs for betraying him, thanked the Lord for his longevity, and blessed his children for their loyalty. He summed up the balance with the assertion that he had "tried to find a happy way of living because you only live once."

> I don't believe in this heaven or hell because no one ever came back to tell us about it. Whatever there is, for certain, is here. You can take it or leave it—and we all will leave it in "the fullness of time"—but meanwhile I enjoy whatever I can. Just yesterday I noticed that a rather attractive woman moved in down the hall. So we'll see what happens. I understand she's a widow. . . . "

PATRICK HEALEY

When Frank was alive, his son spoke of him with a mixture of admiration and exhaustion. "For all his frailty, my father is, in other ways, very tough: he's a strong-willed, sharp-tongued man. The weaker his body gets, the angrier he becomes . . . the more he strikes out with what strengths he has left. And, I must tell you, he can be pretty powerful."

Patrick was Frank's most faithful and beleaguered visitor: he could never escape from either his own sense of responsibility or his father's wrath. With his wife Effie's help, he was always trying to put things right or, at least, listen patiently. On the negative side it was roommate problems or arguments with the aides. On a more positive note, it could be his father's veiled, romantic interest in one of the therapists or, quite undisguised, his pursuit of a new female resident. But some of Frank's most characteristic moments were barbed ones: the shafts were thrown both at those he considered pretentious and, when all else failed, at his admired and admiring son, who did not have the power to extricate Frank or his body from their fate.

One of Frank's favorite japes was to cut the outside world and its representatives down to institutionalize size. "Some of the retired professors who live here—and I'm talking about the ones who are *not* senile—if they were as stupid in real life as they are in this home, then the university where they taught must have turned out three generations of fools. Please don't take offense," he went on, excusing me in a very disingenuous way, "because I know you're a professor yourself. But they should have given these men tea and sympathy instead of tenure. They had to be from the faculty without its faculties."

The thrusts at his son came from a different angle. They were aimed not at his mind but at this actions . . . or at what his father sometimes saw as inaction. Frank grew impatient, for example, at the slow pace of arranging for a transfer out of John Carmichael's room and took Patrick to task for not making it happen more quickly. When a prolonged bladder infection stopped his weekend trips to Patrick's home, Frank repeatedly urged his son to override the doctor's recommendation that he stay at Elmwood until the condition had completely cleared up. Clothes provided another occasion for complaint. Several times a year, a local department store brought a van load of apparel to the home so that the residents could shop without having to leave the institution. Effie usually came to help her father-in-law buy on these days, and when necessary she altered the clothes for him. Frank was truly appreciative of her help, but not above criticizing her choices and her sewing. Yet he always voiced these judgments to Patrick and never to Effie herself. What compounded the difficulty of such father-son encounters was Frank's finely tuned sense of timing. He and Patrick would often sit and talk in the first floor lounge—one of Elmwood's relatively private places— but when there were enough people around, either staff or other visitors, Frank would choose that moment for an outburst. At least that was the way it felt to Patrick. "He's generous—he likes everyone to get the most out of my embarrassment."

Frank's relationship with his family was not all criticism and carping, however. There were also good visits and warm times at Patrick's home, a sense of connection that dissolved the shadows of daily life and gave Frank the rewards of anticipation. He loved his family and they knew it, though he made them take more than their fair share of the burdens of his frailty. Patrick and his oldest son delighted in Frank's wit, even when they were among its targets. "My father does have this knack for seeing through people," Patrick acknowledged. "Sometimes it used to disturb me because it made me feel that no one and nothing was sacred. But as I've gotten older and less naive about human nature, I can sense the justice of his remarks. I can feel the courage it takes to be so candid. There's also a skill to it that I admire: his use of language, the way he can take people's own words and turn them back on them."

As he himself aged, one of the other things that Patrick came to respect was what his father's history had been like.

He almost never spoke about it when I was growing up or even later, after my mother died. When he lived in the first nursing home in Syracuse, I don't remember that my sister—who saw him the most then—I don't recall that she talked about his past as something that he spoke about a lot. But when I'm with him now, especially if one of my children is there, he tells about the poverty, the paintings on the sidewalk, the kind of food they could afford when he was a kid. What I am impressed with is that we never knew much about that part of his history; that he was able to overcome it and make a success of himself in American, middle-class terms—a family, good jobs, a decent place to live; and that he was able to learn so much on his own, develop his intellect, become a self-educated man. He has such a good mind! It's only in the last few years, too, that I've been able to grasp how much he wanted to be a painter and performer, how disappointing that must have been to him. It's a shame, really, that he has to live out this last part of his life this way— I can understand the bitterness that's there. The irony for me is that if this had not happened, if he wasn't so physically sick and near us, I don't think I ever would have seen this much of him or learned so much about what he's been through.

Frank's kin felt more anguish than guilt. They thought that Elmwood was the best place for him, but were frustrated, sometimes maddeningly so, in their attempts to help him make the most of his situation. Staff were sympathetic to the family and often went out of their way to be actively supportive. The main impediment was Frank himself.

There was the bread and butter incident, which left a mark not only on the floor, but on everyone concerned. Of the many foods which appeared on his meal tray each week, the bread and butter were the ones Frank found most objectionable. It seemed a curious and minor choice for complaint, but he was insistent and serious about his displeasure. Finally, Patrick and his wife brought it up with Nina Breckner, who put them in touch with the dietitian, who agreed to switch whole wheat slices for white and a whipped spread for a hard pat.

But even the best laid trays can go astray. When Florence, a dietary aide, proudly put the new fare in front of Frank one lunchtime, he sat and stared at it, said nothing for a moment, and then exploded that he had asked for rye bread. That said, he picked the tray up and hurled it at her, splattering Florence's dress and the nearby floor with meatloaf, gravy, peas, whole wheat crumbs, and smears of butter.

Patrick was left to pick up the pieces in a social if not a literal sense. He was called in that afternoon to calm his father; and while there, he sought out Florence to apologize, and then arranged to see Nina to discuss the whole incident. Later in the day, when he and Nina met in her office, they traded weak, rueful smiles. They thought they were going to make some small progress this time, but instead found themselves going over the wreckage. While nothing permanent had been destroyed except the week's expectations, they were also tired, worn down by their would-be beneficiary. Nina's view was that their attempts to help "had only made him feel more helpless. It's unpredictable. In this case it simply added fuel to his anger. It's a real double bind. Each time we try to do something *he* wants, he is reminded that only *we* can do it for him."

Patrick found himself pleading. "But he is already dependent in so many ways. Can't anyone do *anything* for him without his getting resentful?"

"Maybe. Sometimes. But that," Nina offered, "is what we're up against. He has so many reasons to feel this way. *That* is what he really threw at us today."

BONNIE DUMOND

The War of the Words

Bonnie Dumond was locked in a war of the words. The weapons were names and nouns, the enemy was memory itself. In the midst of everyday conversation, it was appalling to be plunged suddenly into the unequal struggle inside her. It was as if the mind itself had become arthritic: somewhere within, it saw what it wanted but could not get the fingers of speech to reach out and firmly grasp the object of its desire. When Bonnie was at a loss for words, her face—to compensate, perhaps to explain—broadcast other feelings through the silence: cheeks and mouth curved into embarrassment, the eyes flashed terror.

She once told me a story, a courtship tale whose telling combined the twin gods of comedy and tragedy that had come to rule her life.

> At one time I thought my mother was rather foolish, though later I saw how smart she was. When I was seeing my beau, long before he and I were married, she'd make it hard for us to be together. Sometimes she'd even forbid me to see him. But she knew what she was doing. The taboo threw us together: the defiance felt as good as love. I think they were almost the same emotion! Later, when I was married . . . when I married . . . ?

The name had fled. Bonnie's eyes froze on the half-empty cups of coffee on the table between us. Losing her husband's identity was one of those time-shattered moments, a failing that no afterthought could redeem. In less than a minute she had recovered his name, but not her balance. She had been lost in a way that only those with faded memory will ever know, cut off at least momentarily from the history that had made her who she was.

Years ago, Bonnie would have been described by the affectionate term "dotty." But her dotage had carried her into the clinical age, and she was now stuck with the label of "senile." There was a particular vulnerability for institutionalized people like her when they got caught in wordless time. They did not have the means to dissemble that the rest of us do. They could not pace, they could not move about the room fingering objects, or stand to stare out the window in feigned distraction. When talk with them stopped, the silence and stillness were total.

From the fragments of Bonnie's memories, from the vibrant way she often redeemed them, it was possible to make a kind of conventional sense out of her past. She had been born in Mississippi in 1902, but her father, a railroad man, eventually moved his family to Texas. She grew up in a small town within one hundred miles of the Mexican border. Later, living in Houston, she attended religious schools and a Baptist college, studying to be a teacher. She returned to the Texas community she had been raised in and established its first kindergarten. Within a few years she married, but continued to teach until the first of her two children was born. She recalled the next few years as a period of great domestic tranquility and fulfillment. She spoke with animation of raising a son and daughter, owning her first car, singing in the church choir, participating in the life of the local women's club. In retrospect, at the age of 82, she saw the years of teaching and parenting as the best of times.

> I loved to watch children grow. If I were a college student now and I could live my life over, I'd choose to teach again. I had always had a picture in my mind of working with the young. In the first school where I taught I saw that the children learned as much from one another as they did from me. I loved the challenge of their curiosity: after each answer I'd give them there'd be another "Why?" With my own son and daughter, I wondered if they'd turn out well [she laughed] just like me and my father. It was exciting to see things in them that they were not conscious of—family mannerisms, pet peeves, even tastes in music. How I loved Mozart and Bach, and oh, how happy I was when they discovered them too!

Talking about teaching often brought her around to the subject of her father.

> He gave me more encouragement than my mother did, plus most of my advice. He was a businessman, out in the world: when my brother and I were in college, he'd tell us what courses to take. And he was almost always right about what would do us the most good, what would really be useful in the long run when we got out in the world. He died after I finished my schooling and by then I could see how well his words stood up.

In the light of what Bonnie's own memory had become, it was ironic that words, and the very structure of language, had been two of the most passionate parts of her education.

> I loved book-learning and taking notes and especially grammar. As I went up through the grades, I loved to remember the hard words and pronounce

them correctly, to diagram sentences, to learn the parts of speech: alliteration, metaphor, euphemism—those names were like magic or music to me. It was grand, in the elementary school I worked in, to teach all those lovely things to my pupils.

Now, when she struggled to recapture what she had learned and taught over three score years ago, Bonnie's déjà vu was doubly strong. "I feel like I'm getting back into my first childhood—and theirs—when I speak about those days. Maybe that's what 'second childhood' should mean—reliving your own through someone else's."

Although she sometimes joked about her forgetfulness, Bonnie was also embarrassed and anguished by it. The points of confusion and contradiction covered the compass of her life. She was 94 . . . or 84. She had been married once . . . or twice. Her daughter was a teacher . . . or her son was . . . or they both were. The relative who visited her every few weeks was a niece . . . or a cousin. And the little boy who accompanied this woman was Bonnie's grandson . . . or nephew . . . or "someone just like a godchild." She sometimes spoke of all the other residents at Elmwood as "being retired teachers like me." When a name escaped her, she was more likely to halt her speech than search her mind out loud. The need to stop, rethink, correct, confess, or suffer through the silent uncertainty took an almost physical toll on her. In midconversation she could be gasping for breath as well as grasping for words. She almost never asked for help in finding the fugitive name or noun, but she let those who knew her well know that it was alright for them to fill in the missing parts of a sentence or thought.

Where biblical prophets were sometimes forced by God to speak against their will, Bonnie tried to force her will upon speech itself. There were moments when, exasperated with her failure, she became exasperating to others. Sometimes for staff there was a question of whether Bonnie was confused or simply contrary. Once, in response to an aide's gentle encouragement that she be more active in bathing herself and caring for her room, Bonnie complained, "I don't know why they keep expecting me to do all these things for myself when I'm spending so much money to stay in this fancy hotel."

Depending on what day you spoke to Bonnie, you were likely to get widely divergent versions of how she had ended up living at this "hotel." She had come to town to visit her grandson and decided to stay. Or she had to sell "the various properties" that she and her late husband owned because they were too much for her to care for. Another time it was "exhaustion"—the need to rest up after "all those trips with the retired teachers to Mexico, Europe, and other such places." Each week she had a slightly different history. When I wasn't wondering whether or not to feel sorry for her, I was jealous over how many lives she had led.

The accuracy of Bonnie's memory, her awareness of its inconsistent claims, would come and go. When its fragility or vividness were foremost in her mind, she sang a kind of broken song, spun out and spelled out a word, a moment, an image at a time. Her short-lived teaching career had been worth a lifetime of remembrance, yet she was also haunted by its brevity. She loved her own children, but had given up the chance to nurture so many others for the sake of raising just those two. At a pet session, Cathy had once remarked to Bonnie that women could now be as liberated as men, and that "it's never too late" to achieve this. But Bonnie had answered with a look that asked, "Never too late for whom?" As her silent response implied, Bonnie felt she had been young before her time.

It was not possible to feel just one or even two ways about Bonnie. Her mind and her mood changed too often. The experiences of her best friend and roommate, Barbara Hernstein, testified to the push and pull of Bonnie's effect on people. "The day Bonnie moved here I saw her come into the dining room. We were about to have lunch, so I motioned to her to sit near me at my table. Well, she did, and we've been having our meals together ever since. What I like about her is that she's private, she minds her own business—that's an important quality in people."

Barbara liked to take some license in describing both Bonnie's character and her own. For all their shared sense of propriety, the two women loved to gossip; and like diligent librarians, they could spend hours cataloguing the failings of other residents. They laughed like schoolgirls once they got launched, and floor staff would check in to see who was being flayed that day. But even with the leaven of shared mealtimes and judgments, the two also got on one another's nerves. They occasionally quibbled over who should sit where at the table. Another time, Barbara found her way blocked by Bonnie's wheelchair when she tried to leave their room. She asked her friend to move. Bonnie, either out of forgetfulness or feigned distraction, was so slow to respond that Barbara erupted at her. Reva, the aide who cared for them both, had to referee their quarrel in the midst of bathing her other patients. Bonnie's contrariness also got to staff at times. Once, when Denise had especially recruited a new volunteer to read to her, Bonnie refused to come down because she claimed she was "too tired and not in the mood." The volunteer tried to cover her own confusion by saying she understood, but Denise, who had put a lot of effort into making the arrangements, felt both embarrassed and betrayed.

Bonnie's own reading of the nursing home was also a mixture of emotions: in her case, the signs of gratitude, disappointment, and expectation took their turns in the foreground. She spent her days in a routine of PT, planned activities, and sitting in the lounge "to study the people and the happenings." She praised the care she received, and liked to single out the value of regular therapy. "Even from a wheelchair you can exercise your arms, hands, and legs. Without that, people like me would almost be like mummies sitting here." Along with many others, Bonnie loved to be out on Elmwood's lawn in the nice weather and "watch the scenes of the village move by." She appreciated the security that home life gave, though she often put this in third rather than first person terms. "Take Barbara. She's happy to be here because her arthritis left her feeling so inadequate in her own house. She says her family 'got rid of her and kept the dog,' but you know, she really didn't want to live dependent on them."

The nursing home, however, was not all that Bonnie had hoped for in her own case either. Grouping herself with some of the very people she objected to, she confessed:

> I've been disappointed that there are so many here who are deformed, or in bed, or in wheelchairs. It's too much of the same. This leg, the one that's so weak, I thought I would be able to walk on it [in six months], but it's already two years I'm at Elmwood and I still can't use it. I like to be active and get out and go places. I feel I could almost be independent enough to live in a home by myself. It's alarming to consider that you can't do what you feel you should be capable of.

Disability was also disenfranchising for her. Along with other residents— as well as healthy people outside—Bonnie had found that the price of security was a certain loss of privacy, a lack of say over her surroundings. The most constant reminder of that for her was the need to live with three roommates. At first, Bonnie recalled, "what was hard was having three voices besides my own." Later, it was the loudness of one person rather than the tyranny of numbers that prevailed.

> There is a woman in my room who is so loud and noisy that we hope to get rid of her. June, she's never had much education. She's not only crude, she takes the floor whenever she gets a chance. We have to threaten her down. We just hope, well, not that she won't live too long, but we pray we won't have to have her with us forever. Barbara and I think we can trade her off for someone else.

When Bonnie was not in one of her "hotel" phases, she compared Elmwood to another institution from her past.

> Maybe I expected the nursing home to be something like the dormitory I lived in at college. I shared with two girls there. But that didn't last as long as this. I mean, if the women in my room now stay for five or ten years, I could have them with me the whole time . . . you know, like a marriage. But just like the way college was, I guess, some stay and some go.

Compared to her relations with roommates, Bonnie's ties to her family were less ambiguous but also less intense. Her son and daughter still lived in the South and each traveled to see her two or three times a year. She enjoyed their visits but did not anticipate or remember the details much. Her "nephew" David—her great-nephew, really—was the person whose presence excited her the most. Once every few weeks he came to Elmwood with his mother, Emma, Bonnie's niece. "I've enjoyed seeing him grow up. He has such animated eyes," said Bonnie, opening her own wide to illustrate. "He makes me think of a newspaper reporter—collecting all the information, asking all the questions. When he talks, instead of that awful noise that June makes, it sounds more like music."

Despite her periods of confusion, then, Bonnie knew something of what she wanted: she preferred a certain tone and tenor in other people's voices; like her friend Barbara, she had her standards for companionship; and as a person used to her independence, she harbored a hope for its return. But in these and in other parts of her life, she increasingly experienced a loss of control rather than a fulfillment of her desires. An accident she suffered in her third year at Elmwood wove the threads of her frailty together in a disconcerting way. Bonnie fell and badly injured her hip. She had been standing at her dresser, arranging some letters and books, when she leaned backwards to sit down: the wheelchair which should have been there was gone. She had forgotten to set its brake, and the chair had slipped far enough behind to fool and elude her. She did not break any bones, but the contusions spread a sunset of colors over her buttocks and thigh. Falls such as this were among the most common accidents at the home, and most of them, as this one, were nobody's fault. Staff could not monitor every resident at every moment. Furthermore, because one of Elmwood's goals was to encourage people to do as much for themselves as they could, employees had to leave opportunities for residents to put that ideal into practice. If mind or machine failed, however, self-reliance could be a risky business.

In the aftermath of her accident, Bonnie was indignant as well as hurt, her ego bruised worse than her side. The lapse of attention to the brake was another reminder of how forgetful she had become. It left her bedridden for weeks, irritable, depressed by both the immobility and the heightened sense of her vulnerability. Two months later she had recovered enough, in body and spirit, to talk about the accident in a chastened, philosophical way. She concluded that "the way of all flesh wouldn't be quite so bad if the mind didn't collude with it." Then she suddenly became quiet, and when she came back from the silence—half a minute on—she had switched to her former role as teacher and mentor. Without prelude, she asked me what my students were like, but before I could offer much of an answer, she began to admonish.

> Tell them not to be intimidated. Not to be afraid of other people's bragging. Lots of young folks are scared of growing old and dying, of what the future holds for them. But I feel that if they are sincere, if they've done everything

they think they can do, and it still doesn't work out for them the way they want, then at least they won't go around blaming themselves.

When you're afraid, fear eats up your life. It only makes the worst happen, or happen sooner. Don't be old before your time. It'll come soon enough.

She paused, considering her own words.

Well, maybe that all sounds too brave. I know it's hard. Like my husband's death. It came so suddenly: he got cancer, a growth in the stomach that seemed to come out of nowhere, and he was dead in just a few months. At first I couldn't accept it. It was like a void. For half a year I just went through the motions of being alive. But then you recover and get on with what you can get on with, with what you've set yourself to do. . . . There's a song, a hymn I sort of remember, that says something about "blessing each day," I think. I've always been musical, though I don't sing much any more. . . . Anyway, what I mean to say is just tell those children, those students of yours, not to just go through the motions. They need to live as much as they can while they can—before they get like me. Then they'll have something to remember.

Looking at her wheelchair and touching her hip, she added, "It doesn't redeem any of this, I guess. But what could?"

EMMA STONNICK

Bonnie's niece Emma enjoyed visiting but was almost apologetic: she spoke as if someone else had more of a right to be there than her. She came once a month, and sat with a composed, attentive attitude while her son Jamie played with cars and trucks on the rug in the lounge. Bonnie was stationed beside them in a wheelchair, rhythmically moving her head back and forth between Emma and the boy: with pleasure, and just a hint of anxiety in her eyes, she tried to register all the details and hold on to them for as long as she could. Jamie, with only an occasional glance at the two women, carried on a monologue about his game: he had a three year old's knack of being oblivious to all those around him and yet engaging them in everything he did.

Although Jamie only directed a few comments to Bonnie at each visit, she loved to speak about him. "He has such a hungry look. He wants to take in and talk about the whole world. When you listen you find he sees details in the places we only glance at." She watched him with her own hunger, her teacher's memories, which transformed the lounge into a classroom's echo. When he posed a question to her and she answered, she smiled broadly, becoming her old self, the one she liked best, the educator. "He is my latest student," she beamed. Skipping over the motherly phase of her life, she saw before her more of her former pupils than her own children.

Emma had inherited the role of visiting Bonnie from her father. Henry, Bonnie's younger brother, had been a widower and after Bonnie's husband died, she had moved upstate to be near him. They checked in on one another regularly, but led quite separate lives. Bonnie enjoyed an active, good health then, traveled a lot, and lived in her own apartment. After a few years, however, osteoporosis and joint troubles began to cripple her body. Henry and Emma assisted her with housekeeping, but eventually Bonnie became so constricted that the only viable move left was to go into a nursing home.

This was almost a year before Henry's death from a coronary. In the weeks before the move, he and Emma—who had just bought a house with her husband—helped Bonnie sort out her remaining possessions. Bonnie had been through this scaling down of memories once before, when giving up her last home in Texas prior to heading north. A few rooms of furniture, several cartons of clothes and books, some favorite pictures, and a small box of precious jewelry had made the journey to upstate New York. Now she had to reduce the tangible pieces of history even further. "I remember thinking," said Emma, "that I had more stuff jammed in one closet of my new home than Aunt Bonnie was going to be able to take with her to this whole place.

> I thought, at the time, it was cute that she still had some of her notebooks from college, and the folders with lesson plans from her teaching days. But she didn't have them because she was absent-minded—I mean she *was* getting a bit peculiar and forgetful then—but no, she hadn't forgotten to get rid of them. Those were the things she knew she wanted to keep. She smiled and talked a lot and shook her head when we took them out: she made me stop everything to show me certain pages, and her professor's comments, and some of the children's drawings. She even remembered the names of some of those students: they must be sixty years old now!

Emma sometimes just sat and watched Bonnie watch Jamie. The two women's moments of silence were as natural as the boy's chattering. Bonnie often broke the quiet with a comment, some random association pulled out of the grab bag of her memories. For the first months, whenever this happened, Emma would pepper Bonnie with questions, trying to put the older woman's remarks into some kind of normal, narrative order. "What church was that?" "Where were you living then?" "Was it before or after you got married?"

"I don't understand my aunt some of the time, but I always enjoy her," Emma later confided.

> You can't always pin her down but I've decided now it doesn't really matter. It's a bit like a scrapbook she once showed me from one of her pupils. It had all these pasted pictures in it, cut out of magazines, choppy around the edges the way little kids cut with scissors. You could never guess what was going

on in the boy's head, except that those images all must have meant something to him at the time, and he liked them, whatever his reasons. Somehow, they were all him, they all added up to him at the time, like a collage.

It's hard to add my aunt up too sometimes, but I get pleasure hearing the pieces of her life. Also, it's nice to like someone and not feel responsible for her in the way my father did when he was alive, or her son and daughter still have to be. The two of them, they visit five or six times a year from Texas, and in between they count on me to keep track of how Bonnie's doing. But if anything serious happened, I'd have to call them and it would be up to them to decide what to do. They'd need to come up here to deal with it.

It's kind of an accident that I ended up closer to her than them—physically, I mean, living here in the same town. But when they ask her if she'd like to move to a home nearer to them, she tells them no, she's quite happy here, and as long as they don't mind traveling to see her, she'd rather stay put. She is pretty happy: she has some friends, and is used to the place, and she gets on with the staff from what I can see. Maybe at her age you don't want to move any more, and because she does get confused, it helps her to stay where she knows the people and the routines. Nina feels it must make her feel secure, which is no small thing. It's just funny how we end up where we are, and how we feel about it, or make our peace with it. . . . But it's a long way from Texas.

CODA

The Enemy of Denial

Frank, the pundit of South Wing, once encountered a young woman trying to distract a resident by showing off dance steps in the lounge. The little ballet passed unnoticed before the elderly woman's eyes, but Frank was attentive and found the performance dismaying. Gently, he tried to put the well-meaning visitor straight by informing her that "old age is coming to all of us. It's only a matter of time." Then he turned to me and translated his own remark: "You can dance around it, but that won't exorcise the demon."

Frank was the enemy of denial, and for people who had a need for strong defenses, he was a major annoyance. But he had many allies among those residents for whom reality was the dominant principle. Many echoed Stavros's comment that he and they were "paying the price of longevity." Most knew where they were and why they were there, regardless of whether they liked it or not. Tilly enjoyed it, Frank did not, Stavros was resigned, and Bonnie fluctuated, depending on how homelike or hotelish she felt the home to be.

Even these verdicts by residents were subject to periodic reconsideration. In their own ways, each of the people I came to know changed their feelings about Elmwood from time to time. Which parts of its reality loomed largest in their minds—its security and services, its indignities and restraints—

depended on people's health, wealth, and well-being on any given day. Stavros was most irritable (though still controlled) when his daughter was out of town. Bonnie related best to her surroundings, and her friend Barbara, when the frailty of her body loosened its grip on her mind for a while. Frank's most agreeable periods were spent in anticipation—of a weekend away, or a special meal—but since few things lived up to his expectations, he could be at his worst in their aftermath. And Tilly, reversing the enthusiasms of the normal childhood she had never known, was most disheartened when school was out of session.

Late life had many ironies, and these were not lost on the people whom they touched. Bonnie had gone from loving language to being betrayed by it. Tilly had left a home that had locked her away from the world in order to enter an institution that opened the world up to her. Frank ended up finding a chance to perform as a result of losing the ability to walk. And Stavros knew he would live until the end of his time in confinement in a promised land.

These ironies, rewards, and punishments were central "themes" in how people spoke about their lives and sense of self: they provided an infrastructure for their ongoing concepts of identity (Sharon Kaufman 1987). Frank stressed his talents, his gratitude, his passions; Stavros, his enduring politeness in the face of loss. To Tilly, it was a lifelong sense of mission, now married to the long-sought status of student. And for Bonnie, continuity came from the complementary role of teacher—once active, now retired—which gave shape to both her past and her present.

The cast of people's characters probably had the most influence on their view of home life. Their personalities and memories not only gave the content of who they were and what they could look back on, but also formed a prism that bent and spread the light of the present. None of them were living in a way they had ever done before. In late life, when adjusting to the new is supposed to be particularly hard, they had a surfeit of novelty to contend with. Their bodies were frail and some of their minds were weakening. They resided with roommates, not spouses or kin. Their ties to the outside had changed and taken on different shapes and personae: for the four people considered here, contacts were now occasional visits, a weekend at home, a classroom, a walk; the key people had become a son, a daughter, a niece, and a neighbor. The symbols and metaphors they each used to speak of their lives comprised a very personal language. And what residents expressed in words was often more honest and wistful than innocent, making their accounts of growing old so dismaying and, at times, so disarming.

5 MEMORIES AND SYMBOLS

A quartet of lives is a small-scale composition. In it, orchestral range gives way to the clarity of each instrumental voice. While a handful of players can develop the same themes as a larger ensemble, they can also treat that material with more detail, more personal embellishment. Bonnie, Frank, Tilly, and Stavros comprised such a quartet of voices. On one level they spoke only for themselves and did not claim to represent all the residents at Elmwood Grove. Yet they also had enough in common with their peers for their words to suggest how others felt about and dealt with the most basic problems of institutional life. In what follows, the memories and symbols that these four individuals stressed are brought together to illuminate several important themes. They will show us how people looked at the past and used language to describe it; how different residents came to enter the home; how individuals coped with roommates and the decline of domesticity; how the loss of autonomy and privacy were interpreted by them; and how they developed distinctive styles for adapting to daily life.

The insights presented here are essentially those of the articulate—the residents, visitors, and staff who could put thought and feeling into words. But these individuals shared the home with others who could not remember or, in some cases, talk. And what was unexpressed or forgotten by those others still needs to be acknowledged. Attention will therefore turn, in the next chapter, to the people who lacked the powers of speech and recall, who lived out their lives in a private world of silence. We will see there how they coped with their condition, and how their peers reacted to their presence. Their fate, their haunting example, was one of the main preoccupations of those who still possessed both memory and language.

MEMORY AND LANGUAGE

Reminiscence provided the fabric upon which some residents pinned the facts and ornaments of the present. But for others, the past was foreground rather than backdrop: it stood as the main tapestry of meaning into which the events of the moment receded. In remembering their histories and recounting their current lives, Tilly, Stavros, Frank, and Bonnie treated time differently, and they each used language in characteristic ways to weave in the colors that expressed what experience felt like.

Bonnie sometimes drew on her past to measure the present. Like the baroque composers she admired, she never hesitated to borrow from her own work, taking opinions on one subject and transcribing them to fit another. As a footnote to her childhood memories, for example, she once observed, "What I liked about cats was not just their cleanliness, but their discretion: they didn't announce things to the world the way dogs did." Then, on a different occasion months later, she praised her friend and roommate Barbara "for being discreet. We tell one another what we hear, but that's where it stays. What we learn about everyone else is really no one else's business."

For Bonnie, one phase of life clearly stood out as the most fulfilling— her early years of marriage when work, children, material comforts, and community involvement all combined to make for a rich existence. Only a third of the residents asked were able to identify "the best period of their lives" as quickly and as unequivocally as Bonnie. Nor did she hesitate to pinpoint her father as the most influential person in her youth, or to speak of her college education and her brief career in teaching as two of the most satisfying of her endeavors. A person, a profession, and a particular span of time were thus the most memorable for a woman whose memory often failed her.

Stavros spoke about his life in such a self-effacing way that the dramas of persecution, war, and immigration were all muted. His mind and memory were clear: he could give dates of departures, the names of ships, and the grades his grandchildren got in school. But the facts did not rouse him as much as his reflections on the darker side of human nature. A lifetime had shown him people's weaknesses and capacity for hatred, their ability to neglect problems and deny the obvious, their failure to use the potential gifts of brain and body.

Living in the nursing home brought much of this, and some human virtues, into close compass for him. He appreciated people's solicitousness and good intentions, just as he recoiled from their crudity: Tilly's cheerfulness cast a warm light on moments of his day, while just next door, Frank's outbursts perplexed and embarrassed him even more than Karl's silence or the incontinence of less competent residents.

Losing his wife, losing his health, and losing his home and freedom had condensed Stavros's world and his expectations into a small circle of needs: a daily visit from his daughter, regular meals and baths, and an easing of the pain in his spine were the desires that absorbed and assuaged him. But even fulfillment could be frustrating. The pain medication he was on sometimes made him drowsy and disoriented, adding insult to relief from injury. He had heard stories of nursing home patients being drugged into submission and was wary of suffering the same fate. Though Katina and the staff could assure him that Elmwood was largely innocent of that sin, the escape from suffering still cost Stavros some of his sharpness.

Because Stavros prized the mind and his own clarity of thinking, to cede these for mere comfort was a sad bargain. He was also uneasy about being housed with so many demented people, but got even more exercised over being lumped with them by employees. Both he and Katina were particularly sensitive to the patronizing, infantilizing ways and words which some staff used with patients—a pattern of behavior noted at virtually every other nursing home that has been studied.[1] To Stavros, the humiliation of such categorical treatment reminded him of the one adolescent experience he remembered with strong emotion, namely, the discriminatory Turkish law that had prevented him from attending university and that had thus shaped his career and whole future life.

Tilly had had to deal with physical handicaps from birth, and her years had been so limited in scope, so meager in retrospect, that a handful of memories served to summarize much of her first six decades. Whereas entering a home had cost others their freedom, it had brought her opportunity. Tilly had made friends and found roles instead of losing them. And rather than lapsing into silence, she relished the chance that the institution gave her to talk about her experiences—in therapy, in school, at church, and at work. Language for her, then, was not so much a vehicle for expressing memories as the means to celebrate a new life with which reminiscence alone could not compete.

For Frank, on the other hand, speech was both a tool and a weapon. He was articulate, graphic and, at times, cutting. He told emotive stories of his childhood poverty, his latter day romances, his artistic ambitions. In the autumn of his years, he experienced the cruelty that T. S. Eliot ascribed to April, its bent for "mixing / Memory and desire" ([1922] 1963: 53). Unlike Tilly, then, the past was memorable to Frank, and he loved to relate and embroider it. He had the narrator's knack for building drama and the moralist's sense of irony and closure. He told some of his tales in tragic terms: artistry that never fully flowered; passion cut short by a sense of ethics.

On the positive side he was proud of his talents, his moral stature, his children's accomplishments. But the unfulfilled dreams he lived with—the artistic, the intellectual, and the romantic ones—left him with a bitterness that also broke through. His accounts of past and present were a blend of hubris and regret. There was also a strong tension between the public and private sides of him, neither of which was easy to satisfy in a nursing home. He hungered to perform and be attended to, just as he craved protection from the invasive, open quality of Elmwood's life. On any one day there was too much, or not enough, of either the publicity or the privacy.

Being outspoken and sharp-tongued, Frank's feelings were rarely kept secret from those around him. When he displeased others, it was not simply to please himself: it was to express himself. He felt that to grow old gracefully was to acquiesce to the way others want the aged to behave. In the process, in order to satisfy them, Frank said, "You are no longer true to yourself." He made sure that people knew the story of his past and what he felt about its outcome. Lusty, cynical, grateful, and skeptical, he made the point that *to be* was to be *known*, and that this, for him, was one of life's necessities: people could be content or offended, but they should not ignore his presence.

ENTRÉE

Entry into a nursing home can be the result of people's social situation as much as their medical condition. Studies of geriatric facilities reveal that a disproportionate number of their residents have fewer social ties than individuals of comparable health who continue to live on their own or with kin.[2] Admission to an institution may thus reflect not only a person's physical status, but the paucity of caregivers who might have enabled that individual to remain in the community. About a quarter of the women and men at Elmwood were in that kind of situation. Of the four residents featured here, Tilly was the one example of such an "unconnected" person. Her mother's death deprived her of the only relative who had been there to care for her; so while Tilly's health did not decline after her mother died, she had virtually no alternative but to move to an institution.

Bonnie *did* have other options, yet these turned out to be more apparent than real. Her grown children lived far away. Nearby were a widowed brother and a niece with a family of her own, but these relatives felt they were in no position to take Bonnie into their homes and provide for her when her condition began to fail. Like a number of the other patients, Frank was already in a geriatric facility when he was transferred to Elmwood. He changed from an institution where he had had regular visits from his daughter to a community where his primary contacts were with his son. Stavros, like Bonnie and Frank, was widowed, but unlike them he had moved in with a married child after his spouse passed away. His medical situation quickly worsened, however, and the attempts of Katina's family to secure good care for him at their house proved unsuccessful and unaffordable. For them, as for many Americans, the lack of adequate community-based home care was a decisive factor. In the struggle between his daughter's reluctance and Stavros's insistence that he enter a nursing home, his will won out.

These four histories show several of the routes by which other people also came to Elmwood. One path was through the loss of a caregiver, such as a parent, child, or spouse. A second catalyst was a major change in health, such as a stroke, incontinence, or immobility. And a third course was transfer from a different institution, such as a hospital, another home, or a lower care facility. While Elmwood had patients brought there through family neglect or indifference, most residents belied the myth that the old end up in institutions because their kin cast them away. All four of the people featured had, in fact, been cared for at home for at least a time, supporting the argument that "parent care is a normative family stress" (Elaine Brody 1985: 19).

The vast majority of patients, as was true of Stavros, Frank, and Bonnie, had had one or more episodes of hospitalization prior to entering a nursing institution for the first time. Such a hospital stay was a prerequisite for certain Medicare benefits. There was also a minority of people, including Tilly, who had moved to the facility directly from their own residences. People living at Elmwood also had different kinds of ties to the immediate community. Of the four individuals considered, only Tilly had no connections to a family: in the absence of kin, she had instead built up bonds with a school, a work place, and a church. Bonnie saw her children five or six times a year, and a niece and nephew about once a month. Frank's son or daughter-in-law came to see him several times a week, and he occasionally stayed at their home overnight. The most frequent visitor was Stavros's daughter Katina, who stopped in on a daily basis and telephoned on those rare days when she could not be there. To Stavros, and some other residents, the telephone at the nursing station was, in fact, both a symbol and lifeline for family contact—a feature also found at other homes (e.g., Gubrium 1975: 92–97; Powers 1988a: 55–56). At the opposite extreme from those with kin were some dozen Elmwood patients who received neither calls nor callers. Sole survivors, or estranged from their relatives, these were the people who considered the aides or the volunteers—because they came from the outside—to be their "true" or their "new" family, the residents for whom the home was indeed a last refuge.

While Elmwood had only a dozen or so patients cut off from their kin, the very fact of institutionalization still caught the other residents and their families in a conflict of values: counterpointing the desires of the elderly to not be a burden and yet be attended to were the wishes of their relatives to be caring and responsible. Unlike those facilities that try to dissuade families from visiting (Sheldon Tobin 1987: 44), Elmwood encouraged relatives by allowing visits during all hours of the day and evening. But for the families involved, showing that you cared *about* someone you could not care *for* was not an easy thing to convince yourself or the patient of. Though Stavros claimed for himself the decision to enter Elmwood, Katina ended up wrestling with her guilt in both the daylight and her dreams. And while Frank praised his son for his dedication, he also made Patrick pay a price for the lost freedoms his visits could not endow. In his own way, Frank made sure that his son experienced some of his own helplessness.

As recipients of the most regular contacts with family members, Stavros and Frank showed some of the similarities and differences in how such visits could impact on people's well-being. Both men derived a measure of power and visibility from the presence of their relatives—a benefit that visitors have been found to bestow on patients at Murray Manor (Gubrium 1975: 97–99), Franklin (Shield 1988: 59–60), and Bethany Manor (O'Brien 1989: 29). Katina was able to be a particularly effective advocate for her father both because of her own skills and Stavros's charm and gentility with staff. But Frank's relatives, while equally concerned and conscientious, were less successful in helping him adjust: though employees liked them, the family's efforts were often undermined by Frank's bitter outbursts and his rejection of well-meaning attempts by those who worked with and cared for him. As Powers found in her study of another New York facility (1988a: 55), visits by relatives could sometimes be stressful instead of rewarding. In Frank's case, people from inside and outside the institution were often at a loss about what they could do, feeling like actors at the whim of a writer still uncertain about how, or where, to end his script.

People who move to nursing homes willingly and knowingly have been shown to make a better adjustment to this new world (Rodin 1986). With the exception of a few people like Tilly and Vivian, however, almost no one at Elmwood had really wanted to end their days this way. Residents nevertheless all had to come to terms with it, and the terms and metaphors they used to describe their entrance showed how they wished to see and be seen. There were some, such as Barbara Hernstein, who portrayed themselves as victims and spoke with anger at what they felt was their abandonment by family or friends. Others sought for and found a more positive image. Stavros described his decision as an act of will rather than one of resignation, a choice that he felt had spared his daughter and her family from an insupportable burden. For Frank, entering his first institution had been like an audition, and the subsequent move to Elmwood a testimony to his son's concern. Tilly saw her conduct in almost religious terms as a form of obedience to her mother's last wish. And Bonnie, freed from the fetters of realism, could picture herself a resident of the hotels and dorms of more attractive times.

From words alone it was sometimes hard to judge how voluntarily some of Elmwood's residents had entered that institution. It appeared, in many cases, that people developed a version of the experience that gave it the meanings they needed it to have. A similar quality has been found in the stories that other elderly persons tell about their relocations to homes (Morton Lieberman and Sheldon Tobin 1983: 124–134; Tobin 1987: 51). The accounts and images developed by Frank, Bonnie, and their peers suggest, then, that admission to Elmwood was an imaginative as well as an adaptive challenge. Residents had to find or create a meaning for their fate, and they found its source in such themes as betrayal, sacrifice, deference, respect, and their roles from the past. For institutional life to be endured, people had to be able to explain it, and with their words they had to convince not only others, but themselves as well.

DOMESTICITY

Just as residents had followed different paths to enter the home, they looked inward and outward from it with their own ideas about domesticity. Stavros and Tilly provided one of the sharper contrasts in this regard. Tilly had probably lived in one home, her own home, for longer than any other resident or staff member or volunteer at the facility. Yet she had adjusted to life at the institution more successfully than most of her peers. She found a new and larger family, and rarely looked back to the place she left behind. There was a small clutter of books, note pads, and religious objects on her night table, and a mélange of plastic flowers, wooden animals, and plaster curios on the bureau she shared with Vivian. These were the tokens of newfound friends, the signatures of a new life.

Stavros, on the other hand, saw the whole idea of "home" evaporate with his wife's death and the subsequent need to go live with his daughter. If he had harbored any thoughts about recapturing a domestic feeling from being a permanent guest in Katina's house, these were soon shattered by his declining health and his resigned decision to move to a nursing home. In his room at Elmwood, Stavros had put his feeling that "no home can be a home" into practice. Compared to Tilly and some others, he had made only the most minimal effort to domesticate his living space. One family picture sat on his shelf; occasionally, briefly, a birthday or greeting card stood beside it. Katina brought in other items to furnish his corner, but they pleased her more than her father, and he rarely drew them to the attention of visitors. This was not where his home or his heart lay, and the objects seemed almost foreign, drawn from another person's lifetime or household.

Other people made much more expressive and personalized use of what space they had. As Carobeth Laird found herself doing at Golden Mesa, they set about assembling a new identity kit (1979). Stavros's coffee companion, Dave Dorenberg, had a richly decorated environment. In the room he shared with his wife Mollie, the wall behind his bed was adorned with awards and plaques from the community organizations he had belonged to, and there were also photographs of his daughter and Mollie and their summer cottage. Each item was worth a story, and visitors were taken through them if they showed any hint of interest. In comparison, Frank actually kept few objects around him, but the can of paint brushes on his night table, and the small stack of sketchpads beside it, made a strong statement about him. On the nearby wall, a series of his watercolors threatened to overshadow the family photographs his son had tacked up behind his headboard. The space, and its contents, were emphatically Frank's creation.

There was more to some of these areas than met the eye. In the corner behind Bonnie's bed a small bulletin board had been fastened: snapshots, cards, clippings of country scenes, and some small religious plaques had been mounted on it. There was one photograph of Bonnie, her husband, and their Siamese, which she particularly liked. The elements of this exhibit changed from time to time, but the space was almost always fully used. Most of what was on display had been chosen for Bonnie by others—her children and niece, and Reva, the aide who worked with her—but in a drawer, out of sight, Bonnie kept her old lesson plans. She was not secretive about these, but was selective about who she chose to share them with. It was a sign of intimacy to have Bonnie take the papers out and to be invited into that part of her life.

Compared to the paints, photos, and curios with which some people personalized their rooms, Stavros and others seemed determined to stay in sparse surroundings. There were residents, such as Eddie, who left their walls and bureau tops bare except for the most utilitarian of objects. In Eddie's case, it was his harmonica, portable and audible, that stood for what stationary props meant to others. Denise and Nina and several of the aides encouraged people to decorate their rooms, and they sometimes gave residents pictures, knickknacks, and other small items with which to do this. Staff also put up posters, photographs, and printed sayings around the building to enliven the atmosphere. But there was a consensus among personnel—even the most dedicated and conscientious—that ornamentation and decoration could, at best, humanize the facility, but not make it homelike. Many were emphatic that, of all the losses residents suffered either prior to or after their admission, the hardest of all was the loss of their home or apartment. "For some," said Kate, a nurse's aide, "that is even more devastating than losing a husband or wife."

I don't say that to sound cruel or make people seem callous. But having to move can be worse than dealing with a death. When someone dies you lose one part of your life. But when you have to leave the place where you lived, it's like *you* fell out of your life. Everything that was familiar, everything that made it feel like home, all the things you had memories about—you can't replace those.

Staff found that where domesticity could not be visualized, it could sometimes be verbalized. The pet visits, and the reminiscing they evoked, provided opportunities for employees to speak with residents about their home lives and memories. On a week-to-week basis, the animals gave patients and caregivers an immediate event, a symbol of the past, about which they could converse. Denise emphasized that the richness of such conversations could belie the impression left by bare walls. Nina agreed, and once remarked. "Some residents who don't show or ask for much have a lot to say when they feel there's someone to listen." But, she added, one had to look inside, or draw them out—with pets, or poetry, or your own presence—to learn what kind of past they carried around inside them. Stavros's memories of the cats in his mother's kitchen, and Eddie's quatrain about the sweet smell of his cows, were cases in point. These two men, and some of the others without decoration, still had a firm sense of attachment and history. But they did not project it into the space around them. In the austerity of their rooms, the domestic environment was an inner world, not a visible wall.

ROOMMATES

Nursing homes require a kind of compulsory coexistence that few forms of family life prepare people for. Elmwood had no private rooms, and so everyone began by sharing a space with strangers. Residents' accounts of their lives invariably included their experiences with roommates, and the stories they told showed how variable such relations could be. Bonnie's closeness with Barbara Hernstein, for example, was a tie based on common values, gender, and personalities, a bond whose foundation was laid at Bonnie's very first lunch at the home. Inveterate gossips, these two women never tired of commending one another for their sense of propriety. Yet once or twice a week they also quarrelled over minor matters: "B and B are at it again," their aide Reva would say, showing how exposed even the better friendships were to the abrasions of daily life. The true extreme of enmity for both these women, however, actually lay within their own room in the person of June—the loud, upstaging patient whose behavior provoked both Bonnie and Barbara to the very edge of a death wish.

In Stavros's situation, reticence spoke louder than words. Disinclined by habit to approach people, he was safe with his daughter, and took only occasional risks to reach out to others. The slow, incremental loss of his hearing made his attempts to communicate even more uncertain with time, and having a tentative, emotionally fragile roommate like Karl only deepened the difficulty. Stavros eventually found a coffee hour comaraderie with Dave Dorenberg and Frank, but since neither of these men roomed with him, Stavros was often left with a choice between silence or the telephone

If Bonnie did well with one good friend, and Stavros stayed with what was familiar, Tilly moved in a widening circle of people. She had become close not only with staff, but with fellow students and coworkers from outside the home, and with one of her roommates, Vivian Grote. These two women appreciated each other's tolerance and company, and shared a regard for books and Tilly's growing capacity to read them. They could talk or be quiet with equal ease, and had discovered in the act of reading a comfortable way both to be together and be separate, within the same space.

For Frank, life in his room was neither literary nor conversational; and when it came to his relationship with John Carmichael, there was more war than peace in the plot. The two men carried on a kind of civil conflict, fought with words and tones of mimicry, and broken up by boredom or the interventions of staff. As roommates they were, perhaps, too sharp for one another: they each had a talent for exposing the frail nerves and tissues near the heart of the other's character. John punctured Frank's pretenses, while Frank could not resist taking John to task for hiding from life behind his blindness. There were jokes and unkind laughter. The verbal blows drew on small habits and details, one assault bringing forth another in defense. On some days time passed like the rhythmic steps of a cautious boxing match, each fighter feeling out the other, with meals marking the breaks between rounds. Though Denise surmised that the two men secretly liked one another, her feeling was that they were "too proud to admit it. They sense how vulnerable they each are, but they deal with that by attacking the other's weakness instead of admitting their own. They could have been supportive . . . though I know that's easy for me to say. I guess fighting has been their way of relating."

Studies of older people in other types of communities have noted that conflict, by its very nature, can serve to promote cohesion. The elderly Jews whom Myerhoff worked with in California told her "we fight to keep warm" (1978: 153). Political differences were a source of unity and community in the French retirement complex described by Keith (1982). But few researchers have ascribed this unifying role to conflict among nursing home residents. This is probably because people in such institutions face their lives in a more individualized, fragile, and dependent way, and this prevents them from forming active groups that could build on disputes as a source of solidarity. At Franklin Nursing Home, Shield suggested that bickering was a way for residents to guard against the closeness that they could not risk (1988: 138, 155). She attributed the lack of talk there to people's fear of appearing senile, and the paucity of their friendships to the absence of both resources and common interests as a basis for sharing. There, as at Elmwood Grove, instead of contending jointly with the conditions of their lives, patients were left to fight with one another.

Relations with roommates thus placed a kind of unnatural burden on many residents. Shared living with strangers had none of the built-in restraints or rewards that had made domestic tranquility possible in their own homes. Some of the people from rural areas, such as Karl and Eddie, had lived their whole lives with only modest social contacts outside their families. Now, only the outside remained, and it was in the bed or the room next door. For many residents, the cultural ties of blood and marriage were gone, or they existed only at a distance. In their place stood the natural facts of age and gender, and the random hand of infirmity, to bring people together.

Nina and the staff tried to pair residents with individuals whom they thought would be suitable partners. Elmwood even had a policy, costly and rare among nonprofit homes, of keeping the beds of hospitalized patients open for them so that they could return to their old rooms. But the initial step of making compatible matches was necessarily somewhat random: it depended on the availability of beds, which in turn waited upon the chance events of deaths and transfers. No one had as much control or choice in the process as they would have liked. In some cases the timing and the judgments dovetailed to match a Bonnie with a Barbara, or a Tilly with a Vivian. In another instance, Laura, who had already seen two roommates die, suddenly found herself with Jan in the next bed. Though it was a risky step to take, she eventually reached out to this new stranger in spite of the losses of the recent past. The success of these friendships showed, as Powers also found, that some residents can play an active role in shaping their social ties (1988a). The women of Elmwood, in fact, generally made a better bargain with their fate and their relationships than did the men— a gender pattern which has not always been found in other institutions (e.g., Joan Retsinas and Patricia Garrity 1985). For Stavros the result of the roommate process was an uneventful, unstimulating arrangement, while Frank found his to be a test of wits and wills. The ideals of friendship and companionship, so hard to fulfill at any age, were thus particularly elusive in a place where intimacy was a gamble, and the very idea of home itself an unlikely achievement.

PRIVACY

One of the most intimate areas of life that the nursing home infringed upon was personal privacy. The combined effect of small spaces, unlocked doors, and Elmwood's architecture was a building with few places where residents or their visitors could be alone. Claire, the physical therapist, once commented on the irony that a private, not-for-profit institution was really a not-for-privacy one too. Patients had difficulty controlling their doors, drawers, clothing, belongings, and the surface of their bodies—all of which were exposed, at one time or another, to others who lived in or worked at the home. Despite the best intentions of even the best of staff, employees' responsibilities sometimes compelled them to encroach on people's space. This was also true of roommates, thrown together in a small living area, who had hardly any means to block out the sights and sounds of their companions.

People dealt with these situations in a number of ways. For some, crowding and the lack of walls simply led to more covert methods for keeping person or possessions apart from others. Bonnie secured her lesson plans in the out-of-sight depths of a drawer. When Stavros sat in the dining room between meals, he not only occupied his favorite corner place, but he held others at bay by turning his wheelchair so that it almost faced into the corner itself. Barbara Hernstein sometimes escaped from the "privacy" of her four-person room to sit in the public space of the open hallway; she claimed her solitude there by periodically putting on a blank expression that led others to ignore and pass her by. And Dave Dorenberg used naps in the lounge as a ruse to get peace and quiet from his wife. I was once settling in to do an interview there with Eddie when I realized Dave was sitting a few feet from us. When I started to apologize for disturbing him, he reassured me. "Don't worry. I'm not asleep. I'm just away." Even the television was used by some patients as a chance to tune out rather than tune in. People could thus get their privacy by hiding in public, or by changing the posture of furniture and faces. Like Dave and Stavros, Barbara and Bonnie, part of what some residents wanted out of each day was a chance to be overlooked, to be granted a bit of anonymity.

But these various ploys were not suitable or successful for everyone. Frank, though he was usually a very public figure, was also particularly sensitive to the lack of solitude. Unattracted by many of the activities offered at Elmwood, he often sought refuge in painting and in the quiet of his room. This was possible some of the time, but there were other days when he had to deal with the interjections of John's comments, or with the interruptions of aides and housekeeping staff, who came in to clean the floor, change the linen, or claim his laundry. The room was then no longer a sanctuary but a disputed territory. He sniped and griped, feeling that "not to be left alone is the final indignity."

There were other kinds of intimate spaces that residents had learned, sometimes with surprising equanimity, to cede to institutional needs. Both Stavros and Frank had come to terms with being bathed by female staff: though they had each found the experience disconcerting at first, modesty had yielded to gratitude for the pleasure of being able to keep clean. Bodily needs, in fact, often took precedence over bodily privacy: Frank was more likely to express thanks for an enema and a good bowel movement than to complain of any indignity in the pursuit of regularity.

As a private domain, then, the body took some surprising turns. Though some residents were appalled by age's assault on their vanity—"wounded in their narcissism," as the analysts have said (Ronald Blythe 1979: 9)— others were more occupied with the body's inside than its outside, with function rather than form. Some entered into a special relationship with their organs and limbs, carrying on a dialogue with their own flesh. Frank, for example, could curse his legs and praise his bladder, Stavros swear at his spine but bless his mind. The tones were variously grateful, bitter, or perplexed, the speakers wary about where the next assault might come from.

There were some residents, however, who got exasperated hearing of other's ills. Vivian Grote herself refrained from complaining a lot because she did not want to give people "second-hand pains." But she was an exception. Volunteers, often equating age with wisdom, were shocked to learn how concerned the elderly were with the physical rather than the philosophical, with the state of their stomachs rather than the condition of their souls. But Louise Santorini, as a nurse, was more accustomed to seeing residents attend "to what others wear as a given—teeth of your own that naturally fit, a varied diet that the palate can taste, the freedom and self-respect of controlling your bowels and your other movements."

AUTONOMY

Issues with roommates and privacy were only two parts of people's responses to living within an institutional regime. Residents knew that much of their day-to-day life was governed by a clockwork schedule of meals, medications, therapies, bathing, and changeovers in work shifts. Individual needs or preferences, whether it was for a type of food or the timing of treatments, had to be accommodated to the routine of the home, to the necessity of accomplishing a great number of caregiving tasks for some seven dozen people in an orderly way. Most residents responded by creating a daily routine of their own, building it around some meaningful activity: it was school for Tilly, painting for Frank, recreation events for Bonnie, and visits for Stavros. Though these people realized that the home's own priorities were reasonable—or at least rational—they often found them irksome nonetheless. For Bonnie, the regime conflicted with her image of the hotel she sometimes felt she was in. Tilly found that it interrupted her own schedules for prayer and study. For Stavros and Frank, the invasions violated their sense of personhood and individuality.

Some people fought the potential indolence of institutional life by creating their own responsibilities. Stavros and Tilly helped Alzheimer's victims and other confused residents in order to feel useful and good about themselves. Tilly also studied, preached, and reached out. Frank fed the animals and performed. Even the apparent inactivity of certain patients could be meaningful to them. Bonnie and Stavros were two of many who liked to sit and watch people from the hallways, lounges, and lawns, participating in the world in a quiet but involved way. This apparently passive pursuit of "watching" has been found to be a meaningful, engaging activity in other nursing homes, such as Murray Manor (Gubrium 1975: 180–184) and Bethany Manor (O'Brien 1989: 168–178). Denise suggested that even when Elmwood residents refused to participate in certain events, this was not necessarily a mark of apathy. It gave individuals like Bonnie and Frank a sense of power: they can, argued Denise, "at least say 'yes' or 'no'."

Having a sense of control has been found to enhance the subjective well-being of the elderly (Rodin 1986), and at Elmwood it not only took the form of "yes" and "no," but also expressed itself in other ways. Frank and Bonnie tried to achieve it by getting others to respond to their needs, whereas Tilly and Stavros sought it by responding to those in more need than themselves. As a form of adaptation, the latter kind of "helpful" role has been described among residents at Murray Manor, where such people were called "supporters" (Gubrium 1975: 119), at Bethany Manor, where they earned the name "guardians" (O'Brien 1989: 224–225), and at several other institutions (Lieberman and Tobin 1983: 45–46; Powers 1988a: 49–51; Shield 1988: 164–165). At Elmwood, these self-appointed roles as guides or assistants enabled helpers to feel productive and to indirectly reciprocate the home for its services. Frank's performances had some of the same significance for him. These were the things that people gave in return for what they got.

The scope of such reciprocity was limited, however, and could only partly offset the burden of living under institutional rules. Members of the floor staff, such as Louise and her aide Kate, were sympathetic to the complaints of competent residents: they knew the routines could be invasive and boring to them. But from her perspective as a charge nurse, Louise also noted the other kinds of people at Elmwood who were confused and in less command of their lives, who needed and welcomed the standardization of each day. She mentioned Karl, the new admission; Eva Rayburn, the "wanderer" next door to Bonnie; and Sarah Kavalick, who sat in the hall most days clinging to her teddy bear. The schedules gave these patients a feeling of security, the experience of control that came from the predictable. It was important for these women and men to know not only where their next meal or shower was coming from, but when it would happen, and who was going to provide it.

At the heart of this dilemma between individual and institutional needs was the fact that Elmwood was home to people of such widely different levels of ability. Some could walk, others could only wheel; some spoke, others were silent; there were people with full bowel and bladder control and others who were doubly incontinent; there were individuals gifted with sharp intellects and those whose minds and bodies both wandered. It was impossible for staff not to recognize these differences, but sometimes equally difficult for them to respond to everyone individually. And there were usually a few employees who, out of indifference or obtuseness or haste, paid scant attention to what set people apart, or the behaviors that set residents off. An astute, dignified observer such as Stavros was deeply wounded at being treated as if he were infantile or insane. The decline of his body had in no way compromised the acuity of his mind, and while he found a measure of purpose in helping his senile peers, his sense of sanity and integrity were threatened by his silent neighbors and the condescending conduct of some staff. Though Stavros acknowledged that many personnel worked hard, and that many of his neighbors were ill, he nevertheless felt burdened by "the amount of stupidity" around him.

Frank chafed under the home's rules and his own lack of freedom. He periodically lashed out at employees, residents, and his own relatives for their failure to satisfy or anticipate his needs. To be immobilized was humiliating, and criticism was his way of expressing that rage. Whenever he felt pandered to his anger grew, leaving both family and staff confounded about where the boundaries lay between tolerance, consideration, and the need to set limits.

There were also instances where the lack of autonomy masked the rewards that some residents found in their dependency. Though Barbara Hernstein was disinclined to admit it, she had been content to trade her fragile independence for the company and security of Elmwood. A more dramatic case was that of Eva Rayburn. Long before she lapsed into her senile pattern of stalking, Eva had been admitted to Elmwood for purely physical reasons. A fractured hip had first led to her admission, and after six months of healing and physical therapy, staff felt she could move to Hillview, a domiciliary facility for people in relatively good health. Eva moved there, but did so with a noticeable lack of enthusiasm. Within three weeks of the transfer she became listless, occasionally abusive and, worst of all, incontinent. Hillview, not equipped to deal with the latter condition, was compelled to make Eva leave, and Elmwood—in Nina's view—"got her back because that's where Eva really wanted to be in the first place: in the home, in her sick role, well taken care of, and relieved of responsibility." It was disability as a form of identity.

There was quite a different cast to Yvonne's way of handling her loss of autonomy. It was both more positive and, in a sense, more political. Though a poor black woman on Medicaid, she could be as demanding as some of the residents she called the "uppity folks"—the private-pay patients who felt entitled to more services because of the fees they paid. But as Gordon Morrell observed it from his administrator's chair, Yvonne saw her fate in a different light because lifelong poverty had often forced her to work for white families in menial jobs.

For her, it's the reverse of what some white residents feel about the black aides. To Yvonne now, though she's old and frail, she can finally turn it around and demand to be served. She relishes that part of it. She once confessed to me she loves "telling white folks what to do for me." I think she's waited her whole life for this.

CONCLUSION: THE ELEMENTS OF STYLE

People in their eighties in the 1980s were survivors. When their turn-of-the-century births occurred, life expectancy in the United States was 48 (Richard Crandall 1980: 25). The average man and woman at Elmwood were thus 35 years ahead of—or behind—their allotted span. The more coherent and thoughtful of them used some of that time to create an account of what they had done with their lives and how they saw themselves.

Such residents did not parade about with emblems or name tags that announced their identities. But many did have personal symbols that said something about who they were, or what they had done, or what they needed. With Tilly it was the pen and notebooks in her pocketbook. For Bonnie there were the lesson plans from her teaching days. Stavros had the telephone at the nursing station—his lifeline to his daughter. With Frank it was the painter's brushes and sketchpads by his bedside. These symbols made up a kind of personal heraldry: the fields for these four displayed artistry, literacy, an instrument of communication, and the tools of a cherished trade. They were visible reminders of how people thought of themselves, self-portraits done with objects.

On a verbal level Frank probably had the best sense of timing, but he and all his peers each had their own sense of time as well. The past was more a presence for some than for others, and even in the present-orientedness that everyone shared, each person focused on distinct problems and promises: these ran the gamut from bowels, meals, and pain relief to visitors, religion, school, and passion. All residents felt, and most suffered, Stavros's truth that "no home can be a home"—though this was less of a burden for Tilly and Barbara than the others.

People's use of memory as well as time was selective, and their choices about what and how to remember were, in effect, a subtle form of control. It was a process in which individual meaning took precedence over abstract notions of truth. In a benign, highly personal way, they bore out Orwell's prediction for *1984* and their own time in history: "Who controls the past controls the future; who controls the present controls the past" (George Orwell 1950: 204). Frank, the de facto existentialist, put it in the homespun terms quoted before: "No one ever really knows what happened anyway," he said. "We just have our stories about it, our recollections. The so-called facts are just someone else's memories." He had hit upon the psychoanalytic truth that sees all life-history as personal "myth" (Robert Jay Lifton 1976: 60), a set of tales in which deceased spouses become "sanctified" (Helen Lopata 1979), our families "mythicized characters" (Tobin and Lieberman

1976: 220), and the past itself "an image that changes with our image of ourselves" (Herman Feifel 1961: 62).

As these women and men of Elmwood showed, personality and history shaped the way residents coped with nursing home life. They each sought to distinguish themselves from those around them—Frank, for example, from the incontinent, Stavros from the senile—in order to foster a positive sense of self. Some of the issues that confronted them—privacy, autonomy, intimacy, and domesticity—were cultural ideas and ideals that they also dealt with in distinct, often surprising ways. One could, for economy's sake, condense their adaptations to one- or two-word statements of style.

—Stavros, for example, was accommodative and passive: he placated his caregivers, but did not suffer in silence because of Katina's efforts on his behalf.

—Tilly was an optimist and opportunist: for her the institution offered a richer life than her past, a new arena for her religious sense of mission.

—Frank was dramatic, working his theatrical strengths into a reputation and a source of attention: he was passionate, demanding, appreciative, and articulate, gifted with a knack for turning art and anger into a sense of presence.

—And Bonnie coped in part by recreating Elmwood and its residents in her own image: with the license granted by the state of her confusion, she converted the home into a hotel and most of her companions—like she herself—into retired teachers.

To speak of these four individuals as pacifying, missionizing, dramatizing, and fictionalizing would be, of course, an oversimplification of complex lives and behaviors. But it gives some sense of how people organized their conduct and attitudes around the exigencies of age, institutional life, and personal symbols. Their words, actions, and emotions expressed a great deal of their individuality, and belied the image of residents as uniformly quiet or cowed by their surroundings. They developed their own routines, created their own networks, made their own meaning out of memory and the materials at hand. People's style may not have been all that it once was, or all that they wished it to be, but those with the means to express themselves could still give it voice and form.

6 SILENCE AND STIGMA

Many elderly people have a great deal to say, but not all of them have the ability or the opportunity to say it. Only some individuals at Elmwood Grove were as articulate as Stavros, Tilly, Frank, and Bonnie. Yvonne, for example, could hold her own in a conversation, as could John Carmichael and Dave Dorenberg when they chose to. But there were others, such as Greta on her mobile bed, Sarah with her teddy, Bonnie's neighbor Eva, and Stavros's roommate Karl, who were mostly silent or barely verbal because of a medical condition. One of the most dramatic and distressing contrasts at the home was this difference between speech and silence, between those with memories they could express and those with recollections locked inside a private realm. And there was an even greater chasm between people whose lives were memorable, and others who had lost, by virtue of dementia, their own history. When Alzheimer's was the cause of such a condition, it slowly and inevitably added the culminating indignity of destroying the individual's control over body as well as mind.[1]

Stroke, senility, Alzheimer's, and other dementing disorders could wipe out the past, suspend speech, and compromise people's best attempts to "act their age." Disability and deformity could then so stigmatize or limit a person that proper conduct became impossible. Alzheimer's was a particularly painful and disconcerting case in point because it subverted, from the inside of what may have been a normal-looking body, all of an individual's earnest efforts to act and appear in appropriate ways.

To be demented is, literally, to be deprived of one's mental capacities. It can be the result of overmedication, neurological or circulatory disease, stroke, depression, or causes that science has yet to discover; and it is the most common, chronic illness among all nursing home residents (Barry Reisberg 1983: 3). But beyond dementia's medical roots, it also has a cultural meaning. At Elmwood, as in most nursing facilities, people suffering from

Alzheimer's and similar illnesses bore a special stigma that transcended the disabilities of their disorder. In a culture that values self-sufficiency, coherence, outward appearance, and youthfulness, they were dependent on others, inconsistent in their dress and comportment, illogical in their discourse, and—of course—old. Though their disease was not catching, the stigma that it carried could be contagious. To be around such individuals was to run the risk of being seen in the same light as them: it was guilt, or diagnosis, by association. Some residents consequently tried to avoid victims, just as certain sufferers denied their own condition as a way of maintaining a positive identity. Bonnie, who found her memory lapses upsetting, was even more disturbed at any suggestion that she was even mildly senile. She took refuge in the argument that "everyone forgets things from time to time, so why make a big deal of it?" But the very fact of being institutionalized made avoidance and denial more difficult for residents like her than for people living on the outside. Like the residents of Bethany Manor who tried "covering" their confusion (O'Brien 1989: 94–95), Bonnie and her peers were in a suspect place where insiders and outsiders alike were subject to doubts about the competency of those who lived there.[2]

This chapter examines the stigma of silence and senility that dementia sufferers had to bear, and considers the kinds of communication and contact that they were able to achieve. It goes on to compare their situation with the way similar conditions are dealt with in other age groups and societies. It suggests that silence and randomness are not invariably qualities of affliction, and that the stigma they carry is partly the product of culture as well as the result of an aging body.

STIGMA

For some residents, the answer to dementia was distance. Not wishing to be viewed as sharing the same space or status as Alzheimer's victims, they tried not to associate or be seen with such individuals. They emphatically pointed out to visitors that they did not live on the same floor or unit as "those people," "those crazies," or, as Frank once put it with genuine compassion, "those poor vegetables." Residents at other institutions have also been noted to use such statements of "relative deprivation" (O'Brien 1989: 39) or "downward comparison" (Powers 1988b: 313) to set themselves above and apart. At Elmwood, Tilly's roommate Vivian was uneasy around the senile because she was "never sure what they'd do next." When she was outside her room, she moved to lounge areas where she would not be near her demented peers. Such a pattern of "distancing" or avoidance has been observed in members of the "alertness cliques" at Murray Manor (Gubrium 1975: 108–113), and among competent residents at Franklin (Shield 1988: 56), Bethany Manor (O'Brien 1989: 32–33), and other facilities. Frank, who had so much finesse with language, who played with and shaped it like clay, put as many layers as he could between himself and the senile. His face lost its color when he heard Mr. Howard in the next room repeating to an aide, over and over and over again, the same question about his pajamas. "The tops or the bottoms? The tops or the bottoms?" echoed Frank under his breath. "Who the hell cares! She should just dress him and shut him up." But Frank did not really despise the demented: he rather recoiled from the potential they stood for. He said they made him feel "ill with pity and anticipation."

Frank was one of a handful of residents who criticized Elmwood's management for even taking in demented patients, arguing that this changed the nature of the home and, thereby, the reputation and self-image of all who lived in it.[3] His objections highlighted one side of an ongoing debate in geriatrics over whether to separate confused from competent residents (S. Salisbury and P. Goehner 1983). The intensity of Frank's negative reaction, suggested Louise, was rooted in people's attempts to evade the possibility that they themselves might eventually suffer some form of senility. In the act of avoiding the afflicted, they were holding at bay their fears for their own future. Vivian, who suffered only a physical disability, bore out Louise's theory when she complained that "because Alzheimer's is all the rage now, it terrifies us into looking at everything we do or say for signs of it." Not only did people "monitor" one another for signs of decline (Shield 1988: 165–166): they were self-monitoring as well.

The fear or experience of contamination was far from universal, however. There were also residents unaffected by dementia who took on a caretaking role with the senile. People such as Tilly and Stavros responded to their requests, redirected their wanderings, offered words or touches of comfort, and explained their condition to perplexed visitors. To the confused people around her, especially agitated individuals such as Eva and Karl, Tilly voiced the same spirit of hope she bestowed on others. Some of Tilly's and Stavros's acts of kindness derived from their own sense of bewilderment over the condition in which they found their contemporaries. Stavros once asked, after guiding Karl back to their room:

What happens to people after eighty that their minds start to go? Most of the people I have met here who are over eighty have lost some of their mental powers. Very few are "all there." The Bible says our normal life should be seventy years. That is the gift that God has given us. And then afterwards . . . what do we live on? You're a professor, perhaps you can explain it. What do the doctors know about this? It puzzles me because most people do not really use their brains a lot in their lives. Their jobs and the other things they do don't seem to demand it a great deal of the time. The other parts of our bodies, our organs and muscles, they get used a lot . . . and yet they seem to hold up much better sometimes in old age than the brain. Why should such an underused organ get so run down?

Out of the compassionate behaviors that Stavros, Tilly, and others engaged in, they derived a sense of self-esteem, a feeling of usefulness. Being volunteer caregivers was also a way for them to emphasize their own abilities by literally putting them side by side with others' disabilities. For Tilly, it was a chance to practice what she preached about. To Stavros, it was a means for combating the implication that just because he was in Elmwood, his mind was in decline. Unlike those who avoided the demented because of the stigma, then, these two sought such people out to accentuate their differences from them. Like elderly people who volunteer or reach out to others in their retirement, they had discovered that helping was itself a form of self-help.[4]

One of the patients attended to in this way was Sarah Kavalick on South Two: hers was a benign dependency, all meek and mild and well meant, making her a favorite among staff. She only asked for things with her eyes, and agreed to almost every suggestion her caregivers made. On most days she sat for hours in a chair near the nursing station, watching what there was of the world go by, seeming to take a silent pleasure in it. At random moments she would stand, stroll the length of the corridor, end to end, again and again, and then just as suddenly stop. Tucked under her arm was a stuffed woolly bear, deer colored and plush, which she frequently smiled at and stroked. People passing by would ask her about it, and she would answer by giving it another caress. At pet visits she took to and held Mandy's cat with the same absorption, occasionally breaking her silence to meow to it in her only other form of conversation.

For all her dreamy innocence and harmless journeys, however, Sarah could also frighten the nurses. She had no direct way of telling people when she was ill, or what hurt, or how good or bad a treatment felt. Once, when she developed a florid, infected sore on her ankle, a trio of women—Marian Portline, the nursing director, Claire from PT, and Louise, the charge nurse on her floor—all stood over and around Sarah's chair. They consulted with one another, and tried to get what information they could by asking the seated woman questions and reading her face. In that moment, Sarah looked like a lost child inside a circle of adults, each of whom offered her phrases of comfort while trying to determine where she lived. The three women were compassionate yet tense, burdened by Sarah's silent trust. Their patient smiled attentively at their voices, pressed her pet to her chest, but stared at her own leg as if it were a foreign object.

Eva lived out a different story, a tale told partly in her own words, but accented by the marks of her agitation. To Bonnie and the other residents on South One, Eva was "The Wanderer." She slid along the corridor's walls in an endless patrol, sometimes refusing to detour around chairs or carts, impatiently waiting for others to move them. Whereas Sarah loved to touch what was—or seemed to be—alive, Eva clung to the firm, inanimate walls and followed their direction. She slipped into people's rooms, rummaged their drawers, and took the things that struck her strange fancy. Some items she hugged to her breast or tucked into the pockets of her house dress; others she held up to no one in particular to lecture about. Once, snatching up the cloth and brush from the top of Barbara Hernstein's bureau, she moved out to the hallway to proclaim: "In my house we always kept this kind of doily: every night I'd take the brush from the lace on my dresser and"—holding the brush aloft—"I'd give my hair 50 strokes." Eva groomed herself as she talked and walked along the wall, continuing her round till Reva, an aide, stopped her to ask where she had gotten the objects in her hand. Eva's face froze into a rage, and she raised her stroking hand in threat. "My hairbrush, my home! This is where I do *ma toilette!*...." Where had the French come from? There was no clue. Only the gesture. And then, with a practiced calm, Reva disarmed her.

Most of the time, Eva was quiet: her store of energy went into strolling, though items that had some private association could touch off her outbursts of speech. Having said her few words, she would then quickly step back inside herself and press mutely against the walls again. Residents gave her a wide berth, keeping a wary eye on her movements to guard their rooms.

Staff were watchful in a different way: instead of constantly tracking Eva, they monitored her moves by periodically scanning the halls. Eva was one of the people caregivers tried to keep around the corridor near the nursing station on South One: the collection of patients seated there gave the impression of a sociable gathering, though little interaction actually occurred. Rather, residents quietly watched what was going on, giving housekeepers a chance to clean their rooms and make their beds, and providing caregivers a vantage point from which they could keep an eye on those who wandered. The hallway that Eva prowled usually had a complement of aides, nurses, and housekeepers during the day, which enabled employees to keep in touch with one another about Eva and those like her. Sometimes the system failed and a person slipped away: Eva was once discovered over on North One, where she had removed all her clothes and curled up inside Dave Dorenberg's bed. Though Millie laughed when she heard about her husband's uninvited guest, Dave was badly embarrassed when he found Eva, and he was teased for weeks about the company he kept.

People like Eva were rarely restrained or medicated at Elmwood unless—like Mr. Howard—they had a tendency to fall and injure themselves. But the freedom such patients enjoyed did not diminish the strong, contradictory response they engendered in others, who were commonly left torn between scorn and sympathy for them. To be attacked, embarrassed, stolen from, or met with empty looks and wordlessness, were affronts to the common code of civility. Residents, staff, and visitors had different thresholds of tolerance and understanding, which meant that some moved in close and others stepped away from the demented. Sometimes it was not enough to know, intellectually, that certain individuals simply had no control—especially if their behavior cost you *your* self-control. To be sorry for the indignities of their dress and undress, their confusion and detours, their sentence of silence, was merciful. But it did not bring the demented back inside the realm of acceptability. If it could have, reflected Stavros, "they would probably not have been in an institution to begin with."

CONTACT AND COMMUNICATION

For volunteers at Elmwood Grove, the first contacts with confused people were as unsettling as culture shock, but compounded for them by experiencing the alien in their own hometown. By adding uncertainty to the daunting qualities of age and confinement, these encounters intensified all the difficulties visitors faced in working with the institutionalized elderly. For a new volunteer, the striking orderliness of the nursing home could pale beside the disordered speech and behavior of the demented (see Figure 6.1 for a sample of a structured and busy monthly schedule). Wandering minds and bodies were random elements, proofs of indeterminacy, moving about in a world of clockwork, Newtonian regularity.

Volunteers who came with their pets often experienced considerable anxiety about how to approach and relate to people—such as the confused and the senile—whose needs and reactions seemed unpredictable. They feared being intrusive and inappropriate with individuals who were themselves defined by their very inappropriateness. These visitors wondered about whether to approach residents who seemed withdrawn, whether to continue talking to people who did not respond, and whether to respond to persons who made requests that they did not feel authorized to comply with.[5] Was it alright, when Karl asked you, to close his door, or wheel him to another floor? And how did you reply to Eva, who implored you to "call my daughter now—it's urgent"; or to Mr. Howard when he said, each week, "please take off these belts and help me pack: I'm going home tomorrow for good"? Mr. Howard's voice and eyes both argued his case with passion, and he backed up his pleas with details about his son's impending arrival and the ramp that he had built for his father's wheelchair. With no outward signs of senility to alarm Mr. Howard's listener, it was easy to believe his story if you did not know the nature of his history.

Decisions about how to deal with such situations depended not only on the volunteer, but on the setting of these encounters. At pet sessions, visitors who were unsure of how to react to people could turn to their peers or to staff for advice. Perplexing speech or behaviors could often be interpreted by another person who had had some experience with the resident in question. Being told that Eva could only hear in her left ear, or that Karl enjoyed touching but not being touched, were valuable guidelines. It also helped to be told by Nina that you could nod agreement with Mr. Howard's account

Figure 6.1
Bulletin Board

YOU ARE ON EAST 2

ACTIVITIES FOR MAY

Sunday	Monday	Tuesday	Wednesday	Thursday	Friday	Saturday
		[1] Exercise	[2] Baking	[3] Crafts	[4] Pet Day	[5] Bible class
[6] Catholic Communion	[7] Protestant Worship	[8] School Play	[9] Kiwanis - Birthdays	[10] Exercise	[11] Patients' Council	[12] Talking Books
[13] Bingo	[14] Clothing Sale	[15] Baptist Service	[16] News	[17] Bird Watching	[18] Craft Sale	[19] Square Dancing
[20] Bowling	[21] Westman Club - Crafts	[22] Exercise	[23] Poetry Club	[24] Kitchen Band	[25] Pet Day	[26] Bake Sale
[27] Garden Club Outing	[28] Player Piano	[29] Movie	[30] Slide Show - China	[31] Card Party		

TODAY Is: **TUESDAY**

THE DATE Is: **MAY 8**

THE WEATHER: **SUNNY**

NOTICES

Wed. May 9	Birthday Party
Fri. May 11	Patients' Council
Mon. May 14	Clothing Day
Fri. May 18	Craft Sale
Sat. May 25	Bake Sale

of his homecoming, and still decline to assist him without making him angry. To learn, from Denise, that Greta's squint was a smile and not a sign of pain, encouraged visitors to stay close to her bed instead of drawing back from it. But when such understandings were not clear, or the translations not forthcoming, volunteers tended to pretend to comprehend, reducing the interaction to a respectful fiction.

New staff were often in the same position. Some took the caregiving path of least resistance and insight by patronizing people. As Katina once remarked, "It's 'dear,' 'honey,' or 'love' to nearly everyone," said with tones of condescension that presumed that all were impaired in the same way. Though rarely meant maliciously, such language dismissed the individuality that mattered so much to residents like Stavros. Other staff were prepared to attend and respond to what set people apart, but they also came to appreciate that goodwill and the right words were often not enough.

Nina, for example, remembered how much help she had needed when she began her job in social work.

> I walked around like a well-meaning blithe spirit. I would read someone's chart and then speak to the person as if words were all that mattered. But what does "mildly confused" on that page mean? And how confused on this particular day? Sometimes a casual remark from an aide who had just been, say, with Eva—"Oh, she's feeling up today, talking about her garden"—that would tell me more about what to expect and what would work than all the charts in the world.

As Nina observed, experienced staff could often smooth the path to rapport by presenting people to patients with simple comments about the latter's interests and lives. From her position in Activities, Denise helped volunteers in the same way to anticipate unorthodox speech patterns and meaningful subjects of conversation. When she introduced a mildly disoriented woman to the recreation room by saying, "Marjorie just had her eightieth birthday and she's wearing the sweater her son gave her," a great deal of awkwardness could be avoided. The conventions of such a simple, opening remark—tightly wrapping a name, age, family tie, and event of note all inside a single sentence—put marks of character on a strange person's face. And the act relieved the anxiety of the less articulate residents too, for it introduced those who could not present themselves.

There were other lessons that people learned about behavior and speech. Sometimes movement alone could be eloquent. This was true on North Two, a floor that had a cluster of confused and frequently wordless people. To walk down its hallway in midafternoon was like touring a soundless town where each person spoke her own dialect of silence: some talked with their eyes, some with their hands, some with the rhythmic swing of a foot. One Alzheimer's victim there, a roommate of Greta's named Queenie Jones, hummed almost inaudibly to herself in a wheelchair for much of the day: her fingers tapped out a cadence that her head would nod in concert with. Whatever music she beat time for clearly pleased her, and the fact that it was unheard by others did not seem to matter. When a passing aide would ask what she was listening to, Queenie's most common answer was an upward sweep of her arm, an echo of a conductor cuing his orchestra. Occasionally, she would loudly pound both her palms on the wheelchair's tray as if offering applause for some private concert. To Steve Nakara, a volunteer who visited that second floor unit most weeks, strolling through the quiet, constant movement was like "being backstage at a mime show," watching each performer rehearse her moves "in deep concentration."

The clock was another character in the landscape of the confused. Late afternoon and early evening were the most common times for senile patients to become agitated. Staff at Elmwood called this "sundowning" and referred to this period as "the witching hour." Kate pointed out, however, that even agitated residents had their peaceful times most days. It varied from person to person, with some being better in the morning, others later on. When staff recognized this, the more conscientious tried to adjust the schedules in order to bathe or walk patients during their calmer periods, or at least know when to watch such individuals more carefully. "Mr. Howard is actually quieter at night," Kate observed, "while June downstairs is at her best after breakfast." Even randomness, then, had its rhythms.

There was also an issue with the terms used to describe the senile. Though *dementia* was largely about language, the word itself was loose and imprecise. Clinically, at least, it clung to patients showing a great range of emotions and symptoms and behaviors. Their responses to pet sessions, for example, were as varied as those of unconfused residents. When volunteers and pets approached people who had some form of dementia, there were a few who declined both types of companionship, some who were receptive to the animals while ignoring the people, and yet others who focused on the person and treated the pet as incidental. In their conversations, the less disoriented— such as Bonnie—showed an appreciation both for the attention they were being given, and for the opportunity to converse, complain, laugh, and reminisce. The more impaired and withdrawn participants—individuals such as Sarah, Karl, and Greta—would variously hold, pet, smile, and sometimes talk to the animals, reaching a kind of communion they could rarely enjoy with people. The animation shown by even the most confused persons belied our culture's assumption that, when old and infirm, we can only kill time until time kills us.

Even the best of these encounters could occasionally alter course and change tenor, however. When individuals experienced agnosia, memory lapses, or the loss of a desired name, their frustration and chagrin could turn into anger or sadness or self-denigration. The tone of a visit could then sud-denly shift from ease and warmth to intense self-consciousness. Karl offered some painful moments of this kind. He was undemanding, understated, and usually wary of speech itself because he was so unsure of his words. As a young man he had built barns and sheds with his hands, but could now barely construct a sentence without fear. Even small conversation felt like a risk, and he was often content to sit with a visitor, and a pet, in comfortable silence. Janice, one of the older volunteers, gradually got to know him because she and Midnight, her cat, spent time with Karl most weeks. Usually they shared a brief ritual of greeting and a time of quiet sitting, with the cat by Karl's side on his bed. The man would stroke the animal and periodically say a few admiring words about her. Occasionally he ventured into real talk. Janice once found Karl reading a letter. "It's from my cousin Gene in Pennsylvania," he explained. "We grew up together. Used to hunt a lot when we were boys. His mother and mine were . . . uh . . . were. . . . "

As he fumbled for the term, his lips tried to help by making the shapes of different sounds. But nothing emerged. Then the hand with the letter began to tremble and he crushed part of the paper in a fist, beating it repeatedly into the mattress.

At such a moment, a volunteer could be as lost as Karl: uncertain about which feelings to show, unsure whether to intervene with suggestions to lead him out of the confusion. But Janice had learned from Denise, and she offered Karl the missing term: "Sisters? Were they sisters?" And Karl nodded, letting his hand and his lips come to rest. His face was covered with exhaustion.

Most confused residents preferred to be prompted towards the word or name they were fighting for, but many volunteers did not realize this (cf. Nancy Mace and Peter Rabins 1984: 44). Confronted with a stuttering, struggling individual, some visitors became paralyzed with indecision. And their embarrassment, their lack of assurance, only amplified those of their companion. Both receded beyond what Yeats called old age's "curtain of distorting days" ([1932] 1983: 253). Times like these had several layers of silent anguish. There was the older person's pain and humiliation, and the visitor's own strata of fears: the worries about being too active or too passive, more hurtful than helpful, more intrusive than supportive.

Experienced staff and volunteers learned not only that their words were welcome, but that with some residents, touch could be a more appropriate means of communication than talk. Holding hands, embracing a person's arm or shoulder, and placing a dog or cat where a patient could silently stroke it, were rewarding and much less stressful for some people. Greta and Sarah, both literally bereft of words, could each be reached in this way, the one responding with caresses, the other with purring sounds. For Karl, Janice's presence and Midnight's fur were as sufficient as conversation. The value of these types of contact has also been observed in other research on Alzheimer's victims and the institutionalized elderly.[6] For volunteers and animals, as well as for residents, these were moments of simply being together in both a literal and an existential sense. It required time and some practice, however, for most visitors to get over the need to talk and be spoken to, and to become comfortable with the experience of silence itself. They had to work to grasp what Caro Spencer, May Sarton's elderly protagonist, had learned, that "sometimes silence is the greatest sign of understanding and respect. It is far more consoling than words of false comfort" (1973: 49).

The animals at Elmwood were of considerable assistance in this. They not only provided contact for the patients, but a kind of tactile, totemic security for the volunteers. They could be petted and turned to in awkward moments, lending shape to the silence by centering people's attention on touch. For many visitors, the animals legitimized their presence at Elmwood. Janice compared them to a security blanket without which she would have felt "vulnerable and naked" inside the institution's walls.

It was reassuring for volunteers to recognize, as many eventually did, that while confused patients had special qualities, they nevertheless resembled other residents in their varied reactions to both human and animal visitors. Volunteers were sometimes also unaware that their own responses to dementia sufferers were often much more open and accepting than those of relatives who had lifelong ties to such individuals. Nina once explained this by pointing out that both staff members and community visitors had fewer expectations about how a particular resident should act because their relationship to that person did not predate his dementing illness. This lack of history reduced their tendency to be judgmental. Volunteers and staff thus had one important advantage over family and friends. They had no previous, healthier image of the person to compare the resident with, and so the patient, who may have suffered from comparison with others, at least did not suffer from comparison with himself.

SILENCE AND TOUCH

Cultural attitudes towards stigma, silence, and contagion, and social expectations about communication, all affected the way the elderly and the demented got treated. Not only at Elmwood Grove, but in the United States in general, people respond not just to symptoms, but to the names of the diseases and disabilities that victims wear: to be "old" or "senile" or "blind" is to be part of a category, not simply a bearer of a particular quality. Individuals who are deaf, retarded, or brain damaged may, in part, resemble demented people symptomatically, and yet the latter still evoke much more intense reactions from those who are healthy. These differences go beyond the boundaries of clinical concepts because they reflect still deeper cultural attitudes and the burden of stigma. Furthermore, our responses to the senile and the elderly are not only categorical—they are also distinct from the attitudes towards illness, age, and communication found in other societies. A comparison of these cultural differences is worth considering here because they illuminate the nature of our society's reactions to aging and dementia. Four factors that merit special attention are the ways Americans and others respond to silence, touch, contagion, and uncertainty.

The significance of touch and the value of silence provide important points of cultural contrast. The experiences of residents and caregivers at Elmwood Grove demonstrated that tactile and nonverbal forms of contact could be very effective with withdrawn and disoriented people. But it was often difficult for volunteers, visitors, and staff to accustom themselves to these types of communication. Silence demanded an exceptional form of intimacy, one in which intuition was more important than information, where gesture and posture had to say all that words and voice could not. Americans claim that "silence is golden," but with the exception of circumstances requiring extreme respect and awe, they are more likely to experience silence as awkward. It seems to lock patients in and others out. Under most conditions, the ability to speak is a defining quality of adult competency and full humanity. Its loss is depersonalizing, the losers less than human. In our etiquette, it is only children who should be seen and not heard, whereas old people who cannot be heard should not be seen.

Americans tend to be much less comfortable with silence, be it in their speech, their poetry, or their music, than is true of individuals in many other cultures. In Indian oratory, for example, silence can be eloquent. An Iroquois anthropologist has observed that silence among Native Americans is "half of speech: speech is half of silence. . . . Silence is the continuity which integrates ideas and words. . . . Silence is a thing of power. Beyond any utterance, the power of silence stands vast and awesome" (Shirley Hill Witt 1972: xxiv). Tribal patterns of communication can dictate the circumstances under which people should refrain from speech. The Papago expect individuals to greet one another with silence rather than words, thus "absorbing one another's personalities" (Ruth Underhill 1979: 10). The Western Apache remain silent or "give up on words" in a variety of situations: when dealing with strangers; when courting; when being reunited with relatives after a long separation; when in the company of people who are grieving; and when in the presence of a patient for whom a curing ceremony is being held. The common element in all of these contexts is that social relations have momentarily become uncertain and unpredictable, rendering silence either the safest or the most considerate of responses (Keith Basso 1970).[7]

Silence can also be part of sociability, spirituality, and creativity in other cultures. There are forms of Native American music that are silent in that they are never supposed to be performed or voiced out loud. Such "silent music" exists only for the seeker who has received a song in a spirit quest, whose music retains its power only in the privacy of his heart and mind (Edmund Carpenter 1978). Arctic peoples with whom I have lived in northern Canada can visit one another's homes in silence for hours, sipping tea and sitting in quiet throughout an entire evening. Such a visiting pattern is largely nonverbal but very satisfying in the undemanding companionship it offers (Savishinsky 1974). The writer John Berger had described how migrant workers in Europe, separated from family and homeland, create a private world of silence within which memories and anticipations are housed (John Berger and Jean Mohr 1975: 167). Dispossessed people in developing countries also sustain a "culture of silence" in the face of their oppressors (Paulo Freire 1970: 10–13).

In many religions, silence is the space out of which meditation, reverie, and prayer arise. Within it, people discover or recreate who and what they are. Plutarch declared that "from men man learns to speak, from the gods to keep silent" (Soren Kierkegaard 1954: 258). In South American tribes which ritually seclude people for months or years at a time, remaining in isolation and refraining from speech are means of reconstituting one's social identity (Thomas Gregor 1970). In the mime performance of someone like Marcel Merceau, silence becomes art. With a contemporary composer such as John Cage, music becomes silent again: the empty spaces in his scores open the doors for sounds "to come into being of themselves" (John Cage 1961: 7–8, 70). While none of these forms of silence are predicated on a disability, they demonstrate how acceptable silence can be when it is made socially meaningful. But when the reverie celebrated in our folklore comes from a person whose integrity is in doubt, the act of contemplation becomes artless and sad.

Our society's discomfort with silence is matched by our insufficient awareness about the importance of touch in human development. There is great cultural variation in how much tactile experience people have with one another in daily life and at different stages of the life cycle. Members of Japanese, Jewish, French, Russian, and Eskimo communities are significantly more physical in their everyday relationships than are most middle-class Americans (Ashley Montagu 1986: 292–392). In our own society, we are just beginning to learn that the nurturing that individuals can readily give to babies can be just as essential to women and men in late life. For older persons with few other means of communication, the importance of touch can be particularly pronounced. Rocking, for instance, can be satisfying for the aged as well as for infants because it is soothing, self-caressing, and stimulating for large areas of the skin (Montagu: 158–171). Caro Spencer found that "the body remembers *for* the mind," that memory itself was "kept alive partly through the *senses*" (Sarton 1973: 55, 60). Such direct, sensory experiences meet the special needs of the very young and old, among whom "the bodily state is such a large determinant of well-being" (Myerhoff 1978: 18).

Researchers have stressed how crucial physical contact and other forms of nonverbal communication can be for demented and brain-impaired individuals. Opportunities to experience touch with people, with inanimate surfaces such as smooth wood, or with animals, are all of potential value. Events that help trigger memories for institutional residents—such as visits that include family photographs, children, or pets—can also help sustain morale, promote reality orientation, and enhance intellectual functioning (Reisberg 1983; Mace and Rabins 1984). Where social contacts with others are limited for the elderly by stigma, anxiety, or inadequate opportunities, animals can be an important alternative source of comfort and enrichment. When pets, photographs, and other stimuli are accompanied by people who are prepared to listen, talk, touch, or simply commune in silence, there is a great enhancement of the healing value of time spent together.

CONTAGION AND UNCERTAINTY

Social attitudes can disable the elderly as much as illness. To be old and sick is to bear a double stigma. To be senile or silent is to be pushed even further towards the margins of the human community. Though our understanding of dementia has improved, scientific insights into it can be overshadowed by cultural assumptions about how the aged and ill should be treated. In particular, the conventional wisdom about contamination may negate medical assurances that senility is not contagious. The candid comments of Vivian and Frank show that the stigma of Alzheimer's pertains not to what is physically transmitted—for nothing is—but to what is socially communicated about those in the company of sufferers. Elderly residents in institutions who avoid the demented are afraid of what contact with them will do to their public and self-image. At Elmwood Grove, some also felt that being around "people like that" was demoralizing and thus debilitating. Frank and Vivian were not the only two who realized that contagion could be social, not just biological, in nature.

Residents' concerns about contamination, then, were based upon an astute appreciation of environmental influence and cultural meaning. They were acting out what others had warned them about: they did not want to play a supportive role in a self-fulfilling prophecy about senility. This was one reason why Stavros, though fully competent, was wary of speaking with peers and staff: he did not want any slip of the tongue to be misconstrued as confusion, or his presence in the home to be seen as a sign of dementia. In that sense, his reticence was articulate and powerful, asserting the claims of a speaker who wanted to hold some of himself in reserve. This kind of sensitivity, Vivian once implied, was very much a product of the times in which she and Stavros were living—a period in which dementia, as she put it, was "all the rage," pressing residents into a fearful examination of their every word and deed for telltale signs of its onset.

The social treatment of the demented in our society is also shaped by the fact that they are deviant individuals. Though their departure from cultural norms is obviously involuntary, they nevertheless suffer the same fate as many other nonconforming populations. Specifically, dementia sufferers go through two processes that distinguish the Western treatment of deviance from responses to it in simpler societies; namely, they are subjected to both institutionalization and labeling. The process of labeling transforms people's identity by restructuring it around their deviant condition. The ill *become* their disorder. No longer primarily husbands, grandmothers, teachers, or farmers, afflicted persons *are* simply demented, nothing more . . . and potentially much less. The label makes stigma more evident and more verbal, embedding it in the very vocabulary that others use to refer to and describe such individuals. And although such a labeling process is characteristic of American culture, it can also be found in other complex societies. In contemporary Japan, for instance, people soften references to the confused elderly by describing them as being in their "ecstasy years," but this is a widely recognized euphemism for senile dementia (David Plath 1983).

If labels are a way of symbolically confining people, institutionalization in American society turns the symbolism into physical reality. For Alzheimer's victims and other dementia sufferers—as is also the case with mental patients, criminals, and the retarded—it is the inability of the general populace to treat or countenance such people in public that underlies their placement in specialized facilities. And while nursing homes are a relatively modern medical development, they are simply the most recent example of this Western tendency to institutionalize deviant populations. It is an approach to abnormality which has been used increasingly with mentally, morally, and physically deviant groups since the eighteenth century. This trend, which social historian Michel Foucault calls "the great confinement" (1973, 1979), substitutes formal, external restraints for the internal and bodily ones that certain people are judged to be incapable of exercising. It is social control in place of self-control, and for the senile, it presumes the absence of the "self" itself.

The isolation of demented persons is predicated, in part, on their unpredictability. Normal life in all societies depends on a high degree of regularity in human behavior, and in a clockwork culture such as our own, senile and confused patients can often not conform to that. The routines of nursing homes thus provide such individuals with what they cannot provide themselves. Yet uncertainty is not always an unmitigated evil, for there are circumstances—both in our own and in other societies—where people try to induce randomness for the greater social good. The Montagnais Indians of northeastern Canada, for example, were a nomadic hunting and fishing tribe who created a bit of chaos to contend with a scarcity of food. Their periodic lack of meat was partly a result of their tendency to fall into predictable patterns when searching out and stalking game; this enabled the animals in their region to adapt to and avoid the hunters. When this happened, Montagnais shamans would practice a form of divination called scapulimancy, in which the random burn marks produced on a heated deer scapula were "read" as a map to indicate where the hunters should seek for game. The ritual thus served to counter the human propensity for patterned behavior under conditions where predictability had itself become counter-productive (O. K. Moore 1957).

In Western culture, the search for randomness lies behind a great deal of the twentieth century's avant garde art. Painters, sculptors, composers, and choreographers, including Marcel Duchamp, Robert Rauschenberg, Jean Tinguely, John Cage, and Merce Cunningham, have purposely introduced unpredictability into their work in order to eliminate the formal structures and aesthetic canons which have traditionally dominated their fields (Calvin Tomkins 1976). In their artistry, such devices as chance operations, coin tosses, the use of the *I Ching*, and tables of random numbers, are substituted for the ordered content of the individual mind, thereby reducing the role of the will and personality in the creative act. These aesthetic ideas echo the Principle of Indeterminacy, described by physicist Werner Heisenberg, as the basis for the scientific perception of physical matter (Lincoln Barnett 1962: 23–24).

Although it is provocative and creative, the uncertainty that inspires artists and scientists cannot easily be accommodated into daily life, or accepted in the behavior of those seen as ill. Bonnie's niece Emma enjoyed the play and serendipity of her aunt's mind, but Reva, the aide who tried to get Bonnie ready for a doctor's appointment, was understandably less entranced by this woman's refusal to acknowledge that she even lived in a home. While the randomness of creative endeavors is intentional, the acts of Alz-heimer's sufferers such as Bonnie and Eva could be uncontrolled and there-fore unsettling for others. Their fugitive memories and untimely conduct branded them. Eva's thefts, Bonnie's denials, Queenie's sudden outbursts of applause, Mr. Howard's ardent pleas for his freedom, and Sarah's random pacing with her teddy were all cases in point. Just as silence can make a person seem less than human, unpredictability may produce something of a monster. Composer John Cage in fact describes some of his music as "inhuman" because chance operations have brought it into being, and the score then controls the people who perform it (1961: 36). But whereas artists and scientists are seen as productive, the demented are perceived as destructive. Yet in the end, ironically, these three categories of people—the scientists, the artists, and the senile—still share a common fate: the unpre-dictability of their acts compels society to confine them. Whether it be in laboratories, artists' studios, or institutions, the general view is that they are best kept in facilities that house the eccentric.

YOUNG AND OLD

There is another paradox in the stigmatizing, the labeling, and the insti-tutionalization that victims of dementing disorders undergo. The irony is that these illnesses mimic the qualities of early childhood, which is a stage of life whose traits our culture otherwise cherishes and even romanticizes. When their disease takes the form of Alzheimer's, its progression is actually a regression—a loss, in reverse order, of a young person's acquisition of the abilities to smile, sit up, walk, talk, go to the toilet, bathe, dress, and remember (Reisberg et al. 1988: 14–15).

Late-life disease and the first phases of human development also share a mixture of other attributes, including innocence, freedom, forthrightness, dependency, irresponsibility, and unpredictability. But the childhood qualities of old age generally stand condemned in a condition such as Alzheimer's, whose victims are seen as childish rather than childlike. The candid remarks of a youngster, for example, become unbearably rude when uttered by an aged adult. The attachment to stuffed animals, which is affecting in children and adolescents, is viewed in a bemused, patronizing, or pitying light when witnessed in an elderly person such as Sarah Kavalick. Our culture's model of the life cycle pictures it as a linear process in which our capabilities progressively increase. Some of us can accept, with a measure of grace, the decrease of our powers over time; but few of us can countenance their reversal and regression. Compounding this problem for those who are senile is the fact that institutionalization often exacerbates the very conditions it is meant to alleviate by further infantilizing older residents.

In contrast to these attitudes and social responses, some other cultures recognize and prize the fact that old age has many similarities to early childhood. The Mbuti Pygmies of Central Africa see purity as a state that the very old and the very young share because of their proximity to nonexistence and their distance from active, adult responsibilities. Wisdom to them is the result not just of experience, but of a liberation from too much engagement in the mundane affairs of the world (Colin Turnbull 1983: 51–59). This suggests that the concept of disengagement may sometimes be a misguided interpretation of what others see as the penchant for older people to seek out "passive mastery" (Guttman 1976), or the state of simply "being" rather than "doing" (Turnbull 1983: 223–262). Yet only a handful of Western thinkers, such as C. G. Jung (1933), de Beauvoir (1972), and Montagu (1989), have praised the youthful qualities of the old, seeing late life as a developmental opportunity to recapture what maturity has cost us: spontaneity and outspokenness; primary feelings and curiosity; easier access to the unconscious; the primacy of touch; the nearness of birth, death, and nothingness; the ability to ask questions; and the freedom not to answer them. As Baudelaire once suggested, "Genius is childhood recaptured."[8]

The symptoms of dementia also overlap with certain adult traits that are often perceived of in a neutral or even a positive light. Abstractedness, candor, eccentricity, and absentmindedness may be seen as amusing, challenging, or even professorial qualities in others, but they shade and slip off into illness, disability, and stigma when people become elderly patients.

The point where endearing traits become unendurable failures can be a very personal judgment; and such judgments can be just as arbitrary as the cultural standards we use for determining what it means to act your age.

CONCLUSION

At a time in history where many families are finding it necessary to put elderly Alzheimer's sufferers and other senile individuals into nursing homes, there is a growing need to put the behavior of demented people into context. Institutionalized patients with dementing disorders are often triply out of touch. They may, at one and the same time, be divested of control over their cognitive and motor functions, just as they are deprived of social and physical contacts with kin and friends. Yet their need for company is crucial, and the rewards of companionship critical. "Patients who have visitors, live; those who do not, die. The statistics are literally that dramatic" (Reisberg et al. 1988: 16).

The confused elderly are also caught in the paradox of a culture that values youthfulness, but requires that people act in a way that befits their years—a contradictory set of expectations to which the old in general, and the senile in particular, cannot possibly conform. The stigma and silence that surround demented people, or with which they surround themselves, can aggravate their condition by increasing their withdrawal, depression, and isolation. Being out of touch with parts of their own minds and other bodies compounds the sensory and social deprivation that human and animal companionship can help reduce.

People's experiences at Elmwood Grove, and the other research noted here, indicate several areas that warrant more careful study. These include the following:

1. The need to explore further the social attitudes toward dementia and its sufferers, and how these relate to broader cultural perceptions of health and illness, aging and deviance, and curing and caring;

2. The need to consider whether silence, touch, and unpredictability can be looked at in new and more creative ways;

3. The need to understand more clearly how people with Alzheimer's and similar illnesses perceive themselves, their disorder, and their treatment by others;

4. The need to identify the ways in which staff, volunteers, and other caregivers relate to and feel about dementia sufferers, and how these responses compare with the treatment of institutional residents with other disabilities; and

5. The need to assess the impact of specific recreational and therapeutic programs on those afflicted with mental impairments.

Insights into all of these issues could improve both the image and the treatment of demented people in our society. When greater understanding is achieved about stigmatized individuals, the result is generally a more humane consideration of their human needs and civil rights. This can be seen historically in the way American reactions to other disapproved conditions have been altered in recent decades. Members of certain populations that were once discriminated against or excluded from public life—racial minorities, homosexuals, and the blind, deaf, crippled, and retarded—are now much more readily accepted in society. Improvements in their status have been the result of both scientific knowledge and political activism. As a group with a new visibility and social identity, Alzheimer's victims and others with dementia may also ultimately be accorded a greater degree of tolerance, though this too will require more research and more advocacy by both sufferers and their families.

Anthropological studies can be of relevance in this process by enabling caregivers to recognize the impact of their own culture and behavior on the nature of life within an institutional setting. It is particularly helpful to know that other societies, and some groups within our own culture, respond to aging, silence, touch, randomness, and disability in very different ways. The more conscious we can be of how our own patterns shape people's experiences and expectations, the more capable we become of developing behaviors that will better meet the needs of both aging individuals and those who serve them.

7 THE STAFF

"INVISIBLE IN THE MOST OBVIOUS WAY"

Sitting with me in her kitchen one evening, Louise Santorini, who had been a nurse at Elmwood Grove for ten years, described the varied ways in which residents coped with institutional life. She spoke of those who accepted it with equanimity or relief; those who fought it with anger or incontinence—two of the few weapons at their disposal; and those who withdrew into silence and the privacy of their minds. She called the latter "the shadow people."

In contrast to those who were in retreat, staff at the nursing home were very evident in every room, corner, and corridor of the building (see Figure 7.1). They were bathing patients or taking them for walks, supervising a game or showing a movie, updating charts or taking a life-history. Others were cleaning the floors, preparing meals, conducting an exercise class, balancing the books, or fixing the plumbing. But to outsiders and occasional visitors, employees may still have had only a shadowy presence. Their jobs not only fit into the home's daily routine, they *were* that routine. The more efficient staff were, the less apparent they became. They were, Louise suggested, "invisible in the most obvious way."

At times, they seemed to be supportive players in a theater whose central characters were the elderly. It was the residents, after all, who had been uprooted from their homes, who faced the daily task of adjustment, who wavered between life and death. While the nursing home could not have functioned without the staff, then, these people could easily be overlooked in the midst of the dramas and traumas that colored the lives of those they served.

When given a voice or an audience, however, employees had a great deal to say. They spoke about the rewards and frustrations of their labor, about residents who valued and others who abused them, about people's bravery or withdrawal in the face of loss. And they talked about the need to talk.

NINA BRECKNER, SOCIAL WORKER

"A Hopeful Realist"

When Nina Breckner retraced her career, she spoke mostly about other women, especially their promise and their vulnerability. In her present and past jobs, she had often been their advocate. Dropping out of college in Ohio, she first went to work for her church. In a rural area of a neighboring state, she helped run a home for pregnant teenagers. The complexity of the girls' situation forced itself upon her like the urgency of the new lives that grew inside them. It was not just problems of sexuality and contraception. Their condition was often the product of poverty and poor education, alcohol and violence, and the responses of their families and communities: when it came to the question of adolescent pregnancy, their parents and peers could be both encouraging and discouraging in the worst sense of each word. After two years, Nina went back to school, chastened by her discovery of how overdetermined the lives of some people could be.

Studying social work worked on Nina's sense of history and conscience, turning experience into skill and Nina herself into "a hopeful realist." She was less naive about human nature, more sanguine about making the agencies that serve people truly responsive to their needs. After graduation she took her degree and her priorities to a shelter for runaway children in a midwestern city. In impressive, often startling and disconcerting ways, the young people she found there had decided to take their lives into their own hands. Many had done it, in fact, because they had been battered by the hands of others. Some had left, others had been thrown out of their homes. The tides of misfortune and Greyhound buses had brought them into the twilight zone of urban life.

Unlike the runaways she had once worked with, the residents who now surrounded Nina had lost control over much of their lives. And where she had once helped her adolescent clients move away from their pasts, she dealt now with old people trying to hold onto their history. Their futures faced in different directions.

A primary responsibility of Nina's was deciding who could come to stay at Elmwood. Sometimes it was a question of life and death; at other times it was an issue of means and ends. The case could be like the one presented by Yvonne Williams, an elderly woman living alone, with failing eyesight and the worsening tremors of Parkinson's disease: no longer capable of caring for herself, she badly needed a sheltered place to reside. Or there could be a call from the Department of Social Services: the caseworker had Tom Shaugnessy, a 75-year-old diabetic man, a widower who had just had

Figure 7.1
Elmwood Grove Nursing Home: Selected Residents and Staff

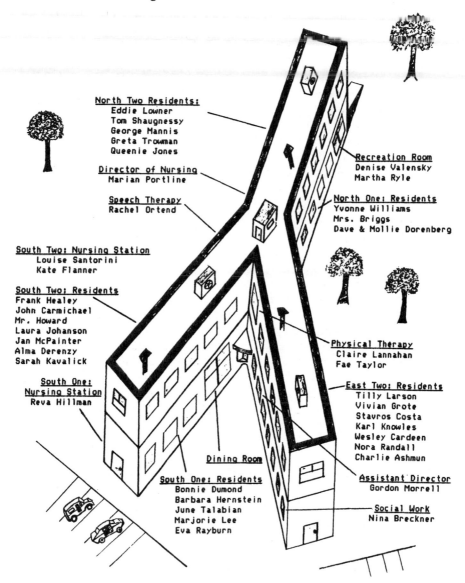

North Two Residents:
  Eddie Lowner
  Tom Shaugnessy
  George Mannis
  Greta Trowman
  Queenie Jones

Director of Nursing
  Marian Portline

Speech Therapy
  Rachel Ortend

South Two: Nursing Station
  Louise Santorini
  Kate Flanner

South Two: Residents
  Frank Healey
  John Carmichael
  Mr. Howard
  Laura Johanson
  Jan McPainter
  Alma Derenzy
  Sarah Kavalick

South One:
  Nursing Station
  Reva Hillman

Recreation Room
  Denise Valensky
  Martha Ryle

North One: Residents
  Yvonne Williams
  Mrs. Briggs
  Dave & Mollie Dorenberg

Physical Therapy
  Claire Lannahan
  Fae Taylor

East Two: Residents
  Tilly Larson
  Vivian Grote
  Stavros Costa
  Karl Knowles
  Wesley Cardeen
  Nora Randall
  Charlie Ashmun

Assistant Director
  Gordon Morrell

Social Work
  Nina Breckner

Dining Room

South One: Residents
  Bonnie Dumond
  Barbara Hernstein
  June Talabian
  Marjorie Lee
  Eva Rayburn

his leg amputated. Currently in the hospital, he was to be discharged within a week, and was eligible for Medicaid. The appeals and inquiries that came to Nina were sometimes phrased in a way that made her feel

> like I'm not a social worker but either God or a stockbroker—two of life's most compromised roles nowadays. It's often a question of who's entitled to what, or how to use the public's money—or a family's funds—for health care. No one authorized me to decide all that, yet here I am, opening or closing doors.

While she was a key person in the admissions process, Nina herself was not in sole possession of the key, and that at least eased some of the burden from her conscience. In this, as in several of her other tasks, she worked as part of a team, in this case sharing the job with Marian Portline, the director of nursing. The waiting list which these two women dealt with often had over a hundred names and it was constantly under revision. When someone died or left the facility, they spoke of it as "a bed opening up." And while Elmwood did not have a strict quota of men and women, gender was very much a factor affecting who got in at any given time. Since people shared rooms with members of the same sex, a female death meant a bed for a woman.

The interval between requesting and being offered admission was unpredictable. Some of the names on the list had lived there in limbo for months. When others who had risen to the top were called by Nina, she frequently found that they had gotten better, or moved into another facility, or died. Individuals ranked below them would then move up in rapid order. The admission process thus ran on two tracks: there was orderly succession, but also the opportunity created by gender and the fate of others.

It seemed strange when I first heard Nina describe entry into Elmwood as "an opportunity," but there was in fact a local shortage of nursing home beds. People had to compete, wait, and hope to secure one. For those without the financial means to pay as private patients, the scarcity was even more acute: they could only seek a place in those institutions, such as Elmwood, that accepted Medicaid recipients. The cost to facilities of providing care was great, and staff, residents, and families at the home were well aware of this. Gordon Morrell, the assistant director, emphasized that the institution had only a small endowment, and that it depended directly on private and government payments for most of its operating revenue. Elmwood was not only a not-for-profit facility, it was less than that. It operated at a loss: the private and public fees it received did not actually cover the expense of sustaining its 84 residents. The rising price of health care had outstripped revenues and reimbursements in recent years. The home's modest endowment had thus become more than just a monetary cushion: it was a financial safety net that administrators fell back on to balance the books. If getting into Elmwood, then, was competitive and costly, keeping the institution going required ongoing prudence and drawing on a debt to the past.

The past was also a presence with each potential admission to the facility. Nina spoke with every applicant, or a family member, to compile the person's social and medical history. This included information on the individual's background, current living situation and finances, previous illnesses, and records of treatment. All this went into the PRI, the Patient Review Instrument. The PRI also gave the person's current medical status, and this was later updated if an actual admission became imminent. When a man or woman became a serious candidate to enter Elmwood, several considerations figured in the last stages of the process. The home had to look at the information on "The Screen,"—the assessment form used by the hospital to determine the appropriate level of nursing home care. Nina explained,

> For reimbursement purposes, people have to fall within a certain range [of disability] so that we can accept them. The state has specific criteria for who needs skilled nursing care, and we must take that into account. Sometimes there are also applicants who have special medical or behavioral problems that we can't handle, and the review we do is meant to bring that out. Once we've decided on a likely person, we contact them at their home or at the hospital. If it's the latter, we speak to the social worker there. And then usually Marian and myself, we go to the hospital, read through the chart, and meet the man or woman. Or I'll go to people's home and speak with them there, or maybe with their relatives here in my office.
>
> After we've agreed on someone who is appropriate, I contact the hospital or family with a decision. If the admission is directly from the hospital, I speak to their social worker, and she talks with the family. . . .

Nina paused to measure her words.

> Actually, it's not as open and shut as that may sound, it's not that simple. Usually the hospital or the patient's relatives are also in touch with other nursing homes in the area, so we aren't always their only possibility. Sometimes I'll consult with the social workers at those other facilities too. Who has a bed, whose need is greatest, who can pay what—those are some of the weights that get thrown on the scales. . . .
>
> A person who's been admitted needs to have a doctor. If they don't already have one we have certain practitioners [from the community] who've agreed to take on people here. The home also has a medical director, Dr. Krigstein, but he doesn't actually have a caseload of patients in Elmwood. So residents see their own physician, and my impression is that, over all, they're as satisfied, or as dissatisfied, as people in general are with doctors. You hear praise, you hear complaints. There are a few who make quick, really perfunctory visits. I've known some families who've changed doctors almost every few months

because they can't find one that they or their mother or father can get on with and trust. But then I've also seen physicians, like Dr. Sheren, who'll spend longer with Yvonne—even having coffee with her in the dining room some days—which is more time than my doctor spends with me!

Sheren once said to me that the problem for the better doctors—and by that I think he meant the more conscientious ones—is that some patients still think their bodies are like they were twenty or thirty years ago, and that most of what ails them can be cured. But much of the time their problems are chronic ones, the kind—Sheren says—that a physician can only relieve. If people don't or won't see that, they're going to be unhappy and keep changing doctors. . . .

Nina felt that another crucial ingredient in how individuals adjusted was what they experienced at the very start of their life at the home. There were several critical issues both for new residents and their relatives, including reassurance, roommates, and Frank's old nemesis of denial.

At an "intake," on the day a person actually enters Elmwood, I meet with them and the family, though there is more paperwork than social work to what I do with them just then. On the unit there is a lot to be sorted out: clothing, medicines, possessions, introductions, getting oriented. How much time I spend with people—on the floor or in my office—depends so much on what they need. Some hardly look to me for anything. With others— either the resident or the family—there are a lot of questions, a lot of reassurance they're looking for. . . .

Roommates are a big concern, both at the start and for long afterwards. We have our "marriages made in heaven"—Tilly and Vivian, for example— but those are really quite rare. Much of the time residents basically manage to get along or just ignore one another. In the perfect world, we would try to match up a new admission with people who would be compatible partners: similar interests or temperaments or backgrounds. But who they get largely depends on what bed's available when they enter, unless there's some other opportune switch we can make just then. Otherwise, to make the "perfect" matches, we'd have to be rearranging the home every week, which would only create more problems. Besides, you can't move people around at will because that violates patients' rights. And who knows what is perfect anyway, especially with a new resident who you barely know? But trying to explain that to an anxious, and maybe a guilty, son or daughter is not easy.

If there is one human quality I really underestimated before I came to work here, it was denial. Some families deny the condition of an elderly relative right up to the time that moving them to an institution becomes necessary . . . and some continue to deny it afterwards, pretending that this situation is only temporary. Perhaps they're trying to be kind—to their family member or to themselves—but it gives the resident a false picture, a false hope. So some of those who claim they're going to be leaving here soon are not delusional: they're just saying what they've been led to believe, what others need to hear.

In an age when most social workers have redefined themselves as therapists, Nina still practiced old-fashioned social work. She did problem solving, trouble-shooting, and mediating with the bureaucracy. More often than not, she went to see people rather than waiting for them to come to her. Like the nearly mythic doctors of the past, Nina still made house calls, and saw herself and her role in very practical terms. She resisted the idea, in fact, that she really did counseling. "I drop in on people, I check up on them, we have coffee, we talk. It's not what I would call therapy."

Most days Nina spent some time on each of Elmwood's units, and there were certain individuals she made a point of seeing regularly. These were often new residents like Karl, or people going through a difficult period, or a person such as Eddie to whom she felt particularly attached. She also spoke with family members—fielding their requests, hearing their complaints, supporting those like Patrick Healey through some of their anguish. She spent much of her time—too much, she felt—doing paperwork. Social histories had to be updated, quarterly reports written on each resident, intake interviews recorded, and insurance, Medicaid, and Medicare forms filled out.

If the flood of paper was one of Nina's biggest regrets, it was people's gratitude that gave her the most satisfaction.

I've never worked before with a population so appreciative and polite and respectful to me. My friends sometimes ask me: "How can you be there? How can you spend your days with old people?" My response is I don't have any difficulty with it. To me, one of the things about human services is that oftentimes you're with people who *don't* want your help, who don't want to be working along with you, who aren't particularly cooperative. But the elderly are the one and only population I've ever worked with who are enthusiastic about me. That's one of the biggest rewards I get. To wheel someone down the hall and hear "thank you" or "you look so nice today," whereas I worked with teenagers for years and much of what I got was "fuck you." How can I complain? My career has gone from "fuck you" to "thank you."

While Nina valued the appreciation, the fact that her small acts elicited such gratitude struck her as disproportionate.

For so much to come from so little tells you how little they have. People miss their power, their families, their homes—most of all their homes. It means eighty years of life packed into two boxes, a whole house reduced to half a room. The body declines, the living space shrinks, the witnesses grow fewer. People, it's true, also miss their privacy, but some are even hungrier for the personal—someone who will give them undivided attention, be there just to be with them. Staff try, and we succeed in small ways, but we can't fill the void. And we know it.

The note of realism struck by Nina also echoed from other departments. Kate, Louise's aide, once said:

> Elmwood will never be the kind of real home that most people would want. Even the most sensitive institution is still, in the end, an institution. The only patients who don't seem to mind at least somewhat are those who are so out of touch they have little sense of where, and maybe who, they are.

If the quality of residents' lives was one issue for staff, so was the quality of their own work life. If no institution could please all who lived there, Nina suggested, perhaps no work environment could satisfy everyone employed there. Salaries at Elmwood were low, especially for direct-care staff such as nurse's aides, LPNs, housekeepers, and dietary aides. While most of these people recognized that such pay scales were ubiquitous to the whole health care economy, the realization itself was not much of a comfort or compensation. Administrators and board members acknowledged that nurse's aides were underpaid and often overworked, but they also argued that the local supply and demand for labor, as well as government ceilings on reimbursement, limited what they could pay and how many they could hire.

The most commonly voiced complaints of Elmwood's employees, however, were not related to such external factors as the economy, or contracts, or the statutes of the state. They centered on qualities internal to the daily fabric of work, especially the amount of cooperation between departments, and the nature of supervision and accountability within them. The crux of the matter was usually communication: not so much who said what, but how it was said—a question of style rather than substance. It was the charge nurse who bawled out an aide in front of her colleagues; or the housekeeper who would not watch a resident while a therapist went to get a chart; or the administrator who said things in memos rather than in person.

Nina ended up being privy to more of this than she expected because, without intending to, she had become a confidante to many staff. If not a counselor, she was at least a confessor to them. They came to her partly by default: some were in departments where workers and supervisors gave one another little support, or where the informal code of conduct was simply "not to get personal." There were also, she acknowledged, "cliques and clusters" among staff where people did help one another: these included pairs of relatives, or colleagues who took coffee and lunch breaks together, or friends who were neighbors and shared car rides and child care. But these people also had problems, and there were still many who were left out of the "in" groups. Nina provided them with an outlet not because it was part of her job, but because it was part of her persona, her way of responding to people who expressed their needs. It was what her friend Claire in physical therapy called "an occupational hazard—the disinclination to draw a boundary between those you're supposed to help and those who simply ask for it."

The current of opinion also flowed Nina's way because of her place in the structure. As a relative newcomer in a department of one, she was seen by others as novel, neutral, and unattached. In addition, since she moved throughout much of the building on a normal day, she regularly came into contact with personnel from many different levels. Serendipity brought gossip and grief her way.

Receiving so much in confidence from her colleagues left Nina feeling ambivalent. The trust was flattering; the information itself could be a burden. She had been thinking of starting a support group for staff—and perhaps a second for patients' families—but so far she had lacked the time, and the institutional means, to do either. So she continued to shoulder what she could, along with the poor timing with which it sometimes arrived.

> I sit down to work on the charts upstairs [on one of the units] and the employees will get to talking about their problems. I don't want to say "Don't talk to me now. I need to get this done." It's because I feel that even though these are usually issues I can't do anything about, *they* need to say it. And I'd rather they say it to *me* than get frustrated later on and yell at a resident. The two things that trouble me the most are the paperwork and the frustrations of staff. The real burden of helping people who work here is not the listening, it's knowing that there's little I can do to change what bothers them. I walk off the floor knowing more than I want to.

CLAIRE LANNAHAN, PHYSICAL THERAPIST

"Gearing Down"

In a sense, Nina was a staff social worker who did social work with the staff. She spent her days supporting others, but was able to find one source of support for herself from the same quarter. It came from Claire Lannahan in physical therapy. The two women were close in outlook despite the differences in skill, time, and space that set them apart. Nina dealt with finances and feelings, Claire with bones and muscles. There were almost thirty years in age and ten inches of height between the two, and even their offices were on different floors of the home. Yet the ideas they espoused brought them to a common ground. Both were emphatic about treating what Claire referred to as "the entire person, body and soul." She favored the word "holistic" while Nina was partial to "integral"; but their vocabularies were less important than the underlying convergence of attitude.

Both women felt the pull of their professions, sharing a sense of "calling" in the work they did. They managed to find at least a few moments, most days, to spend together over coffee. Walking down a hallway side by side, they set one another off like notes in counterpoint: Claire at five feet ten inches striding strongly in her long white coat; Nina in blue skirt and jacket, a thick file of papers hugged to the side of her five-foot compact frame. For her friendship and integrity, Nina found Claire to be a "lifesaver." Describing herself, Claire said she was "facilitator" as much as "rehabilitator." Reflecting on the number of younger employees who unburdened themselves to her, she also conceded that—at 58—she was something of a "staff mother." Others, struck by both the affinities of these two and the differences in their stature, their ages, and their jobs, joked about them as "Motion and Emotion."

Claire's background was small town, large family, farmer's daughter—"no jokes," she'd say about the latter, "my sisters and I have heard them all." She trained as a physical therapist at a time when it was largely a male profession, earning with her diploma a history of quiet personal triumphs: an education—in a family that had never stressed learning; and a career—in a field built around the other gender. Having mastered the art of improving the body, she went on to apply her skills in various medical settings for the next three decades. She held positions in Boston, Hartford, and Philadelphia, eventually coming to upstate New York because her husband's career had brought him to the area. The move had cost her a hard-won hospital job, but she gave over, tempering her liberation for the sake of her marriage.

Elmwood Grove was the first skilled nursing facility where Claire had worked full time. Compared to the big-city "rehab unit" where she had most recently been, she said that "coming here required that I start gearing down." She explained that hospitals offered

> a range of treatment modalities, with doctors, technologies, and laboratories all available right there. A nursing home offers fewer services, and despite the fact that there's a discharge plan for each patient, relatively few leave and fewer yet go home. It's a matter of means and ends. The hospitals have the means because they treat people for whom a reasonably normal life back in the community is a realistic goal. But that is rarely the case here.

Gearing down for Claire, then, meant less of an emphasis on curing, more of a stress on "making life bearable and the body more movable."

The thrust of her efforts at Elmwood ran on two levels: one was restoration, the other maintenance. If a resident's spirit was willing despite the weakness of the flesh, Claire tried to restore diminished capabilities. "Ambulation" (i.e., walking) was the most fundamental goal, but improvement in being able to sit up, stand, reach out, dress, eat, and carry things were also significant achievements. Some of the people who came to her had such severe contractures that it could take months to make headway in straightening their limbs. Claire and her assistant Fae worked one-on-one for part of each day with individual patients. They walked people, they massaged, they used whirlpool and ultrasound; they encouraged, joked, cajoled. The physical burdens under which residents labored or lay were various: stroke, arthritis, palsy, amputation, disk problems, osteoporosis. It was a late life catalogue of brittle bones, weak muscles, lost powers, poor nerves.

If Claire and Fae could bring people to the maximum level of functioning they were capable of—the most basic task of their work as they saw it—then they moved residents into "maintenance." That could involve a program of exercise classes, or ongoing therapy to reinforce and sustain recovered skills. Maintenance, however, was neither a plateau nor a condition of permanence. Claire had to face the fact that people's abilities would fluctuate with time, that she helped but did not cure them, and that a condition alleviated today might reappear at a late date.

This is not the kind of practice where you can take someone you've worked with for a long time, go to the front door with them, pat 'em on the back, and send them off smiling to a full life. It doesn't have those Hollywood endings. I'm more likely to go with a woman to the door of my therapy room, and see her walk slowly down a corridor she used to be wheeled through.

There are also people like Frank Healey, who work and work at it but can probably never regain the use of their legs. All he feels is frustration, and it is hard for him to believe that the effort itself is worth it because it keeps up his muscle tone and exercises other parts of his body. The really sad thing is that there are other people who *could* be walking, or using an arm, but who are so dispirited that they don't try, and nothing I've attempted—pep talks, tricks, bribes, pleas—can get them to make the effort. So Frank has his frustrations and I have mine, but I know his are a thousand times worse. I'll have other patients, but he'll probably never walk.

It sounds like small victories and defeats, but believe me there've also been some very dramatic, some very moving moments. Yet they're often so quiet. One of the hardest for me was Alma, maybe because she had a nobility that almost no one got to see, even her own family. She was about 86, with a mind as clear as crystal, and a leg, a right leg, that you could hardly look at without crying. Diabetes was taking it, from the bottom up. She could still use it, real gingerly, and she walked on it each day with the help of an aide. But it was going to develop gangrene, and it was only a matter of time. The doctor told her son, who lived in Iowa, and the son said it was alright to tell her. I was in her room, changing a dressing when the doctor came in. Alma said it was okay for me to stay while they talked. So he told her what was going to happen to her leg, and that they needed to operate, to amputate it.

"And what happens if you don't?" she asked. And I said to myself, because I knew the answer: "This lady looks the beast right in the eyes."

The doctor, who was a no-nonsense type, not crude but just straight with people, said to her. "If we don't take the leg off it will spread"   and he hesitated for just a second . . . "and you'll die from it."

Alma nodded her head. "How long do I have before I have to make up my mind?" she asked.

"What?" he said. He was stalling, trying to grasp whether she really felt she had a choice.

She tried again. "By when do I have to decide about my leg?"

"It's not really a matter of deciding. If it spreads . . . I mean *when* it spreads. . . ."

"Yes, I understand," she interrupted him. And she did. "Come back in a few days, on Friday, and I'll tell you my decision." Then she thanked him and waved her hand, dismissing him from the room.

For those four days, Claire walked around the edge of Alma's small world, alternately feeling like a daughter, a servant, and a spy. She did not know what Alma, or she herself, might do. They were briefly together each morning either for a treatment, or to change the dressing on Alma's leg, but neither woman said anything about the amputation.

I'd find a reason to be near her unit when the aide took her for a walk. Alma seemed as intent and as talkative as ever. I tried to read her face, but there was nothing grim there, just her usual concentration. It was only at the end, when the aide helped her into a chair, that Alma did look more exhausted, but she also had this look of contentment. It was almost beatific, as if inside she was still walking along on her own.

Thursday, when I was changing the bandages on her leg, she did moan in pain—that was something she almost never did. And I couldn't contain myself any more either, so I said to her, "Alma, what are you going to do about this leg? The doctor is coming tomorrow." She sighed and gave me a look which seemed to say, "This was decided a long time ago." Then she told me:

"I've been walking through this life and I'm going to walk out of it. You may not understand or agree, but it's that simple for me. I know what I'm doing. It's not vanity—it's how I want to live. If I can't move about in this world, I won't have any joy being in it. I want to walk for as long as I can, as best as I can. If that means a few more months or a few more weeks, then I'll take it, and I won't regret missing what would have come afterwards. It wouldn't have meant anything to me by then anyway."

She said she was sure, that she'd explained all this to her son, and that he'd abide by her decision. He was going to fly out the next week to see her. And he did come, but what he never saw was what she was like in the days after he left—as if she had achieved a kind of fulfillment, a dignity she thought she was going to lose.

She was more at peace than any of us. Some of the aides, once they found out, were very upset: one of them wanted to know why no one was doing anything to stop her or change her mind. It was hard to explain and Alma didn't help much because she felt that she really didn't owe anyone an explanation. She was right, of course, but that left those of us who did know—Nina and me, for example—in this terribly difficult position of trying to put it in our own words. But since it was coming from us and not Alma, I don't think it was clear or convincing for a lot of the others. Some of them were the same staff who can't stomach DNRs [Do Not Resuscitate orders]—they think patients and families who make them, and doctors who abide by them, are immoral. Reva, who's an aide on another floor, she called what Alma was doing "suicidal," and blamed the administration. But I didn't. I think what Alma had was a life wish, not a death wish.

As Elmwood's physical therapist, Claire had a job description, but she also had an agenda of her own. Beyond helping and healing residents, she felt she could—and should—educate other staff. She believed that good physical therapy not only made life better for patients, but that it also made work easier for personnel. Running her own department in a small institution pleased her because she had the freedom to put that belief into practice. So she did in-service training to show aides how to move, transport, and handle residents; and she urged employees to recognize that the more capable an individual was, and the more positive that patient's outlook, then the more cooperative such a person's relationships with caregivers would be. A resident who could transfer herself from a bed to a chair made fewer demands on the staff. A man who could dress or wash himself was likely to have better morale and fewer complaints because he felt more in control. Claire knew that she and Fae "could not do it all" with exercise classes or individual therapy sessions. Residents needed follow-up—that is, nurses and aides who would then encourage them to take more care of themselves by walking or propelling their wheelchairs, reaching and carrying, dressing and brushing.

Three decades of experience had convinced Claire that what limited the body was not just age but motivation. And what tempered motivation were the limitations of hope and example. She had trouble getting floor staff to work on range-of-motion exercises with residents: they often forgot or found themselves too busy with other tasks. Furthermore, she argued, patients at Elmwood lacked reinforcement because they were surrounded by peers who occasionally improved but who usually, eventually, declined.

In another facility I worked at there was both a health-related and a skilled nursing unit. The people with deep disabilities there, those getting skilled care, could see that there was another place for them to be if they could get better. They knew of residents who had recovered enough mobility to move downstairs to a lower level of care. But here—though it's no one's fault—there's no immediate model, no better level to aspire to, and so I feel there's less motivation than there might be.

Too many people get invested in the "role" of being sick—like Eva becoming incontinent so she could move back in here from Hillview. Nina calls it "disability as identity." It's a hard one to overcome. What we really need is a rethinking of the whole idea of the nursing home so that people will have some goals, something to strive for, some larger reward than just surviving. We helped Tilly to find it. I think Alma had it too . . . though in her case it probably came from inside her, not from anything we gave her.

The prophetic effect of appearance on reality was also part of Claire's gearing down—for if residents had few chances to see healthier models, she had few opportunities to see the results of her work translated into revised, revived forms of living. The rewards were smaller—smiles, thanks, steps, a good laugh, a wider reach, a better posture, less pain—and Claire enhanced these with the leaven of her own faith. The small shelf behind her desk boasted a dozen books of inspiration: religion, pop psych, self-help, how-to. She bought paperbacks avidly but read with discrimination, trying to grasp the most practical of what others preached. When filtered through her mind, their ideas made for a new brew of moral uplift and down-home folk wisdom. She sometimes hugged the people she helped and felt, in that act, a genuine giving and getting of grace. In a field where the laying on of hands was the central act, she was touched by those she held. She testified to, and bolstered her sense of mission with, well-considered rhetoric.

> I think of someone like Alma a lot, but what I remember is not just the pain, or her strength for it, but how she was in that moment of knowing herself. I like to think that I could be that way, that I could see myself in her, in my own age. We are all dying. In the meantime, the only issue is who of us are really going to live?

Though the question was rhetorical, Claire also gave an answer in the way she spoke about her profession. When she supervised PT students, she would admonish them about the ethics of their work, not just its techniques: she stressed the need to respect people's values as well as their bodies. She cut away both the glamor and the gore in front of their eyes. Indirectly, through speaking to them, she addressed herself as well. "We are treating people, not diseases," she once admonished a new group of interns.

> Physical therapy is a very involved field, very gritty, nothing pretty about it, nothing fancy. Cute little white uniforms don't count. They're usually plastered with antiseptic anyway. You can do a lot for people *if* you don't let your ego get in the way. But remember, if doing it doesn't also do something for you, you'll have nothing left to give to anyone else.

LOUISE SANTORINI, NURSE

The Fingerling

Louise Santorini gave until she almost gave out. Then she gave a little more. And then she quit. After working as a nurse at Elmwood Grove for ten years, it was a long good-bye. When I visited her a few weeks later and asked why she had resigned, Louise—who usually wielded language with surgical precision—had trouble finding the words to explain. She finally left the kitchen we were sitting in and came back a moment later with a large photograph of fingerlings, a swarming school of young salmon swimming in a stream. They were packed together like the silvery strands of a wire cable. Louise put her finger on one fish in the middle of the mass and said: "*That* is what it felt like. On the inside, I mean, not the outside. Too many people asking for too many things. Me and my stomach feeling like we were at the center of it all. I kept it together, understand. I'm a good nurse, and my people were well cared for. But after a decade I knew I had to get out."

At Elmwood it would have been almost impossible to detect the turmoil beneath Louise's skin. In the home her work space was a model of organization: an uncluttered desk with rows of patient charts; cups of medicine lined up for distribution; a schedule of baths, therapies, and treatments for the fourteen residents on the unit she supervised. Her uniform was crisp, her manner controlled. But at her own home, Louise's living space turned her insides out: it was a warm, family mélange of laundry baskets, tea bags, brick-and-board bookshelves, teenage tape decks, and cat food. Here the fingerlings moved apart, the school of demands scattered in the stream.

But in the nursing home, Louise's role as a charge nurse put her at a point of convergence, a place of concentration. She described herself as

> the "pivotal person." It means you got it from the top, you got it from the bottom, you got it from the patient, and you got it from the family. The information, not just the people, flowed to where you were, especially if anything was wrong. Or if something changed in a resident's situation. Say someone develops a UTI [urinary tract infection]. You would have to alert the PT people, and inform the staff in dietary, and all the other departments. I mean if there was anything that had to be done differently, you were the one that took charge of the change. I'm very relaxed on the outside normally, but sometimes there were days on the inside where I felt like the salmon, like I was going in all those directions with everyone else rubbing against me.

"What you can't lose sight of," Louise once warned, "is the task of a nurse in this kind of institution." Using terms reminiscent of Claire's, she said:

> You have to treat the complete person. You're the family that they don't see, the words they may not hear. It's easy to get absorbed by the vocabulary of what we do—IVs [intravenous procedures], intubation, decubitus sores—and then you lose touch with the basic language of caring. You could end up like a nurse I once talked to from another unit, who felt she just "tubed people in and tubed 'em out." To be compassionate is not simply to pay lip service

sympathy to someone else's pain. Being a nurse, and a Catholic—even a lapsed one like me—I know what "compassion" means: it's to share, to be *with* another person's suffering. What scared me the most was not someone dying— that happens all the time. No, it was forgetting why I was there, waking up some moment to realize that when they died, I really wasn't there for them.

For a person whose profession was caring for other people, Louise made one disarming confession about the limits of her own capacity to give: she would never want to be responsible for a member of her own family. The problem, in her view, was not that the stakes would be too high; it was that familiar expectations, the ways she and her relatives usually related, would crowd out the possibilities of proper treatment. "It happened with my own mother after gall bladder surgery—she came home to recover and drove me and my aunt crazy. I had to hire someone to care for her, and *I'm* a nurse!"

Indirectly, Louise was acknowledging the dilemma of other individuals who put family members that they might have care for in a nursing home. Their dilemma, and hers, made her job necessary. In her own case, faced with a frail relative, she felt she would get too caught up in being a daughter or niece or granddaughter to be an effective nurse. As her mother's illness showed, family history and the reversal of roles would stand in the way. "You can't be acting out twenty years of love and irritation with someone while adjusting that person's catheter."

This kind of incompatability hit home for her in the very first year of her training. "I'll never forget this," she began.

> I was a student on a postoperative ward of a hospital near Elmira, and my supervisor put me in charge of the first elderly person I'd ever cared for. The curtains were still drawn around the bed while this nurse told me about the procedures I'd need to do. Then she pulled the sheet aside and I looked down at this small, white-haired woman, and I gasped. It was my kindergarten teacher! "Oh God," I said to myself. I didn't even think she was still alive. I never felt so embarrassed as I did those next three days. This woman used to wipe my nose, and here I was changing her bedpan.

Of all the students Louise graduated with, she was the only one who chose to take her first full-time job in a home rather than a hospital. Two feelings dictated this other direction for her. One was the draw she had long felt to old people, an enchantment she traced to her own grandmother. "She was a tough, talkative woman. When she was young she lived through the West Virginia coalfields, and later, in her sixties, she stood up to the mining companies when they tried to bulldoze her house. She held her own sit-in, and they backed down. Granny and her friends were the best storytellers I ever met. Every old person isn't like that, of course, but if you're ready to meet them, they're out there."

Louise's second reason for choosing a nursing home was the fulfillment of caring for patients for the long term. "I found that two or three or six days of a hospital stay cut off relationships just as they were beginning. It didn't take long for me to realize that I liked to get involved and know my patients as people, even though that made it hard when they died because you *do* get involved... and some *will* die." At the hospital where she trained, there was a long-term geriatric unit where she worked one summer as part of a rotation. In her senior year she had to pick a ward to go back to for specialization, and she chose geriatrics for another three months. "I did it, just as I do this job, because I like old people. I *really* do. To live that long you have to be feisty, and because they've seen so many changes, you can learn a lot from them. One other thing that's so great about them is their directness. They know what they want and they'll tell you straight out. They don't have words to waste or time to wait."

Though the medical needs of her Elmwood patients were considerable, experience had taught Louise that often it was the little things that mattered even more to them. "Some residents were readers, not TV watchers," she noted, "and now they can't do much of that."

> One woman, Laura, had a talking book machine, but people would pass her room and forget to turn it on. Small acts like that can mean a lot, like picking out your own clothes—even if it's the aide who dresses you. That's the kind of daily thing, the everyday freedom, we take for granted. Being able to choose your own place at the dining room table becomes very important to some residents here. Meals themselves—the getting down to the dining room, the food, the ritual—all that takes several hours a day when you add up breakfast, lunch, and dinner. No other activity in a nursing home takes up so much of people's lives. So where you sit and who you're next to are almost as important as what gets put on your plate.
>
> What doesn't get said also has to be heard. There was one man, George Mannis, who couldn't speak, yet he moved around pretty well with a walker. But if someone slower got in front of him in the hall, he'd get furious. For that moment, it became the last straw: he'd push the person aside, sometimes almost knocking them down. With George it basically boiled down to the fact: "I can't express myself, but you'd better understand what I'm saying anyway."

The little things got to residents, Louise felt, because these were all they had left: the tone of a greeting, the type of bread, the place for the call bell. What seemed picky was really powerless individuals trying to practice the art of assertion. But it was hard for caregivers to be tolerant of the demands and the details all the time, she confessed, especially with so many people needing so much of their attention. "What I have to struggle to remember," said her aide Kate, "is that even on a bad day I get to go home to a real home when work is over. They don't. This place is *it* for them—their last home. They have a right, or at least a reason, to be angry and fussy."

The floor that Louise was in charge of had 14 patients. It was small, the way she felt such a unit should be, and as part of caring for its people, she supervised another nurse and two aides. With this staff Louise was responsible for administering residents' medication; seeing that they had baths, changes of dressing, massages, and other forms of treatment; and monitoring their diets and basic medical condition. Her workday had some of the orderliness of a well-planned meal. There was a sequence of tasks and events, a rhythm of responsibilities, and a structure to who and what got served. Where meals have an etiquette, nursing had protocols. And despite their obvious differences, nursing and feeding were both designed to nourish—a word, Louise reminded me, which had its Latin root in *nutrire*, from which the verb "to nurse" derived.[1]

While nurturing people was Louise's primary task, there were also dues to pay to the bureaucracy. So much record keeping was required, she felt, that the state "regs" often threatened "to replace patient work with paperwork." Acknowledging that records were necessary for good management and good nursing, she still argued the bureaucracy got absurd. "If you didn't chart it, you didn't do it. Now that's crazy from a caregiving point of view, but the records take on a life, a reality of their own. Fiction can replace truth if something invented gets written down, or if something real gets omitted." Her real concern, however, was not with some unlikely fiction, but with the time and talent being wasted filling out forms. She suggested that a well-trained secretary could do most of the paper work that ate up her day. So what would she have done had she been freed from that task? Her answer was that it would enable her

> to give patients the time to explain their real needs. You can't walk in and give somebody a medicine, spend three or four minutes with them, and expect them to tell you all their problems. And I think that finding out what patients want and feel is the hardest part of my job. Without that, I get reduced to a technician, and competency can't take the place of compassion.

One of Louise's compromises was to take her piles of record keeping to where her neediest patients were and work beside them. When I joined her one morning while she was still employed at Elmwood, she pointed to a stack of charts at her station: "When I have a glut of paperwork like this I sometimes take it down to their room and sit with them just so they know I'm there. It's a lot different to have someone sit with you when you're sick than to have them up the hall. The patient may know you're up there, but they also know you're busy and think you may not want to be bothered. But it's really not an imposition if they need to talk and you're right there in the room with them, writing. The act of being there is a way of saying it's okay to speak."

What was not strictly part of Louise's job, then, was the way in which she chose to carry out its formal responsibilities. Her manner of working and relating created other roles for her too. One of these, reminiscent of both Claire and Nina's experience, was that of confidante. "Maybe I still see things through Catholic eyes, but I feel like a 'mother confessor' to certain residents. Sometimes I'm the first person they see in the morning. Maybe the last one to see them before they die." The dying itself was sadly misunderstood in her eyes.

> Death is a taboo subject. It's where sex used to be, but now they've changed places. We have sex all around us, but we avoid old people because they remind us of death.
>
> You may see someone die on television or in the movies, but that's in a different context. I mean you never really see death [there] like it truly is. You get the picture of it usually as a violent ending. Most people don't die that way. It's a very quiet finish to life. There are residents here who starve themselves to death. They don't want to go on the way they are, and this is how they've decided to do it. I feel you've got to respect that. But however it happens, they do want somebody there, and I've always thought that that was very important. If a resident was dying, the most important thing was to just have somebody be near them. You don't even have to say anything. You can just sit there. Try and make them as comfortable as possible. Try to take care of their last wishes if you know what they are. . . . And notify the family before they die. This may be their final chance to see this person alive. You're not sparing them anything if you let that moment pass. I think it's important because it's easier for someone to mourn after they've had that experience.

The Janus-like face of her profession—angel of mercy *and* angel of death—did not trouble Louise, who saw each side of the mask as part of one outlook. The DNR orders were, for her, a means to bring the two halves together in "merciful death." She knew, however, that dying—like the DNRs themselves—evoked a range of emotions in her colleagues. Some wanted no steps spared to preserve life and were not amused by the disaffected daughter who responded to the news of her elderly mother's head cold by joking, "Please, no extraordinary measures in her case." But there was dark humor among the nurses and aides as well, some of whom called patients with multiple, major disorders "train wrecks." Staff from various departments had strong opinions about death. For Louise, who handled people's bodies every day, "deterioration was worse than death." To Denise, the choice was for "death over disability."

Of all the people Louise dealt with—patients, administrators, aides, other nurses, and volunteers—the families of residents were the most poignant and perplexing. This was because their feelings were often the most intense and confused. While she tried to be honest with patients, Louise sometimes ended up lying to their relatives.

Families come in, saying we hope Auntie or Granny will get better. And you know you're gritting your teeth when you say, "Yes, she does look a little improved today." I remember doing that with the son of Celia, one of Laura's roommates, who had terrible edema and a recent heart attack and was barely hanging on. To the staff, the fact that she was dying was an open secret. But sometimes you lie just a little to make people feel better because so many of them are so guilty for placing Mother here.

Maybe, however, the false assurances were not all made just for the families. "I'm not sure how much we lie to the relatives to make ourselves feel better for working in a nursing home. You know if you've been around it a long time there's a point you reach where you ask: What do I do to make peace with myself?" Louise's guess was that offering false hope was one concession to her own and other people's frailty, to the staff's need "not to always be the bearers of bad tidings."

The issue of honesty became infinitely more anguishing when nurses dealt directly with residents. How much should they be told? How much do they want to know? And what is to be done when the resident and the family ask for opposite things? Louise felt that elderly patients resented it when secrets were kept from them. "I think they want you to be straight-forward. But there are a lot of families that don't want that kind of candor. 'Don't tell Dad that he has . . . ' and they can barely get themselves to say 'cancer.' But Dad may *want* to know because he needs the time to put things in order. You realize at some point that even if you keep telling him he's alright, one day the light in his brain is going to turn on and say 'No, I'm not okay.' "

And then what?

If he would ask me I'd have to tell him the truth. Sometimes residents don't say it directly, but you know they want to know. In that case I may not come out with it in words, but I would let the person know by signals or body language. They understand. And like with Alzheimer's patients, words don't have to say it all. But tell them *somehow* because it's only fair. I would want to know if I were really ill so I could get my affairs and effects in order. I think it's important for people to have that option, to be able to make that decision. It's respectful to give them the choice . . . if they want it.

Of course, a lot of people *don't* want it, just like a lot of people avoid making wills and things. I know because I've been trying for the last five years to talk my parents into writing a will, and I haven't been successful. Some people think that a will is another end. "If I write it down, oh Lord, I may be letting myself in for a disaster." But I think it's just one of those acts of preparing, taking a step. People should be given the time. Making a will doesn't mean you're going to die next week or next year. And letting someone who is dying know that fact doesn't hasten anything. It only gives them the time that belongs to them.

Time framed two other figures in Louise's world of work. One was the presence of history that the residents themselves embodied. "On any given day you can look at a corridor or lounge, and if seven or eight people are sitting there, then six hundred years of living are present.

You can still learn from the old even if they're in a wheelchair. But you have to look beyond the chair, which a lot of people can't . . . as if the steel was a sign that said "Do Not Disturb."

What have I learned? Patience. Humor. Survival. That things change and a lot of people don't. . . .

We were odd ducks in our family in that we always read books, especially history. But besides an author's viewpoint, I wanted to learn what the past was like from those who lived it, and the only way I could do that was to talk to people who were older than I was.

Different kinds of things come out when you take the time to sit down with somebody. Most of the residents really want someone to listen. They don't want to be forgotten. You may not have done anything important in your life but you want to be remembered somehow. Karl, for example, lived his whole life on a farm, and someone else owns it now who probably doesn't even know Karl's name. But when Karl talks about his farm and his animals, his horse, his whole face lights up. He doesn't do it often, but when he does he becomes a different person. And a lot of the patients here seem to be the last in their family line: they've outlived their friends, they've outlived their kin. Who is there to hear them? . . . The people who are ninety years old have gone through an incredible period of time. They've seen planes fly, which was once thought impossible. They've been through radio, they've lived through television. They've seen a man land on the moon. I mean who thought in 1895 that any of this would happen?

The art of listening was, for Louise, its own reward; the act of telling was, in turn, the way residents changed experience into identity. So she felt it was important to respect not only people's sense of propriety, but also their sense of time. "These people do not need to be rescued from the past: the past preserves them in the present. Karl's farm, Bonnie's classroom, Eddie's songs, the women Frank has loved. . . . I think sometimes they have to talk to their history to relate to what is around them."

If the past was the shape of the present for many residents, if this was one of the time-framed figures inhabiting Louise's world, then a second was the "time-out of time" that she felt caregivers needed to escape to. She argued that staff and family required a "time-out" from their tasks—a place, a moment's permission, to talk or cry or rage about what it meant to be responsible for the elderly, whether their particular charge happened to be moral or legal, financial or physical. Louise took that time on her own time. After a terrible day at work, she would go home and march over to a special bookcase where she kept some "deranged, disposable paperbacks." Where Claire turned behind her to volumes of inspiration, Louise would heave her throw-away books at a wall, unburdening herself with an outburst of energy.

At Elmwood itself, however, the relief from feelings was not that simple to arrange. Louise spoke of a quartet of primary emotions that embraced both staff and relatives: these were anger, guilt, grief, and the affront of being abused. When one of these overwhelmed employees, she said, people either failed to do their jobs, or they passed the buck. "Something goes awry and the person says: 'I wasn't there.' " And, to Louise, "a lot of that is true: they *aren't* there if they're upset—either because they're literally absent or just psychologically off in a different place." But she felt that instead of having people drop out of sight or lose concentration, "there should be a room where they can say 'Time out! I can't take any more of this. The pressure is just too much. I need to get away, at least for a few minutes.' " She explained this sense of urgency by describing one of the most troubling experiences that caregivers have.

> Residents curse or hit and strike out at staff sometimes. An incident like that happens almost on a weekly basis. When it does you need to get by yourself for a while and just recover your cool. But no facility I've ever worked at had something like that—a place where you could calm down. When you get hit—well, you know you wouldn't take it from someone out on the street, so why should you take it at work? If it happened on the outside you could do something: you'd call the police, or struggle with the person, or run away. But you have to take it here because there's such a thing as patients' rights. So when you can't strike back or run off, how do you keep your sanity, your self-respect?

When one of Louise's nurses or aides got hit, she let the woman escape to the bathroom. It was not that private a place, but at least for a few moments it offered some refuge. A far better option, she felt, would have been "a support or a counseling group for staff, a set time where they could say, 'I really feel pissed today,' or 'He made me so angry,' or 'I was upset because no one came to help.' "

> It wouldn't even have to be once a week, just so long as they knew there'd be some chance to blow off steam. A lot of rumors and bad talk begin around here because nobody has a place to put their anger. You build up your adrenalin and you don't know what to do with it . . . or with your sadness. If one of your patients, someone you've been attached to, if they die, you need a space to retreat to, a place to go to cry. But where is there?

Though death was democratic in its equal claim on everyone, its toll was uneven for staff because some of the residents it took occupied a much larger emotional ground for them than others. To Louise, for example, the death of Wesley Cardeen was one of the most devastating I think I experienced at Elmwood. It was not because he died horribly... he didn't. He didn't even die here at the home, but in the hospital a few days after they moved him there. And he wasn't that old—68 at the time—but he had developed multiple sclerosis in his fifties and had been living at Elmwood for 17 years. I remember when he died they got upset with me because the administrators wanted to move another patient right into his room and I... well, the rest of the staff were very close to Wesley. And I said, "I can't do this." I told Mr. Morrell, "I have to give them time to mourn. I cannot ask them to move this new person in. We'll do it tomorrow, but we cannot do this today."

You know I felt that staff really needed that time because for some it was like losing a family member. If you've taken care of a resident for that long, and a number of caregivers had because they'd been here 13, 14 years when this happened... I mean, you need a bit of space just to realize that someone's died, to let it settle in. And though Wesley did pass away at the hospital, he'd been here up until a few days before that. We'd kept his room for him because we expected him back. But now that the girls knew he was never going to return, they had an awful hard time packing his belongings, his clothing and things. They were crying in his room and here in my office. So you've got to give them some respect.

Yeah, I got in trouble for that one.

For Louise, the most trying parts of nursing the old were not explicit in her contract or job description. They were the deaths, the affronts, the need to be at the center of things—the aspects that put caregivers themselves at emotional risk. "There is a lot of burnout and stress," she emphasized, "a good deal of turnover."

I think nurses, like teachers, should really have sabbaticals where they could take off time and just go somewhere. For education. Or for a rest. You need to get away from all this for a while.... It's a hard job and people don't know the amount of work, not just paperwork, that it demands. You carry a lot around in your mind and on your mind. Most nurses don't simply sit at their desks and write things. If residents were only charts and notes and medicines, then all you'd be aware of is what you put into or took out of their bodies. Then you've reduced them—and yourself—to being a machine. If you looked at my med sheets you'd see we don't "snow" [oversedate] people here: we rarely use drugs to control patients... which means that staff have to be even *more* attentive to people.

I'm not claiming every nurse is good, but good nurses are more than technicians. They're out on the floor, talking to patients, trying to understand their whole situation. Because you don't know your patients unless you spend time with them. And if you don't know them, you can't care for them the way you should.

Louise had seen family members, including the most conscientious and best intentioned, experience some of the same kinds of stress and abuse that staff went through. She spoke about Eva's brother William, who had begun to visit his sister at Elmwood long before the tenure of her senility set in, when she had first been on South Two with Louise. William was invariably solicitous and gentle, but everything he did for Eva became the subject of her next reproach. Louise remembered how "she'd ask him: 'Why haven't you come to see me before this?' 'Why did you do this?' or 'Why didn't you do that?' He would send her flowers. 'I don't like that sort of flower' or 'Stop sending me flowers–I don't need them.' " So William would come to Louise or one of the aides, looking for reassurance. "Are all my judgments really that bad?" he'd ask.

What William got from Louise was the same observation she offered to new employees, the realization that

> residents may be angry, and it may come out *at* you, but they're not necessarily angry *with* you. If they've had a stroke, they may be outraged at the uselessness of their arm. Or it may be the loss of their home. Or the death of their loved one. The people who have promised to come see them have not shown up, so they get irritated. And maybe it's not fair to be angry with *you*, but you were the person who walked into the room right after that, and so you got it. The target matters less to them than taking a shot at someone . . . anyone.

Like relatives, staff also needed to absorb anger, or at least try to, even when they had not earned it. For the money they did earn, that burden was sometimes too high. A few occasionally lost control, paying back patients with some of the same behavior they had received. In Louise's case, however, the stress that drove her from her job was neither the abuse nor the money. It was being what she called the "pivot person"—caring for the patients, supporting the families, being accountable to the administrators above, and responsible for the staff below. This was what burned her out, or at least what made her take her own "time out." Over tea in her kitchen she said she knew she would be back nursing some day: it was her livelihood and her passion. And she would probably look for a job with the elderly. But since her profession did not grant sabbaticals, she had decided to sacrifice and create one for herself. She felt it was the nurturing thing to do.

GORDON MORRELL, ADMINISTRATOR

An Argument with Society

An assistant director at Elmwood Grove, Gordon Morrell was disturbed by the direction of medical care in the United States. His was a general dismay, quite distinct from the particulars of his own facility. He took his responsibilities and his residents seriously, noted the quality of patient care with pride, but felt—as did others on his staff—that insitutionalization was often an unsatisfactory, expensive alternative to other kinds of support. It was unfortunate, he argued, that private and government health insurance rarely covered the costs of treatment at home, for this forced the frail and chronically ill elderly to move into nursing facilities.

He was emphatic, however, that his personal feelings did not get in the way of his professional role. "That's because," he explained, "my argument is with society, and not with this institution." He smiled when he said this because it was a safe quarrel and he acknowledged his limits to pursue it. He knew he made policy only at Elmwood Grove, not at the national level. To be even more precise, his job was to implement the policies agreed on by his board of directors.

But national policy and state politics did affect what Gordon could do, as well as what he and his board had to worry about. Finances were an endless problem, the kind of thing that kept him "company at night" when he "was up with a backache or indigestion." Most of the home's residents were Medicaid patients, and the facility "was losing money on them every day." In the mid–1980s, for example, Medicaid payments were about $25 less per patient per day than what it cost to maintain these people at Elmwood. Gordon's account of his money difficulties was served up alongside the alphabet soup vocabulary of health care: he and his director not only had to pay strict attention to SSI (Supplemental Security Income), Medicare, and Medicaid laws, but also to the impact of DRGs, RUGs, and the CMI, which governed federal and state levels of compensation for acute and long-term care. On occasion, he noted, New York State had retroactively lowered the payment rate for some of the RUGs categories into which patients were put. "In effect," Gordon complained, "since they reimburse us only six to eight months *after* we've treated someone, they wanted money back that we'd already spent. And since 72 percent of my operating costs are staff salaries, what was I supposed to do? Ask people to give me back their pay?"

The dilemma hit home on the board too, for its members were the ones who were legally responsible for the major debts that the facility incurred. One member said "being 'not-for-profit' doesn't mean we can afford to be 'for-loss'." A local businessman, he pointed out that the home had operated in the black until the early 1980s. Then the costs of care, the start of union wages for most staff, and the inadequacies of Medicare and Medicaid payments caught up with the institution's budget. "We've been running red ever since," said Gordon. Elmwood's endowment had so far covered the deficit each year, but much of that financial cushion had now been worn away. In the near future, he predicted, the home would have to undertake a major fund-raising program just to cover its operating expenses.

Elmwood ran with a work force of 120 individuals, and Gordon's assessment of his staff was a mixture of respect, candor, and criticism. "The patients we have to deal with now are much frailer than in the past, both because they're older, and because, with the DRGs, hospitals won't keep them that long. . . . So we get them sicker, quicker, and for longer. Which means fewer discharges for us . . . which in turn frustrates the older staff, who dealt with more hopeful cases in the old days.

"Most of the day-to-day issues we face are practical ones in the literal sense of how can we best practice what we are obligated to do. The residents here deserve our care, our concern, our love. And," he felt, "they get those from us." There were caregivers, indeed, who gave what Gordon, Denise, and other administrators admitted they themselves could not provide. "I could not be a nurse's aide for all the tea in China," confessed Gordon. "I could not work up to my elbows in excrement, even for my salary . . . let alone theirs. I admire them for that capacity to deal with people in such a raw, unprotected way."

What Gordon could not claim to envy was the pay that aides and housekeepers received. He and most administrators agreed that the home's preponderance of female staff was largely due to the twin facts that most men could not afford, and would not be willing, to do this type of work. The low salaries, the periodic indignities, the kinds of nurturing required, were not what males were prepared to endure. "Men who have the same lack of training as my employees here could go out and make a living with their muscles—and earn two to three times as much," Gordon observed. "There's a pride factor for them in not doing this type of work. Those men who can take it on are unusual and," he wistfully added, "they're blessed."

While most staff were conscientious about their work, Gordon knew that they were sometimes harried and occasionally abrupt with residents. But outright abuse or neglect were rare, he contended: people were encouraged to report it and, from time to time, employees were fired if they behaved improperly. "We once hired a 19-year-old," he recounted, "the niece of an older woman who had already been working here for seven years."

Wanda—the niece—she seemed bright and personable, and a family tie like that's usually been like a reference, a good clue to people's character. So Wanda went through the usual training and orientation, and then she apprenticed with one of the more experienced aides for a few weeks before we put her on her own.

She picked up things quickly and was very reliable. But that first month her supervisor had to speak with her about the way she was talking to residents: she was sharp with them, not really abusive, understand, but dictatorial some of the time, ordering them around. Then she was heard shouting at some of her people, and the charge nurse asked her aunt to speak to her about that. Everything was quiet again for a while, but then she lost it. One of the aides was helping her move a woman—I think they were changing June's bed— and this other aide had to leave the room for a minute, and when she came back in she saw Wanda wrestling with June to get her to stay in the corner, and she saw Wanda slap her.

This other aide didn't directly report this, but she did talk to other people, and by the end of the day word had gotten to the supervisor.

We fired her.

Now, she wasn't a mean person, and she was actually pretty skillful at what she did, but she didn't have the kind of control you need to work with some of the people we have here. There are those who are no problem at all—they're a pleasure to be with, and help and care for, they're grateful—but others are difficult, a real trial, and you need a degree of restraint in order not to be provoked. Wanda did not have it. And luckily we discovered it pretty quickly. I admit that information like this doesn't always come through the normal channels, but Elmwood's still small enough for something of this sort to get around. Gossip may be bad, but it has its uses when bad things happen. And in a case like Wanda's, I think she'll be happier working somewhere else, because you can't be at peace with yourself when people get to you that way.

Acknowledging that abuse was real if rare, Gordon also felt it was sometimes invented. He said, "There are staff who overreact to one another, seeing things that didn't happen in the way they thought they did. We've even had one or two disgruntled employees who've reported things to the state out of vengeance."

Gordon got just as exercised about the reverse situation, the abuse that some residents inflicted on caregivers. This was, in his view, the hidden side of nursing home life—the dimension that families, the media, and the muckrakers missed. It was, for example, one of the leading causes of lost staff time. Such work-related injuries as back problems often developed when a patient stopped assisting during a transfer by suddenly dropping all her weight. Resistance then turned passivity into a source of real pain for the aides. But the abusiveness of residents could take more aggressive forms as well. The scratches, the bites, the pinches, and the objects and verbal insults that got hurled at staff also took their toll on work time and morale. These were the experiences that drove employees to drop out of sight, or take a day off, or—as Louise put it—"to not be there in spirit even if they're there in the flesh." Gordon felt that just as caregivers needed to be informed about patients' rights, they also had to be aware of their own rights and how to protect themselves. His opinion was that "outrageous behavior is tolerable if someone is truly out of their mind and they don't know what they're doing."

Then workers learn to duck. But if you're a person who is capable of acting like a human being, then you're going to do it, by God, or else the staff will be directed not to go near you. I know how angry people can get, and I also understand the reasons for it. But there still has to be some spirit of reciprocity and respect here. The fact that you live, or work, in an institution does not suspend the code of decency.

When Gordon came to Elmwood Grove at the age of 43, his own code of values had been shaped by several waves of desire and experience. An engineering student in college, he had gone on to graduate work in psychology and management, but still harbored—mostly in private—the wish to divest his life of all its details and "drown in philosophy." Some day, somehow, he wanted to dissect people's ethics, not their pocketbooks, to give up medicine for morality, and trade the body for the soul.

He had worked as a medical administrator in other, larger institutions—mostly in planning and development—and was no stranger to the informal structures that lay behind the formal organization of any facility. Beyond the division of Elmwood's work force into departments—nursing, activities, dietary, and so forth—he knew there were other distinctions that set people apart from and occasionally against one another. Some were based on legalities, some on loyalties, still others on background. His view was that administrative staff tried—with uncertain success—to be sensitive to the class differences that separated them from most caregivers. Many of the latter were relatively poor people, including both married and single parents working at minimum wage: their chances for advancement were as slim as their salaries; and the motivation of some was modest. But, he quickly added, it was also at this level of staff that one found the employees who had worked dedicatedly at the facility for over a decade, the personnel who took particular pride in Elmwood's reputation. These were the staff, in fact, who were still likely to be at the institution long after he, and most administrators and specialists, had moved on to other positions. The home's sense of self was derived as much from them as from its corporate identity.

Another organizational distinction was legal in form. LPNs, nurse's aides, housekeeping staff, and dietary aides were all represented by a union, whereas RNs, consultants, therapists, department heads, and other administrators were not. This heightened the feeling of separateness laid down by differences of class, education, salary, and title. During contract negotiations, this sense of distance between union and nonunion people became more pronounced, even though most employees had no role in the negotiations themselves. The latter were the prime responsibility of the director, the board, and union representatives. As one of the facility's chief officers, Gordon would have preferred not to be dealing with a union at all, but confessed he found the one at Elmwood to be generally cooperative and understanding. When it came to imposing standards and monitoring people's performance, in fact, he felt that union officers were often more demanding of employees than he was, which he saw as an expression of their pride in the work place.

The staff divisions that most troubled Gordon were the ones he thought people had created among themselves: the cliques and factions, the alliances and antipathies. They fed, in his view, on rumor, backbiting, and petty gripes, and found expression in techniques of provocation—a favorite one being to withhold information so that others would flounder or make mistakes. "The functional level for some employees here is: 'Don't tell them what they need to know; but as soon as they blunder, get 'em.' Last month," he illustrated, "there was a situation where a nurse knew that a patient's diet had been changed, but she apparently failed to tell the kitchen. So when the meals came up during the next shift, the resident was upset, dietary got criticized, and the floor staff got hassled. Eventually it ended up in my lap, with everyone blaming someone else."

Part of what undermined cohesion, from Gordon's perspective, was that the various shifts—the 7:00 A.M. to 3:00 P.M. "mornings," the 3:00 P.M. to 11:00 P.M. "noons," and the 11:00 P.M. to 7:00 A.M. "nights"—were "a different world, each with a mentality of its own." The pace of the work and the routines of each group differed: some staff felt that those who labored at other times got off more easily than they did; or that others left their problems for the next shift to deal with. Right or wrong, the perceptions fostered resentment. Though Gordon thought the level of mistrust at Elmwood was better than it used to be, his feeling was that "the fallout still falls on me." At the end of one of his more exasperating afternoons he proclaimed: "There are 17,000 reasons a day to commit murder around here. But I only commit it about three times a year. It's a long fuse."

When it came to issues of war and peace among personnel, Gordon did not perceive Elmwood to be any more divided than comparable institutions he had been at. He felt that the degree of conflict or togetherness in any facility depended mainly on the mix of personalities in the home at a given time. He knew that some of the administrators he worked with, not just the caregivers, were likely to engage in character assassination as an occupational sport. After Elmwood's financial worries, he considered the games people played there to be the second biggest stress of his job. But he admitted that he was probably more sensitive to this than he had been in his previous positions, and attributed this to Elmwood's small size. Larger institutions insulated top administrators from what was happening out on the units. Here, however, he noted that his office was a stone's throw from South Wing, a nursing station, and the dining room, which put him along one of the main pathways used by visitors, residents, and staff. People, gossip, and crises all found their way to him "too easily," and there were few intervening layers of bureaucracy to filter the flow. "Short of building a private entrance for yourself," he decided, "you couldn't cut yourself off from it even if you wanted to."

Gordon felt he got along fairly well with personnel, and rated himself a "B+" as an administrator. Some of those who worked at the home were afraid of him, others—in his judgment—were overly familiar.

Overall I think they see me as fair. I see myself as humanitarian, which is sometimes a handicap in running a place like this. It's hard to find the time or the will to evaluate staff and give them the feedback they need. Some think of me as unapproachable, and information doesn't always get to, or from, me in the way it should. Whenever people judge how I handled a situation, there are always layers of interpretation. . . .

He faulted himself for not having sufficient meetings with staff, for not coming in enough on evening shifts, for not sitting down and talking with employees as often as he should. He felt he put in long hours, but that too many of them went into budgets, battles, and state regulations. "I'm here too much and yet not enough," was his guess. And there were the inevitable bureaucratic traps.

There is so much that needs to get said—so, for lack of time, you're forced into the habit of putting things down in memos. And no matter how nicely you do it, there's always going to be someone who'll misinterpret it . . . or resent the fact that it got written rather than spoken. A lot of it comes down to endurance, forbearance. I survive here because I'm good at separating. I can usually leave this place and it cares behind when I go home. If I couldn't, I might be *in* an institution, not helping to run one.

Such ease of separation was not always the case for Gordon. There were invariably some people who did affect him more, residents who, in his words, "I do worry about when I'm away. I'll call up first thing in the morning and ask: 'Is Sarah [Kavalick] still with us?' I was like that about Eddie, too. He was someone I cared for very deeply. Eddie is buried with my tie on, and I'm glad about that. It moves me whenever I think of it."
There were also those who moved Gordon in different directions.

There are certain residents who I keep a safe distance from, with whom I'm very much in my role as administrator. Some I wish God would call home very quickly, even though they are the ones who seem to live on and on. The nasty live longer. Is it that they live longer because they're nasty, or do they become nastier the longer they live? I once asked Nina: "Is nastiness a weapon? A means to survival?"

He shrugged.

I'm not sure, but I do know I have to set limits with people like Frank, or tell them to stop behaving in certain ways, or remind them about our policies and rules. I get into a kind of parental role with them at times. And I don't like that. When I want to be a parent, I want to do it with *my* children, not with someone else's parents.

The families that had put *their* parents or grandparents in the nursing home filled the entire emotional spectrum with their feelings about what they had done. Gordon found that there were some who, out of pride, would lie about their resources "so that Mom or Dad could be admitted as a private-pay patient—even though they were fully eligible for Medicaid." Others would not come in to visit because they found their parent so mean, or so impossible to deal with, that time spent together became intolerable. There were others who left it to a granddaughter or niece to take care of the whole situation. In general, and with notable exceptions such as Stavros and Frank, Gordon found that most residents enjoyed only a modest level of family contact. The saddest cases of all were those who had outlived all their relatives, leaving just staff and volunteers as candidates for the role of kin. He added that there were

> even some patients *with* families who find them so distant—or are themselves so needy—that they latch onto personnel or visitors as substitutes: they talk about and treat them as family. Some staff are much more comfortable with this than others, and they're the ones who reciprocate. They do favors for residents, run errands, even cook food for them at home. You take Reva, one of the aides on South One. She's been adopted in this way by Barbara Hernstein, who takes this constant interest in Reva's life: she asks about Reva's kids, and sends them gifts, and keeps track of Reva's course work in night school. It's a kind of vicarious life for Barbara, or maybe it's having the kind of daughter she would have wanted. I know Reva's even accompanied Barbara on some weekend trips—helping her out for pay, it's true, though I don't think she would have done it unless she felt connected to Barbara.
>
> There are others who'd *never* agree to be put in that position. Being "family" is being too close. Believe me, I know it! It muddies everything. You can't pull back without hurting people. They get to expect too much.

The most intriguing and the most troubling real families for Gordon and his staff were those who were so guilty about putting a parent in the home that they would go to almost any length to compensate for their sense of remorse: they became obsessed, for example, with making sure that their relative got the best care in the world—even if they themselves had never been attentive or solicitous to their mother or father before.

The demands of such people could be insistent, sometimes belligerent, and caregivers then ended up bearing the burden of that family's history. "*We* work out their guilt," Gordon explained.

> If there's been anger between parents and children in the past, then when the sons and daughters come in here they're likely to be very protective and concerned so long as *you* provide the services. The guilt becomes anger turned outwards at the home, even though they're really still mad at Mom. And they're mad at Mom for getting old, for causing the guilt. "She made me put her in the home" is what they're feeling . . . even when they don't know it.
>
> It's fascinating but also so common after a while. They complain, they push, they bother you like a bulldog. You can tick off the steps like a recipe, like Kübler-Ross.[2] It's an absolute scenario. But very few ever come to a

realization of what they're doing. Perhaps it's not our job to educate them, yet we end up with the work of sustaining them. Both them and their parents—anger, guilt, love, and all.

Whatever the issues—residents and families, staff and morale, finances or abuse—many conversations with Gordon cycled back to his quarrel with the social order. Its policies and priorities were an enigma that often appalled the moralist in him, bringing out his muted, religious sensibilities couched in the language of sin. When he spoke of health care and aging, he took on Descartes' machines as well as the machinations of Congress.

I think we have a strange society. It's not a caring one. It's a technical society. All the machinery shelters you from feeling. You turn on the medical equipment . . . and you've done your job. People walk away without compunction like Descartes' scientists, thinking that the creature at the other end feels no pain. It's sinful that it's now a hell of a lot easier to act that way than to just hold someone's hand when they're dying. We don't even ask people if this is what they want. We just plug them up, turn on the motor, and feel we are being responsible. In our theology we kill God and then in life we usurp his role. But what we have really done is take away the human right of the old to decide how they want to live and *if* they want to live. There is no dignity in that, not even the decency of finding out how they feel and what they desire. We are not improving life, we are simply prolonging death.

Some of the realities that consumed Gordon were, to him, obscenities: by funding huge defense budgets, we are forced to choose which human services to support because "military costs cut down on our capacity to pay for everything else.

The money given to the army would be so much better spent on helping the people I am responsible for. The truth is I think there *are* other groups out there who need our resources even more badly than the elderly, but who can quibble over *that* when we're throwing away so many dollars on bombs and bank bail-outs—programs that really don't benefit anybody.

This is a small planet; there is just so much to go around, and I know that. That's where the politicians fail us: it's a failure of the will, a failure of the imagination. It's funny: twenty years ago I thought I had all the answers. Now, every week, I lose another one.

CODA

A Right or a Privilege

Going home after a day—or night—at Elmwood Grove was the right of staff, but it looked like a privilege to residents. Louise appreciated this, seeing it as the heart of why the elderly, and their caregivers, experienced the institution in such different ways. At the very least, she felt, it required that those with freedom have a special tolerance for those without it, that they recognize this as one of the taproots of the elderly's anger and sadness, their irritability and longing.

To know, literally, that you could not go home again raised the curtain on the final act of life. It was the task of staff to make this last drama a secure and humane experience. Some saw their role in this as merely custodial: their work was a job, and most did it well, but they bridled under the poor pay, the low status, and the grudging attitudes of certain colleagues. Others, including both caregivers and professionals, embraced a wider ambition: it was to create hope against hopelessness, to practice the skills of their training, to fulfill themselves in the act of nourishing, comforting, or strengthening others.

Strength for the staff, the substance of their coping, came from many sources. There was Claire's faith in acts of will, Nina's politics of caring, Gordon's sense of injustice, and Louise's love for the grandmotherly gifts of the old. These assets hung in a balance, weighed each day against the frustrations, bewilderments, boredom, and losses that work inevitably entailed. People got struck and struck out—rarely in a literal way, more often metaphorically or verbally—leaving the spirit more bruised than the body. Perhaps, Nina once suggested, the caregivers' success at self-control was what sometimes undid them: they took their rewards quietly to heart, but took their displeasure with residents and relatives out on one another. The result was dissonance. So they reached for words and books, they took walks and coffee breaks, or they hid in the bathroom, in order to heal and steel and replenish themselves. Elmwood may have been, as Kate once said, "a world of its own," but it was still very real, often too real, leaving some people living their roles, and not just playing them.

8 ROLES AND REALITIES

Elmwood Grove was a home to paradox as well as people. Though it had evolved into a geriatric institution, few of those employed there had been formally trained to work with the elderly. It was ironic that the exceptions were usually not found among the professionals, but rather among the newer nurse's aides: though most of these women had limited formal education, they did receive classroom and in-house training during their first few months on the job. This hands-on apprenticeship gave them more direct experience with the aged than many therapists, nurses, or administrators could claim as preparation for their work.

The general lack of geriatric background among staff at all levels had some curious effects. It did not compromise people's competency so much as it affected their sense of justice and tolerance and fulfillment. The elderly brought into question what they assumed life, work, and career would hold in store for them. Finding the ends of time directly in front of them condensed the daily frame of reference to the dimensions of a small island inhabited by intimacy, threat, and promise.

When employees looked at their work, it sometime seemed that they were standing in a mirrored room. They saw in the reflection not only residents, coworkers, and families, but also gratitude, criticism, and the vicissitudes of hope. They took different meanings to heart. Some, like Gordon, had lost their hold on answers; others, like Louise, had rediscovered a sense of history; Nina was one of those drawn into a world of unprecedented thanks and unexpected clients; and still others, like Claire, saw a reflection of how they wished their own aged selves might act.

Staff members' accounts of their lives and jobs revealed how their work had affected their emotions, expectations, and sense of morality. Six of the major themes raised by them will be explored here: their training and previous patterns of employment; the sources of satisfaction and dissatisfaction they found in their jobs; the effects of gender and hierarchy on their work; their handling of time and space; their methods for coping with stress and support; and their reflections on aging, social responsibility, and institutionalization. Each of these was a factor in the way they tailored their roles to fit the reality of nursing home life.

CAREER PATHS

The decision to enter a profession, be it social work or physical therapy, nursing or health administration, is not the same as deciding where you want to practice your skills. Among staff who had been specially trained and licensed to do the jobs they were employed in at Elmwood Grove, only a handful had planned on pursuing their career with the elderly. Nina had wanted to do social work with adolescents; Claire had originally been employed as a physical therapist with acute care patients in hospitals; and Gordon had held positions where he planned and developed new medical facilities. Of the four staff members featured, only Louise had clearly decided, while still in nursing school, to work primarily with the aged.

Louise traced her affinity for the elderly to family background and adult experience. Her maternal grandmother, a colorful, vocal woman raised in the Appalachian coalfields, had clearly impressed her with the strengths of character and history with which some older people are gifted. Years after knowing this childhood model, Louise found new exemplars in the geriatric ward where she trained. She saw the patients there as survivors who embodied lessons about humor and human durability, about the mind's transcendence of the failing body. They revived her empathy for the elderly, and led her to choose a nursing home for her first job. In this regard, Louise was different from a number of her colleagues, as well as peers at other institutions, who commonly feel that "real" nursing only takes place in acute care settings (e.g., Shield 1988: 101). But for Louise the mirror of age held several rewards. She especially preferred the home to a hospital because it allowed her to develop relationships: instead of treating people briefly and then seeing them leave for life, residents were individuals she could get to know and work with a continuing way.

The paths that led Claire, Gordon, and Nina to Elmwood were much less direct and, to a degree, more a matter of practical opportunity. Nina's social work schooling was preceded and followed by jobs in the Midwest that involved children, adolescents, and young adults. She eventually moved to upstate New York to be near her sister, taking a post at a nearby medical complex. But she later applied for the opening at Elmwood to get away from "hospital politics," and—like Louise—to work with a more stable population of clients. While the elderly did not represent the kinds of people or problems she had originally prepared herself for, Nina found them to be surprisingly, sometimes dismayingly, grateful.

Claire had trained as a physical therapist in New England, and after working in major medical centers along the East Coast for over two decades, she came to upstate and Elmwood as a result of her husband's career. The scale of the facility appealed to her, as did the chance to run her own department and design its programs. But the nature and size of the home were also the source of its drawbacks. For Claire, Elmwood's aged turned out to be more challenging in an interpersonal than in a strictly therapeutic sense. The array of treatment modalities she could employ with them was modest. And since poor motivation was at least as much of an issue for her as weak musculature, she felt more limited in what she could accomplish than had been true with her patients in other places. In a number of regards, then, her training had equipped her to do more than she was able to here.

With a background in management and engineering, Gordon's main goal had been to work with buildings rather than bodies. And he had realized this call in planning medical facilities across Pennsylvania and New York. But life had a different construction to it now. In his mid-forties, with a family of his own, he was not as mobile as he had been in his bachelor days. Several years ago, when his last supervisory job finished up, he had taken the administrative post at Elmwood as an interim move. But as time slipped by and the size of his family increased, the young at home made it harder to leave the old at work in order to build new complexes elsewhere. Instead, Gordon became more embedded in the community and wedded to what his job required. If the latter was not all that he would have wanted, neither were the attitudes and social policies that made it necessary. The engineer—and the philosopher—in him had a different sense of proportion than what he found in the dimensions of institutional life.

Direct care staff—the aides, dietary workers, and housekeepers—lived in a world of smaller horizons and opportunities than Elmwood's professionals. Most were women from the local area with modest economic and educational backgrounds. Reva, for example, was a high school dropout with two young children, and Kate, a single mother of one. To a considerable degree, the work that such caregivers did at the home constituted an extension of the traditional female domestic skills they had already practiced in their own houses, namely, cleaning, cooking, caring, laundering, and nurturing. Their pay and both the job prerequisites and opportunities for advancement were minimal. A number of the women had school-age children and, in some cases, a second job: Elmwood's schedule of work fit in with the regime of their family life. Domestic ties also exerted another kind of influence: a fair number of floor staff had taken positions at the home because a female relative was already employed there. Daughters followed in the footsteps of their mothers, nieces echoed the choices of aunts. Kate, for instance, got her cue from an older sister, who had been employed as an aide for five years before Kate herself began.

Given the circumstances and backgrounds of these employees, it was striking to learn that many remained at their jobs for five, ten, and even twenty years. Periodically, some of them did quit, or change shifts, but it was administrators and health professionals who were more likely to leave for other positions. Among the varied groups that served the elderly, then, the most highly trained and the best paid were often the shortest lived at Elmwood. An unplanned but salutary result was that it was the caregivers— the people most often seen by residents each day—who gave the home's work force its continuity.

SATISFACTION AND DISSATISFACTION

Gordon thrived on novelty, and the fact that Elmwood ran on and required routine had begun to wear on him. The facility's periodic crises— contracts, cash flow, new state regulations—were mostly reruns of old ones he had already dealt with. But in his third year as assistant director he found some adrenalin in the possibility of building a new wing for the home. As soon as the sleep of the year's summer passed, he began to develop plans for this project with the chief administrator and board of directors. Meetings with committee chairs, fund-raisers, architects, and engineers were exciting in a way that few staff meetings could be. He was finding, in this enterprise, a way to turn his current job into the same channel where he had found much of his fulfillment in the past.

But there were other features of the present that continued to disturb and dissatisfy him. Two of these were quantities: one was the size of Elmwood itself, the other the deficits in its budget. The scale of the institution made him privy to more petty disputes and gossip than he would have cared to know about. Though the information sometimes turned out to be useful, he felt its circulation basically undermined morale. He surmised that the smallness of the home tended to exaggerate the smallness of people, and he would have preferred a kind of blissful ignorance about some of what happened around him. Other accounts of larger homes, such as Gubrium's Murray Manor (1975), document the insulation of "top staff" from the workaday reality of "floor staff." But at Elmwood, with less bureaucracy and fewer layers of separation, the qualities that buffered administrators at big institutions were not there to protect Gordon.

Like the scale of its relationships, Elmwood's endowment was also proportional to its size. Gordon lived each day with the worrisome awareness that the pool of money from the past was quickly evaporating, being burned off by the excess of costs over income. He had to argue with government officials over levels of reimbursement, monitor the ratio of private-pay patients to those on Medicaid, and remind the board of its fiscal responsibility.

On a day-to-day basis, what satisfied Gordon the most was the quality of care that the institution provided, and the personal quality of his own relationship with certain residents. Those who treated him like a peer, rather than a parent, brought out a strong, nurturant respect in him. He enjoyed giving of himself when those who received were not presumptuous about what he could or should offer in return. If they could reciprocate in some small, even silent way—a smile, a wave of the hand, a joke—he felt acknowledged as a person, not just as an administrator. Here, for a change, numbers did not count. For Gordon, as with the more reflective residents, a handful of good memories overcame a spate of unpleasant experiences. The remembrance of a person such as Eddie, peaceful in the face of death, wearing Gordon's tie to the grave, was sometimes enough to take the sting out of a difficult day.

Nina was gratified by some of the very things that burdened her most, and one was the tendency of staff to confide their problems to her. Like Gordon, she knew more about Elmwood than she cared to; but whereas his knowledge often came in the form of complaints, hers arrived in the cloth of confession. Some of this was very private and unrelated to the workings of the home; but other pieces detailed the insensitivity of supervisors, or what caregivers felt was the failure of administrators to lead and clarify. The reward for Nina in hearing all this was the personal knowledge that, in her role as confidante, she helped diffuse some of the tensions of staff, thus making their workdays and the lives of residents more bearable.

Like most other employees, Nina also found emotional satisfaction in her relations with particular patients. Stavros was one of her favorites. Though they had little that was obvious in common—neither age or gender, nor religion or ethnicity—they shared a sensitivity to the tragedy of other people's frailty. They spoke with one another about senility, puzzling over and never resolving the conundrum of its random assaults on human dignity. But when such a condition began to assert itself in some competent person whom Nina had gotten to know and care for, the enigma was less compelling for her than the anger she felt.

What dismayed as well as pleased Nina about the closeness she enjoyed with patients was that people's gratitude seemed disproportionate to the amount of attention she gave them. For residents to be so thankful for the modest amounts of time and care she could offer was, for her, an expression of how hungry they were inside. Their gratitude was thus a gift and a weight on her mind, an embarrassment of emotional riches which she never quite knew how to spend or repay.

For Claire, the rewards of work lay in a balance between rehabilitation and renunciation. Just as Nina disclaimed that she really did counseling, Claire felt she was rarely involved in curing. This "gearing down" was a bind, or at least a disappointment, since the medical model that she and other professional staff had been trained with was based on the concept of curing and not simply caring. But the conflict between the two goals—a tension found in nursing homes such as Martindale (Vesperi 1983) and Franklin (Shield 1988)—meant that instead, Claire's labors comprised a less dramatic trio of restoration, maintenance, and education. The satisfactions, though real, were relative and sometimes subject to reversal. The regained powers of residents lapsed, releases from the home were rare, and the skills she trained staff in were largely cautionary—designed to prevent injury and make their work with patients easier. The three themes converged on the key of amelioration.

There was, however, a fourth challenge for Claire, and this was to foster motivation. Her desire to "treat the whole person" meant getting people to believe in the possibility of improvement through effort. But this was often a difficult case to prove. Floor staff were sometimes far less helpful in this regard than Claire had hoped because they were either too busy or indifferent to work with patients on range-of-motion exercises. Also, in a skilled nursing facility like Elmwood, Claire found the elderly totally surrounded by agemates of comparable frailty; without the presence of healthier peers to model what hard work might have yielded, residents had difficulty finding the motivation to try. Without a built-in set of examples, then, Claire had to fall back on what inspiration she could provide. And though her spirit was willing, it was often insufficient to undo what age had imposed on the flesh.

The main feelings that Louise voiced about her work had much to do with the ways language was lost and found. She knew colleagues for whom the keeping of records and the vocabulary of technique had become the center of nursing, a tendency that dismayed her even more when she saw signs of it in herself. She felt best about the home when it left her in peace to give care, rather than distracting her with paper or the need to keep peace among others. A lapsed Catholic, she could not muster the kind of faith that moved Tilly or Claire, but she was jealous of preserving the spirit of her profession.

A reader of history, a lover of oral tradition, Louise was naturally drawn to words and their etymology: she knew that the Latin root of nursing lay in "nourish", and that compassion was the ability to "endure another's suffering." The heart of her job, she felt, was finding out what people needed, but this meant discovering it in their own terms, in their words, and in their time. Though the paperwork often threatened to get in the way of this, she had found ways to bring her charts into people's rooms, keeping company at the same time she kept records (see Figure 8.1, a patient review form).

She regretted the continuing, taboo nature of death as a topic at Elmwood, particularly because she found it so important to be there with and for people when they were dying. Too many workers denied or sanitized or muffled the death that was around them, she argued, and the staff who talked about it often did so in a way that distanced such losses. There were

Figure 8.1
Patient Review Instrument (Selected Items)

```
                                                    Page 1
 I. ADMINISTRATIVE DATA
      Operating Certificate Number    Social Security
      Patient Name           Date of Admission
      Date of Birth          Sex
      Medicare No.           Medicaid No.
      Date of PRI Completion


 II. MEDICAL EVENTS                   IV. BEHAVIORS
      Decubitus Level                      Verbal Disruption
      Medical Conditions                   Physical Aggression
       Comatose                            Disruptive, Infantile, or
       Dehydration                            Socially Inappropriate Acts
       Terminally Ill                      Hallucinations
       Diabetes Mellitus
       Stasis Ulcer                    V. SPECIALIZED SERVICES
       Contractures                         Physical and Occupational
       Urinary Tract Infection              Therapies:
       Ventilator Dependent                 Level; Day and Times Weekly
      Medical Treatments                Number of Physician Visits
       Tracheostomy Care/Suctioning        Medications
       Wound Care
       Chemotherapy                    VI. DIAGNOSIS
       Nasal Gastric Feeding               Primary Problem
       Dialysis                            Name of Assessor
       Catheter (Indwelling/External)
       Physical Restraints             VII. UTILIZATION REVIEW
                                            Resource Utilization Group
 III. ACTIVITIES OF DAILY LIVING (ADLs)        (RUG)
       Eating                               Level of Care (HRF/SNF)
       Mobility                            SNF Medical Coverage
       Transfer                            Utilization Review Physican
       Toileting                           Next Scheduled U.R. Date
                                           Race/Ethnic Group
```

exceptional situations that opened a dialogue, such as Wesley Cardeen's death, and the conflicts over Alma's decision not to lose her leg. The DNRs were also a source of contention. While Louise's aide Kate welcomed these directives for the "moral clarity" they brought, Reva—an aide on the floor below—resented them as orders which imposed "other people's moral choices" on her. Still other staff could be just as upset by the reverse kind of situation—one, for instance, where a family insisted on a life-sustaining NG tube for a resident who did not want one. The aide in just such a case railed: "If I was Celia, you know what I'd be saying about my family? 'If you put me through that [kind of torture], I'll haunt you for a long as you live.' "

Residents themselves spoke about life and death in several ways. Denise observed that patients sometimes used the visiting animals as an indirect means to talk about the deaths of their loved ones and their own mortality. But the elderly could also be very direct about these same subjects, and generally agreed with staff that the dying could be worse than death itself. Death nevertheless evoked different responses from patients as compared to personnel. Residents related the passing on of their peers within the home in a regretful yet matter-of-fact way, whereas caregivers were more anxious and evasive about it. Employees were likely to comment on death with respectful silence or a nod of the head, whereas patients offered such remarks as, "We've all got to go"; "I'm ready when my time comes"; and "She's better off out of that suffering." At the end of a month with the unusual number of five deaths, workers' comments focused more on the number of losses than on who had actually passed away; but Vivian observed, "How sad it is we've lost so many of the real old-timers like Celia, Tommy, and Marina."

This difference between staff and the elderly—the greater readiness of the latter to confront death—has also been noted in other nursing homes, including Murray Manor (Gubrium 1975: 203–206), Franklin (Shield 1988: 69–71), and Bethany Manor (O'Brien 1989: 128–130). Watson and Maxwell observed how caregivers at the Jewish institution they studied set up "refuge" area for themselves in order to avoid the dying and the severely disabled (1977: 73, 92). In their work on hospitals and geriatric facilities, Glaser and Strauss found that staff recoiled from the deaths of patients they identified with, treating these events as if they were "dying rehearsals for their own fates" (1968: 231). At Martindale, older nurses were more aloof and hostile towards the elderly because they "saw in their patients a foreshadowing of their own demise" (Vesperi 1985: 152). This distancing of death by doctors and nurses has been interpreted as a form of self-protection among those who not only confront their own mortality every day, but who measure the worth of their work by their ability to preserve life itself (cf. Feifel 1961).

Louise stood apart from the latter view, but she was not alone in this. Dr. Sheren, who shared responsibility with her for some of the same Elmwood patients, echoed Louise's sentiments well when he described part of his own code of ethics: "One of the most satisfying things I can do here is help people die—with dignity, with respect, and in their own time." This was not the way other practitioners saw their role, and some had the reputation—accompanied variously by the staff's praise or damnation—for sending failing patients to the hospital for life-sustaining treatment. But Sheren's attitude fit with how Louise herself wanted to deal with death. When she could be part of a process that accepted "that death has its time," it did not necessarily make the resident's loss any less painful, but it made her experience of it, and that of the patient, more humane, more fulfilling, more reassuring. She felt the same attitude could be applied when life itself was over. "When someone dies and the family comes to get their belongings," she once explained, "you shouldn't shun them the way some do here. I feel we should spend some time with them, help them pack, talk about the person who died, and share our regrets. It can be a way for everyone to say good-bye: to the person and to one another. That's basically how I try to relate to the patient when they're dying. People should know," she emphasized, "that they don't have to be alone in death any more than they have to be alone in life."

Elmwood's small scale drew staff into an order of intimacy with residents. The more vocal and visible patients had each earned a reputation or a resume of traits among those who cared for them, and these judgments were often at the heart of what was most disturbing or fulfilling about work at the home. Talk about the elderly was one of the most common forms of conversation among employees, who regularly compared notes on how their patients were getting on, and how they—as staff—were getting on with residents. There was consensus about some individuals, but diverse opinions on others.

Staff were of two minds about Stavros. One view expressed a benign approval of his charm and accent and inherent gentleness, the other an uncertainty about what to make of his self-effacement. Stavros was very articulate but, as Nina observed, he had lost much of his voice when his wife died. He asked for little, or at least did not ask for much directly. Nor did he lie or rage or exaggerate about his condition: he was easier to help than Frank, for example, less demanding and more prompt with thanks. Yet he was sadder all the same. He keenly felt what he had lost with his wife, whereas Frank was deeply frustrated by what age withheld from him at that very moment. Compared to Stavros, Frank's conduct and his outspokenness required a more activist response. He had people guessing, not just commiserating. Where he could not find love, he at least laid claim to people's attention. Denise, Nina, and the aides tried to stay one or two steps ahead of his fire, but they were frequently caught in its heat. Despite their well-meant measures, words and food sometimes flew through the air.

Frank, however, could also flatter and amuse, and he was the wellspring for a good deal of laughter. To Claire, he made fun of "doctors who couldn't tell the difference between the fainthearted and the light-headed." He remembered, to Louise's delight, the old days of vaudeville when "audiences voted with fruit and eggs." He spoke to Nina of "a young, middle-aged lady" he was once on the verge of marrying: "She was a woman of many parts, but they didn't fit together very well." In Gordon's estimate, Frank's practiced tongue was often "an entertainment," a welcome diversion in a place where the good use of language was "a form of music."

Staff sometimes found their own terms turned back on them by the more sharp-tongued residents. With solicitude, Denise once asked Frank whether he had recovered from a recent head cold. He laid a finger above his upper lip, mocking a moustache, playing Chaplin playing Hitler. "Nein, Liebchen," he mimicked. "Ich shtill habe ein incontinent nose." Bonnie once broke through her customary courtesy when Claire, finishing up a treatment, praised her faith as a "rock of ages." Not to be bought off with pieties that day, Bonnie admonished her: "Let me tell you, after 83 years and all these illnesses, I'm being crushed to death by these rocks of ages!"

There were also behaviors and values that tested people's tolerance. Those, like Gordon, who loved Frank's gift of speech, could still not hear his abusiveness without feeling outraged themselves. Some staff found Tilly's piety cloying, though not enough for them to discount her sincerity or forget her intercession with her agitated peers. They felt that they and Tilly each ministered to people in their own way. Even Kate, one of the most ardently irreligious of the aides, found merit in the way Tilly expounded her faith. "She pleads with people, but she does not lecture." And better yet, Kate felt, "she does not condemn." Though Tilly had lived her whole life in a limited, sheltered world, she impressed Kate with having somehow won from it a wide acquaintance with human weakness: it was a type of knowledge that staff could also esteem, for their work put them in the way of more frailty—physical, emotional, *and* moral—than most of them had expected or suspected. So they applauded Tilly's tolerance for failings, seeing in her, as Kate once suggested, "an innocent person" who had nevertheless "escaped from being naive."

Beyond the difficulties of caring for the old, staff at Elmwood had to deal with such workplace tensions as management issues, personality conflicts, and clashes between cliques. There were some who saw their job as just a paycheck, who resented both the conditions of their employment and what they were paid for doing it. But others found satisfaction in their labor. They felt their jobs were important and caring ones, even if they were insufficiently rewarded or poorly appreciated by the people "on the outside." Kate once commented on the widespread feeling among the aides that the feedback they got on their work was one-sided. She observed that when residents or their relatives assessed the general quality of care at the home, the consensus was that Elmwood did a very good job; but when people spoke up to make more pointed remarks to—or about—caregivers, they were more likely to register complaints than offer praise. "You might *know*," Kate said, "that people feel you're generally doing a good job; but what you *hear* them say are mostly critical things, like, 'Why can't you do it this way?' or 'My father liked it better when he got his pills before dinner.'" As a number of the aides also argued, they were doing meritorious work which, in Reva's estimate, "others were incapable of or refused to do." In other words, and in their own eyes, then, the aides were both undervalued and indispensable.

There were also times, however, when job satisfaction got reduced to the minimum of getting through the day. And for staff at all levels, there were certainly many such harried times. Though Elmwood ran on a system of routine, the fact is that to many employees, crises of one sort or another were common. Events such as a resident's death, a spate of new admissions, a breakdown in some key piece of equipment, an unannounced inspection, or the illness of a colleague could all disrupt the day's regime. In the life of a small institution, occurrences of this type affected employees at many levels—not just the nurse dealing with the death, or the therapist coping with the breakdown, or the administrator shepherding the inspector. In such circumstances, people had to cover for one another or do additional work or improvise.

But what generally satisfied or dissatisfied employees about their jobs was distinct from their feelings of the moment about how work was going. It was a case of general sentiments versus daily details, of feeling good (or bad) about their job overall, but being stressed (or gratified) by the situation at hand. Whereas days were fairly uniform for residents, then, this was less true for staff: their work life included both the routines of care and the random nature of the things that went wrong. These were the "levels of reality" that Denise once described as "what had to be done, what might have been, and what was."

GENDER AND HIERARCHY

Most staff members could give, or even quote from memory, a job description of their position. But while the formal nature of their work was clearly laid out on paper, employees at all levels agreed that they did more than was specified in the letter of the law of contracts and union rules. People found themselves taking on a variety of tasks that were not strictly part of their jobs. Nina, for example, occasionally found herself helping to serve meals. Kate, though a nurse's aide, sometimes assisted at recreation activities by setting up games or staying with participants while Denise transported other people back to their rooms. And Rachel, the speech therapist, periodically agreed to take the families of prospective residents on tours of the building.

These unwritten, informal parts of their jobs alternately pleased and irritated staff. On the one hand, the tasks were a welcome break from routine, a chance to mix with different people in a different way. But the novelty was less attractive when requests for such help came at inopportune times, or were phrased in a manner—and said in a tone—that presumed upon the willingness or inherent availability of others. While complaints about timing and tenor came from all quarters, it was the aides who felt most put upon, claiming—in Reva's words—that some of the "people with titles" treated them as if they were "always on call."

Although some of the work at Elmwood was carried out in this ad hoc fashion, responsibility usually had a very clear structure to it. There were the visible realms of departments, the lines of authority, the levels of hierarchy. And underlying these divisions of labor was the reality of gender. The female quality of life and work at the home was evident in the preponderance of women among staff, residents, and volunteers. For Elmwood's employees, the female majority held at all levels, but it was particularly marked among those giving direct care. As Gordon noted, the reasons were neither surprising nor uncommon in American health facilities. The modest pay, the minimum requirements for education, and the emphasis on such traditional female tasks as cleaning and nurturance all made the lower level jobs in housekeeping, dietary, and nursing the province of women. Locally, this gender pattern was aided and abetted by the informal process of family recruitment among female staff. By contrast, the men employed at Elmwood were found mostly in typically male jobs in maintenance and in the higher-paid administrative posts.

Women in the lower echelons, while proud of their work, were often critical of the way their superiors behaved toward them. They were conscious not just of differences in salary and privilege, but of what some felt to be a lack of respect in the treatment they received. These were among the issues that regularly surfaced during union contract talks, but no one had yet found a way to resolve these concerns either on paper or in practice. A reason once suggested by Kate, a two-time member of the negotiating team, was that "you can't legislate tact in a contract." Aides and nurses on certain units frequently found themselves being publicly taken to task by their superiors, which added an unwarranted element of embarrassment to a situation that would have been difficult enough in private. Gordon periodically heard complaints about this from employees, but admitted he found it hard to find the time to supervise all the supervisors, or press them to be more sensitive. Conscious of himself as part of a male minority, he observed—in self-defense—that there were female supervisors who were as roundly criticized for their manner as any of their male peers.

Among top staff at Elmwood Grove, women as well as men, there was both sympathy for and some disagreement with the way caregivers saw things. There was a consensus that the latter were underpaid, but an objection from Gordon and others that "the real problem with their workload is not the amount—it's that they're poorly organized." Among administrators there were also discrepant views on the sources of disrespect. Nina, for one, supported the caregivers' contention that they were unfairly and often insensitively dealt with. But one nursing supervisor complained that some of the care staff aggravated their treatment by "failing to work cooperatively" with people from other departments and administrative levels. Louise was less sanguine about cause and effect, acknowledging that she was not sure "which came first here, the chicken or the egg, the abuses or the refusals."

Personnel who administered and supervised often spoke candidly about the deep differences of culture and class that lay between them and other employees. And while they were equally emphatic about their respect for the aides, they usually expressed this in terms of their own inability to carry out the routine tasks that these employees performed, that is, to bathe, toilet, and clean up after residents, "to work up to your elbows," as Gordon bluntly put it, "in shit." Their respect, in other words, was phrased in terms of the jobs that others did, but what some of the aides felt was a lack of regard for them as people—a difference in attitude that hinged on the distinction between the work and the worker.

These same attitudes could color how different staff perceived the identical events. Elmwood's health professionals and administrators, for example, took pride in their occasional, hands-on care work. They sometimes pitched in to help dress residents, or take them to therapy, or get them bathed or shaved. But caregivers tended to see these forays by supervisors and specialists as mostly token in nature. "They drop in and drop out," observed Kate. "It makes them feel good," she said with a smile, and dismissed it with a wave. Yet these contrasting views—pride on one side, shrugs on the other—were not so much distortions as refractions: helpfulness versus tokenism, regard opposed to disrespect, were each "reality" as seen from the stance of people at different points in the system of care.

TIME AND SPACE

The relatively principle for staff was not only a product of hierarchy and gender, but also a matter of time and space. These dimensions often separated workers in very concrete ways. Administrators and department heads had their own offices, charge nurses had desks at their stations for record keeping, and therapists had separate rooms in which to do treatments. But there was no comparable work or personal space for direct care staff. Their jobs were conducted much more in the public domain, and they could neither retreat nor perform their tasks in private.

Yet if privacy was a privilege of rank, the lack of some other kinds of space could also level these differences. None of Elmwood's employees had their own lounge or eating area, which effectively turned the home's dining room into a commons for all the workers. It was, in effect, the informal social hub for the whole institution. Even there, however, the separations among staff were quite visible. Between meals, the housekeepers, aides, and dietary workers "owned" three tables at the east end of the hall near the kitchen. Professional and administrative staff never joined this kaffeeklatsch, except to give messages or ask questions. Instead, they usually took their coffee breaks in their offices, or sat in a cluster on the room's west side. Those residents who used the hall as a gathering place also had their own well-known tables; if Stavros, Dave, and Frank met over coffee, or sat with visitors, they could be found near the water fountain along the south wall.

These customary groupings were casual but clear, separate but equal. And they were accomplished without the benefits of architecture. The dining room had no internal walls or even pillars to break up the space, and yet its social divisions were well marked by age, appearance, and agreement. As students of other nursing homes have shown, people create their own domains when designers fail to do it for them.[1] Any knowledgeable person walking into Elmwood knew where to sit and what the distances between the groups meant.

The regime of the home also divided up staff along the dimension of time. The main separation here was the organization of caregivers into three shifts, each of which, as Katina Glover put it, was "a world unto itself" with a cast of characters, and a rhythm and work ethic, of its own. The two daytime groups—the "mornings" and "noons"—had distinct routines for meals, baths, medications, and cleaning, and they did much of their work in the public eye. They were in charge of residents during their waking hours, labored while administrators were in the building, and received the most scrutiny from family and visitors. It was the night shift, however, working largely out of sight, that meant the most varied things to different people: depending on who you spoke to, it involved the worst hours or the best, the easiest tasks or the most boring ones, the minimum responsibilities or simply those that were the least recognized and appreciated. People's feelings about their own jobs and those of others were thus quite discrepant.

Each shift actually overlapped for a quarter of an hour with the one following it by staying until 3:15 P.M., 11:15 P.M., and 7:15 A.M., and employees were expected to leave the residents and the facility in good order for the next group to take over. Therein lay a recurrent problem for administrators—that of insuring the continuity of Elmwood's operation and handling the complaints of staff over the way an earlier shift had left things. Gordon described an example of this having to do with medical treatment. On a Tuesday morning, a doctor visiting Yvonne on North One ordered a change in the kind of dressing and ointment to be used on her leg. The new regimen was dutifully written down, but staff on the next shift found that their predecessors had failed to get the required bandages and medicines for them to use. It was then too late in the day to secure the right materials. The charge nurse claimed that this was not the first time the people at her station had been "set up" by the workers on the previous shift. Yvonne protested, the staff groused, and on Wednesday morning Gordon had complaints on his desk from both the afternoon shift and Yvonne's son.

Incidents of this kind were not common, but when they did occur they usually indicated the lines of cleavage that divided groups of employees. Cliques and personality clashes could sometimes be as salient here as the work shift or staff level to which a particular person belonged. At other nursing homes that have been examined, the major splits have pitted Murray Manor's "top staff" against "floor staff" (Gubrium 1975) and Franklin's social workers against nurses (Shield 1988: 65–71). In the latter situation, the human service emphasis on "rehabilitation" and "quality of life" clashed with the nurses' concern with "maintenance" and the "quantity of life": it counterpointed the medical staff's model of Franklin as a "hospital" with the social workers' image of it as a "home." At Elmwood the difference was more commonly phrased as a distinction between "caring" and "curing," and it did not neatly fit within departmental boundaries. Social work only had one position, and while Nina occupied it, she tended to be a resource for a broad range of therapeutic and nursing staff. The split over philosophy often occurred among the latter, leaving people like Kate on one side and Reva on the other. Up in physical therapy, Claire wanted it both ways—curing *and* caring—choosing her stance on the basis of what she felt her patients wanted and what they were capable of achieving.

From his "view near the top," Gordon felt that Elmwood was no better or worse than comparable institutions in the degree of cooperation and conflict among workers. Nina once tried to sum up the situation by observing that the home was large enough to have numerous specialists, yet small enough for everyone to know something about other people's business. There were times, she said, "when employees feel others know too little, or too much, about what they do. When information doesn't get communicated, or when it gets out of control, the feelings are usually not far behind."

STRESS AND SUPPORT

As if she were planning a family trip, Nina once asked me "where do you go when you want to get away from it all?" But the question was rhetorical: it not only related to work instead of play, but had to do as much with Nina's colleagues as her own ways of coping. In one of the most telling departures from the official routine at Elmwood, Nina herself was one of the sources that employees went to for escape and assistance. This was not what she was paid for, but it revealed both the open-ended nature of her role—or at least the way Nina chose to play it—and the needs of staff to deal directly with the stresses of work. Nina gave employees an outlet by listening to them, even tough she felt that the free moments she offered them each week were hardly sufficient. She would have preferred to run support groups for personnel and families in order to offer both sets of caregivers a chance to help themselves.

She was quick to add that staff members were not without support from within their own ranks. The social worker in her noted that their cliques were a sign not just of cleavages *between* groups, but of cohesion *within* them. There were, for example, networks of good friends among caregivers, women who sat together over lunch, who were drawn to each other by gossip, who on the outside shared child care, carpools, and other tasks. What they also had in common, however, were some of the negative features of work on the inside, including the imbalance in the feedback they got from those they were responsible *for* and those they were responsible *to*. One of Kate's lessons from her peers was that things done well by aides were too often taken for granted by others, whereas their mistakes were deemed worthy of criticism. Her estimation was that "when it comes to words, ours is a pretty one-sided world."

From the vantage point of her desk at the nursing station, Louise offered a perspective on some of Elmwood's other stresses. Talking specifically about the nurses and aides whom she worked with, her idea for a "time-out" room grew from their need for a place to vent their anger and rage or simply retreat from the emotional demands of their jobs. Residents, she noted, could not only be critical but manifestly abusive at times, and if caregivers were to avoid responding in kind, they needed a refuge where they could "complain, bitch, or, if need be, cry." She added,

> I'm pretty good at controlling myself and I can keep it in 'til the end of the day, and then go home to fling my throw-away books at the wall. But it's not realistic to think that everyone can be like that. If they can't take it out safely, they'll just take it out on someone. It's only human. . . . I've seen relatives get mistreated by residents in the same way. I try to make them and my staff understand that they're the targets of people's anger, *not* the cause of it. But that doesn't always help at the moment you're under attack.

Despite the need for a place to deal with the stresses of work, there was no time-out room, support group, escape hatch, or even staff lounge at the home, and the dining room tables that workers laid claim to afforded only a minimum of privacy. So people created ad hoc opportunities to cope with the immediate need for refuge and support. When a resident she cared for died, Denise took a walk, or a series of walks, around the block. She and her assistant Martha had some privacy in their office and could talk to one another or fume and cry there. Claire periodically looked behind her desk to her bookshelf of inspiration. At times of crisis, she and Nina sought one another out, though they also made a point of getting together for a few minutes almost every work day just to check in and see how the other was doing. Louise let her staff go off to the bathroom or the supply room when upsetting things happened, and she or someone else covered for them. Kate, one of her aides, vouched for the wisdom of this. "She knows we're not very good at those times: people become inefficient when they're under that kind of strain, so you don't lose anything by letting them leave for a while."

Though the home had its divisions and its cliques, its personalities and shifts, then, it was not without ways to sustain the staff. But these were mostly informal rather than institutional in nature and were the result of personal decisions rather than official policy. This informality also meant that there were some people who did not get the support they needed, or who ended up looking for it outside Elmwood's walls. Several got it from their spouses or families: Denise was one such person, and she saw this as one of the strengths of her marriage: "My husband," she said, "should get a salary for listening to me talk about this place." But there were others, such as Gordon, who resolutely refused "to take it home" with him. "When I leave here at the end of the day," he declared, "I want to leave it all behind me."

Louise, who coped so well inside the facility, found it increasingly harder to leave it all behind or outside as the years went by. The current of demands got too strong and she eventually quit, a casualty of caring and coping in a vortex. Working near the midpoint of Elmwood's hierarchy, she had been torn by the claims of the people above and below and beside her: she felt administrators, aides, residents, and relatives had "all wanted a piece of me." When she resigned it was because this seemed the only way to honor some of the legitimate claims she wanted to make on herself, not the least of which, she said, was "to regain my center." In her wake, she left hanging one of the most vexing questions in medicine and mental health, the issue— as Nina once put it—of "who shall take care of the carers?"

MORAL REFLECTIONS

The experiences of staff also raised some difficult moral concerns. There were residents who befriended and tried to "adopt" employees, treating them, for example, with the kind of parental interest that Barbara Hernstein took in Reva. But most employees found such behavior problematic as well as flattering. It could sometimes lead to what Nina called "the kind of blunt, borderline behavior, not just the affection, that family members indulge in with one another," and she catalogued "the demands, the tongue-lashings, and the possessiveness" that kin felt entitled to. Furthermore, some aides and housekeepers found that too much familiarity bound them with expectations for a kind of reciprocity they could not provide. Shield found the same hesitancy to become "family" among Franklin's employees (1988: 74–76). At Elmwood, however, this was less true for volunteers: because their contacts with residents were far more intermittent, they were also far more comfortable in the surrogate family role than the staff.

Another dilemma hinged on what workers, in their turn, could legitimately expect from patients. Black aides sometimes bridled at the racism of a handful of residents, but more often chose to ignore it as another symptom of "people's crotchetyness." The nastiness of some residents—a trait which, as Gordon guessed, has indeed been found to contribute to longevity[2]—could generally be absorbed by staff if it stopped short of abuse. But caregivers and therapists had more trouble deciding when patients could reasonably be expected to do more to care for themselves. Some staff emphasized the goal of not reinforcing unwarranted dependency, but others—

feeling overburdened—found it easier to do things *for* people rather than help them to help themselves. It took extreme cases—such as those of Greta, Sarah, and Eva—to leave people's minds untroubled about how active a role they had to take with residents.

Patients wanted not only to be cared for, but to be listened to and remembered. Yet this was not technically part of anyone's job. Individuals such as Louise built the role of listener into their work, but not without some emotional cost to themselves. The decision to engage, for example, brought up the ethical dilemma of how honest to be with residents about their medical condition and their life chances. Did you honor their requests to be told the truth or respect their hints to leave things unsaid? Could you take the responsibility of interpreting their nonverbal cues about how much they really wanted to know? Was it ethical to lie to their families to make relatives feel better? And were some of the lies told, as Louise concluded, to ease the pain for staff rather than kin?

There were employees who evaded these issues either by avoiding people at crucial moments or by leaving the decisions up to others. But some had a clear moral stance and were not afraid to assume it. Louise was insistent on giving patients the choice of whether or not to be told the facts about their health. Her view was that the elderly were entitled to be informed and prepared for their death. This took precedence over a family's request "to spare Mom or Dad the truth." Nina and Claire concurred with Louise's judgment that most residents did know what was happening, and that being honest with them was more in the nature of a confirmation than a revelation.

Death cast the moral sense of staff into bold relief. There were some for whom death remained a taboo topic, even in an institution where it was a fact of daily life. But for those who had taken the risk of getting close to residents, decline and loss exacted a heavy toll in both the choices and feelings that ensued. Part of the anguish lay in the lack of consensus about how to handle certain life-and-death situations. When Alma and her son decided she would walk with her own two feet to meet her demise, Claire concurred, but some of the nursing staff were outraged. When Wesley Cardeen passed away after 17 years at Elmwood, the sense of loss was nearly universal . . . but then his empty bed became a disputed ground between Louise and her superiors. On one level the fight over whether to keep it open for a day or fill it quickly was a matter of staff feelings versus institutional needs. To Louise and her adversaries, however, the struggle was also a conflict between the ethics of respect versus those of fiscal responsibility.

In a different sense, Alma's case had raised a comparable dilemma between employees who felt responsible for sustaining life and those who wished to respect the right to a dignified death. Reva said she could "sympathize with the anguish of losing a limb," but felt people could "cope with more than they realized if given the chance." To Claire, however, Alma knew that the amputation was only a way of buying time and that the kind of time was not worth the price. Gordon expressed the thoughts of a number of his staff when he spoke out against prolonging the lives of those residents who had indicated a wish or a willingness to have their life end. Talking more personally and emphatically, he said he felt it was "obscene" not to ask and respond to what people wanted. It was, to him, the crime of a society that valued "technique over compassion."

Several employees were outspoken about ways that they and the home could allow people to die with dignity. For Claire this included touching and holding residents when words were no longer possible. For Louise, it meant offering your presence in a person's room during their final hours so that they did not have to leave his life alone. For Dr. Sheren, it involved a decision not to rush patients off on "repeated, tortured trips to the hospital" just because it was part of some medical protocol. When we do the latter, in the words of Gordon quoted before, "we are not improving life; we are simply prolonging death."

The most basic and at times embarrassing issue for staff was the very idea of institutionalization. While proud of Elmwood's reputation, only a handful found the nursing home concept a desirable solution for the elderly—except in the most extreme cases of frailty and dependency. Like a number of the residents, their problem was not with their institution, but with the idea of institutionalization itself. Yet few could offer viable alternatives because, when pressed, they also came up against the realities of finances and family life that precluded home-based care for most older people. There were moments of candor and contradiction when employees considered what they were capable of. None of the administrators felt that they themselves could do the kind of bed, body, and bowel work that care staff did. Louise, who had carried out all of these tasks, nevertheless admitted that while she could effectively nurse and care for residents, she would not choose to do the same for her own relatives.

Among themselves, employees chastised certain families for putting their elderly in the home unnecessarily, but they were even more likely to take such relatives to task for their behavior *after* institutionalization occurred. Elmwood staff spoke critically of the families who neglected their kin or who foisted off responsibility for them on a distant relative. And while not morally outraged, they were oppressed by those guilt-ridden individuals—spouses, children, and siblings—who took out their anguish by badgering personnel to care for their husband or parent or sister in a way that they themselves never had and never would. This pattern has been observed in other facilities too, where the anger of families at themselves and their relatives gets "displaced onto the home" (Tobin 1987: 49).

None of Elmwood's employees claimed the institution was perfect, but many were offended and hurt when the limitations of their work were thrown back at them as personal faults. Just as Gordon resented being made into a parental figure by residents, he and other staff were dismayed when families made them the victims of their misplaced rage. What also perturbed them was the failure of such outsiders to consider the levels of pay and abuse that caregivers endured. Gordon saw these kinds of censure and ignorance in even broader terms, viewing them as symptoms of a society that consigned the elderly to late-life limbo, and their caregivers to the margins of respectability.

CONCLUSIONS

Many staff at Elmwood espoused a work ethic of caring for the total person. A commendable ideal, it was not, however, a total picture of the conditions or the results of their labor. Employees at each level specialized in satisfying one set of patients' needs, be they physical, financial, medical, nutritional, or social in nature. This did not prevent some particularly committed people from making significant efforts to attend to the complete person of residents, but the demands of work limited how much even the most conscientious could achieve. The reality of this was explained, in part, by Gordon's observation that Elmwood's patients now came to it in a more debilitated state than in the past, and that they were far more likely to live there for the rest of their years. By the dawn of the 1990s, such long-term frailty had become a feature of life in many American nursing homes (Sheryl Goldberg and Carroll Estes 1990). For Gordon, the effect of this trend on Elmwood was to saddle the institution with high costs and the staff with unrealistic expectations.

> People have grown up with the notion of being "nursed back to health." Well, yes, we're a nursing home, but we can't do what some expect us to. The hospitals can't do it either. That's why they send the old to us so quickly. With current reimbursement policies, it cuts their costs. But that just means they pass the patients and the problems on to us.

The daily world of the work force also had other attributes. Elmwood's staff was divided by a number of formal and informal qualities, many of which were inherent in the nature of an institutional setting: differences in gender and viewpoint; in union or nonunion status; in levels of pay, power and professionalism; in the quality of morale; and in personal affiliation with support systems and work shifts all created distinctive experiences for employees. These, in turn, affected their relationships with other personnel and with residents, their families, and visitors. The materials presented here suggest a dozen features that defined the backgrounds and the work lives of staff.

Preparation. Most employees had not trained or planned to work in a nursing home or with the elderly. They either had no specialized education for this, which was true of Kate and most caregivers; or, in the case of people such as Nina, Claire, and Gordon, they originally intended to work as professionals in other kinds of community or medical facilities.

Choice. A contrasting point was that although Elmwood had its short-comings, a number of staff had nevertheless chosen to work there in pref-erence to other places of employment. Many direct caregivers, who could have had comparable jobs in other nursing facilities in the area, had selected this home because they liked its atmosphere or size and, in some cases, because they wanted to work alongside friends or relatives. A number of professional staff, such as Nina and Louise, preferred a residential facility to a hospital because it gave them the opportunity work with patients on a long-term basis. It thus enabled them to come closer to the ideal of total care, even though they did not pretend to have reached it.

Fluidity. The content of people's jobs were often open ended. Many staff at all levels felt their work entailed more varied tasks than could be found in a formal job description or contract. This applied to therapists who helped to serve meals and aides who assisted at games. Employees raised occasional objections to these informal additions to what they did, but some took much stronger exception to the *way* in which this extra work was requested or taken for granted by colleagues. On the other hand, the confessional role that Nina and Claire chose to take on was one of the most gratifying aspects of what these women did.

Scale. Employees were pleased with—and took pride in—Elmwood's reputation for providing a good level of care for its residents. When dis-cussing this and their own degree of job satisfaction, most staff argued that the home's relatively small size made a positive contribution to the quality of life and work there. Gordon agreed with this in principle but demurred as far as his own position was concerned: he felt that the scale and structure of the institution left him too exposed to its gripes and frictions. Claire raised two caveats of a different kind: the range of disabilities she dealt with left her limited scope to use her skills, and the population of the home provided residents with few models of the physical improvements they might have achieved.

Paperwork. There were other, more commonly voiced complaints. One of these pertained to formal responsibilities at the institution. Administrative and supervisory staff railed about the amount of paperwork they had to do, identifying this as a major impediment to giving residents the kind of attention they wanted to. Louise innovated by making her charts into a portable task so that she could get to the bed-bound, but this was not a luxury that the more desk-bound of her peers could afford.

Divisions. The work force at Elmwood was divided up in several ways, only some of which reflected the home's formal organization. Beyond the shifts, departments, and levels of hierarchy, there were other separations that grew out of gossip, cliques, and a perceived lack of sensitivity. While the hierarchy codified people's powers and responsibilities, there was also the de facto reality of gender, which at Elmwood meant a predominance of women in the work force, and a concentration of males at the top.

Perceptions. Elmwood's divisions affected not only the distribution of authority, but the way staff saw and heard the reality of home life. Administrators thought of their occasional hands-on work as an expression of their engagement, while direct-care staff dismissed it as tokenism. Gordon found gossip to be a major irritant, whereas Nina heard it as a key to people's discontents. Supervisors could make straightforward requests, but what caregivers heard was not just their words but their tone. People's perceptions thus varied with their place in the structure, leading them to derive different meanings from the same sets of experience.

Support. The fundamental issue of support for staff included both the emotional needs that people had and the ways they tried to get them fulfilled. Workers required a place to escape from conflict, a setting in which to grieve, an opportunity to rage about abuse or injustice or neglect. Some individuals satisfied these by having a special confidant among their colleagues. Claire and Nina, Denise and Martha were paired in this way. Many employees, however, wanted more sustenance than they could get from their peers. The pattern that some developed—that of turning to Nina or Claire for a friendly ear—was symptomatic of the tensions in their situation, and the need to go to a neutral outsider for help.

Faith. Religion provided a different kind of assistance for some staff. Claire and a number of caregivers found an important source of support in their faith. They did not talk about this in the same evangelical way that Tilly did, but their beliefs sustained them through the declines, the deaths, and the lesser stresses of their jobs. One of the most disturbing aspects of work at Elmwood, for example, was dealing with the victims of Alzheimer's disease: while it was difficult for workers to cope with their outbursts, their decay, and their silences, it was even more perplexing to contend with the mystery of why the illness struck some and not others, why its victims numbered those who had once been among the most articulate and fastidious. What faith gave to some staff, such as Claire, was not specific answers to these questions, but rather the general reassurance that while they could not know the reasons why, they could nevertheless fulfill their calling by caring for those in their charge.

Abuse. Abuse was another feature of people's work life, and it had all the power of a double-edged sword. The more visible edge was the mistreatment of residents. Staff acknowledged its occurrence but stressed its rarity. Gordon was emphatic that employees were encouraged to report instances that they saw or heard of, and people whose abusive behavior was confirmed or highly suspect were let go. During his years at Elmwood, however, only a handful of cases had come to such an end.

The sword's hidden side was the mistreatment of staff. Gordon and Nina, along with Kate and other aides, argued that much of the abuse experienced by the elderly had to be understood in relation to the behavior of the residents themselves. Several people living at the home could be highly provocative, and the extreme responses of workers were often a reaction to this. Employees mentioned these situations not to excuse the behavior of their colleagues, but to underline its occurrence as part of a mutually stressful relationship. They felt that this was a piece of the home's life that families and casual visitors never saw, because their focus was on the quality of care rather than the nature of work within the institution.

Family. The relatives of residents were one of the most contradictory elements in the world of staff, and employees were not shy about characterizing the virtues and failings of the kin they met. Some, such as Stavros's daughter Katina and Frank's son Patrick, were well liked and respected. They were friendly, made reasonable requests, and acted with an appreciation of the demands that work placed on caregivers. Furthermore, they were attentive to their relatives, and—in Katina's case—even spent time with several of the more isolated patients when they visited. A few individuals were hardship cases, such as Eva's brother William, who seemed to pay for every good-faith effort he made. None of this escaped the notice of staff, who contrasted such behaviors with that of other families who neglected or rarely saw their kin, or who came to the home more in the role of complainant than companion. The latter individuals included those who treated the home as a stage upon which to act out the final scenes of a domestic drama—a "theater of guilt," as Gordon called it, in which employees found themselves cast in the villainous roles.

Morality. Moral judgments by staff were a recurrent aspect of their experience. They evaluated families, coworkers, and the institution as a whole. This was not done systematically, but was an element of their reaction to the people and the situations that work confronted with them. The tendency to judge grew out of the fact that Elmwood was, in many ways, an emotionally charged environment: compassion, hope, indifference, anger, decline, and death left few witnesses to life there feeling neutral. This intensified relations among the staff, informed their assessment of family members, and highlighted—for some workers—the merits and failures of institutionalization as a solution to aging and frailty.

Staff as a whole were also caught between two contradictory models of what the home itself stood for. The expectations of some residents that they could recover their health was fostered by their relatives, but rarely realized. With much more fragile patients than had been true even a decade before, Elmwood's emphasis had shifted to a model of *caring* rather than *curing*. While this change was difficult even for some staff, it also raised ethical dilemmas for all personnel about how honest to be with residents and their families about people's health status. The choice between deceit and truthfulness was complicated by related concerns over kindness and respect...

including what Louise named the employees' own need "to be kind to themselves."

Almost every staff member was vehement about not wanting to end his or her days in a nursing home. Only Gordon phrased some of his objections in political terms, castigating society for prolonging life without regard for the physical and social conditions in which this left people. Others talked in more visceral language, agreeing with Louise's judgment that "deterioration was worse than death," or concurring in Denise's preference for "death over disability." But Denise may have also spoken for others as well as herself when she admitted that this judgment reflected her weighing of her options at the healthy age of 38. She acknowledged that she might feel differently about such a choice after the passage of another three or four decades. "Life can get more precious when there's less of it left. I don't want to end it in a home, but maybe I'll decide to take it on whatever terms I can get. This is not a bad place to be if you have to be in a place like this."

9 THE VOLUNTEERS

To volunteer is to offer one's time, which is a gift that can never be reclaimed, in exchange for people's gratitude, which is a reward that can rarely be bought. The gift of service is one whose deepest motives and rewards lie within the giver. For some, volunteering is a way to lay hold of a small amount of quiet honor. It sustains the spirit, deriving its sustenance from the cultural wisdom that sees service as a special form of virtue. While we are promised honor and security for laying up the ways and means of life, our folklore also holds that it is better to give than to receive.

Morally speaking, this tension between giving and getting is one of our culture's favorite dichotomies. It seems to embody the basic ethical choice between selfishness and altruism. To many volunteers at Elmwood Grove, however, the acts of offering and receiving were not inherently antithetical. They felt that they were part of one of those fortunate human situations where the two could comfortably coincide. Rather than having to choose between being a donor or a taker, they insisted that being of service allowed them to be both. Their relationships with residents provided them a chance to prove their own worth. As some visitors attested, the benefits of what they did—as companions and as witnesses—were implicit in their role rather than in something external to it. For these people, the moral of the tale was a variation on the theme that virtue was its own reward.

What seemed inherent in the role of giver was not that simple or that uniform, however. Virtue was rewarding for some, but not sufficient for others. The experience meant different things to different volunteers. For certain individuals, the nursing home was a place to escape to rather than a place to escape from. They found it a relief from the tedium of school, the routine of marriage, or the repetitiveness of work. For others it was relevant experience for a future career in gerontology, veterinary medicine, or recreation. There were also those who needed to see visible signs of improvement in the patients they visited in order to feel that their own presence had been worthwhile. Thus, while volunteers were sitting in the same room, saying similar words to the same group of people, they could still be separated from one another by gulfs of purpose and meaning. Their accounts of what they saw and felt, earned and learned, were too varied, too Rashomon-like, to be reduced to a single version or vision

Even the same volunteer could sound like a different person at different points of time's trajectory. Cathy, for example, was one of the visitors who had become deeply attached to Eddie. But in the course of one year—as his speech slurred and his mind slowed—her feelings about him changed from life-sustaining compassion to a compassionate death wish. Fridays would come around, and when she got on the bus to Elmwood, she found herself wishing he would not be there. She wanted him out of his misery, and his misery out of her life. Well before she had made this explicit in her own mind, she had become convinced that a convergence had developed between her needs and his, that his death would satisfy both of them. When she realized this one Friday night while sitting with Mandy over coffee, Cathy's self-image collapsed in a small rubble of guilt and grief. At first she thought she was crying for Eddie; later she recognized that the tears were also for herself. In the subtle mix of her emotions, Cathy was trying to balance her feelings for and her feelings about Eddie. She was one of several volunteers whose affection for this man had grown up at a time when Eddie's own powers had just begun to decline. The changes that were hard to face at first eventually became hard not to see. Finally denial no longer worked. Riding home together each week, Cathy and Mandy began to surrender to the reality principle. They found that they could acknowledge outside of the home what they had witnessed without comment on the inside. Cathy would ask, "Did you see how hard it was for Eddie to grasp what was going on?" Understood, if unstated, was the implicit message: "And do you hear how hard it is for me to watch what he is going through?"

CATHY MONTOYA

"Not the Center of Everything"

In some situations, the border between feeling and perception becomes diffuse. The two currents mix in the mind the way sea and river flow in an estuary. The lives of volunteers involved a similar blending, one of inner and outer experience. While new visitors could sometimes guess at what they would see in a nursing home, few were able to anticipate how these events would invade and shape their emotions. The difference between those who persisted in their work and those who decided to leave after a short while had to do in large measure with how people coped with this unpredictable mix of river and sea, sense and feeling.

Some individuals were better equipped for this challenge than others, not because they knew more, but because they were better prepared to deal with what they felt. Nor was their ability to relate to the elderly with integrity and compassion proportional to their age. At 21 years, Cathy Montoya was already a veteran volunteer who could look back on two years of work at Elmwood. While her time of service had given her much to reflect on, her initial decision to get involved had itself been unpremeditated. She had seen a notice about the pet program on a bulletin board during her freshman year and decided the same day to join. There was no meeting scheduled for new volunteers that month, and so after contacting the organization's director, she simply began to visit Elmwood at the appointed time on Fridays. Her choice of this facility was pure circumstance: it was the one visit during the week that fit into her schedule of classes and laboratories.

She acknowledged that the sessions were difficult at first: there were only two other volunteers going to the home at the time, and they did not always come each week. Cathy would show up some Friday afternoons to discover that she was the only visitor present, presiding over several dogs, a cat, and the expectations of a half-dozen residents. The hardest part about being alone was that the elderly people themselves were often very quiet; normally the volunteers would talk to one another and the recreation staff to "keep it going." But when she had no peers with her, Cathy found herself doing monologues. She remembered feeling a bit like an actress whose partner had forgotten to come on stage, leaving her with the task of improvising lines until the cast and the plot caught up with her.

Though Cathy believed in the value of what she was doing from the start, she also felt the need to expand it beyond the scope of a one-woman show. After a few weeks of uncertain rewards and occasional Friday afternoon stage fright, she worked out her best improvisation by recruiting her friend Mandy as a volunteer. From that point on they went and worked together as a team. Eventually a few other reliable visitors began to attend, and Cathy was then able to enjoy two of the qualities she felt essential to the program's success—continuity and sociability. What had begun as a solo act had become an ensemble of players.

While she had never done pet therapy before, Cathy was not a novice at volunteering. In high school she had belonged to an organization through which she had made weekly visits to Delia, an isolated elderly woman in her hometown neighborhood. As part of that school program she had also helped to take groups of handicapped adults to a local fair each spring. She recalled the disabled people taking a special pleasure in visiting the stalls and exhibits that featured farm animals. But working with the aged and the handicapped was not an unmixed blessing. The home visits to Delia were "frustrating at times. She was stubborn, often depressed." Cathy remembered wondering "if we were doing much good going to see her. But Delia really had no one else, no one who she regularly spent time with. If she was hard on us occasionally, maybe it's because she needed someone to take it out on. Basically, we were the only company she kept."

Though these earlier experiences involved neither pets nor institutions, they set a precedent, a level of awareness for Cathy. Watching what happened at the livestock pavilions reinforced what she had already read about the value of using animals with disadvantaged people. Walking into the emptiness of one older person's apartment brought home to her the way in which isolation bred anger, and loneliness fostered retreat.

Some of these insights into adversity helped to mediate and motivate Cathy's later experiences at Elmwood.

> What I went through in high school was like a preview of what I now see in the nursing home. A lot of these people, nobody ever visits them. We've noticed that new patients [i.e., the recent admissions] who come in can be really talkative at first, but after they've been there a couple of weeks they start withdrawing into themselves. And you never know whether or not it's because of their health problems or, I thought at first, drugs. But I don't believe it's that. Mandy, me, and the rest of us feel it's more psychological. If you can imagine being surrounded by people you know all your life and then suddenly waking up in a place where you hardly see anyone familiar. So we figure if we could talk to them, be somebody else who visits them, *become* familiar, that would help. If we can at least do that, it has to make some kind of difference.

The satisfaction that came to Cathy during the pet sessions was occasionally tempered by what she saw immediately afterwards.

> Sometimes we take them back to their rooms or we wheel them to the hallway, to a place where they like to sit, but then they may not even be near another person. Many of them just do not talk or relate. Do they think that no one will listen or have anything worthwhile to say? To watch the ones who don't seem to connect makes me feel empty. You wish that there could be just one person to sit down with each of them and talk to them during the day. Other times you walk down the halls and people you don't even know look up at you. You wish you could spend a few moments speaking with each of them, but there simply aren't that many hours in the day. Besides, I'm really not sure which of them would want that anyway.

Despite her desire to draw patients out and engage them, Cathy had also come to recognize—almost with reluctance—that withdrawal and illusion were strategies that worked best for some residents.

> I have often asked myself what it would be like to live here. I wouldn't like it, I know that. Trying to put yourself into that situation makes you see why

people might act the way they do—either silent or bizarre. Sometimes I wonder if the people who act kind of strange aren't the ones who are really the smartest. I think of Bonnie, who's usually smiling when she comes in, and then there're days when she seems to be staring off into space. She'll talk about all kinds of things. You ask her about her past, and every time you go to visit she's done something different. One day you ask her if she ever traveled and she'll say, "Oh yes, all the time . . . to lots of countries." And then the next week, "Oh no, I stayed in the South my whole life." But she seems happy. I'd rather be like that than withdrawn or not talking to anybody. For someone like Bonnie, it's as if she keeps inventing different kinds of histories. Maybe that's what fills up her life now, living out all the things she never got to do.

While Bonnie clung to what her imagination could give her, time gradually divested Cathy of some of her own illusions about what she could accomplish as a volunteer. She had first hoped that pet therapy would lead to lasting improvements in the condition of residents, but later felt that for many of the people, the benefits were more likely to be immediate and short-term in nature. This was not to devalue what patients derived from them, including comfort, company, and variety in a life with few diversions. They were also a beginning for the friendships she slowly formed with Eddie, Stavros, Bonnie, and Yvonne. But she knew as well that for some residents, people like Eva and Sarah, there was no carry-over from week to week. In their eyes she was a first-time visitor each time, a person who had never been there before. Like Bonnie's varied versions of her history, the sessions for these patients were a recurring novelty that made the present pleasant, but did not build into a coherent past.

If volunteering had carried no more of a reward to it than pleasantness, however, Cathy would not have lasted for two years. In both tangible and emotional ways, she found the experience of more enduring worth. At the animal level itself, the dog whom she borrowed to visit with each week helped to fill the gap left by the pet she had had to leave with her parents when she went away to college. It gave her "a dog away from home." But a more compelling reason for Cathy was the insularity of her own university life: she thought that the visits not only diminished the loneliness of residents, they helped break down the isolation of her and her peers.

It gets us off campus, which is important because you sometimes forget that you need to see people of other ages, not just students and professors. Here you're with men and women with different problems and different ideas about the world. You remember that there's more to life than school, and that there's life *after* school. It puts your own existence and all of its problems into a new perspective. At least for a moment you are not the center of everything . . . and believe me, that's a relief.

Moving into another setting, a special kind of space each week, also helped Cathy to rethink the way she experienced time. For her, the flow of events fell into shapes that were different from those seen by some of the elderly. Cathy's own time frame, for example, was more expansive than what Bonnie or even Stavros could muster: they were concerned about and content with each week, and did not look much beyond it. But when Cathy thought about what the visits meant to her, her vision was a long-term one, embracing months rather than moments.

It is the way the visits feel when I look back over the winter or the whole year that stays with me the most. There are special times that stand out in my memory too, of course. I know I get a lot out of it, even though that isn't always the case each week. Sometimes I don't know why I do it. Maybe it's something I simply feel I *can* do. I want to do something other than just be closed up studying, inside my own world. When people recognize us from the week before and smile and say, "Hi. How are you doing?" that's wonderful. When Denise or Louise tells us that someone like Frank was in a bad mood all day, angry or throwing things, and that it somehow changed when we came with the animals, that makes it feel worthwhile. There's one woman, Marjorie, who the staff say never speaks, either when she's in her room or out in the hall. Then one day she was wheeled in and she started shouting at the dogs. First I was scared. But she was happy. She yelled and talked to them for half an hour.

There aren't many times when it's that gratifying . . . I mean so immediate or dramatic. Week to week, something explosive or poignant, like having Marjorie open up, isn't that common. What feels good is usually quieter. But maybe if there weren't those special moments it would be harder to believe we're really doing something that matters. In two years I've gotten to know some people well. At least I've gotten to feel close to them. For all the residents who don't remember us one visit to the next there are also people like Stavros and Yvonne, who I can pick up conversations with right where we left off the last time. With them there's a carry-over: it's a relationship. What I mean is that it's more than just a contact, a brief encounter. It's not that I don't think there isn't something valuable that we're giving to the others too. But when there's at least some kind of history, I feel connected to what I'm doing.

The residents who most perplexed Cathy were the ones who simply did not respond to her or the animals or other visitors. Unless it was someone she had dealt with before, she did not know whether to keep trying, or whether repeated attempts amounted to a form of harassment. There were also problems with people who did talk but who could not make logical connections in what they said. Cathy admitted that sometimes the illogic was funny—the day, for example, when Bonnie greeted her and Mandy as "the new guests at the hotel," or when Eva insisted on doing Cathy's hair as if she were her sister—but at other moments, especially when someone was trying desperately to be understood, she found it more painful than amusing. If the others who were present in the room began to laugh, she found herself getting upset. "I know the laughter's part of the way people deal with this, a kind of defense, but it's one of those rare moments when I'd prefer the whole place to be silent."

Loudness could be as problematic as logic. If a patient had poor hearing, volunteers had to raise their voices to be hard, and then the entire recreation area became a party to the conversation. It made it hard, Cathy felt, to talk either with candor or without self-consciousness. Visiting residents in their own rooms was a more confidential experience, and she did that from time to time. But even there volume just gave way to privacy as the main problem. Cathy pointed out that

> no one lives alone here, so there are usually roommates or staff around. In the recreation area we're generally sitting in a circle, which is great because it makes things more sociable, but if someone gets upset, then everyone else notices. When people remember their spouses or children, or pets who have passed away, or when they *can't* remember them—that will do it. A person may start crying or get agitated, and it's hard to know how to respond then. You feel bad for them . . . and conspicuous yourself.

The residents who evoked the most compassion from Cathy, however, were those whose minds were all in place but who had lost the freedom of movement—the people who had wills but not the ability to put their desires into action. They were, in her view, "prisoners of their bodies." The energy and frustration they felt within were sometimes visible on the surface of the skin. "I can catch it on Frank's face and hear it in the tone of his voice; I can read it in Stavros's eyes even though he doesn't say much about it. Anger in one case, dignity in the other: but the source is the same." She could also see and sense their intelligence, knowing all the while that "they still think a lot about the things they can't do." She found it painful to witness their captivity.

Witnessing it fed Cathy's own sense of frustration because there was no easy target to blame. Though she was less politically minded than Gordon, she also felt that the residents' "captivity" was not just medical but also social in nature. She laid it at the feet of a world that "still can't face up to growing old."

While Cathy hoped she would never have to move into such a facility herself, being a volunteer had given her a different awareness of what it was like to live and work in such a setting. She had considerable respect for the staff, most of whom she found to be genuinely concerned about the patients they cared for. Their ways of handling some of the residents at first disturbed her, but Cathy later concluded that this had more to do with her own naïveté about certain patients' needs and capabilities. When she saw patronizing behavior it still upset her, but she was also candid enough to recognize that she slipped into it herself. "Mandy sometimes mimics what I sound like at times, and then I can hear how much I've talked down to people that day." It was this recognition that made Cathy less likely to leap to a judgment about what she saw and heard others doing. She had become diffident in this regard. Perhaps, she suggested, being patronizing was "an occupational hazard."

Though Cathy became much more aware, over the years, of the limits to what pets and volunteers could do, she remained an advocate of this form of therapy. What she felt she could also offer in retrospect was a more realistic appraisal of what it took to be effective in such an activity. She identified the key quality as the ability to "put oneself in the place of people who don't have what you have: people who once had pets and health, and families and freedom. Then you must be able to see something of what this means to them." It was not that you could really fill the void, she added: the animals you brought were temporary, the health and home and freedom residents wanted could not be restored . . . either by you or anyone else. "If you think you're going to remake their lives by offering your presence, you're going to be disappointed and probably depressed yourself."

But, she continued, volunteers could still do something "meaningful, even if it seems modest." This was to "acknowledge what these people want, what they have been, and what they have lost." In the act of doing that, she argued, "we can reaffirm the residents as people. And they *are* still people in spite of everything that's been reduced. That's what we have to fight not to lose sight of." Being even a small part of their lives, bearing witness to them, Cathy felt, could give the elderly "a measure of humanity, a measure of meaning," to help them "break through the silence" in which age had enclosed them.

STEVE NAKARA

"Putting Her Ghost to Rest"

It took ten months of volunteering before Steve Nakara talked about the ghost and the guilt that accompanied him each week. Fifteen years before, when still in high school in Maine, one of his grandmothers had been placed in a nursing home. He had visited her regularly at first, but then, as she became increasingly senile and frail, it grew more and more upsetting to talk with or even look at her. He eventually stopped going. She died a few months later without his seeing her again. "She quickly lost her memory, her awareness, and then just lingered on," he recalled.

I stopped visiting eight or nine weeks before she finally died. I never even made a clear decision to do that. Maybe that was typical adolescent behavior: I just drifted into not going. You know—passive resistance. But afterwards

I had a bad feeling for abandoning her that way. And I had really bad thoughts about institutions, too. Maybe I needed to blame them instead of myself, but at the time I felt she didn't just die there—I felt that in some way, maybe in *their* own passive way, they helped to kill her.

These feelings slept for over a decade, however, and during that time Steve never entered a nursing home. Ultimately it was his own domestic life that revived the memories by bringing him inside another facility. By the time he was thirty he had gone to college and graduate school, chosen a career in agricultural development, acquired a dog, and gotten married . . . all in that order. He had met his wife Beth in a canine obedience class, which they continued to attend with their two dogs after the four of them were living together. "We joked that we knew how to love and honor, but *they* needed to obey."

It was the dogs and Beth who led Steve back to his unfinished past. Every month the people in their course got a newsletter, and one issue carried an article about the pet program's need for new volunteers. It was the kind of notice Steve would normally have overlooked, or have read and forgotten. But Beth saw it as an answer to a personal dilemma. Her grandmother Laura had recently entered Elmwood, and Beth was finding it hard to face up to the ordeal of visiting her each week. The few times she had gone, she felt awkward, unfocused, self-conscious. The whole environment was unsettling: Beth was dismayed by the ranks of residents seated along the corridors in wheelchairs, by the stares she felt were fixed on her, by questions patients asked that she could not answer. But since Elmwood was one of the institutions where the pet program held its sessions, Beth thought it might be easier to go there as a volunteer, bearing an "official" purpose and a built-in topic of conversation.

More out of loyalty than enthusiasm, Steve agreed to accompany her. It was a bit of a lark at the start—"The dogs' day out," as he remembered it. After the animals had been screened, they all went through a brief orientation to the home, and then began attending sessions. At first the novelty was diverting, and Beth found it less troubling to be with her grandmother because they had, in the dogs, something immediate and easy to speak about. The format also deflected Beth's attention from the disabilities of other residents. But this period of distraction had a relatively brief half-life. Within a few weeks the dog talk wore thin, and during the moments of hesitation and silence, the afflictions and the voices of nearby patients grew more noticeable. Beth withdrew more to her grandmother's side, spending less time with the other residents around her. Steve, meanwhile, had been moving further afield. At first, while Beth was with her grandmother, he had wandered aimlessly through the lounges and corridors, letting his dog lead him. Encountering a few of the same people several weeks in a row, he began a routine of small talk with them. Some were interested in the dog, others more interested in him. Then, in a search for a bit of structure, Steve found himself seeking the same residents out on successive visits. The result was a series of intermittent but ongoing dialogues, and the weight of habit slowly settled itself into a pattern. He had his "regulars."

Although Steve was in demand, it took him several more weeks to realize what this meant. People expected him: it was not simply flattering—it took the burden of proof, the need to initiate, off his shoulders. He found it easy to be with the talkative ones, such as Tilly and Frank. Her smile and his animation set the tone: "It was like going to my grandmother's apartment before she got sick," Steve said, "just visiting and chatting." But his walks around the floors also took Steve into the world of the silent and the confused. Perhaps because his dog approached them, or because he himself felt compelled to know something of who they were and what they were like, he tried to talk to some of these people. He made himself go see a few of them each week. "The residents who're deteriorating before my eyes— sometimes I can't believe this is happening to another human being. Maybe I go out of disbelief, because they're the hardest for me to accept."

Steve created a rhythm, a sequence, to balance the extremes.

> I go to Bonnie and Dave and Yvonne first, the people near the kitchen on the ground floor. They're a delight. They help me to get into it. Then, the far end of North Ward on Two, that's where the hard part starts. Most of the people on that floor, like Marjorie, don't recognize me from week to week. Sometimes I get depressed when I come off that unit. It feels like there's no way out, that it's a one-way street going nowhere. Those patients will never be themselves again. So it helps to go over to East Two and South Two, to see Frank, Tilly, and Stavros to finish. There're a lot of times on my way to North Two, I get into the elevator and just lean against the wall, saying, "Why am I doing this to myself?" There's a little bit of dread going up there, but I always feel better coming out for having done something. Maybe I get a rise out of Sarah and, small as that is, it can change me for the rest of the day. Somewhere in my mind, also, North Two's connected with my grandmother, even though there's really no one up there who actually reminds me of her. The whole unit does. It's four hundred miles and half my life away, but that's where she was living in the end.

Once, during his second year as a volunteer, Steve did stop visiting North Two for a while. The end of his graduate work was looming ahead, he was having trouble finding a job and, as he put it, "I was already depressed enough. I couldn't take the risk of getting even more depressed by going up there. I guess I 'pulled a grandmother' again, you could say. But then it passed and I felt better, so I started back on that unit and thought more— or was it less?—about myself because of it."

His experiences made Steve sensitive to the depth of individual needs, the hunger for constancy.

When we visit Elmwood, I believe we make life a little better for people there. But the other side of the coin is how residents react when we don't show up. One woman there, Yvonne, has gotten so attached to Mandy that on a week when she doesn't visit, Yvonne starts to worry that Mandy may never come again. It's not quite like a drug, but people do come to assume that certain of us will be there. It becomes a kind of dependency in that they do depend on us to show up. That makes sense to me if I think about it, but it's something we really didn't think through at first. A couple of them even prepare for a visit, and then, if it doesn't happen, the let-down can be pretty steep. Yvonne, for example: she lines up bits of cheese on her dresser each week for when Mandy brings Yussy. Tilly and Frank once lectured me the week after a Friday when I didn't visit. They told me I was "not to do that again." I said to myself: "Hey, I didn't sign a contract." But then I thought: well, maybe I did make a kind of social contract.

Once he recognized their nature, people's expectations were not that difficult for Steve to live with—even when he could not fulfill them. A resident's death was another matter. The loss of someone he had gotten to know could be painful enough. Their rapid "replacement" made it even harder by making the death feel unreal.

You see them one week and then, within a few days, someone new has moved into their room. It's almost like they didn't exist. Just within that week, all traces of them have disappeared: their clothes, their pictures, their name outside the door. That's hard to take. I know, as an economist, that the economics are against it, but they should leave their room empty for a while, or do something like that, to show that there is an emptiness where they once were.

There were other kinds of shock. Once, Sarah Kavalick, a woman Steve had regularly visited on North Two, had suffered a stroke and gone to the hospital. Steve had heard this news by phone from Denise, and when he asked about her on his next visit, a resident on the floor said, "Oh, she's gone." The tone of finality was accented by a slow, heavenward wave of the hand. It was a gesture of farewell, a last good-bye. The next time Steve came, he went by Sarah's old room, saw again that neither she nor her name were there, and once more registered the fact of her death with sadness. Near the end of that afternoon he was up on South Two and almost collided with Sarah as she was being wheeled out of the lounge near her new room. It was a terrible moment, he recalled, one in which "the shock of seeing her was far more powerful than the relief. I hadn't seen a ghost. I'd seen a resurrection."

Despite the surprises, the bouts of dismay and depression, the rewards of going remained dominant for Steve.

The best part is being needed, doing something that matters for someone else. . . . Obviously we're not all cut out to do this kind of work. I think those who stick with it are people with a lot of self-discipline, who manage their time well and really want to accomplish something for others—even if there're days when it's painful or disturbing. There are hard things to face up to and deal with. You have to *want* to be able to deal with them. Otherwise they'll put you off right away. About half the time I'm getting ready to set out for Elmwood I can think of a thousand reason why I can't go. But I've just decided I'm going to visit every week regardless. Because as soon as I start making excuses for not going, then I know it'll be easier and easier not to go.

Beth found the excuses. Except for her grandmother Laura, she could not commit herself as Steve had. The images and sounds of the home assaulted her: the bent bodies, the pleading voices there, overshadowed the people who were doing well. Her mind moved to what was worst: she knew that, but could still not stop the pull. And there were other binds: "I should have stuck with it," she once reflected, "because I realized how much it meant to them. But it was almost like I couldn't win. Sometimes when I went I felt guilty for the times I *didn't* go because I saw how good it made them feel." She paused, then added: "Perhaps I gave all that I had to my grandmother. The others frightened or depressed me. They looked like something she might become. But Steve," she pointed out, had "already seen his grandmother go that way." The present did not seem to haunt him the way the past did. She guessed that Elmwood's patients gave him the means "for putting her ghost to rest."

Over the months, however, Steve found himself wrestling not just with memories, but with his feelings about institutions. His regard for the home and its staff were high, and he recognized, almost reluctantly, that it was the right place for some residents to be. His opinions about caregivers echoed those of Gordon:

I have total respect for the people who work on the units there forty hours a week. It's sometimes hard for me to visit just for an hour and a half. I can't conceive of anyone with that sort of patience. Those who can last there honestly amaze me, regardless of whether it's saintliness or doggedness. All I know is that I couldn't take it day after day.

I've had bad feelings about nursing homes since I was a teenager, and I guess I still do. But now I also know that there are residents at Elmwood who love it there. Tilly is one. Her roommate Vivian's another: she thinks going there was the best thing she's ever done. She couldn't keep up her house or take proper care of herself because of her bones and her nerves; she worried about that and her safety all the time. So she moved to Elmwood, and now she feels like she's died and gone to heaven.

But Steve could not picture himself in the same place. The only role for him in the home was that of visitor, not resident.

In the beginning I remember that going to North Two was almost like going to the zoo. I'm sorry, but that *is* what it felt like—as if you were on the outside looking in. Later, when it got to be more comfortable, when I was closer to some of the people there, it still felt bad telling them about all the everyday things I did—like taking the dog to the vet or going shopping—because they haven't gotten out of that wheelchair in months, and probably won't get out of it until they die. They're going to stay on that same unit to eat, sleep, dream, despair. They exist in that chair, except to be put to bed. . . . I think when I get that old there's no way I'm going to go into a nursing home, even one with healthier people. Because once you're there, if something happens to you, they move you upstairs. If I get that bad, I'd want to die. Honestly, I'd take an overdose or something. I don't want to sit there and wait and try to be content when someone like me comes in for an afternoon. I can be *me*. I couldn't be *them*.

JANICE ASHLER

"More Good Energy Than Good Sense"

After a visit to Elmwood Grove one cold Friday in March, Janice Ashler offered me a lift home. We packed our pets in her car, scraped the ice off the windshield, and dumped our down coat-covered bodies onto the front seat. I commented on how tired she looked. Janice laughed as she slumped behind the wheel. "I have more good energy than good sense."

She was, in some ways, a classic community activist—politically astute, religiously connected, and overextended. But where some well-intentioned individuals fail at their good works because they are not good at dealing with people, Janice possessed social as well as spiritual graces. She had warmth, a reassuring smile, a soothing voice—qualities that encouraged others to trust her and talk.

She could be motherly or empathic, without stooping to condescension. This was a skill she had honed raising three children, all of whom had now grown into adolescence. She once reflected:

As they got older, they became, in an unexpected way, more demanding. The didn't need just food and a bath or a car ride; they wanted to be listened to and given respect, to be acknowledged as individuals. They helped me learn how complicated people are, how their needs change. It wasn't instant insight, and I wasn't a perfect mother, but I found your children can teach you if you let them.

While her sons and daughter were still young Janice embarked on a series of community projects. She did volunteer work with Asian refugees, ran a church fund drive, and later drove in a meals-on-wheels program. But the most difficult enterprise she ever faced was the nursing home—not because the people were so old, but because they were so vulnerable, so needy. What heightened her dismay was a mental picture, carried in her mind from the start, of all that was desperate in institutional life. It was like a photographic negative just waiting to be developed, and it came from her fellow activists. "People at the church were always being asked to visit places like this—but while many claimed they were willing, most didn't follow through because it was too hard to just walk into one and start talking to whoever was there. Or they'd visit once or twice and not know what to do. They painted a pretty bleak picture, and then begged off."

The full story of Janice's own ambivalence was more complex, made up of part image, part biography.

> I had strong doubts about this kind of place because my mother is in one in Arizona. She started to go senile about two years ago and my brother—who lives out there—he and I realized that this was the only alternative for her. I feel bad she has to be in a home, and yet I want the experience to be a good one for her. When I heard about the program here, I was sitting in my half "empty nest"—not feeling lonely, but in between things, waiting, you might say, for my next enthusiasm. It was me and [my setter] Striker, out walking each day, keeping one another company. The notice about the pet visits caught us at a good moment. It got to me like one of those patriotic, wartime posters, you know the ones with General Kitchener or Uncle Sam pointing a finger and saying "I need you" . . . and your dog!

There were other figures in the background too.

> A year or two before, I had been to Hillview a few times for a church project—it's a retirement home, a place for people who are not totally independent, but who're still in pretty good health. I liked it there: the residents had their own rooms and furniture, and could organize a lot of their own lives. But the nursing home scared and depressed me even before I stepped inside. I thought, "These people have come to this point in their lives: they can't even take care of themselves; they are so physically incapacitated. My God . . . my mother's situation is like that."
>
> What can I say? It galls me to see her that way.
>
> In the beginning, going to Elmwood the first few times, I just had to steel myself for it. I needed to somehow get over that anger, or get past it for that day. Each week I had to rethink it. Some afternoons I went in and out of the place without trouble. Other weeks I came out and just fell apart—especially if I had thought of my mother. You never completely accept that kind of decline, not for your parents: they were the strong ones who once held you up.
>
> And you fear for yourself too. Some day I'm going to be old: am I going to be in that situation? That's partly why Hillview wasn't quite as scary. I can see coming to a point where I'll want to give up caring for a house, doing the cooking and shopping and cleaning, and I think I could probably be happy in a residence like that because it doesn't feel or look like an institution.

But I know the people there also have their anxieties: "How long can I keep my health?" "Am I going to wind up in the nursing home?" Residents there didn't actually talk to me much about that, but there was this way they had of speaking about others they knew: "Oh, Bill, hmmm, where has he gone? Oh yeah, to Riverside Nursing Home." They'd say it and then they'd kind of drop it. It's a bit like what happens with those who die there. At first, as a visitor, you only notice their absence. But where are they? "Oh yes... last week...," the others say, and their voice sort of trails away. It's a very quick kind of oblivion, very self-protective for those who are left.

Having visited with healthier people at Hillview made Janice sensitive to how different a "real" nursing home could be.

It's an enclosed world, but one that's cut off more by circumstance than necessity. People could get out more but they rarely do, except for day trips, or a family visit for those with relatives who invite them. Yet it's still not the depressing, awful place I was afraid it would be. Once I got to know the staff and saw how some residents do relate to each other, I started to think of it in a new way. One thing you learn is that the priorities there are not the same as yours. What is important to people on the outside is different from what's important to those on the inside. For example, you might say: "Oh, look at how they're dressed. Wouldn't they feel better if they were fixed up more?" Well, maybe yes, maybe no. Some are not even aware of this. A lot of that [attention to appearances] matters more to those who visit. What many residents care about is that you do some little thing while you're there that has meaning to *them*: you ask about their grandchildren, or you bring in a poster they can see every day. I liked to hear their stories, and then one day it hit me how much they just wanted to be listened to. So *my* priorities, and how I saw and heard things, also changed.

When I first went to Elmwood I was very critical of details, of what didn't make sense or seem necessary: of all the noise, all the people moving around without any purpose that I could see. But after I'd been there for a while, these things became less crucial. The "buzzing, blooming confusion" was in my mind. I began to see the routine and how things worked. I still heard the "dears" and the "sweeties", but I also noticed the aides who stopped to talk with people while they worked, the kind of moment your eyes miss when you're a newcomer and overwhelmed by it all. It's not that there aren't things that could be improved, but you begin to understand what does work and what matters most.

Aging also began to take on some new aspects. Janice became somewhat more interested in, if not accepting of, it because residents helped her to personalize what the experience could be like. They made growing older less of an abstract idea because their personalities gave it character. Now when she spoke of aging, she did it in terms of particular individuals.

I've learned you can still meet people who are animated, who carry with them interesting memories, who've had good or at least full lives. I think of Yvonne and Tilly in that way, even though Tilly's life would look paltry to most. There have been lots of ups and down for these women, but somehow they've come through. When you look at Stavros or Frank, you feel bad that physically they are breaking down. But you also learn from them that you can live to an old age and still be alert and mentally active. There's something here about human nature too, something stubborn and durable and funny. You see personalities grow old that were probably just the same way when they were growing up. . . . [The aide] Kate calls it her "more so" theory: as people get older they just get more and more like what they were, rather than less so. In my mind I can just hear Frank as a young man, cutting people and pretenses to pieces, and I end up laughing then at something I've never even heard. The sound of his voice sets my imagination going. I can predict how he'll act, guess at things he once might have said. Now he's a character in my life, not just a person in the home.

Elmwood's residents also showed Janice some poignant exceptions to this static image of human character.

Maybe, like Cathy says, the old are imprisoned by what age has done to their bodies, yet they also break free of other things. I notice that some, as they get older, are much more relaxed, even liberal in the way they think about certain issues. I don't know whether or not it's because they're not personally dealing with them any more, but they're much more accepting, say, of modern morals than you'd think. Bonnie and I were once talking about unmarried couples living together, and she said, "Oh, these young people nowadays. . . . " But she wasn't judging them: she was interested, almost amused by it. "They must put their parents into such a state," she said, and she was smiling! I think she was imagining herself doing it. Now maybe if it were her own son or daughter she'd feel differently. I don't know. But I do know of elderly couples who are living together now and not marrying, both for emotional and practical, usually financial, reasons. Yet it doesn't seem to bother them. Maybe they feel free to let go of some of the appearances they felt they had to keep up before.
   The letting go is there even in small ways. In the years before my mother went into the nursing home, she became so much less compulsive about cleaning up dishes and tables right away. She practically used to take the plate from under your food! Later on, but before her dementia, she'd casually leave dishes in the sink overnight, and just shrug about them. It wasn't indifference: it's not that she didn't care; it was that she'd stopped worrying about that kind of thing. To me it shows people's ability to let go of some of the structures they grew up with. Of course everybody isn't like that: there are those who have felt the same way since they were young. But many do change. They get free. That's hopeful—for me, at least—because it means there are new ways and new ideas to look forward to. I even find I'm loosening up now, and I suspect that raising three children and getting older myself is part of it.

On the darker side, however, Janice also saw other facets of aging where insight did not mean acceptance.

I can't reason myself past my mother's fate, the indignity of her life now. It is unfair, unjust. At times I feel she has been violated and stolen from me. So many outcomes make no sense. She and Stavros are like two sides of the same coin, her with a sound body and weakened mind, and him as sharp as ever, having to watch his health slip away.

I don't know whether people get more resigned to disability and death when they get older. Talking with some of the residents here convinces me that if you live long enough, you start to absorb that this is going to happen: to you, your family, to your friends. As I get on in years, I'm no different inside than I ever was, but I look in the mirror, and I see that I am. Bonnie and I once had a very lucid, a marvelous, bittersweet conversation about this. She brought it all up. I remember she said: "I don't feel any different now, inside here"—and she tapped her head—"or here"—and her hand went over her heart—"I don't. But then there's this old lady in the mirror, and she can't get around. Yet in my mind I look out and see things the same way I always did. Which one is me?"

Like Bonnie's views of her inner and outer self, Janice could not look out at the world of the nursing home without reflecting on her own inner uncertainty about institutional life. Alternately sad and angry about her mother, she tried to resist blaming the Arizona facility for her parent's situation. At a distance, Elmwood was a way to work out the ambivalence, to create meaning where neither hope nor acceptance could be found.

In the past I felt I wanted to get out of these places as soon as I walked into them. I didn't know what to say or do when I was there. I didn't see that I was helping, and it certainly wasn't making me feel very good.

Many of the people here, like my mother, have some kind of dementia. I know where their minds are at and realize they're deteriorating. But now I see something of what can be done to make them feel better, to reach those who seem out of touch or beyond recall. I can pick out the personalities, the names, the faces, and talk to them. You get to know the ones who can communicate directly, and the ones, like my mother, who can be made to feel something in other ways—even if the moment is a brief one that leaves no trace in the mind. I hope some volunteer out there with my mother feels the same way. If you can recognize at least the possibility for this, then the nursing home is not such an alien or alienating place.

For Elmwood to be that for Janice, however, it had to provide her at least the reward of reciprocity.

It feels good when residents begin to give back to you. That doesn't usually happen for the people who go in trying to be jolly, who tells jokes or something uplifting just to be cheerful, because then you find there isn't much coming back. It's nerves—I understand that—but it doesn't ring true, and the patients can hear it. I'm convinced that kind of visiting isn't terribly satisfying to elderly people. I don't think residents like you to jabber at them and joke and leave. You have to sit there for a while, and with someone who's demented it helps to bring something familiar. That's where my dog helps. He's not just an icebreaker: he reminds people of other things—their pets or being young or some place they once lived. When they can talk to you, instead of you just speaking to them, then you get more out of it. It becomes a relationship, not just a well-meant monologue.

Years of unpaid work had shown Janice that volunteers did get paid, but that it was in their own kind of currency.

I'm convinced that people volunteer for lots of reasons. But probably the bottom line, to be really honest, is you're getting something out of it. Whether it's a good feeling, or an escape from bad ones, or the knowledge you're helping someone, or your conscience telling you it's the right thing to do. It's different for each person. But if you don't get paid in some way, you wouldn't continue doing it. When it comes to the point where you're so bored or so anxious over the situation that you're not giving or getting what you can, then it's time to change.

I have a friend who used to be in pastoral work, and he said that whenever he got depressed he'd go visit a hospital. I thought at the time that this was crazy. I said, "Doesn't that make you even more depressed?" He answered, "No—it's the opposite. Those people can be going through all sorts of sadness or pain, but somehow they're offering me something that I need. It's not," he added, "that they're a reminder that 'there but for the grace of God . . . ,' or of how much worse off I could be. It's that they enable me to give them something." I never understood this at the time, but now that I've done this kind of work, I think I do. It's what I think of as 'selfish altruism.' I want to go not just because I'm doing something for them, but because they're doing something for me.

In Janice's version of voluntarism, then, the emphasis was on reward rather than sacrifice. Though her church had taught and inspired her a great deal, she insisted she was no martyr. "I don't go in for futility," she claimed, "I can get my exercise in better ways.

I do this because I feel I can make a difference. I know what it's like to be lonely, to live in a new place. And from my mother I now know something of what it means to lose control. At Elmwood it *can* be depressing, at times, but it's also satisfying to see people happier because of something you've done. It's not that I always have the time, but it's still far more interesting than most of the stuff I've got to do at home.

Sometimes it's easier to work with people and problems you're not living with. I wonder, for instance, if I would be so patient with my own mother. I can listen to Frank complain, or sit with Eva while she rambles and grips my hand, and not get irritated . . . or bored. But I have to be careful about getting overinvolved. I did that when I was teaching the refugees: I took on all their family problems, and I can feel the temptation to do that with certain people at Elmwood. I fall into that too easily and then [she laughed] I feel like a fallen woman. My sister-in-law, when she was being facetious, once put it well: "The church is a homewrecker," she joked. "It takes people away at the expense of their own families, their personal lives." Except that some of the residents here really *are* part of my life now. . . . But maybe that's what my sister-in-law meant.

FRIEDA RICHTER

"In a Few Years, There Go I"

Layers of ordinary life were being peeled away from Frieda Richter when she launched her brief career as an Elmwood volunteer. A year before, at the age of 65, her husband Al had died. Then, six months later she moved from Maryland to upstate New York to be near her daughter. Though in reasonably good health, Frieda had gone through cataract surgery soon after Al's death, and living close to family now felt reassuring. It was nevertheless a new community and a new world of widowhood, and she wanted to offset her sense of vulnerability by finding something of value to give herself to.

Frieda was no stranger to giving. While her three daughters were growing up, she had volunteered for 12 years with the Girl Scouts. She had been everything from troop leader and publicity chair to picnic organizer and fund raiser. But she and the girls had long grown out of marshmallows and summer camps, nature trails and bake sales. Since moving to upstate Frieda had been holding down a part-time job; and despite its dividends of pay and company, it was a bit of a bore, a shape without much content; "In fact," she thought, "a kind of marshmallow."

When Frieda heard about the animal program from a woman at work, then, she was drawn to it as something of more substance and risk. But it might not have struck her that way had she not already been a devoted pet owner. In the spring after her husband died, she had bought—at her oldest daughter's urging—a miniature poodle. While Colette was not the first dog Frieda had owned, it was the first pet she had ever purchased: all its predecessors had come to her as gifts. But Colette was also unique because she came into Frieda's life at the empty point of widowhood, and thus took on a role quite disproportionate to her size. By offering Frieda something worthwhile and sociable to do with her companion, the pet program felt too opportune to ignore.

Volunteering at Elmwood was nevertheless the first time Frieda had worked with the elderly. Within just a few weeks, however, she made several astute observations about what the visits meant to the women and men she had met. "To have someone or something to talk to seems like the most important thing," she noted.

Residents can't sit there and speak to themselves all day—I mean they *could*, but then people would think they're going off their minds. But they can sit there and talk to the dog because that's something that a sane and sweet person would do. Almost all the people I took Colette to see spoke with her. She was a living thing they could hold or touch, and that made all the difference between looking crazy and feeling caring. She was small enough to get up on the chairs and laps of patients who couldn't bend over to pat her. So even for the dog lovers she had all the virtues of a cat.

"It was funny," she digressed, "how the sessions affected Colette too. Poodles are pretty high strung, and before those visits, she wouldn't let people get near her. But after a few weeks, she became much less fussy, much more outgoing. The residents helped her to enjoy herself. It was like she went through the next stage of becoming domestic."

The visits were not always that heartening, for Frieda also noted a good deal of the sadness in what animals evoked for some people.

I brought Colette in to Barbara, and she held her and started telling me about the dog she had owned, the one she'd been forced to get rid of because she was entering a nursing home. I suppose this was part of what depressed me. I don't think I could ever give my pet up that way . . . but if you go into an institution like this you have no choice, and when I came with Colette it reminded her of this.

I think that behind the dog, so to speak, were all the other things in her life she had to give up: her home, her furniture, her record collection. The dog *was* very important to her—it was the only companion she had—but I think it was also her way to grieve for everything else she had to leave behind. You know people felt better for talking about this kind of thing, but while it was good for them to share it, it didn't feel so good to hear it.

Frieda's voice tapered off and she shook her head. "One lady said she took her dog to the vet and had it put to sleep because she knew no one else would take care of it the way she had. She felt so loyal and yet so guilty about that. Sometimes, when she spoke about it, her voice sounded proud and other times ashamed, as if there was no choice that wasn't in some way wrong."

Like other volunteers, Frieda eventually came to feel that her own role as visitor was at least as important as the part played by the pets.

I think there are residents who enjoy the people more than the animals. It's talking to us that seems to satisfy or excite them the most. The pets are of real interest to some, but they work more like a magnet for others: the animals bring us in and they bring them out. To tell you the truth, I had never been to a nursing home before I began doing this. I was surprised: they're not as bad as what you read about—at least Elmwood wasn't—but you still don't like to think of ever having to move to one yourself. It is safe and comfortable, but people obviously get lonely and demoralized too. I was hoping it wouldn't rub off on me.

While the volunteers were welcomed and needed, Frieda once punned about "not taking every visitor at face value." She explained that

the residents were actually friendlier with young people. With me, it was just another old person, and there were old people all around them. Seeing a different kind of face made the biggest difference to them, I think. A few times a young woman came who must have been in her late twenties, and she not only brought her dog but her daughter, who was about two years old. Well, I never saw the old people there so animated and interested as they were in that little girl. Their faces did truly light up. You'd think they'd never seen a child before in their lives, or at least in years. And I bet that for some of them that was probably the case.

What Frieda herself saw, then, was a case for how the age of the volunteer affected the response of the aged. College students as well as children were a part of both the outside world and people's pasts, and no older visitor could duplicate what they represented. A new, old face was not unwelcome, but it was still familiar in a way that diminished what elderly people could see in it. Such a reaction was not just a matter of appearance or association, however: Frieda felt there was a different kind of energy and humor to the young, an unguarded type of interest and enthusiasm, which brought residents out in a way that the simple good will of an older person could not. She echoed some of the same bias in an unguarded moment of her own: on reflection, she confessed, she might have "gotten more out of working with children" as she had in the past.

In the end, what finally compelled Frieda to stop volunteering was not her assessment of what she could do for the elderly, but her admission of what they were doing to her. She quit in her seventh month. When she had reached out to those who were especially frail, she had been overwhelmed by their neediness, by what she described as "their literal hold on me."

The people were too ill there. They sort of hung on to you, and I'm too old—I was too near that myself. When Eva took my hand it was different from what happened with Sarah. They were both gentle, but Sarah would allow me to let go after a while, and Eva didn't. Even when I indicated to her that I had to move on, she held on. Having to pull my hand away, to actually extricate myself, felt so bad, like I was abandoning her, like she was going to sink away. I thought: maybe there, in a few years, am I, and it was very depressing. I think the people really need the company, and they like the animals. They love the visits, in fact, I know they do. But I think it needs to be done by younger people... people who don't identify with them so much. I have only admiration for the students who can look at them and listen, who can be touched and not troubled by it.

For Frieda, however, who enjoyed being needed but cringed at being clung to, the nursing home was too much to bear. She explained that she "liked the residents who weren't so ill, but you just couldn't go up to them and ignore the others.

> It took me a long while to realize that this was why I was becoming so depressed—that I was seeing myself in those people. In a few years, there go I. . . . It *is*, after all, a real possibility. But I don't want to live my life now dwelling on that prospect. . . .
>
> I just stopped visiting. I looked for excuses for a few weeks, telling myself I had to do this or do that. But then, after a bit, I really knew why I didn't want to go. So I quit. With regret. I keep thinking now I should go back, but I know I can't. It means a lot to them, but it means too much to me.

CODA

It was not unusual for volunteers to get caught or caught up in their chosen role. The part they played was often more, or less, than they expected it to be. Beth found it too much or, to be true to her honesty, felt herself inadequate to its demands. Frieda could not match *her* needs to those of Elmwood's neediest. Steve, however, learned to think of himself in a new way, allowing the role to redefine him.

Elmwood was a place of confinement, yet it gave free rein to the fantasies of visitors: hopes, horrors, death wish, and death fear were all there. Cathy, who came to give relief from loneliness, also wanted to witness Eddie's final release from suffering. Janice found her mother in the body and spirit of others, the same places where Frieda saw the seeds of her own future.

The ability or the inclination of volunteers to continue with their work depended, then, on what they saw in others and what they felt about themselves. Experience filtered these visions and feelings, just as age tempered them. In the special pleading that volunteers did, there were echoes of what staff sometimes asked for themselves: to be able to bear witness to residents' lives, to be acknowledged for being at emotional risk, to leave the rooms of the dead empty for long enough for death itself to feel real.

And there was a good deal of the volunteers' behavior that was unpremeditated and unconscious: Janice's fall from grace into too much familiarity, Cathy's call for Eddie to die in peace, Frieda's postponing of her next visit from week to week, Steve filling the vacuum left by Beth. People were more attuned to what was particularly pleasurable or disheartening: Lilly's smile and Bonnie's moment in the mirror, the silence of Sarah or

Frank's angry words, Stavros's dignity and the grip of Eva's hand. The hardest task, for those with the moral curiosity to take it on, was to make sense out of what their senses told them. Of a different order was the challenge to simply accept what was and carry on in its name.

10 ALTRUISM AND AGING

Volunteering has a kind of fearful symmetry. It seeks to balance the generosity of some with the neediness of others. The offerings of time and attention may be recompensed with gratitude, or they can be seen as rewarding in their own right. While the perfect symmetry of such altruism is attractive, this idealized image conveys only some of the many meanings that voluntarism has had for individuals in our culture. Beyond altruism, people have used their voluntary work to achieve grace, to further their careers, to assuage guilt, to fulfill vows, to combat boredom, to lay ghosts to rest, and to confront a myriad of existential problems. For all its bad press and poor pay, voluntarism has long occupied a substantial place in the American search for meaning and fulfillment (Wendy Kaminer 1984).

Many observers of the United States, including native sons such as Ralph Waldo Emerson (1844), and perceptive visitors like Alexis de Tocqueville (1848), remind us that Americans have a long tradition of grassroots reform and community activism. Historically, some of the voluntary groups they created were designed to further the interests of their members, but others have been developed to help disadvantaged people from other segments of the population. The latter organizations have focused their energies on a range of political, philanthropic, and humanitarian issues. These have run the gamut from the abolition, temperance, and prison reform movements to efforts for securing the rights of women, animals, children, minorities, and the poor. Whatever personal rewards participants have derived from working for these causes, they have tended to see their actions as rooted in altruism rather than self-interest.

In the twentieth century, voluntarism has also become a potent element in various therapeutic programs. Recipients of the help offered by unpaid workers include the emotionally disturbed, the physically impaired, the developmentally retarded, and the institutionalized elderly. The concept of therapy itself has also undergone a great deal of change and expansion in recent decades. There has not only been a proliferation of specialities in the helping professions, but also a range of new treatment modalities using forms as diverse as poetry and plants, pets and dance. One of the more innovative movements in which volunteers have come to play a key role centers on the use of companion animals as a medium for education and therapeutic growth.

A number of the visitors who came to Elmwood Grove did so as members of the community's pet therapy program. But they were not alone in serving the institution. Others were there as part of church groups, local service organizations, or the Linda Westman Club—Elmwood's own women's auxiliary. Despite their numbers and their importance, volunteers such as these have often been overlooked in both the popular and the academic image of the nursing home. Public attention has understandably been focused on residents and their caregivers, even though a complete picture of geriatric facilities would include portraits of those who are there purely by choice rather than as a result of incapacity, the need for income, or family ties. Unpaid and unheralded, the impact of the volunteers' work, and the impact of their work on them, have usually gone unrecognized.[1]

Frieda, Cathy, Janice, and Steve were four individuals who illustrated the varied backgrounds, motives, and experiences of visitors. There were differences in their ages, genders, family situations, and previous levels of activism. They and their colleagues had diverse expectations about what Elmwood would be like, and they associated the residents there with different people from their own history. The accounts given by these four, along with information from other volunteers, raised several basic questions about what it was like to meet and work with the frail elderly. Why did people get involved in this kind of activity, and how did they feel about their encounters? What were the most satisfying and problematic aspects of visits for them? How did volunteers see their role, and how much turnover was there? And why did people choose to continue or terminate their involvement at the home? These issues will be examined here through a consideration of three sets of factors which deeply affected visitors: the relationship between intimacy and emotion; the sources of people's motivation and self-image; and the limitations on their voluntary role imposed by age, gender, and other personal qualities.

INTIMACY AND EMOTIONS

When volunteers and residents met at Elmwood Grove, they did so in various timeframes and places and moods. There was the group format of a pet session; there were scheduled activities where two or three volunteers came to assist the staff; and there were visitors who worked one-on-one with individual residents, reading with a woman, taking a man for a walk, or helping a person to write letters. There were also volunteers who made the rounds of one or two units each week, stopping to talk and spend time with a series of patients. People thus met in large groups and in pairs, while active or at leisure, in public or in private.

The most satisfied visitors were those who had discovered the format that best suited their own needs and abilities. For Cathy it was the sociable setting of a group, whereas Janice found her fulfillment spending separate half-hours with single residents. Steve sought variety by searching out a number of people on different units and floors. And Frieda, who began in the same serendipitous way, eventually found the whole experience to be too close, too overwhelming to continue with.

Not only did volunteers have distinct responses to these various ways to visit, they also had to deal—each in their own manner—with Elmwood's different levels of disability. The home accommodated both the moderately healthy and the seriously impaired, and most visitors gravitated to individuals at one or the other of these two extremes. Among those who had been coming for the longest time, and with great consistency, were people who regularly went to units with the frailest patients—individuals who were bedridden, confined to a wheelchair, or suffering pronounced forms of dementia. The particular satisfaction for these volunteers lay in the fact that many of the elderly they saw were especially in need of contact because they got fewer visitors than more capable residents. Furthermore, since these frail people were less mobile and active, there was more potential for volunteers to interact with them in a rare spirit of leisure and intensity. As Janice once put it, betraying a self-conscious sense of irony, these residents comprised "a captive audience." For various reasons, then, those areas of Elmwood where visits were least expected proved to be well cared for. In a twist on the conventional wisdom, the most disabled often got the most attention.

Many of the volunteers who kept to their role for a long period found that their relationships with residents deepened as the months went by. Their initial contacts with the elderly were often polite, superficial, and repetitive. New visitors, in fact, were sometimes puzzled and disconcerted by the way patients repeated the same stories or returned to the same topics, week after week. But for people who persisted, subsequent sessions yielded new levels of novelty and rapport. Regular contact with particular individuals became a rewarding part of their routine, creating what Cathy called an "unexpected intimacy."

While visitors generally found this to be a gratifying experience, there was also a note of ambivalence in the way some reacted to the closeness. The richer, ongoing relationships took on aspects of commitment and expectation, leaving volunteers feeling obligated to see the same people each week. Residents could be very explicit about their demands and their hunger for company. Stavros once half-jokingly said to Steve, "You can't go home

again to *your* home unless you promise to come back again to *this* home."
Informal contracts like this could be stressful as well as flattering: they
frustrated visitors who wanted to reach out to other patients, and left a
residue of guilt when people's vacations, illnesses, or other obligations
prevented them from seeing individuals whom they normally dropped in
on each week. Their own emotions sometimes took the volunteers by
surprise. Many recognized that in their personal lives, intimacy could be
both a pleasure and a burden. But most of them had not expected the same
dilemma to arise in their volunteer work, or generate the same type of
ambivalence.

Whether the response they got was more than they hoped for or greater
than they feared, working at Elmwood also had other emotional effects on
people. Some volunteers had no prior experience with either the elderly or
institutions, and they needed to make major adjustments to play their roles.
The rules and the atmosphere that prevailed in the home, and the disabilities
that residents suffered from, could be difficult for them to confront and
accept. Volunteers had to cope with institutional noises, odors, and routines,
with the unanticipated and often unfulfillable requests of the old. In the
midst of a novel and uncertain environment, pet visitors found their animals
to be a source of security and legitimacy; some novices confessed feeling
"naked" without their cat or dog. Moving through the facility without
uniforms, name tags, or family connections, outsiders discovered that their
animals bestowed a sense of identity on them. Some volunteers were not
even known by name to individual patients, but were referred to instead
by such titles as "the man with the two German shepherds" or "the girl
with the ginger cat."

Rejection and acceptance took on many forms in the facility. The residents
at pet sessions had themselves agreed or asked to come there, and so volunteers entered a room of willing, or at least acquiescent, people. But for
visitors who chose to circulate through the corridors and lounges, the element of risk was far greater. Unable to predict the responses of patients
whom they had not seen before, they were inevitably rebuffed by some of
those they approached. On the other hand, they were also the recipients of
unsolicited trust from the staff they met. Employees sometimes turned to
regular visitors such as Janice and Katina for a sympathetic ear, giving the
latter an unexpected but often valuable place in their support system. Workers talked about job-related problems, individual patients, and their own
lives and families, casting volunteers and kin in a kind of confessional role.

While volunteers occasionally risked rejection by residents, this situation
could also reverse itself: from time to time, patients were abandoned by
visitors. Some volunteers who stopped coming to Elmwood failed to do
so in a direct, definitive way: rather than saying farewell to residents and
letting them know of their intention not to return, they simply never showed
up again. In some instances this was partly because the decision itself was

never a very clear or conscious one. But in other cases it was due to the fact that volunteers could just not face those they felt guilty for leaving. In either scenario, the result was a lack of closure for patients, a feeling that visitors had rejected them. Denise was often stuck with the task of accounting to residents for the absence of these "missing persons." To do this as gently as she could sometimes meant telling uncomfortable lies, for while Denise could understand the difficulty of "coming to terms with letting go," she could still not excuse what she had to explain. "Old people who've already lost so much should not have to face a loss like that without the grace of a good-bye."

Long-term visitors with close ties to residents had to face other facts, including depression, decline, and death among those to whom they had grown attached. Neither the training they received, nor the motives which impelled them to serve, necessarily prepared them to cope with these outcomes. Cathy's anguish and dismay over Eddie was a poignant but not a unique development. While some could handle such feelings, others—like Frieda—dropped out because of the immediate strain or the deaths they could foresee. The general consensus echoed Louise's dictum that "deterioration was worse than death." For experienced volunteers, loss became a process rather than an event: they often witnessed the slow decline of people over a period of weeks or months. Death could then take on the prospect of relief rather than terror. During such times, they went through an unfolding, a back-and-forward-looking kind of grieving, and anticipation.

Cathy bore witness to Eddie's deterioration in this way, following him on a downhill journey that lasted from the late fall of one year to the early spring of the next. His health, his posture, and his sharpness each diminished, though the feature that stayed with Cathy most was the withering away of Eddie's voice. Looking back on it from the safe but sad vantage of her grief, she wished there had been more ways for her to share the burden of the dying while it was happening. Afterwards, the support was easier to find. Within the home, a spontaneous and novel memorial grew on a bulletin board near the dining room: staff, residents, and visitors pinned up pictures and paragraphs about Eddie, contributing images and words to a collage of remembrance.

A more private kind of testimony took place a few days following Eddie's death when Cathy, Mandy, Steve, and I met together for coffee. We passed around a number of particularly good and vivid memories, several connected to the holiday parties held at Elmwood the preceding winter, when Eddie had joked and sung and played his harmonica. Cathy, who had been silent for a few moments, suddenly announced: "*That* is the way I'm going to remember him, when he had his humor and his voice. When he could sing and I could understand him. After that he was no longer Eddie, he was not his real self." Steve and Mandy were first shocked by Cathy's act of exclusion, but as they listened to her describe what Eddie had once looked and sounded like, they found something reassuring in this: it was the idea of a fixed yet animate image, a version of the man that helped to center what they too could choose to remember of him.

MOTIVES AND SELF-IMAGE

No one was left untouched by the volunteer experience: empathy, compassion, irritation, bewilderment, sadness, and anger all laid a hand on those who came. The emotional demands, like the intimacy, were unexpected by most, rewarding for some, and too much for others. The way people dealt with them was shaped, in large measure, by the motives that had impelled them to volunteer and the concept they had of their role.

Pet visitors illustrated the varied reasons that brought outsiders into the nursing home. Some, like Janice, were community members with a history of activism. For such people, helping the elderly was an outgrowth of their prior involvement with the handicapped, the homeless, or other special populations. Cathy and many of the students saw their voluntarism as useful preparation for chosen careers in medicine, gerontology, or recreation. Beyond the personal rewards for them lay the potential for professional gain. Still others, such as Steve, were drawn to the home as an indirect result of their work with pets: they had been active, for example, in the local humane society, or in training or showing animals. Some had helped to raise dogs for use in seeing-eye programs. These experiences not only exposed them to the pet program's publicity, but encouraged them to expand their humane interests into more directly human ones.

As commonly happens in voluntary groups, some members identified more strongly with the pet organization's goals than did others. The most enthusiastic visitors to Elmwood even took it upon themselves to introduce new activities there. In this creative role, they initiated an annual petting zoo, a life-history class, special outings, and displays of photographs showing residents with their favorite animals. But these innovators had their opposite number—volunteers who did their home work without much animation, who had lost their sense of mission as time wore its edges away. Finally, there were also callers from other community organizations for whom the home's residents were almost incidental: they came mainly for the sociable time that visits gave them with their own peers. They pushed wheelchairs, laid out bingo cards, and chatted . . . but spoke mostly with one another instead of the elderly. This tendency to avoid residents, shown by members of groups that profess to support nursing homes, has been observed in other institutions (e.g., Shield 1988: 119–120). At Elmwood, in fact, Denise once commented on how difficult it was for her to get such volunteers to come on their own to help with activities. "They only want to attend in pairs or in packs," she observed. "It's their own company they're really here for, and without it they feel exposed or bored or both."

The way people felt about volunteering was also related to gender, to the nature of their own family ties, and to how they wanted to be perceived by the residents themselves. In a pattern typical of voluntary groups in American society, most of Elmwood's community visitors were women: about 80 percent of college age and older members of the pet program, for example, were female, and the home's own support organization, the Linda Westman Club, consisted almost entirely of women. A number of volunteers were homemakers or retired people seeking to vary the routine of their lives and find some new sources of usefulness. Several individuals tried to draw others whom they knew into their voluntary work. As Cathy had done with her roommate Mandy, they recruited a friend, a neighbor, a child, or another family member, turning visits into a shared experience.

Male volunteers found both strength and weakness in their minority status. Some felt conspicuous taking on a traditional female role, but Steve was one of several who thought of themselves as special for the very same reason. He was drawn to the male residents, in fact, and identified with them, because of *their* minority status. "From birth to old age," he declared, "men die first. I'm just visiting my fellow survivors."

There was thus a range of rewards that volunteers derived from their work. These sometimes reached into the empty spaces of social life, where individuals found, among the old, substitutes for missing persons from their own families. So where some visitors tried to bring in people whom they knew, others sought to replace those who were absent. Many students and community members, for example, were separated from parents and grandparents living in other parts of the country, and they often identified particular patients at Elmwood with their own elderly kin. They thus came to value their time with these people as a surrogate family visit. Janice, whose 83-year-old mother was in the Arizona nursing home, acknowledged this fact and the wish it engendered:

> I feel guilty that I cannot see her more than twice a year. But visiting the people here, especially Bonnie, makes me feel like I'm doing what I should be at a distance. I just hope someone out there is standing in for me and feeling good about their experience.

Residents reciprocated this kind of family perception: not only did they point out the way visiting animals resembled their former pets, but they frequently told volunteers how much they reminded them of a grown son or daughter or grandchild. Just as the elderly regarded their former pets as members of the family, some laid claim to the visitors and their animals as elements of a new family.

The domestic image that residents and visitors had of their relationship also carried over into the volunteers' self-image. As Mandy expressed it, they wanted to be seen by patients as "more like friends and family" rather than as institutional staff. Community visitors were thus more comfortable with this kin role than the staff. As outsiders who did not have to deal with residents and their expectations on a daily basis, it was undoubtedly easier for volunteers to maintain this fiction. They played to it in several ways. One was to accept such titles as "daughter" and "grandson" as part of a joking relationship with patients. As a group, most visitors also resisted wearing name tags—as emblem of staff status—because they did not want residents to confuse them with the home's employees. This was not because the volunteers viewed staff in negative terms, however. Rather, visitors saw themselves in a unique, familial role whose distinctiveness they wanted to preserve. Avoiding the label of "staff," then, was not a judgment about other people's merit; it was a decision about separation.

When long-term activists in the pet program recalled their original motives and expectations, most acknowledged that they had not foreseen the many meanings and subleties that volunteering would eventually have for them. On weeks when their animals were ill or unavailable, they came to sessions anyway because of the personal ties they had formed with patients. Their role had changed from being transporters of pets to fully human companions. For someone like Steve, who had joined largely to support his wife, there had also been a transformation from accompanist to soloist. Among the rewards that he and others received was the opportunity to pay some debts: for Steve it was a long-dead grandparent and a sense of remorse, for Janice a distant mother and a sense of guilt. In a moment of great candor, Janice once confessed—as Louise had also done—that it was "probably easier to care for strangers than for your own." Thus, the initial impetus to do good, or to engage in something that sounded like fun, often masked a number of other reasons related to careers, boredom, regret, the pursuit of self-worth, or the search for a way to cope with personal loss or separation from family. Taken together, the collective experiences of visitors showed that voluntarism offered people a broad spectrum of benefits. The more introspective individuals were well aware of this. Without apologizing for it, Janice—in words quoted before—once described the enterprise as a form of "selfish altruism." Doctor Sheren, who overheard her comment, later remarked, "Is there any other kind?"[2]

LIMITATIONS AND AGE

The volunteers' role was complex. They were not therapists, yet they functioned therapeutically. They had positive and negative encounters, gave and received affection, suffered rejection and loss, and sometimes faced uncertainty about how readily they could enter into other people's space and privacy. While their experience was a rich and rewarding one for many, individuals also abandoned it in sizable numbers and for various reasons. Of the one hundred women and men who served in the pet program during its first year at four nursing homes, for instance, approximately 30 percent left the organization after a few weeks to a few months. Some of these dropouts were people moving out of the community, but others were responding to a combination of burnout and boredom. For them, the emotional demands of the visits, the repetitive nature of sessions, the difficulties of coping with human deterioration and institutional life, and the pressures of other commitments were key factors in their decisions to leave the program.

The recollections of former volunteers, Frieda and Beth among them, indicated that few of these individuals had made a conscious or a clear choice to quit. Rather, they had started to find excuses for not going each week, and once they had done that several times, this break in the routine set a precedent for not attending. It was an indirect process of disengagement, a drifting off into leaving. Only a few of these people said a formal farewell to the residents they had been seeing: guilt, embarrassment, and a reluctance to admit the finality of what they were doing all played a role in the lack of closure.

Volunteers who stayed in the program also had to contend with the limits of what they could accomplish: they could not cure people or arrest their decline or return them to the community. There were exceptional moments when a human or pet visitor lured residents such as Sarah or Marjorie or Greta out of a months-long period of silence or withdrawal. But such occasions were rare. More commonly, visitors could share time, compassion, and humor; they could ameliorate; but they could not heal. Recognizing this increased the volunteers' respect for staff, for these were the same borders of hope within which workers had to live.

Just as staff took "in-service," then, and confused residents got "reality orientation," visitors also had to get oriented to the reality of how and how much they could help. For some, these limitations were acceptable; for many who dropped out, they were not. Those who quit stopped coming because the work was too frustrating or depressing or painful; because the preparation and support were inadequate to sustain them; or because the results were not sufficiently evident or dramatic. Turnover of this kind was neither unique or necessarily negative in its consequences, however. It was helpful to recognize not only that it has long been a common feature of most voluntary groups, but that—as Denise argued—it often contributes to an organization's health by removing people who have "lost the fire" to foster its mission. Longevity was not just a mixed blessing for the elderly, then: it was an asset of varying worth among those who served them.

The age of the volunteers was itself a factor in their reactions to the old. Younger visitors were energetic and idealistic in their work, though sometimes unsure of how to deal with people so far removed from their station and stage of life. At times, Steve suggested, they even felt guilty about being so young and free and physically fit. It was as if they looked to the aged, in all their infirmity, to absolve them of the sins of youthfulness and health.

They also differed from residents in their experience of time. Young volunteers saw most of their lives ahead of them; those they visited knew that most of their years lay behind. Yet it was ironically the patients who expected less, and the volunteers who wanted more, out of each moment. Among the elderly, longevity had bred patience in some, resignation in others, and modest hopes in most: care, comfort, and company often summed up what they wanted. Other observers of institutional life have described residents as living in "limbo" (Laird 1979) or a state of "liminality" (Shield 1988). At Elmwood, as at Murray Manor (Gubrium 1975: 158–196), people passed the time by building their days around the routines of meals, therapy, activities, and visits. The orientation of Elmwood's patients was to the present, to the quality of time, not the quantity of things that happened within it: emotional and sensory pleasures were often paramount, commonly taking on a quiet and subtle form, including solitude, simple companionship, and the comforts of touch.[3] In contrast, the younger people who visited them were hungrier, more anxious and impatient for something immediate in each experience, even though the present constituted a much smaller slice of what life still had to offer them. Volunteers such as Cathy and Mandy wanted more *for* the elderly, often more than what the elderly wanted for themselves.

Age also affected how younger and older volunteers dealt with physical and mental decline. Neither old nor young visitors could enter a place such as Elmwood Grove without being confronted by the way of all flesh. Their senses registered odors, immobility, strange postures, and the sounds of walkers, wheelchairs, and aged voices. Within the institution, the volunteers were the least accustomed to these facts of life because the signs of decline only entered their own lives once a week. Younger visitors were at least as sympathetic as their older colleagues to the plight of the patients; but it was only the middle-aged and older volunteers who experienced, with some residents, a split between inner and outer images of the self. When Janice looked at her own reflection, she saw—as did Bonnie—a different person from the one she perceived with her inner eye. Like Eliot's "Gerontion," the journey through the looking glass tended to "multiply variety / In a wilderness of mirrors" ([1920] 1963: 31). Such mirror gazing is, in fact, often a critical part of the process by which older people construct a durable sense of identity (Butler 1968: 489). For women such as Janice and Bonnie, and for others who had reached their middle or later years, growing older helped to create a special kind of disembodied self: the individual's true identity existed inside, outside, or apart from the body, not on its aging and increasingly alien surface.

Conscious of some of these differences, younger volunteers assumed that their older colleagues would have a natural sympathy and a greater skill for dealing with elderly residents. Some of the younger visitors therefore argued that volunteer programs needed to recruit more senior members from the community, that is, people who could draw on the presumed affinities of age. But older visitors such as Frieda had precisely the opposite perception. For a number of them, including several people in their sixties, the sight of their contemporaries in a home cut too close to home. It was a *memento mori*, a painful preview, of what their own future might hold in store for them. Several of these older members subsequently dropped out of the program. Though they thought that their visits had been beneficial to others, "after a point"—as Frieda put it—"doing good no longer felt good." She and her peers concluded that the young were actually better equipped to help the elderly. "They not only have energy and enthusiasm," Frieda decided, "but they are so far away from this point in life that it holds no threat for them. It's ironic, perhaps, but they can deal with people our age better than we can."

ACTS OF WILL

Volunteering is an act of the will, and while its practitioners may know what they want, they are often surprised by what they get. Visitors to Elmwood discovered selfish altruism, the burdens of intimacy, the power of domestic imagery, and the ironies of age and youthfulness. Having set out on what seemed like a simple, generous journey, they took unexpected turns, entering scenes from other people's lives and passing, at times, through halls of mirrors. Depending on personal needs and proclivities, they gravitated towards the relatively healthy or the very disabled, towards a one-to-one relationship or the group setting. What volunteers gave and what they received, therefore, depended not only on their motives, but on the format they followed and the company they kept. For some the experience was too much or, at the very least, not what they had intended. What sustained others was a sense of mission or morality, of family or guilt, of ennui or career, aided in some cases by the familiar presence of a pet, a totemic animal who accompanied them each step of the way.

The value of such good works has been debated for centuries. Does it bestow grace? Is it a responsibility or an option? Do people of a certain class or religious persuasion have an obligation to help or enlighten those who are differently endowed? The medieval philosopher Aberlard argued, in his *Sic et Non*, that works of mercy do not profit those without faith (Charles Homer Haskins 1957: 354). Martin Buber contended that it was only through a combination of great love and great service that individuals could overcome their evil side and "become whole" (Buber 1953: 97). But people with secular as well as religious motives have found a measure of fulfillment and grace in helping others. They have participated in what de Tocqueville, John Stuart Mill, and Lord Acton have regarded as Western culture's ethic of "amelioration" (Hans Kohn 1962: 43). Though disadvantaged groups such as the elderly have been deprived of a great deal, then, they have inherited a gift of service from their own society's moral history.

Many of Elmwood's volunteers had a sense of commitment either to the institution or to the aged. The pet visitors took this one step further: they also had a firm belief in the validity of the novel *way* in which they tried to help residents. They held, as Cathy once said, that "bringing people and animals together is a natural," though they also had to acknowledge that there were elderly individuals who rejected such opportunities. But for those who accepted the visits, volunteers felt there were substantial and fundamental rewards. When they were in a proselytizing mood, these visitors could cite a number of studies, read by them during their courses, their orientation, or their own leisure, that confirmed the benefits of animal companionship. Yet ironically, many of these same individuals deplored the very idea that scientists needed to go around testing, measuring, and proving the value of pet therapy itself. Its merits were so manifest and self-evident to them—affirmed in the weekly reality of their own experience—that they expressed both bemusement and irritation over those who tried to question it. Such research struck them as gratuitous at best, and academic overkill at the worst. This combined attitude of belief and resentment was especially striking in light of the scientific backgrounds and career goals of many who voiced it. Lab technicians, premed, and vet students all joined in criticizing these calculated analyses of what they saw as an undeniably effective and humanistic endeavor. Their words suggested that, as volunteers, they had taken a conscious step away from the technical demands of their workaday lives, only to find that their professional credos—to probe, question, and quantify—had shadowed them into this simpler and purer world, a place where the generosity of spirit was supposed to reign.

Working in a nursing home also had an impact on the way visitors thought about geriatric institutions and the aging process itself. A number of them had had little or no prior experience in such facilities, and so they found their involvement either so depressing or so shocking that they eventually withdrew. Cathy, though she persisted, encountered increasing difficulty in facing people who were prisoners, not of the institution, but of their bodies. Some community members thought that they had been insufficiently trained to deal with the realities of nursing home life and the conditions presented by the frail and the impaired. These feelings of inadequacy were compounded by the fact that the volunteer role was much more complex than most people had anticipated. Some had expected simply to be transporters of animals. They were not prepared to be human resources for residents. While playing the latter role was often gratifying and flattering, it also took an emotional toll that some were simply not ready or able to pay.

Furthermore, some found it impossible to separate the elderly from the image of their own parents or grandparents, or from premonitions they had of their own decline. In a moment of doubt, Janice admitted, "I can't divorce my mother from the old women I see in the wheelchairs." The case of Steve and Beth showed how two spouses could have profoundly different reactions to the same situation. When her husband continued after she stopped, Beth was perplexed and a bit embarrassed by his dedication. But Steve suggested that it was probably easier for him to go because he "did not have to do it." There was no relative inside with whose situation he was compelled to identify. His presence there was a choice he made. While Beth had also chosen to volunteer, he surmised that his decision "was more an act of free will than of family will."

As the experiences of Steve, Beth, Cathy, Janice, and Frieda suggest, other people's late life could take on a very personal meaning for volunteers, regardless of whether the elderly individuals concerned were kin or strangers. The residents' age, condition, and symbolic association with relatives, or their link to a visitor's own future, bestowed upon patients a hidden power and surprising significance. Indeed, given the intensity of their responses to the old, volunteers expressed a desire for more support, more opportunities to talk over the personal and familial reactions that they had to their work. Along with staff, they had become painfully aware that, as caregivers, they needed to be cared for themselves.

The very idea of institutionalization evoked several kinds of judgments from volunteers. Most were impressed by the medical treatment that Elmwood residents received and by the overall quality of institutional life they had witnessed. They felt that Elmwood, and the other facilities in their area, were far better places to be in than the nursing homes portrayed in the media. Yet visitors were also emphatic about not wanting to finish their own lives in such a setting. They felt relieved and reassured that institutions could be run with concern and humanity, but quickly disclaimed any willingness to end up as residents themselves.

Most volunteers saw nursing homes—in Cathy's words—as "a necessary evil." They expressed gratitude for the people who worked in such facilities and compassion for those who lived there. While taking certain staff to task for treating patients as if they were children, a number of visitors came to recognize that they too periodically slipped into a pattern of condescension and infantilization. "I catch myself talking baby talk," admitted Cathy, "and raising topics that would only interest a five-year-old." Some volunteers also voiced vague criticisms of American society for offering the frail elderly few alternatives to institutionalization, but others acknowledged their own incapacity or unwillingness to care for an aged relative at home if the need arose. The confessions came with an embarrassed candor, echoing Louise Santorini's truth that she could nurse anyone but her own kin.

There was one important regard in which the volunteers' image of institutional life differed dramatically from that held by certain residents. Many visitors found it hard to believe that some patients were content and relieved to be in a nursing home. As outsiders, their attention centered on the loss of freedom that institutionalized people had undergone. For these volunteers, independence meant having control over one's own life, a quality that the elderly lacked in their eyes. But to a number of residents, including Tilly and Vivian, independence had a different significance. For them, being in a nursing facility meant freedom *from* worry about the day-to-day details of food, security, shelter, and care, as well as freedom from being a burden on family or friends. Life in an institution had liberated them from having to live as dependents in *other* people's homes.

CONCLUSION

The experiences of Elmwood's volunteers were a product of both personal factors and social forces. They comprised an amalgam of age, gender, self-image, family life, institutional regime, and emotional resilience. Taken together, they suggest some cautionary lessons about the place of altruism and voluntarism in American culture.

First, while people of the same age may be able to sympathize strongly with one another, they are not necessarily in the best position or stage of life to help one another. The converse may in fact be the case at times. Age differences can create enough distance to allow people at opposite ends of the life cycle to be of greater assistance to each other than their peers could be.

Second, females continue to play a large and disproportionate role in the work of voluntary, human service organizations. This applies not only to mature women who have finished their formal education, but also to female college students. At Elmwood Grove, women from the community and its schools far outnumbered their male counterparts. The same imbalance was also true among staff. While there were active and dedicated men volunteering at the home, their minority status reflected a strong, persistent link between female gender and cultural concepts of domesticity, nurturance, and service.[4]

Third, good intentions and good will are not necessarily sufficient to keep volunteers involved in their work. Adequate amounts of training, support, and reinforcement are also required to develop their sense of competency and to foster their feelings of value. One result of our study of the pet program was the recommendation that all the volunteers at each facility periodically get together with a "group leader" to discuss the problems and issues they were facing. The idea was successfully adopted, but was certainly not a panacea for all the things that troubled visitors. With or without such organizational supports, some people will still discover that they are unsuited to the tasks they have chosen to take on. As Denise suggested, a certain amount of volunteer turnover is not inherently a negative feature, but it can leave a residue of guilt among those who depart and a sense of abandonment among those who remain.

A fourth and final point is that while altruism is a cultural ideal, in the reality of voluntarism it can become a subtle alloy of motives and rewards. Volunteers are often helping themselves while in the act of helping others. Intimacy, careers, personal quests, boredom, family problems, and self-worth may each be at issue when people offer their time and energy to assist those whom they see as disadvantaged. Critics of voluntary organizations who focus on the economic exploitation and personal costs of participating in such programs may be overlooking the subtle payoffs that members derive (cf. Kaminer 1984; Kathleen Townsend 1984). Other observers, angry at volunteers who "impose themselves on the aged" (Curtin 1972: 149), often miss the real and mutual rewards that visitors and residents enjoy.

Volunteers also bring different levels of self-awareness to their work, and at Elmwood Grove, some were more conscious of their hidden needs and motives than others. The pursuit of personal goals did not necessarily interfere with people's ability to function well as companions; but when individuals became conscious of their other agenda, they sometimes felt themselves in conflict with the altruistic ideals of American society.[5] Within the walls of the nursing home, then, volunteers were mediating more than just the lives of insiders and outsiders, and humans and animals. They were also playing out a dialectic between culture and the individual, the ideal and the real, and programmatic goals and personal needs. This is one of the dramas of everyday life being performed in every American community, and it can teach people more than they hoped or bargained for.

11 CONCLUSIONS AND RECOMMENDATIONS

In modern medicine, we give as much concern to the health of our institutions as to that of their patients. This is because the well-being of people often depends on the condition of the facilities they find themselves in. Yet the illnesses that lie at the root of this relationship are not simply organic: they are also social and emotional in nature, with each patient's disorder embracing the life of both a person and a family. When an older individual enters a hospital or nursing home, then, he or she brings in a living history as well as an ailing body.

Institutionalization is a response to many of the ailments of the modern world, not just to the ills of the old. The kinds of social circumstances which bring the elderly into nursing homes have also brought other frail, disadvantaged, unpopular, or marginal populations inside the walls of special facilities. We are, in a medical, social, and political sense, an institutional society. The insane, criminal, orphaned, alcoholic, indigent, infected, and retarded are commonly confined. And while they are, of course, afflicted and stigmatized in different ways from the frail aged, they all share the fate of being compelled to live in isolation from the mainstream. The reluctance or the inability of people to care for or cure such individuals within the larger community has led to the birth of the hospital, prison, asylum, poorhouse, workhouse, orphanage, sanitarium, and nursing home. Each of these places focuses not only on a different population but also a different process: they variously raise, reform, confine, cure, sanitize, nurse, therapize, penalize, or detoxify people. And whatever their respective merits or demerits, they each show how mass society tends to institutionalize its marginal members.

Given the prevalence of this social response, *and* the increasing numbers of elderly in both our general population and our geriatric facilities, there is a compelling need to understand what happens to individuals when they come to live, labor, visit, or volunteer in a nursing home. How have people come to this station in life? How do they feel about aging and adapt to the institutional world? And what meanings do such men and women find in their lives and their work?

Anthropology offers one way of answering these questions. Through ongoing involvement in the regular life of a facility, a researcher can experience the day-to-day tone and texture of what residents, staff, and visitors go through. To the extent an anthropologist can gain the confidence of both insiders and outsiders, he or she can discern the fabric of their behavior and attitudes. But where other health sciences mainly attend to the clinical outcomes that medical treatment achieves, anthropology's concern is with the broad content of participants' experience, with the way these reflect and affect the institutions that people are part of. It is the human face of the facilities, more than the techniques of care, that loom largest in what field-workers try to learn.

This book has presented the results of ethnographic research in one nursing home in upstate New York. Over a period of seven years, my students and I observed, participated with, and interviewed the people of Elmwood Grove in order to understand this facility's patients, personnel, and procedures. We worked closely with elderly residents, family members, institutional staff, and community volunteers. Part of our study centered on the impact of a pet therapy program run by a local organization, and so we gained some insight into what older individuals derived from their contacts with animal as well as human companions. Among the other issues we dealt with were role perceptions, communication patterns, the influence of gender and age, the weight of memory and morality, and people's image of the institution itself. Our overriding concern was with the meanings that people found in their lives, their visits, and their labor within the institution.

Findings on eleven of the major issues developed in previous chapters will first be summarized here. In the following section, the practical applications and the significance of these results will be assessed in the light of other studies that have been done on nursing homes. Several recommendations will then be offered for improving the quality of life and work within such facilities.

Though the conclusions and proposals presented here took shape largely inside the walls of one institution, they address experiences that are common to the millions of other people whose total existence or whose labor or whose elderly relatives are to be found within the confines of some other nursing home. They are a scattered but numerous tribe whose presence remains largely invisible to most of the public. Yet the dilemmas they face will eventually confront many of us, for we may one day *be* either the frail elderly or the caregivers of the future. What time has done to all of them should therefore be of interest to all of us.

SUMMARY OF FINDINGS

Adaptation

The image of nursing home residents as a uniform mass of people was belied by the diversity with which patients dealt with the experience of institutionalization. Individuals entered and adapted to life at Elmwood Grove in many different ways. Some came from home, some from the hospital, and some from other institutions. There were those who felt they had control over this decision, and others who thought the matter had been decided for them. Depending on their personalities, health, and backgrounds, different patients adopted styles of coping that ranged from active to passive, cynical to spiritual, and cooperative to belligerent. Stavros, Tilly, Frank, and Bonnie showed some of this variety in the way they respectively pacified, missionized, dramatized, and fictionalized their lives and the company around them.

The lack of privacy was a problem for most residents, whereas relations with roommates ranged from deep friendship to guerrilla warfare. People's experience of the nursing home also varied with the kinds of contact they had with the community. Residents with regular family visitors not only felt less isolated, but they had more leverage with institutional staff. The relatives who came found relief for some of their guilt and anxiety, but could also encounter, as did Patrick Healey, impossible demands and frequent frustration.

Meanings

Recreation programs had unintended consequences and meanings for residents. The pet therapy sessions, for example, were designed primarily to provide elderly patients with an hour or two of animal contact each week. But for many individuals, the social and sensory stimulation of the pets was superseded in importance by the interpersonal ties with the volunteers who brought them. Human rather than animal companionship thus became the most rewarding experience for many. Most volunteers recognized and accepted this redefinition of the situation. On weeks when their pets could not attend, they went on their own so as not to disappoint the people who had come to expect their company.

The visiting animals themselves had multiple meanings for residents, only some of which were anticipated by those who organized and volunteered in the program. Elmwood patients discovered that pets embodied more than just an opportunity for touch and sociability. Some residents came to see the visitors and animals as members of a "new family," thus giving to sessions a broader, domestic definition. Many volunteers were flattered by this promotion in status, and some reciprocated by viewing and referring to individual patients as adopted kin or grandparents. By reinterpreting their time together as an experience of domesticity, the elderly were expressing one of the most deeply felt of their losses—that of home.

Furthermore, the animals offered residents a chance to reflect on several related matters, including their former pets, their family histories, and the moral conduct of persons they had known. In stories they told of their childhoods, households, and work lives, there was the recurrent theme of kindness and cruelty: people's treatment of humans and of animals reflected one another, mirroring the deeper qualities of human nature. This could be heard in Barbara's stress on her adopted dog and abandoned self, in Yvonne's preoccupation with her father's abuse of his horses, and in Stavros's reminiscence about his mother and her cats.

Communication

Residents not only wanted company, they wanted communication. Depending on their needs and abilities, they desired to be seen, spoken to, heard, and held. For those whose speech and memory were intact, polite conversation was usually not sufficient. They needed to be able to share their stories and their lives: listeners were witnesses who affirmed a person's history by hearing, laughing at, commiserating with, and participating in reminiscence. Memories raised both spirits and questions: as Yvonne's childhood recollections of her father revealed, residents continued to puzzle over parts of their past well into old age. They were alert to a lifelong series of issues that remained meaningful so long as they could be talked about.

The experiences of people with Alzheimer's disease and other forms of dementia led to two other insights about comportment and communication. First, these individuals proved to be among the most disturbing and difficult for staff, volunteers, and other residents to deal with. Alzheimer's evoked strong reactions not only because of its medical aspects, but because, behaviorally, it compromised the ability of normal-looking people to act in competent and coherent ways. The nature of the problems it raised varied not just with the particular symptoms shown by each afflicted person, but also with the distinct tolerances of the individuals responding to them. Some caregivers and peers had the most trouble with the sufferers' unpredictability and wandering, others with their memory lapses and incontinence, and still others with their silence. In contrast to what was problematic, the innocence and lack of malice among most of the senile also aroused pity and bewilderment, prompting residents such as Stavros and Tilly to guide and to calm them.

Visitors, staff, and competent patients were puzzled not only by the randomness that dementias induced, but by the apparent randomness with which these disorders struck some individuals and not others. A number of unaffected persons were highly sensitive to living in a facility with the senile, and kept as much real or symbolic distance as they could from them in order to avoid contamination and stigma. The varied symptoms of dementia were thus sufficient to provoke equally varied and intense reactions— ranging from avoidance and denial to helpfulness and compassion—among those who lived with or cared for these residents.

Second, despite the unorthodox behavior of dementia sufferers, there were certain ways of relating and responding to them that proved to be effective. The introduction of pets, the use of touch, and the sharing of company in silence provided calming and fulfilling experiences for a number of these people. Such methods were not appropriate for all individuals, however, nor were all staff and volunteers equally comfortable with touch and silence as means of communication. The cultural etiquette of only caressing one's intimates, and the common view that talk is the essence of sociability, limited the ways in which some caregivers could reach out to and be with others. These social constraints on the behavior of healthy people sometimes stood in the way of their helping the ill.

Roles

Staff and volunteers developed very different conceptions of their roles as time went by. Companion animal visitors, for example, initially thought of themselves simply as transporters of pets, not as support persons for elderly patients. But when the latter began to treat and refer to them as family, many began to think of themselves in this way and accepted this new identity with pride. A number of volunteers refused to wear name tags during sessions because they felt this would lead residents to confuse them with staff members and thus cloud the special status they had achieved. On the other hand, some visitors found this unexpected intimacy to be too great a burden: they eventually withdrew from the program because of the familial expectations, and the deterioration and death with which they were being confronted. One of my students responded to the pressure from patients that she visit them each week by comparing their demands to a quality of her own home life: "They make me feel as guilty as my parents do."

Volunteers brought different motives, backgrounds, and images to their roles. While some had worked with the elderly before, others had never been inside a nursing home. Some undertook this work expecting to be able to foster significant improvements in people's health or morale. But when these visitors discovered the much more modest results they could realistically hope to achieve, the latter were often inadequate to sustain their commitment. There were individuals who gladly incorporated residents into their lives as surrogate elders and others who recoiled from them for the very same symbolic reason. The kinds of fulfillment that people sought from volunteering were diverse and sometimes contradictory: some were acting on a sense of social responsibility and others were reacting to a feeling of boredom; there were those promoting a career and others escaping from one; certain individuals were wrestling with their ghosts while the person alongside them was liberating herself from the self-centeredness of daily life. The "selfish altruism" that defined and motivated these people was therefore very real but very relative, often held together by a fabric of personal rewards.

Staff members also found some major discrepancies between their job descriptions and the content of the roles they played. Therapists such as Nina and Claire ended up supporting their coworkers as well as treating the elderly. Many staff were oppressed by the number of records and forms they had to fill out, feeling that the onus of paper work compromised their ability to enjoy the more meaningful and satisfying parts of their jobs. Conflicts between shifts, cliques, and different levels of hierarchy were another source of concern. Employees also periodically helped carry out the responsibilities of people from other departments, and found that they were expected to think of their own work in flexible terms. Whether they did these extra tasks in a spirit of cooperation or irritation depended less on union rules or the specific task at hand than on the degree of respect with which requests for assistance were made.

Relatively few members of staff had planned or trained to work with the elderly. They had to adjust their goals and learn to value rewards of a different order. Claire geared down, Nina came to appreciate simple gratitude, Gordon took refuge in planning, and Louise found peace in helping people to a good death. Even when they did their jobs well, many employees had to come to terms with being taken for granted. Elmwood's center of gravity was its residents, and while relatives and visitors generally had a high regard for the efforts of caregivers, these outsiders rarely said that directly to the staff members themselves. Criticisms were more likely to be voiced than praise, leaving workers feeling that they were undervalued.

Confession

Work, visiting, and voluntarism led to relationships that were often confessional in nature. Some staff and long-term visitors came to treat each other as colleagues over time. They began to share aspects of their personal as well as their professional lives with one another. Employees spoke about the demands and difficulties of their jobs, and they consulted and commiserated with volunteers and relatives about the declining health or deaths of favorite residents. Visitors and staff were in general agreement with Denise's preference for "death over disability." When people remembered the patients they had literally or emotionally cared for, Cathy once explained, "we remember the person who was—the person who lived before the dying began in earnest." That was the way Cathy herself remembered Eddie, and how Claire fixed an image of Alma in her own mind.

The close bonds between certain volunteers and staff grew out of the fact that employees were often affected by recreational programs, even when they were not directly involved in their operation. A number of nurses, aides, and housekeeping personnel, for example, found the animal visits a welcome break from their daily routine. They briefly interrupted their work during sessions to interact not just with the pets, but with the volunteers and the participating residents. Staff also found that visitors and animals provided helpful topics of conversation with patients during the week-long intervals between sessions. Pets thus served as a catalyst, bringing together different groups of people and enlivening the atmosphere within the home.

The animals also offered an indirect way to talk about death. Residents sometimes spoke their thoughts about longevity by referring to the lives and losses of animals they had owned. Their remarks and stories were often a confession of hope, pride, and fear for themselves—feelings that were expressed through their identification with the pets who had once shared their homes. Even the simplest anecdotes about these animals could thus embrace a series of powerful images about domesticity, loyalty, and mortality.

Formats

Volunteers, relatives, and residents used two main types of spatial and social arrangements during their time together. Some visitors preferred to meet patients on an individual basis, whereas others opted for the kind of collective experience offered by pet sessions and similar events. In terms of relative merit, it was a choice between privacy and intensity on the one hand, and sociability and group support on the other. With the exception of people such as Katina, family visitors usually spent their time just with their own kin. But volunteers had to make more choices. Besides working in either relatively public or private spaces, they gravitated to people with either severe or modest levels of impairment. Some visitors, dismayed by extreme disability and disorientation, worked primarily with the more competent and continent residents. But there were others who sought out some of the frailest and most confined individuals, finding in them a very grateful, needy, and accessible population. Volunteers who found their experiences particularly fulfilling were those who had discovered both the format and the kind of resident that best suited their own needs.

The degree of control that the elderly could exercise over the setting for visits depended on their powers of movement and communication. Mobile residents could more easily agree or decline to go to organized events, and they could spend time with family members and volunteers in their own rooms, a lounge, or the dining area. While none of these places guaranteed total privacy, some were more protected than others. In the case of bed-ridden people, as well as patients who preferred to pass the day in hallways and lounges, visitors clearly had to come to them: such residents could accept or refuse their overtures, but they could only choose between the people who had decided to approach them. Some frail individuals, such as Greta, could be wheeled on a bed to the activities room for recreation, but if their powers of speech were gone, it was up to staff to interpret their willingness to attend such events. For the immobile, the voiceless, and the elderly who chose to sit apart from the home's centers of sociability, then, it was visitors and staff who had the discretion to determine who would see them and where this would happen.

Support

The people who provided for the physical and social needs of residents needed considerable amounts of emotional support themselves. Staff experienced many different kinds of stress: they lived with the contradiction of working in a medical facility where there was little chance of curing or releasing people; they had to contend with conflicts among coworkers and jobs that were often physically taxing and poorly compensated; they came under criticism from supervisors, families, and residents; and they were sometimes subjected to abuse by the latter. Volunteers were engaged in an enterprise that was thought of as being emotionally rewarding rather than costly, yet it too could take a heavy toll of their energies and expectations.

Both of these groups tried to help patients facing serious losses, but in the course of their work they encountered losses of their own as the elderly declined and died. The institutional and organizational supports that were available to employees and volunteers were often far less effective than the special friendships and meanings that some of these people had developed for themselves. The same was true for residents. On a personal level, Claire and Nina had their daily talks and Louise her books; Frank turned to his son, Stavros his daughter, Tilly to a roommate and neighbor, and Bonnie to her niece and to Barbara. On a moral plane, Gordon had his sense of justice, Steve his remnant of guilt, and Janice her strain of responsibility. These were the qualities and ties that sustained some of the people some of the time. But caregivers as well as relatives required more acknowledgment and help than they usually got, which was one reason why some kin withdrew, and visitors and staff burned out.

Religion

One of the most important if largely invisible sources of support for many patients, workers, and volunteers was religion. Spiritual sustenance was central to individuals such as Claire, Janice, and Tilly, and it loomed in the background of some lapsed observers such as Gordon and Louise. While none of Elmwood's employees had based their career choice on a sense of religious mission, some of the volunteers had taken their avocation from this source.

Inspirational books and Bibles, whether on Claire's shelf or Tilly's wheel-chair, and the less visible seeds of faith that had lain inside Janice, Gordon, and others since childhood, bore many individuals through the routines of life and work at the home.

To witness or personally experience the course of human frailty was a test of faith, not just of medicine. Though Elmwood held regular religious services, these were neither the only nor the primary place where people dealt with their spiritual questions. Residents and care providers went through bouts of inner wrestling, reminiscent of Jacob and his angel, over whether God-given bodies and minds were meant for such a fate. It fueled the gratitude of Frank and the skepticism of Stavros, and led those around them to question divine justice and the limits of their own capacity for compassion.

Age

Younger and older volunteers made different assumptions about working with the elderly. Adolescent and college-age visitors felt that their older colleagues had more in common with institutional residents because of the proximity of their ages. Young volunteers felt that this would breed a natural sympathy among these contemporaries. But the more senior visitors, most of whom were in their fifties and sixties, disagreed. For them, ailing elderly patients were a reminder of what they themselves might become. Their time at Elmwood was often a painful voyage into the near future, and many—like Frieda—stopped coming. They felt that younger volunteers, though lacking in experience, were nevertheless in a position to offer more to residents: they were not just animated and hopeful, but also unburdened by the ten-dency to see a prophecy in other people's frailty.

While patients did take a special delight in their more youthful visitors, there was also an important generational difference in how old and young experienced time. Elderly people, who had less to look forward to, made more out of the company, the sensations, and the occasions that came their way. Older visitors were closer in spirit to them than the young, who were more demanding of each moment, and prone to impatience if time was not eventful or marked by some measure of progress.

Gender

Life and work at the nursing home were overwhelmingly female in nature. The predominance of women among residents, staff, and volunteers was a prod-uct of several factors: prominent among these were the demographics of aging; the economics of employment in the health care industry; and the cultural ethos of service and sex roles. That females were the primary donors and recipients of care was a reminder of the strength of certain emphases in American society: women who have traditionally been the caregivers in their families often have no one to provide for them when they become old and frail; female adults with minimum education and working-class backgrounds are likely to take most of the poorly paid, physically demanding service jobs in medical institutions; and middle-class women of various ages are encouraged to donate their time to others as a moral good.

Male residents had to adapt to being bathed and nursed by women, an adjustment that most made with less difficulty than they themselves anticipated. Once attuned to their dependency on others for basic services, they were more concerned with getting proper care than with the gender of the person providing it. Most of the men on Elmwood's staff were in administration, making the boundary lines between the sexes and the levels of hierarchy congruent. Male supervisors, such as Gordon, were sensitive to the preponderance of poorly paid women among direct care employees; but when females from lower levels had complaints about the way their superiors treated them, they focused on the power of these people rather than their gender. The handful of male volunteers felt conspicuous at first, but some—like Steve—turned their minority status into an asset by identifying themselves with the small number of men among the residents. In a world of female longevity and labor, they chose to stress that it was a mark of distinction to be one of the relatively few males among the survivors and the caregivers.

Institutionalization

The ways in which residents, staff, and visitors saw the nursing home itself embraced points of consensus and contradiction. With a few exceptions, patients were pleased with their treatment and praised their caregivers for the way they dealt with them. Employees and visitors also felt that the general quality of care in the facility was good, with workers taking pride in Elmwood's image. Nobody claimed the institution was perfect, however, and everyone concerned was aware that the home's physical plant was inadequate to present-day demands. To varying degrees, residents and visitors knew about conflicts among staff, just as the latter were sensitive to the different levels of commitment that relatives showed to their elderly. The institutional world was a home to moral ambiguity, including DNRs, death, and issues of closure and responsibility. People also realized that on rare occasions, direct-care staff treated patients improperly, but employees were much more cognizant than families or volunteers of how provocative and abusive residents themselves could be.

Beyond these differences in perception, many of the workers, visitors, and patients shared an awareness of two major contradictions embedded in the very nature of the institution. One was the fact that no nursing home could be a real home: whatever comfort, security, and services it provided, and regardless of how well it delivered these, one could not escape the institutional nature of the facility or its distance from the place, the privacy, and the possessions that residents rightfully considered part of their true homes. The loss of the latter, with all its lifelong domestic associations, was more severe than many of the bodily and social diminishments to which people were subjected. "Imagine," as Nina once said, "eighty years of life packed into two boxes, a whole house reduced to half a room".[1]

Relatives spoke almost wistfully about trying to arrange home care for a family member as an alternative to institutionalization. Katina was one of several who recounted her failures and frustrations with this. Kin and staff alike bemoaned the difficulties of this option. They variously blamed its impracticality on government policies, gender roles, family politics, inadequate resources, or community attitudes. Relatives were hesitant to speak of the point that Louise so readily conceded, namely, the great difficulty of nursing one's own kin. Visitors admitted there were some individuals—such as Tilly and Barbara—for whom a nursing home was appropriate, but they nevertheless saw the need for such facilities as an indictment of society at large. When pressed, however, they could offer only the most general ideas for replacing institutions with more homelike forms of care. Most people, then, were positive in their assessment of Elmwood as a place to live in, work at, and visit, but they were critical of the idea of institutionalization itself.

The second contradiction, felt especially by professional staff and some residents, was inherent in a medical facility where the emphasis was on caring rather than curing. The models of treatment that most of Elmwood's nurses and therapists had been trained with defined success in terms of restoration and release. But the reality of nursing home work meant a lower level of expectation and achievement. This gap between theory and practice left doubts in some employees' minds about whether more could or should be done for patients. Such concerns found another voice among those elderly people who had entered Elmwood in the hope of one day leaving it, or at least living in it, in better health. Some of their aspirations were illusory, others more realistic; but only a handful of residents permanently left the institution each year to go to a lower level of care or return to their own homes. Therapy helped Stavros achieve some relief from pain and he was then able to move with more ease, but neither his nor Frank's wish to walk once more was ever fulfilled. Neither man would ever go home again, except on visits, a fate which Bonnie, Tilly, Barbara, and most others shared.

In effect, these two contradictions—the home that could not be a home, and the medical facility that rarely restored people to health—derived from the fact that the institution was neither a proper home nor a hospital. It could not duplicate the feel of the former or the curative powers of the latter. But nor did it claim or try to. Despite its name and medical image,

Elmwood Grove Nursing Home was a different kind of place with a life and priorities of its own: the skills and sensitivities found there were familiar, but they were being played out amidst a unique set of responsibilities for a unique population. Like other nursing homes, it was a brave new world of old age in which the rules, the moral imperatives, and the emotional supports were in process rather than in place. The institution was an answer to the questions that most people chose not to ask.

APPLICATIONS, COMPARISONS, AND RECOMMENDATIONS

Applications

There are some aspects of life that constitute a microcosm of human experience. They offer us the opportunity, as the poet William Blake expressed it, "to see a World in a Grain of Sand" ([1800–1810] 1976).[2] Medical institutions provide such a prospect: they embrace pain and hope, skill and fortune, life and death. They can be looked at from many perspectives, including those of purpose and organization, knowledge and ethics, power and personnel. All these dimensions are instructive, but none are definitive, and many sciences draw on several for insight.

This book has tried to demonstrate that in the realms of human health and institutional life, anthropology also has important contributions to make. The eleven sets of findings summarized here relate to a number of populations, programs, and processes within one geriatric facility. They deal with residents, families, staff, and volunteers; with expectations and changes in people's roles; with recreational and therapeutic experiences; with physical movement and moral meanings; and with the impact of gender and age itself on individual responses to the elderly.

In several regards, these findings had practical applications. Discussions of the research, and the sharing of preliminary reports on it with staff, residents, and visitors, yielded four specific results.

First, volunteers were helped to appreciate the importance of reminiscence and human companionship for patients. Those who had first seen their role from a minimalist point of view were able to appreciate the very substantial value of their presence for people. In addition, they began to grasp that touch and physical company could, in some cases, be as meaningful as conversation.

Second, residents and visitors were encouraged to find the best format in which to spend their time together. Staff members were especially helpful in getting them to recognize the different rewards and demands that individual versus group settings involved. Where possible, efforts were made to match up volunteers and patients who had similar preferences.

Third, employees and outside organizations began to create better support systems for volunteers to help them deal with the practical and emotional dimensions of their work. In the pet program, for example, formal meetings of volunteers were sponsored to give people a chance to learn more about about aging and the nursing home environment. Staff members sometimes spoke at these gatherings to share information and answer questions about specific problems or residents. As a result of the research, this organization also created the new position of "group leader"—an individual who functioned as a facilitator, guide, and support person for all the individuals visiting a particular facility. The informal sessions that group leaders held enabled pet volunteers to share with one another some of their personal experiences and concerns: people were helped to understand that they were usually not alone in their doubts and feelings, and that there were limits to what their good faith efforts could achieve.

Fourth—less apparent, but no less real—staff, family, and community visitors were encouraged to think about the ways in which their age and their expectations affected their relationships with the elderly. Youthful enthusiasm and the maturity of years each had their assets, and caregivers began to recognize that qualities that benefited one patient were not necessarily the most valuable for another. People also came to realize, sometimes in the face of long-held ideas, that a nursing home could actually be the chosen place of residence for some individuals. Acknowledging that elderly persons were there for a variety of reasons, and with different degrees of willingness, was an important step in helping caregivers meet their social as well as their medical needs.

Comparisons

Every nursing home is unique, and the qualities it shares with other institutions are qualified by its own mixture of finances, policies, and personnel. Many geriatric facilities studied by other anthropologists face, with Elmwood Grove, the common task of providing sustained nursing care for elderly people. This applies to all the institutions described in this book's introduction: it was true of Murray Manor, the church-run home in the Midwest described by Gubrium (1975); Golden Mesa in Arizona, where Carobeth Laird lived for several months (1979); the California facility and the National Health Service Home in Scotland studied by Kayser-Jones (1981); the Northeastern institutions—Martindale, Franklin, and Bethany Manor—researched respectively by Vesperi (1983), Shield (1988), and O'Brien (1989); the New York nursing facility analyzed by Powers (1988a, b); the predominantly black and Jewish institutions that Watson and Maxwell studied (1977); and the urban hospital wards and homes examined by Henry (1963).

While all of these facilities included skilled levels of care among their services, they were distinct from Elmwood Grove in several significant ways: most were relatively large, modern and urban; some were private, profit-making institutions; a number were run by the government; and a few had a distinctive ethnic or racial makeup. In comparison, Elmwood Grove was small, privately run, and not for profit. Located in a village setting near a moderately sized community, it served—and employed—a predominantly white and Christian population. Its building was old, its staff partly unionized, its endowment small, and its operating budget—largely dependent on Medicaid payments—had been in the red for several years.

The more grievous problems found in many other nursing facilities were, in most cases, either minimal or modest in scope at Elmwood. It had none of the rampant abuse, neglect, or tranquillizing of people widely reported for the nursing home industry in both the media and in academic and muckraking studies (e.g., C. Townsend 1971, Mendelson 1975, Vladeck 1980). Both employees and volunteers there occasionally infantilized or patronized residents, but this was episodic, not systematic, in nature. There was no evidence of financial exploitation or mismanagement, though the facility certainly had economic difficulties and long-term money concerns.

Problems also existed with staff morale, but these did not approach the level of demoralization found elsewhere by Vesperi (1983) and others. On the contrary, a core of Elmwood's personnel strongly identified with the institution and its place in the community, and their attitudes towards work were improved by the advocacy of their union and the in-service training they received. Yet staff, family members, and volunteers at Elmwood were still in need of more emotional and moral support than they got—an issue noted by numerous observers of the nursing home world (cf. Timothy Brubaker 1987). Nor had Elmwood found effective and meaningful ways to deal with death: the speed and silence that usually surrounded it have been described at other facilities too (e.g., Gubrium 1975, Shield 1988). On the other hand, compared to the predominantly black and Jewish institutions studied by Watson and Maxwell (1977), and the Jewish home researched by Shield (1988), the relatively homogeneous composition of Elmwood's work force and clientele eliminated most grounds for racial and ethnic tension. There were occasional arguments among residents over religion, and a few individuals were uneasy about being cared for by blacks, but these were minor issues in the overall operation of the home.

Privacy, a scarce commodity at many facilities, was very much at a premium at Elmwood Grove. Every patient there had to share a room with two or three others, and people compensated by claiming certain public places for private use—including dining room tables, lounge chairs, and the corners of corridors. Such a pattern of "personal space" has been found at numerous institutions, where conflicts over privacy often derive from the tension between the personal needs of residents and the responsibility of staff to monitor their condition (Sommer 1969, Gubrium 1975, and Watson and Maxwell 1977). The residents' dilemma has been aptly described as that of people trying to lead "private lives in public places" (Dianne Willcocks, Sheila Peace, and Leonie Kellaher 1987).

Unlike Murray Manor and those large nursing homes that combined a health-related with a skilled nursing facility, Elmwood Grove was different in that it comprised an exclusively skilled institution. But like other skilled facilities, Elmwood still had problems clarifying its self-image and sense of mission. Its conflict between caring and curing echoed Martindale's tension between humanitarian and curative emphases (Vesperi 1983: 235), and Franklin's uncertainty over whether it was a home or a hospital (Shield 1988: 65–69). The contrasting pairs of terms used at each of these institutions expressed the general contradiction between "social" and "medical" models of nursing home life (Kane and Kane 1978).

Furthermore, under its official title as a skilled facility, Elmwood still housed people with widely different levels of impairment. A number of its more capable residents therefore distinguished and set themselves apart from the markedly frail and senile. Their efforts at separation brought them reassurance by holding the stigma of "guilt by association" at bay. Measures such as these by elderly people trying to preserve their self-image have also been noted among healthier patients at Murray Manor, Franklin, and Bethany Manor—places where, as at Elmwood, some residents also found fulfillment in trying to help their more disabled peers (Gubrium 1975: 119; Shield 1988: 164–165; O'Brien 1989: 224–225). These contradictory responses to extreme frailty—avoidance on the one hand, assistance on the other—highlight a controversial issue within the nursing home field: that of whether to care for confused and seriously impaired people within the same facility as the more competent. Over against Claire Lannahan's stress on the virtues of diversity stands the potential toll that mixing populations could have on the morale of the more self-sufficient.

Elmwood Grove answered the dreams of some people who hoped to be discharged, but disappointed others who never regained the levels of health they longed for. As at other institutions, patients variously gave staff the credit or the blame for the success stories and failures. Reflecting on their inability to cure certain people, Elmwood employees noted how invested residents like Eva became in their "sick" role—a dependent state of mind which negated efforts to make such individuals more self-reliant. These interrelated issues of motivation and dependency have been raised in other nursing home studies. In her research as an aide at Martindale, Vesperi faulted workers there for dissuading and preventing patients from becoming more independent (1983). But as Powers observed at another nursing home (1988a), residents may also react negatively when staff encourage self-reliance because this threatens to diminish their daily contacts with caregivers. At Elmwood Grove, Bonnie was one of a number of individuals who resisted the overtures of aides who attempted to get patients to do more for themselves. Claire, on the other hand, felt that it was hard to motivate people who lacked models to show them what the rewards of their efforts could be. Individual staff and residents thus gave different emphases to the likelihood, and the means, of curing those they cared for.

Several studies have examined the extent to which nursing home patients remain involved in activities and connected to the surrounding community. Observers at several facilities have noted, as with Stavros and Frank, that residents who receive regular visitors not only enjoy better morale, but also more power and status (Gubrium 1975: 97–99; Shield 1988: 59–60; O'Brien 1989: 29). Assessments of recreation programs, however, have led to more varied results. Critics have pointed out how often institutional activities are reduced to the "BBCs" of bingo, birthdays, and crafts (Johnson and Grant 1985: 135). Curtin was dismissive of the events sponsored by a private facility she examined (1972), describing them as mindless and pointless. Of the few activities offered to Carobeth Laird while she lived at Golden Mesa (1979), only the religious services gave her some sense of fulfillment. Kayser-Jones (1981) found that Scottsdale, the National Health Service home she researched in Scotland, had a recreation program far superior to that of Pacific Manor in California. The elderly people in Scotland were still residing near the town they had previously lived in, and not only did they get out more, but they also received more support from community members. These factors contributed significantly to the better quality of life that the residents enjoyed there.

Elmwood's downtown location in a small village was of some advantage in this respect. It allowed more mobile patients to venture out to shops and nearby streets and made it convenient for volunteers and families from the area to visit. As part of the monthly schedule of activities, a number of community organizations, plus the home's own corps of volunteers, ran regular programs. Some of these were clearly more effective than others, however, and this varied with how genuine the motivation of visitors was. Elmwood's setting had one other asset. The lawn areas surrounding two sides of the facility faced residential blocks, which allowed individuals who were taken out to feel part of the scenes of everyday life. Many more of these opportunities were needed, however, especially for people who were isolated within the facility because they had no visiting relatives. But since outings such as these required close supervision by employees or volunteers, they were very labor-intensive experiences to provide.

A related issue that few studies have considered is the role of volunteers in nursing homes, including their participation in innovative, therapeutic programs. Little of the research cited here deals extensively with community support people. Kayser-Jones praises the ones who helped out at Scottsdale (1981: 28–29), as does O'Brien those attending Bethany Manor (1989: 146–

148). Shield (1988: 119–121), however, notes the distance of visitors who came to Franklin, and Curtin characterizes the volunteers at another American facility as useless and patronizing (1972: 149–150). Yet Elmwood Grove was not exceptional in having a core of active and effective community participants. The growing literature on pet therapy, for example, identifies many nursing homes with good programs run by voluntary organizations.[3] The lack of attention to volunteers by many authors suggests that these people are still a neglected group in contemporary studies of the elderly and their caregivers.

Comparisons between Elmwood Grove and other geriatric facilities indicate that this home had its strengths and its weaknesses. There were problems with staff morale and support systems, finances and privacy, and the handling of death. But there was also a good quality of care, a widespread sense of institutional pride, and a decent level of volunteer involvement. Against a backdrop of frailty and mortality, the interplay of personalities often produced lively drama. There were pundits, protesters, and residents who suffered in silence; dedicated staff working near those who were merely competent; and individuals who found the home a haven alongside others who questioned its moral implications. It was a story without heroes or villains, more a tale of everyday endurance, with Time as narrator and Age the antagonist.

Recommendations

Elmwood Grove had its own history and a unique cast of characters, but it faced a number of the same realities as other nursing homes. These derived from some common institutional experiences. Specifically, many facilities, like Elmwood, are characterized by the following:

—the need for innovative and effective programs for enriching the lives of residents

—the necessity to deal with morale and communication problems within the work force

—the problem of finding productive ways to support staff, volunteers, and families in coping with the frail elderly

—the difficulty of dealing with death in a direct, open, and respectful manner

From research with people at Elmwood, and from studies of other geriatric institutions, six recommendations are offered here for addressing these issues.

1. Programs should be promoted for bringing companion animals into facilities either as full-time residents or as regular visitors. Pets have a positive effect on many of those who live and labor in nursing homes, and there is a good deal of clinical and experiential evidence to document this. Animals can be particularly effective with residents who are often the most

problematic for others to deal with, including the withdrawn and the demented. When people have a chance to *be* caring as well as receive care—be it for an animal or another resident—their self-esteem is enhanced: reciprocity then becomes a route to dignity, help a form of self-help. In addition, pets serve to create or recreate a sense of domesticity, thus providing a means for patients to contend with one of the most emotionally charged losses that they must endure. The feasibility of providing animal companionship to the institutionalized elderly has been amply demonstrated in recent decades. A number of guidelines and models now exist to help those interested in setting up such programs, and there are organizations in many communities that can provide the human and other resources necessary to launch such efforts.[4]

2. A regular process should be instituted in geriatric facilities for airing and resolving conflicts among staff. General and specific grievances damage morale and thereby diminish the quality of care that employees are capable of giving residents. A process for handling disputes must obviously fit within the organizational framework of an institution and take into account the role of such legal bodies as government regulatory agencies, labor unions, and boards of directors. But to tolerate or ignore these work-related problems compromises the conditions under which the elderly live and their caregivers labor.

3. A broad-based effort should be launched to improve the salaries and the image of direct care providers—the people who offer nursing home patients most of their human contact. This would enhance the morale of current employees and attract well-qualified and motivated individuals to enter such work in the future. Since the poor pay and low status of aides are ubiquitous in the health care industry, however, it is difficult for a single nursing home—particularly a non-profit one such as Elmwood—to make significant progress in the area of salaries and still maintain its economic viability. Rather, organizations that advocate for health workers, nursing home residents, the elderly, and improved medical care should all take an active, coordinated role in promoting these priorities.

4. Creative ways should be found to help caregivers of the frail elderly cope with the stresses they face. A much greater social investment in community-based care would enable more families to keep their frail members at home, and thus reduce both the financial and emotional costs of institutionalization for everyone. But when entry into a nursing home becomes imperative, the toll that this takes on a variety of care providers must also be addressed. Institutional staff, community volunteers, and family members are all exposed, at some time, to rejection, anger, guilt, depression, and death. The needs these people have for support are considerable, and they could be met in several ways. Orientation, training, and in-service programs should devote more attention to the emotional demands placed on the caregivers themselves. Louise Santorini's notion of a time-out room

for nurses and aides, Nina Breckner's idea of support groups for staff and for relatives, and the pet program's concept of a group leader to help volunteers serving the same facility are specific examples of measures that could be or have been tried in various places.

5. Volunteers and staff enter and leave the lives of residents as their personal situations change. When caregivers with close ties to the elderly move on, their departure adds another level of loss to individuals already bearing several layers of this experience. Volunteers should be made aware that their meaning for residents lies not just in the programs they run, but in the personal contacts they provide for patients. While turnover among volunteers and staff is inevitable, its impact could be reduced if care providers were urged to say good-bye to residents, thus giving the elderly a chance to achieve a measure of closure and understanding.

6. Death is the uninvited guest whose presence lingers at every nursing home. People who live and work within institutions can have as much trouble dealing with it as those on the outside: denial, avoidance, and haste are common responses. Nursing facilities usually have established procedures for dealing with death in a logistical way, but they should also develop means to address its social and emotional impact on those left behind. Policies should give consideration to allowing staff, visitors, and residents a way to express and experience grief while protecting those who do not wish to share it. A hospice model is one that has been proposed (Shield 1988: 71). Although Elmwood had not dealt successfully with this problem, there were some unplanned events at the home that showed what was possible. When Eddie died there was a spontaneous outpouring from many of the people who had known him. By the day of his funeral, photographs and reminiscences of him appeared on an empty bulletin board near the dining room, and the collection of materials there grew for a week and remained for close to a month. "It was better than a memorial service," said Nina. "All of it came from us, and it lasted a long time, and you could go over to look at it and read whenever the spirit moved you." Perhaps, Nina implied, there was no one way to do this, but she suggested that people at each home should be encouraged to create their own rituals for mourning those they have lost.

THE ENDS OF TIME

There are many ways to view aging, but one of the most revealing and disconcerting is to look in the mirror. This is the prospect that Bonnie once shared with Janice. The sight can be alarming if we discover that we are no longer the person we once thought we were. Narcissus, Dorian Grey, Snow White's stepmother, and Alice in Wonderland all suffered a similar shock of recognition when gazing at their own images.

Studying a nursing home can have the same kind of impact because it reflects our assumptions about aging and causes us to reconsider them. The findings presented here are offered in that reflective spirit, as a corrective to the stereotypes we commonly hold about geriatric facilities. By documenting people's experiences in just one nursing home, the findings indicate how variable and subtle institutional life can be. The recommendations and applications derived from Elmwood Grove also show the value of conducting research that has a practical dimension. Along with other ethnographic studies done on nursing facilities, these results suggest that the "institutionalized" anthropologist is well positioned to see the inside from without, to uncover the behaviors and thoughts that shape the reality of people's daily lives.[5]

Given the widespread criticisms of nursing homes in the United States and other countries, we need the kinds of research that provide in-depth, comparative, and cross-cultural views of such institutions. These can help us identify the factors that promote or inhibit a good quality of care for the elderly. Geriatric facilities are of course always part of the larger society, and so they must therefore be understood as an expression of its policies, priorities, and attitudes. But every nursing home also generates its own way of life, with values, norms, and roles to which residents and personnel must both adapt. This study, and the other research cited, indicate some of the major factors that contribute to each institution's culture: these include a facility's size and financial base; its location and architecture; the backgrounds and health status of its patients; the privacy patterns and expectations of residents; the home's recreational programs and community ties; and the goals, hierarchies, and support systems of its staff.

Finally, whether one looks at the total community or the small-scale world of an institution, it is important to consider the relationship between culture and the individual. The twelve persons who have been featured here—Stavros, Frank, Bonnie, and Tilly among the residents; Claire, Louise, Nina, and Gordon from the staff; and Steve, Cathy, Janice, and Frieda among the volunteers—show that much can be learned about late life by taking each individual's words and giving them a context, not just a token value. It is imperative to try to understand the elderly, and those who care for them, as fully rounded people, each possessed of strengths, weaknesses, fears, compassion, and a history. To accord them less would diminish both their humanity and our own capacity to respond to it.

To hear, to see, and to touch these people within the world of the nursing home also enables us to correct the very partial and very negative image of old age with which the modern world has burdened us. In the literary and the popular mind, the old are often desiccated, vacant figures: they sit like Eliot's Gerontion ([1920] 1963: 29), "an old man in a dry month," his "dull head among windy spaces." They hang empty like Yeats's "tattered coat upon a stick" ([1927] 1983: 193). Or they are reduced to being caricatures rather than characters in their own right. There are notable and moving exceptions: in books such as Florida Scott-Maxwell's *The Measure of My Days* (1979), Ronald Blythe's *The View in Winter* (1979), Jeremy Seabrook's *The Way We Are* (1980), and M.F.K. Fisher's *Sister Age* (1984), writers have given the old a voice and a vision of their own. But the art and the opportunity for doing this are rare gifts.

The everyday lives we hold in common with older people provide us more of a chance to be with and bear witness for them. When we choose to do that, their lives are acknowledged and ours are enriched. It is never too late, or too early, for this. We need to understand that aging begins long before we ourselves become old, because we end up dealing with it when our parents, grandparents, and other relatives reach their later years. And the aging process will touch our own bodies and minds much sooner than we anticipate for, as noted before, we spend only one quarter of our lives growing up, and then three quarters of them growing old.

While the frail elderly show us only one of the possible fates that await us, many of the experiences that they and their caregivers go through are common to each of us. These include the need to deal with loss; the desire to create a meaningful account of our lives; and the struggle to bridge the gaps between expectation and reality. The old and those who care for them can teach us about ourselves if we are willing to listen to them, to consider their questions, and—when necessary—to respect their silence. They show us that the purposes and passions that people live with, the service or the work they perform for others, and the memories they hold to as proof of having lived are among the ends of time that unite us all.

NOTES

PREFACE

1. The emphasis on cultural meanings, developed by Geertz (1973) and other anthropologists, has been applied to the self-concept of older Americans by Kaufman (1987).

CHAPTER 1

1. See, for example, Arensberg (1937) on rural Ireland, Hart and Pilling (1979) for the Tiwi, David Davies (1975) on Vilcabamba, and Sula Benet (1978) on the Abkhasians. The great longevity claimed in the latter two books for Vilcabamba and Abkhasia has not been supported by subsequent research (R. B. Mazess and S. H. Forman 1979; Zhores Medvedev 1974). In regard to the other cultures noted, Guttman (1976) discusses the Druze, Stevan Harrell (1979) the Chinese, Lowell Holmes and Ellen Rhoads (1983) the people of Samoa, Plath (1983) the Japanese, and Marjorie Schweitzer (1983) several American Indian groups. Inuit views of aging and reincarnation are examined by Lee Guemple (1983).

2. The latter two cases are cited by Leo Simmons (1945), who provides information on the treatment of elderly people in 71 primitive societies.

3. For the Parisian building, see Keith (1982); Sheila Johnson (1971) and Arlie Hochschild (1973) write, respectively, about the American mobile home park and apartment house; and Doris Francis (1984) describes the residential development in Leeds.

4. Studies of ethnicity and aging in the United States include Johnson (1983) on Italian-Americans; Schweitzer (1983) on American Indians; and a large body of material on elderly African, Hispanic, European, and Asian-Americans summarized by Donald Gelfand (1982) and Kyriakos Markides and Charles Mindel (1987).

5. Shield (1988) notes several ways in which nursing homes diverge from aspects of Goffman's model.

6. See, for example, the works of Peter Townsend (1962), Robb (1968), C. Townsend (1971), Mendelson (1975), and Vladeck (1980).

7. This diversity can be seen in the studies of Keith (1982), Robert Rubinstein (1986), and Carl Cohen and Jay Sokolovsky (1989).

8. A more recent, comprehensive comparison of American and British geriatric services is provided by William Barker (1987). Neither book covers the crisis in financing and morale that began to afflict the National Health Service during the 1980s.

9. Descriptions and assessments of various forms of pet therapy include Boris Levinson (1972), Leo Bustad (1980), Bruce Fogle (1981), Cindy Wilson and F. Ellen Netting (1983), Phil Arkow (1984), Alan Beck and Aaron Katcher (1984), Odean Cusack and Elaine Smith (1984), and R. K. Anderson, B. L. Hart, and L. A. Hart (1984).

10. The reports appeared as Joel Savishinsky, Rich Lathan, Mari Kobayakawa, and Andrea Nevins (1983), and Savishinsky (1984b). Articles coming out during this period were Savishinsky (1983–84) and Savishinsky (1984a).

11. Decubitus (from Latin *cubare*, "to lie down") is a bedsore; in severe cases, such sores can become ulcerous.

12. For critiques of disengagement theory, see Bruce Lemon, Vern Bengtson, and James Peterson (1972), Dowd (1975), Hochschild (1976), and Jay Sokolovsky (1983). Nancy Foner (1984) provides cross-cultural evidence to show that the status of older people is protected in societies where the elderly maintain command over knowledge, property, or other valued resources.

13. Vladeck (1980) and Johnson and Grant (1985: 5–10) provide histories of nursing homes in the United States, summarizing the roles of demographic, political, and economic factors in their development.

CHAPTER 2

1. Skilled nursing care at Elmwood Grove during this time was approximately 30 percent of the daily cost of extended care in the local hospital. The net loss on Medicaid patients at Elmwood was true of other nonprofit facilities during this period (e.g., Shield 1988).

CHAPTER 3

1. The value of pets as a stimulus for reminiscence has been demonstrated by Levinson (1972), Bustad (1980), Samuel Corson and Elizabeth Corson (1980), Wilson and Netting (1983), and others. The importance of the life review process for older people has been emphasized by Erik Erikson (1963), Butler (1968), Myerhoff (1978), and Kaufman (1987); and the effectiveness of poetry therapy, reminiscing groups, and similar activities for promoting this experience has been described by various authors (e.g., Priscilla Ebersole 1978; Susan Sandel 1987).

2. Some of the material in the rest of this chapter is based on Savishinsky 1985, 1986, 1988a, and 1988b.

3. The works of George Stubbs (Basil Taylor 1975) and other eighteenth century painters contain many such family portraits. Stubbs' oeuvre is also notable for the number of animal portraits he was commissioned to make by owners of favored dogs and horses.

CHAPTER 5

1. See, for example, the instances of infantilizing language and behavior cited at Muni San, Rosemont, and Tower Nursing Home (Henry 1963: 391–474), Murray Manor (Gubrium 1975: 75, 156, 192–193), Pacific Manor (Kayser-Jones 1981: 39–41), Martindale (Vesperi 1983: 225–228), Franklin (Shield 1988: 194–200), and Bethany Manor (O'Brien 1989: 125).

2. Johnson and Grant (1985: 37–51) summarize a body of research showing that many people are likely to enter a geriatric facility because of their social circumstances, not just for medical reasons. Similar patterns have been found in Great Britain (Willcocks, Peace, and Kellaher 1987: 31–52).

CHAPTER 6

1. Parts of this chapter draw on material first presented in Savishinsky 1988c.

2. Goffman (1963) discusses denial and several other methods that stigmatized people use in "the management of spoiled identity." Mace and Rabins (1984: 38), Matt Clark (1984: 60), and Reisberg et al. (1985) recount the lengths that people with Alzheimer's go to in order to mask or deny their illness.

3. Gubrium (1975: 6) observed the same phenomenon at Murray Manor. Older people living in retirement communities also resent changes that result in an increasingly "institutional" image for their residence: this is a threat that the presence of debilitated individuals poses for their healthier age-mates (e.g., Keith 1982: 85–105).

4. This point has been made, for example, about members of retirement communities and senior centers in California (Hochschild 1973: 100–103; Myerhoff 1978: 8), Florida (Vesperi 1985: 49–71), France (Keith 1982: 186–190), and England (Haim Hazan 1984: 570–571).

5. Goffman (1963: 1–19) discusses the dilemma of the "normal" person confronted with a visibly stigmatized individual. If the former acts sympathetically, he runs the risk of being seen as condescending. If he acts as if the stigma were not there, this may be seen as a slight or a denial of the person's condition. The denial may carry with it unreasonable demands that the latter behave in normal ways. Fred Davis (1961: 30) describes this type of encounter as being full of "the familiar signs of discomfort and stickiness: the guarded references, the common everyday words suddenly made taboo, the fixed stare elsewhere, the artificial levity, the compulsive loquaciousness, the awkward solemnity."

6. Mace and Rabins (1984: 151, 244–247, 315) discuss the positive effects of touch on Alzheimer's sufferers, and Shield (1988: 178–179) and O'Brien (1989: 35–37, 174–175) note how commonly used it was at Franklin and Bethany Manor. The importance of pets as a means of tactile contact for the elderly, and the value of various nonverbal forms of communication for institutional residents, is described by Levinson (1972), Bustad (1980), Corson and Corson (1980), Cusack and Smith (1984), and Montagu (1986).

7. As Basso (1970: 215) also observes, the meaning of silence in American culture is situationally defined: it can convey politeness and respect in one context, rudeness and anger in another.

8. The quote is a translation of part of a passage in Charles Baudelaire's *Les Paradis*

Artificiels (1851: 443): "Le génie n'est que l'enfance nettement formulée, douée main-tenant, pour s'extrimer, d'organes virils et puissants?" My thanks to Jane Kaplan for identifying the original source.

CHAPTER 7

1. She was right. According to Partridge (1966: 440–441), *nutrire* originally meant to give milk, hence to feed or nourish.
2. Elizabeth Kübler-Ross (1969) did pioneering work on the emotional stages that people go through during the process of dying.

CHAPTER 8

1. See Robert Sommer (1969), Gubrium (1975: 9–38), A. Lipman and R. Slater (1977), M. Powell Lawton (1980), O'Brien (1989: 170–172), and Willcocks, Peace, and Kellaher (1987: 90–92).
2. In their assessment of how personality affects the adaptation of older people to "relocation stress," Lieberman and Tobin (1983: 180) found that individuals characterized by rebelliousness, assertiveness, and aggression were "less likely to suffer maladaptive consequences subsequent to relocation."

CHAPTER 10

1. There are only a few studies of companion animal programs that examine the role of volunteers. These include Linda Hines (1980), Cusack and Smith (1984), several essays in Anderson, Hart, and Hart (1984), and Savishinsky (1984a). This chapter draws, in part, on the latter article.
2. The nature of altruism has been the subject of a great deal of scientific as well as philosophical and historical debate. Recent discussions have centered on theories suggested by sociobiologists, who have argued for altruism's adaptive advantage in the evolution of human behavior and society (Edward O. Wilson 1979: 155–175). For a view from the fields of economics and psychology that supports the latter thesis, see Robert Frank (1988).
3. Cumming and Henry (1961), Butler (1975), Hazan (1984), and Kaufman (1987) discuss the time and sensory orientations of older people.
4. Kaminer (1984) explores the predominant role of women in American vol-untary organizations, and examines the varied rewards and criticisms that women have earned for their unpaid work.
5. Dorothy Lee (1976: 10–12) has argued that a choice between acting selfishly and altruistically can only exist as a dilemma in a society where the concept of the self is "closed," that is, where people are mutually exclusive objects of one another's actions. But in a society where each person is an "open self," related to others and their value, self-interest and interest in others are not sharply distinguished. Each person *is* to some extent the other.

CHAPTER 11

1. Willcocks, Peace, and Kellaher (1987), drawing largely on research in Great Britain, offer valuable observations on the unhomelike nature of geriatric homes.

2. From his poem "Auguries of Innocence" (1800–1810).

3. See, for example, the programs described in Bustad (1980), Arkow (1984), and Cusack and Smith (1984).

4. Good resources include the materials cited in Chapter 1, Note 9, and the practical suggestions contained in Hines (1980) and Lee et al. (1983).

5. For insightful essays about the role of the anthropologist as an "institutional analyst," see Goffman (1961) and Lorna Rhodes (1986) for accounts of ethnographic research in psychiatric hospitals.

REFERENCES

Anderson, R. K., B. L. Hart, and L. A. Hart (eds.). 1984. *The Pet Connection*. Minneapolis: CENSHARE, University of Minnesota.

Arensberg, Conrad. 1937. *The Irish Countryman*. New York: Macmillan.

Arkow, Phil (ed.). 1984. *Dynamic Relationships in Practice: Animals in the Helping Professions*. Alameda, CA: The Latham Foundation.

Barker, William. 1987. *Adding Life to Years: Organized Geriatric Services in Great Britain and Implications for the United States*. Baltimore: Johns Hopkins University Press.

Barnett, Lincoln. 1962. *The Universe and Dr. Einstein*. New York: Time.

Basso, Keith. 1970. " 'To Give up on Words': Silence in Western Apache Culture." *Southwestern Journal of Anthropology* 26 (3): 213–30.

Baudelaire, Charles. [1851] 1961. "Les Paradis Artificiels." In Claude Pichois (ed.), *Oeuvres Complètes de Baudelaire*, 321–464. Paris: Editions Gallimard.

Beck, Alan and Aaron Katcher. 1984. "A New Look at Pet-Facilitated Therapy." *Journal of the American Veterinary Medicine Association* 184 (4): 414–421.

Benet, Sula. 1978. *Abkhasians: The Long-living People of the Caucasus*. New York: Holt, Rinehart and Winston.

Berger, John and Jean Mohr. 1975. *A Seventh Man: Migrant Workers in Europe*. New York: Viking.

Blake, William. [1800–1810] 1976. "Auguries of Innocence." In Alfred Kazin (ed.), *The Portable Blake*, 150–54. New York: Penguin.

Blythe, Ronald. 1979. *The View in Winter: Reflections on Old Age*. New York: Harcourt, Brace, Jovanovich.

Brody, Elaine. 1985. "Parent Care As a Normative Family Stress." *The Gerontologist* 25 (1): 19–29.

Bromley, D. 1966. *The Psychology of Human Aging*. Harmondsworth, England: Penguin.

Brubaker, Timothy (ed.). 1987. *Aging, Health, and Family: Long-term Care*. Newbury Park, CA: Sage Publications.

Buber, Martin. 1953. *Good and Evil: Two Interpretations*. Translated by Michael Bullock. New York: Scribner's.

Bustad, Leo. 1980. *Animals, Aging and the Aged*. Minneapolis: University of Minnesota Press.

Butler, Robert. 1968. "The Life Review: An Interpretation of Reminiscence in the Aged." In Bernice Neugarten (ed.), *Middle Age and Aging*, 486–96. Chicago: University of Chicago Press.

———. 1975. *Why Survive? Being Old in America*. New York: Harper and Row.

Cage, John. 1961. *Silence*. Middletown, CT: Wesleyan University Press.

Carpenter, Edmund. 1978. "Silent Music and Invisible Art." *Natural History* 87 (5): 90–99.

Clark, Matt. 1984. "A Slow Death of the Mind." *Newsweek* 3 December 1984: 56–62.

Cohen, Carl and Jay Sokolovsky. 1989. *Old Men of the Bowery: Strategies for Survival Among the Homeless*. New York: Guilford Press.

Corson, Samuel and Elizabeth Corson. 1980. "Pet Animals as Non-Verbal Communication Mediators in Psychotherapy in Institutional Settings." In Samuel and Elizabeth Corson (eds.), *Ethology and Non-verbal Communication in Mental Health*, 83–110. New York: Pergamon Press.

Crandall, Richard. 1980. *Gerontology: A Behavioral Science Approach*. New York: Random House.

Cumming, Elaine and William Henry. 1961. *Growing Old: The Process of Disengagement*. New York: Basic Books.

Curtin, Sharon. 1972. *Nobody Ever Died of Old Age*. Boston: Little, Brown.

Cusack, Odean and Elaine Smith. 1984. *Pets and the Elderly: The Therapeutic Bond*. New York: Haworth Press.

Davies, David. 1975. *The Centenarians of the Andes*. Garden City, NY: Doubleday.

Davis, Fred. 1961. "Deviance Disavowal: The Management of Strained Interaction by the Visibly Handicapped." *Social Problems* 9 (2): 120–32.

de Beauvoir, Simone. 1972. *The Coming of Age*. Translated by Patrick O'Brian. New York: Putnam.

de Tocqueville, Alexis. [1848] 1969. *Democracy in America*. J. P. Mayer (ed.). Translated by George Lawrence from the 12th edition of 1848. Garden City, NY: Doubleday.

Dowd, James. 1975. "Aging as Exchange: A Preface to Theory." *Journal of Gerontology* 30 (5): 584–95.

Ebersole, Priscilla. 1978. "Establishing Reminiscing Groups." In Irene Brunswick (ed.), *Working with the Elderly: Group Process and Techniques*, 236–53. North Scituate, MA: Duxbury Press.

Eliot, T. S. [1920] 1963. "Gerontion." In *Collected Poems 1909–1962*, 29–31. New York: Harcourt, Brace and World.

———. [1922] 1963. "The Waste Land." In *Collected Poems 1909–1962*, 51–76. New York: Harcourt, Brace and World.

Emerson, Ralph Waldo. [1844] 1940. "New England Reformers." In Brooks Atkinson (ed.), *Selected Writings of Ralph Waldo Emerson*, 449–68. New York: The Modern Library.

Erikson, Erik. 1963. *Childhood and Society*. 2d ed. New York: W. W. Norton.

Faulkner, William. [1931] 1977. "A Rose for Emily." In Malcolm Cowley (ed.), *The Portable Faulkner*, 433–44. New York: Penguin.

Feifel, Herman. 1961. "Death—Relevant Variable in Psychology." In Rollo May (ed.), *Existential Psychology*. 61–74. New York: Random House.

Fisher, M.F.K. 1984. *Sister Age*. London: Hogarth Press.

Fogle, Bruce (ed.). 1981. *Interrelations Between People and Pets*. Springfield, IL: Charles C. Thomas.

Foner, Nancy. 1984. *Ages in Conflict: A Cross-cultural Perspective on Inequality Between Old and Young*. New York: Columbia University Press.

Foucault, Michel. 1973. *Madness and Civilization: A History of Insanity in the Age of Reason*. New York: Vintage.

———. 1979. *Discipline and Punish: The Birth of the Prison*. Translated by Alan Sheridan. New York: Vintage.

Francis, Doris. 1984. *Will You Still Need Me, Will You Still Feed Me, When I'm 84?* Bloomington: Indiana University Press.

Frank, Robert. 1988. *Passions Within Reason: The Strategic Role of the Emotions*. New York: W. W. Norton.

Freire, Paulo. 1970. *Pedagogy of the Oppressed*. Translated by Myra Ramos. New York: Seabury Press.

Freud, Sigmund. 1961. *Civilization and its Discontents*. Translated by James Strachey. New York: W. W. Norton.

Geertz, Clifford. 1971. *Islam Observed: Religious Development in Morocco and Indonesia*. Chicago: University of Chicago Press.

———. 1973. *The Interpretation of Cultures*. New York: Basic Books.

Gelfand, Donald. 1982. *Aging: The Ethnic Factor*. Boston: Little, Brown.

Glaser, Barney and Anselm Strauss. 1968. *Time for Dying*. Chicago: Aldine.

Goffman, Erving. 1959. *The Presentation of Self in Everyday Life*. Garden City, NY: Doubleday.

———. 1961. *Asylums: Essays on the Social Situation of Mental Patients and Other Inmates*. Garden City, NY: Doubleday.

———. 1963. *Stigma: Notes on the Management of Spoiled Identity*. Englewood Cliffs, NJ: Prentice-Hall.

Goldberg, Sheryl and Carroll Estes. 1990. "Medical DRGs and Post-Hospital Care for the Elderly: Does Out of the Hospital Mean Out of Luck?" *Journal of Applied Gerontology* 9 (1): 20–35.

Gregor, Thomas. 1970. "Exposure and Seclusion: A Study of Institutionalized Isolation among the Mehinacu Indians of Brazil." *Ethnology* 9 (3): 234–50.

Gubrium, Jaber. 1975. *Living and Dying at Murray Manor*. New York: St. Martin's.

Guemple, Lee. 1983. "Growing Old in Inuit Society." In Jay Sokolovsky (ed.), *Growing Old in Different Societies: Cross-cultural Perspectives*. 24–28. Belmont, CA: Wadsworth.

Guttman, David. 1976. "Alternatives to Disengagement among the Old Men of the Highland Druze." In Jaber Gubrium (ed.), *Time, Roles and Self in Old Age*, 88–108. New York: Human Sciences Press.

Hanfmann, George M. A. 1972. *Letters from Sardis*. Cambridge: Harvard University Press.

Harrell, Stevan. 1979. "Growing Old in Rural Taiwan." In Pamela Amoss and Stevan Harrell (eds.), *Other Ways of Growing Old: Anthropological Perspectives*, 193–210. Stanford, CA: Stanford University Press.

Hart, C.W.M. and Arnold Pilling. 1979. *The Tiwi of North Australia*. New York: Holt, Rinehart and Winston.

Haskins, Charles Homer. 1957. *The Renaissance of the 12th Century*. New York: Meridian Books.

Hazan, Haim. 1984. "Continuity and Transformation among the Aged: A Study in the Anthropology of Time." *Current Anthropology* 25 (5): 567–78.

Helyar, John. 1981. "Talking to Your Dog Can Help to Lower Your Blood Pressure." *The Wall Street Journal* 16 October 1981.

Henry, Jules. 1963. *Culture Against Man*. New York: Vintage.

Hines, Linda. 1980. *The People-Pet Partnership Program*. Alameda, CA: The Latham Foundation.

Hochschild, Arlie. 1973. *The Unexpected Community*. Englewood Cliffs, NJ: Prentice-Hall.

———. 1976. "Disengagement Theory: A Logical, Empirical and Phenomenological Critique." In Jaber Gubrium (ed.), *Time, Roles and Self in Old Age*, 53–87. New York: Human Sciences Press.

Holmberg, Alan. 1969. *Nomads of the Long Bow: The Siriono of Eastern Bolivia*. Garden City, NY: Doubleday.

Holmes, Lowell and Ellen Rhoads. 1983. "Aging and Change in Samoa." In Jay Sokolovsky (ed.), *Growing Old in Different Societies: Cross-cultural Perspectives*, 119–29. Belmont, CA: Wadsworth.

Jacobs, Jerry. 1974. *Fun City: An Ethnographic Study of a Retirement Community*. New York: Holt, Rinehart and Winston.

Johnson, Colleen. 1983. "Interdependence and Aging in Italian Families." In Jay Sokolovsky (ed.), *Growing Old in Different Societies: Cross-cultural Perspectives*, 92–103. Belmont, CA: Wadsworth.

Johnson, Colleen and Leslie Grant. 1985. *The Nursing Home in American Society*. Baltimore: Johns Hopkins University Press.

Johnson, Sheila. 1971. *Idle Haven: Community Building among the Working Class Retired*. Berkeley: University of California Press.

Jung, C. G. 1933. *Modern Man in Search of a Soul*. Translated by W. S. Dell and Cary Baynes. New York: Harcourt, Brace and World.

Kaminer, Wendy. 1984. *Women Volunteering: The Pleasure, Pain, and Politics of Unpaid Work*. Garden City, NY: Doubleday.

Kane, Robert L. and Rosalie Kane. 1978. "Care of the Aged: Old Problems in Need of New Solutions." *Science* 200 (4344): 913–19.

Kaufman, Sharon. 1987. *The Ageless Self: Sources of Meaning in Late Life*. New York: New American Library.

Kayser-Jones, Jeanie. 1981. *Old, Alone and Neglected: Care of the Aged in the United States and Scotland*. Berkeley: University of California Press.

Keith, Jennie. 1982. *Old People, New Lives: Community Creation in a Retirement Residence*. Chicago: University of Chicago Press.

Kemper, Peter and Christopher Murtaugh. 1991. "Lifetime Use of Nursing Home Care." *New England Journal of Medicine* 324 (9): 595–600.

Kidd, Dudley. 1904. *The Essential Kaffir*. London: A. and C. Black.

Kierkegaard, Soren. 1954. *Fear and Trembling* and *The Sickness unto Death*. Walter Lowrie, translator. Garden City, NY: Doubleday.

Kohn, Hans. 1962. *The Age of Nationalism: The First Era of Global History*. New York: Harper and Row.

Kübler-Ross, Elizabeth. 1969. *On Death and Dying*. London: Macmillan.

Laird, Carobeth. 1979. *Limbo: A Memoir of Life in a Nursing Home by a Survivor*. Novato, CA: Chandler and Sharp.

Lawton, M. Powell. 1980. *Environment and Aging*. Monterey, CA: Brooks/Cole.

Lee, Dorothy. 1976. *Valuing the Self: What We Can Learn from Other Cultures*. Englewood Cliffs, NJ: Prentice-Hall.

Lee, Ronnal, Marie Zeglen, Terry Ryan, and Linda Hines. 1983. "Guidelines: Animals in Nursing Homes." *California Veterinarian* 37 (3): 1A–43A.

Lemon, Bruce, Vern Bengtson, and James Peterson. 1972. "An Exploration of the Activity Theory of Aging: Activity Types and Life Satisfaction among In-Movers to a Retirement Community." *Journal of Gerontology* 27 (4): 511–23.

Levinson, Boris. 1972. *Pets and Human Development*. Springfield, IL: Charles C. Thomas.

Lieberman, Morton and Sheldon Tobin. 1983. *The Experience of Old Age: Stress, Coping, and Survival*. New York: Basic Books.

Lifton, Robert Jay. 1976. *The Life of the Self: Toward a New Psychology*. New York: Simon and Schuster.

Lipman, A. and R. Slater. 1977. "Status and Spatial Appropriation in Eight Homes for Old People." *The Gerontologist* 17 (3): 250–55.

Lopata, Helen. 1979. *Women as Widows*. New York: Elsevier.

Mace, Nancy and Peter Rabins. 1984. *The 36-Hour Day: A Family Guide to Caring For Persons with Alzheimer's Disease, Related Dementing Illnesses, and Memory Loss in Later Life*. New York: Warner.

Markides, Kyriakos and Charles Mindel. 1987. *Aging and Ethnicity*. Newbury Park, CA: Sage Publications.

Mazess, R. B. and S. H. Forman. 1979. "Longevity and Age Exaggeration in Vilcabamba, Ecuador." *Journal of Gerontology* 34 (1): 94–98.

Medvedev, Zhores. 1974. "Caucasus and Altay Longevity: A Biological or Social Problem." *The Gerontologist* 14 (5): 381–87.

Mendelson, Mary. 1975. *Tender Loving Greed*. New York: Vintage.

Montagu, Ashley. 1986. *Touching: The Human Significance of the Skin*, 3d ed. New York: Harper and Row.

———. 1989. *Growing Young*. 2d ed. Granby, MA: Bergin and Garvey.

Moore, O. K. 1957. "Divination—A New Perspective." *American Anthropologist* 59 (1): 69–74.

Myerhoff, Barbara. 1978. *Number Our Days*. New York: Simon and Schuster.

O'Brien, Mary. 1989. *Anatomy of a Nursing Home: A New View of Residential Life*. Owings Mills, MD: National Health Publishing.

Orwell, George. 1950. *1984*. New York: Signet.

Partridge, Eric. 1966. *Origins: A Short Etymological Dictionary of Modern English*. 4th ed. London: Routledge and Kegan Paul.

Plath, David. 1983. " 'Ecstasy Years'—Old Age in Japan." In Jay Sokolovsky (ed.), *Growing Old in Different Societies: Cross-cultural Perspectives*, 147–53. Belmont, CA: Wadsworth.

Powers, Bethel. 1988a. "Social Networks, Social Support, and Elderly Institutionalized People." *Advances in Nursing Science* 10 (2): 40–58.

————. 1988b. "Self-perceived Health of Elderly Institutionalized People." *Journal of Cross-cultural Gerontology* 3 (3): 299–321.

Reisberg, Barry. 1983. *A Guide to Alzheimer's Disease.* New York: Free Press.

Reisberg, Barry, Steven Ferris, Mony de Leon, and Thomas Crook. 1985. "Age-associated Cognitive Decline and Alzheimer's Disease: Implications for Assessment and Treatment." In M. Bergener, M. Ermini, and H. B. Stahelin (eds.), *Thresholds in Aging*, 255–92. London: Academic Press.

Reisberg, Barry, Emile Franssen, Steven Ferris, and Eduardo Bondoc. 1988. "The Final Stages of Alzheimer's Disease: Issues for the Patient, Family, and Professional Community." In Richard Mayeux et al. (eds.), *Alzheimer's Disease and Related Disorders.* Springfield, IL: Charles C. Thomas.

Retsinas, Joan and Patricia Garrity. 1985. "Nursing Home Friendships." *The Gerontologist* 25 (4): 376–81.

Rhodes, Lorna. 1986. "The Anthropologist as Institutional Analyst." *Ethos* 14 (2): 204–17.

Robb, Barbara. 1968. *Sans Everything: A Case to Answer.* London: Nelson.

Rodin, Judith. 1986. "Aging and Health: Effects of the Sense of Control." *Science* 233 (4770): 1271–76.

Roth, H. L. 1890. *The Aborigines of Tasmania.* London: Kegan Paul, Trench, Trubner.

Rubinstein, Robert. 1986. *Singular Paths: Old Men Living Alone.* New York: Columbia University Press.

Salisbury, S. and P. Goehner. 1983. "Separation of the Confused or Integration with the Lucid?" *Geriatric Nursing* 4 (4): 231–36.

Sandel, Susan. 1987. "Reminiscence in Movement Therapy." *Activities, Adaptation and Aging* 9 (3): 81–89.

Sarton, May. 1973. *As We Are Now.* New York: W. W. Norton.

Savishinsky, Joel S. 1974. *The Trail of the Hare: Life and Stress in an Arctic Community.* New York: Gordon and Breach.

————. 1983. "Pet Ideas: The Domestication of Animals, Human Behavior, and Human Emotions." In Aaron Katcher and Alan Beck (eds.), *New Perspectives on Our Lives with Companion Animals*, 112–31. Philadelphia: University of Pennsylvania Press.

————. 1983–84. "In the Company of Animals: An Anthropological Study of Pets and People in Three Nursing Homes." *The Latham Letter* 5 (1): 1, 9–10, 21–22.

————. 1984a. "What Cornell Has Discovered About Volunteer Experiences." *People-Animals-Environment* 2 (1): 14–18.

————. 1984b. *Staying in Touch: A Report on Pet Therapy Programs in Four Geriatric Facilities.* Ithaca, NY: Department of Anthropology, Ithaca College.

————. 1985. "Pets and Family Relationships among Nursing Home Residents." *Marriage and Family Review* 8 (3/4): 109–34.

————. 1986. "The Human Impact of a Pet Therapy Program in Three Nursing Homes." *Central Issues in Anthropology* 6 (2): 31–42.

————. 1988a. "Common Fate, Difficult Decision: A Comparison of Euthanasia in People and in Animals." In William Kay et al. (eds.), *Euthanasia of the Companion Animal*, 3–8. Philadelphia: Charles Press.

————. 1988b. "The Meaning of Loss: Human and Pet Death in the Lives of the

Elderly." In William Kay et al. (eds.), *Euthanasia of the Companion Animal*, 138–47. Philadelphia: Charles Press.

————. 1988c. "Stigma, Silence, Contact: Responses to Patients with Alzheimer's Disease in Two Nursing Homes." In Richard Mayeux et al. (eds.), *Alzheimer's Disease and Related Disorders*, 49–65. Springfield, IL: Charles C. Thomas.

Savishinsky, Joel S. (ed.). 1970. *Strangers No More: Anthropological Studies of Cat Island, The Bahamas*. Ithaca, NY: Department of Anthropology, Ithaca College.

Savishinsky, Joel, Rich Lathan, Mari Kobayakawa, and Andrea Nevins. 1983. *The Life of the Hour: A Study of People and Pets in Three Nursing Homes*. Ithaca, NY: Department of Anthropology, Ithaca College.

Scheper-Hughes, Nancy. 1979. *Saints, Scholars, and Schizophrenics: Mental Illness in Rural Ireland*. Berkeley: University of California Press.

Schweitzer, Marjorie. 1983. "The Elders: Cultural Dimensions of Aging in Two American Indian Communities." In Jay Sokolovsky (ed.), *Growing Old in Different Societies: Cross-cultural Perspectives*, 168–78. Belmont, CA: Wadsworth.

Scott-Maxwell, Florida. 1979. *The Measure of My Days*. New York: Penguin.

Seabrook, Jeremy. 1980. *The Way We Are: Old People Talk About Themselves*. Mitcham, England: Age Concern England.

Shanas, Ethel. 1979. "Social Myth as Hypothesis: The Case of the Family Life of Old People." *The Gerontologist* 19 (1): 3–9.

Shield, Renee Rose. 1988. *Uneasy Endings: Daily Life in an American Nursing Home*. Ithaca, NY: Cornell University Press.

Siegel, Jacob and Cynthia Taeuber. 1986. "Demographic Dimensions of an Aging Population." In Alan Pifer and Lydia Bronte (eds.), *Our Aging Society: Paradox and Promise*, 79–110. New York: W. W. Norton.

Simmons, Leo. 1945. *The Role of the Aged in Primitive Society*. New Haven: Yale University Press.

Sokolovsky, Jay. 1983. "Background to Sociocultural Gerontology." In Jay Sokolovsky (ed.), *Growing Old in Different Societies: Cross-cultural Perspectives*, 1–8. Belmont, CA: Wadsworth.

Sommer, Robert. 1969. *Personal Space: The Behavioral Basis of Design*. Englewood Cliffs, NJ: Prentice-Hall.

Spengler, Oswald. 1926. *Decline of the West*. Translated by Charles Francis Atkinson. New York: Knopf.

Spiro, Melford. 1965. *Children of the Kibbutz*. New York: Schocken.

Taylor, Basil. 1975. *Stubbs*. London: Phaidon.

Tobin, Sheldon. 1987. "A Structural Approach to Families." In Timothy Brubaker (ed.), *Aging, Health, and Family: Long-term Care*, 42–55. Newbury Park, CA: Sage Publications.

Tobin, Sheldon and Morton Lieberman. 1976. *Last Home for the Aged*. San Francisco: Jossey-Bass.

Tomkins, Calvin. 1976. *The Bride and the Bachelors: Five Masters of the Avant-garde*. New York: Penguin.

Townsend, Claire. 1971. *Old Age: The Last Segregation*. New York: Bantam.

Townsend, Kathleen. 1984. "The Forgotten Virtues of Voluntarism." *Current* 260: 9–20.

Townsend, Peter. 1962. *The Last Refuge: A Survey of Residential Institutions and Homes for the Aged in England and Wales.* London: Routledge and Kegan Paul.

Toynbee, Arnold. 1934–1954. *A Study of History*, 10 volumes. New York: Oxford University Press.

Turnbull, Colin. 1983. *The Human Cycle.* New York: Simon and Schuster.

Underhill, Ruth. 1979. *Papago Woman.* New York: Holt, Rinehart and Winston.

United States Bureau of the Census. 1990. *Statistical Abstract of the United States: 1990.* 110th ed. Washington, DC: Department of Commerce, Bureau of the Census.

Vesperi, Maria. 1983. "The Reluctant Consumer: Nursing Home Residents in the Post-Bergman Era." In Jay Sokolovsky (ed.), *Growing Old in Different Societies: Cross-cultural Perspectives*, 225–37. Belmont, CA: Wadsworth.

———. 1985. *City of Green Benches: Growing Old in a New Downtown.* Ithaca, NY: Cornell University Press.

Vladeck, Bruce. 1980. *Unloving Care: The Nursing Home Tragedy.* New York: Basic Books.

Watson, Wilbur and Robert Maxwell. 1977. *Human Aging and Dying: A Study in Sociocultural Gerontology.* New York: St. Martin's Press.

Willcocks, Dianne, Sheila Peace, and Leonie Kellaher. 1987. *Private Lives in Public Places: A Research-based Critique of Residential Life in Local Authority's Old People's Homes.* London: Tavistock.

Wilson, Cindy and F. Ellen Netting. 1983. "Companion Animals and the Elderly: A State-of-the-Art Summary." *Journal of the American Veterinary Medicine Association* 183 (12): 1425–29.

Wilson, Edward O. 1979. *On Human Nature.* New York: Bantam.

Wilson, Monica. 1963. *Good Company: A Study of Nyakyusa Age-Villages.* Boston: Beacon Press.

Witt, Shirley Hill. 1972. "Listen to His Many Voices." In Shirley Hill Witt and Stan Steiner (eds.), *The Way: An Anthology of American Indian Literature*, xvii–xxix. New York: Vintage Books.

Yeats, William Butler. [1927] 1983. "Sailing to Byzantium." In Richard J. Finneran (ed.), *The Poems of W. B. Yeats: A New Edition*, 193–194. New York: Macmillan.

———. [1932] 1983. "Quarrel in Old Age." In Richard J. Finneran (ed.), *The Poems of W. B. Yeats: A New Edition*, 253. New York: Macmillan.

———. [1938] 1983. "The Wild Old Wicked Man." In Richard J. Finneran (ed.), *The Poems of W. B. Yeats: A New Edition*, 310–311. New York: Macmillan.

INDEX

abuse, 11, 36, 93, 121, 164, 165–66, 168–69, 191, 197–98, 247

activities programs in nursing homes, 11, 43, 45, 50–51, 89, 119–20, 131, 240–41, 253–55. *See also* pet therapy

Activity Theory, 22–23

ADL (activities of daily living), 6–7, 27, 36

administration in nursing homes. *See* nursing homes

altruism. *See* volunteers

Alzheimer's disease, 10, 36, 74, 119, 124–42, 197, 241–42. *See also* dementia art, 87, 90, 96, 114, 122–23, 139

autonomy, 10–11, 102, 119–22

Bethany Manor, 7, 57, 112, 119–20, 125, 183, 250–54, 261 n.5:1, 262 n.8:1

burn-out. *See* staff; volunteers

CAP (Companion Animal Program). *See* pet therapy

caring, contrasted with curing, 6, 22, 148, 152, 180–81, 190, 198, 248–49, 252

CMI (Case Mix Index), 42, 167

conflict. *See* roommates; staff

control, sense of, and residents' morale, 5, 10, 77, 112–13, 120

cruelty towards people and animals compared, 65–67, 241

curing, contrasted with caring, 6, 22, 148, 152, 180–81, 190, 198, 248–49, 252

death, 6–8, 24, 61–65, 84, 90, 102–3, 117, 140, 153–56, 158, 161–62, 164–65, 174, 181–84, 193–94, 210, 214, 221, 227–28, 243–44, 251, 256; DNRs, 43, 155, 161, 182; pet death, 61–65, 219

dementia, 4, 7, 10, 36, 43, 46, 89, 97–105, 109, 120–21, 123–42, 209, 216, 241–42, 252. *See also* Alzheimer's disease

denial as defense mechanism, 105–6, 125, 148, 181, 201, 242, 261 n.6:5

Disengagement Theory, 22–23

DNRs (Do Not Resuscitate orders), 43, 155, 161, 182

doctors, 147–48, 153–54, 183, 194

domesticity, 16, 59–61, 74, 113–15, 219, 229–30, 255; concept of home, 16, 74, 113, 247–49; loss of home, 10, 80, 104, 113–14, 122, 149–50, 219, 248; and pets, 28, 59–61, 67–68, 115, 241

DRGs (Diagnosis Related Groups), 41, 167–68

education: of residents, 71, 80–83, 96, 98, 108–9; of staff, 144, 152, 155, 158, 170, 176–79, 195–96
Eliot, T. S., 109, 232, 257–58
England, 3, 5, 261 nn.5:2, 6:4, 263 n.11:1

families: of residents, 21, 24–25, 43, 55–61, 75–106, 148–49, 153–55, 158, 165–66, 172–74, 240; of staff, 152, 158, 172, 178, 187, 192, 194; of volunteers, 61, 207–13, 215, 217–18, 229, 235
food, 5, 18–19, 36, 73, 96–97, 159–60, 171
France, 3, 23, 116, 261 n.6:4
Franklin Nursing Home, 7, 23, 112, 116, 120, 125–26, 177, 181–83, 189–90, 192, 228, 232, 250–54, 256, 261 n.5:1
friendship, among residents, 74–75, 83–84, 115–17

gender: among residents, 9, 37, 117, 146, 246–47; among staff, 9, 37, 39, 152, 168, 186–88, 246–47; among volunteers, 40, 229, 236, 246–47
Goffman, Erving, 4, 61, 261 n.6:5
Golden Mesa Nursing Home, 5, 64, 113, 232, 250, 253
Gubrium, Jaber. See Murray Manor

home. See domesticity
home care, 24–25, 76, 110–11, 167, 194, 248, 255
hospitals, 7–8, 41, 80, 111, 117, 147, 152, 165, 168, 177, 196, 217, 248

Ireland, 2, 4, 5, 23

Kayser-Jones, Jeanie. See Pacific Manor Nursing Home; Scottsdale Nursing Home
kindness towards people and animals compared, 65–67, 241

labor union, 39, 167, 170, 187, 195, 243, 251, 255

Laird, Carobeth. See Golden Mesa Nursing Home
language: acquisition, 49–50, 72, 80–83, 109; and forgetfulness, 46, 97–100, 107, 124–42. See also silence; ST (speech therapy)

Martindale Nursing Home, 5–6, 181, 183, 250–52, 261 n.5:1
Medicaid, 25, 37, 41–42, 146, 149, 167, 173
Medicare, 25, 41, 111, 149, 167
medication, 5, 42, 75, 82, 109, 157, 160, 165
memory, 19–20, 54–59, 67, 107–23; loss, 19–20, 62, 91, 97–100; and personal meanings, 54–59, 65–68, 78–79, 104–5, 114, 122–23, 241. See also Alzheimer's disease; dementia; language
mirrors, 216, 232–33, 256–57
morality: and human-animal ties, 55, 65–68, 241; issues among residents' families, 78–79, 182; issues among staff, 182, 192–95, 198–99, 247. See also abuse; DNRs; volunteers, and altruism
Murray Manor, 6, 111–12, 119–20, 125, 179, 182, 189, 232, 250–53, 261 n.5:1, 262 n.8:1
music, 44, 89, 93, 98, 102–3, 131–32, 136, 139
Myerhoff, Barbara, 3, 116, 136

nursing, 36–37, 42–43, 127, 146, 156–66, 181, 255
nursing homes: administration of, 18–19, 37–39, 150, 165–74, 179, 186–88; comparisons between, 5–9, 250–54; demographic characteristics of, 9–10, 36–37, 124, 168; financing of, 9, 11, 25, 37, 41–42, 146–47, 167, 179; history of, 25–26, 35–36, 40, 195; as "total institutions," 4. See also under names of specific institutions

O'Brien, Mary. See Bethany Manor
OT (occupational therapy), 37, 42, 82–83

Pacific Manor Nursing Home, 8–9, 23, 250, 253, 261 n.5:1

pets: loss of, 61–65, 219; memories of, 23, 55–68; moral meanings of, 23, 65–68, 241, 244. *See also* domesticity

pet therapy, 14–16, 27, 43, 129, 137, 224, 234, 244, 249–50, 254–55; description of pet program, 13, 27–35, 44–53, 202–4, 219, 226, 228–31; effect on residents, 23, 54–68, 115, 127, 132–34, 240–41. *See also* volunteers

Powers, Bethel, 6–7, 67–68, 111–12, 117, 120, 125, 250–53

PRI (Patient Review Instrument), 42, 147, 182

privacy, 6, 101, 110, 117–19, 164, 188–89, 191, 206, 244, 251–52

PT (physical therapy), 37, 42, 81, 92, 100, 151–56, 178, 180–81

race relations in nursing homes, 8, 37, 93–94, 121–22, 192, 251

randomness, 137–42, 241

recreation. *See* activities programs in nursing homes

religion: among residents, 5, 30–31, 48–49, 80–81, 84–87, 89, 94, 123, 185, 245–46, 251; among staff, 156, 158, 161, 181, 197, 245–46; among volunteers, 212–13, 217–18, 233–34, 245–46

research methods, 16–24, 40–44

residents, 69–106; and death, 61–65; relations with families, 10–11, 21, 55–61, 65–67, 72–106, 110–15, 198, 240; relations with staff, 5–8, 67, 73, 75–76, 93, 96–97, 99–100, 111, 118, 120–22; relations with volunteers, 60–61, 67, 90, 111, 192; and roommates, 63–64, 73, 83, 93, 100–101, 115–17. *See also* memory; pets; silence; staff; volunteers

restraints, physical and chemical, 5, 89, 128–29

retirement communities, 3, 25, 33, 261 n.6:4

roommates, 51–53, 63–64, 93, 115–17,

126, 148; communication, 51, 73–74, 83; conflict, 93, 100–101, 115–16; friendship, 63–64, 83, 100, 116–17

RUGs (Resource Utilization Groupings), 42, 167

Sarton, May, 4, 131, 136

Scottsdale Nursing Home, 8–9, 250–54

"The Screen" (admissions assessment form), 42, 70, 147

segregation: of the demented, 126, 152; of the elderly, 25–26

senility. *See* Alzheimer's disease; dementia

sex, 91

Shield, Renee. *See* Franklin Nursing Home

silence, 50, 124–42, 209, 241–42; in different cultures, 135–36. *See also* language

SNFs (skilled nursing facilities). *See* nursing homes

Social Exchange Theory, 8–9, 23

social work, 39–51, 88, 96–97, 131, 144–51, 177, 180, 190

ST (speech therapy), 42, 49, 81–82

staff: attitudes towards work, 5, 39, 143–99, 243; burn-out, 165–66, 245; conflict, 40, 150, 155, 165, 170–71, 175, 185, 187–90, 183–94, 243, 255; education and training, 5–6, 144, 152, 155, 158, 170; gender and hierarchy, 168, 170–71, 178, 186–88, 196–97, 247; relations with residents, 5–9, 21, 75–76, 96–97, 100, 109, 131–32, 143–75, 180–85, 192; relations with residents' families, 78, 96–97, 112, 147–49, 153–55, 161–62, 165–66, 172–74, 185, 194, 198; sources of stress and support, 150–52, 163–66, 168–71, 175, 187–92, 197, 245, 255–56

stigma, 125–29, 134, 137–38, 141, 242, 261 n.6:5

time orientation: of residents, 108–10, 122–23, 132, 144, 163, 205, 232, 246;

of staff, 188–89; of volunteers, 205, 227, 232, 246
touch: in different cultures, 136; with the elderly, 4, 47, 56, 60, 127, 132–37, 140–42, 242, 249, 261 n.6:6

Vesperi, Maria. *See* Martindale Nursing Home
volunteers, 39–40, 200–237, 242–43, 245, 253–54; and age, 213–15, 220–21, 231–33, 236, 246; and altruism, 200–201, 217, 223, 230, 233, 236–37, 243, 262 nn.10:2, 10:5; and burnout, 218–22, 225, 230–31, 233, 237, 242, 256; families of, 61, 207–13, 215, 217–18, 229, 235, 241; and gender, 40, 229, 236, 246–47; relations with residents, 21, 60–61, 67, 90, 119, 129–34, 192, 200–222, 224–36; training, 227, 231, 234–37, 249–50, 256

Yeats, W. B., 3, 94, 133, 258

About the Author

JOEL S. SAVISHINSKY is Professor of Anthropology at Ithaca College. He is author of *The Trail of the Hare: Life and Stress in an Arctic Community* and numerous articles on pet therapy, Alzheimer's disease, voluntarism, and institutional responses to death and moral dilemmas.